# SAYONARA, ZETSUBOU - SENSEI

## The Power of Negative Thinking ②

# Koji Kumeta

Translated and adapted by Joyce Aurino
Lettered by Foltz Design

**BALLANTINE BOOKS · NEW YORK**

*Sayonara, Zetsubou-sensei: The Power of Negative Thinking* volume 2 is a work of fiction. Names, characters, places, and incidents are the products of the author's imagination or are used fictitiously. Any resemblance to actual events, locales, or persons, living or dead, is entirely coincidental.

A Del Rey Manga/Kodansha Trade Paperback Original



Published in the United States by Del Rey, an imprint of The Random House Publishing Group, a division of Random House, Inc., New York.

Del Rey is a registered trademark and the Del Rey colophon is a trademark of Random House, Inc.

Publication rights arranged through Kodansha Ltd.

First published in Japan in 2006 by Kodansha Ltd., Tokyo

ISBN 978-0-345-51023-5

Printed in the United States of America

www.delreymanga.com

3 4 5 6 7 8 9

Translator/Adapter: Joyce Aurino
Lettering: Foltz Design

# SAYONARA, ZETSUBOU-SENSEI

## The Power of Negative Thinking **2**

## CONTENTS

# Honorifics Explained

Throughout the Del Rey Manga books, you will find Japanese honorifics left intact in the translations. For those not familiar with how the Japanese use honorifics and, more important, how they differ from American honorifics, we present this brief overview.

Politeness has always been a critical facet of Japanese culture. Ever since the feudal era, when Japan was a highly stratified society, use of honorifics—which can be defined as polite speech that indicates relationship or status—has played an essential role in the Japanese language. When addressing someone in Japanese, an honorific usually takes the form of a suffix attached to one's name (example: "Asuna-san"), is used as a title at the end of one's name, or appears in place of the name itself (example: "Negi-sensei," or simply "Sensei").

Honorifics can be expressions of respect or endearment. In the context of manga and anime, honorifics give insight into the nature of the relationship between characters. Many English translations leave out these important honorifics and therefore distort the feel of the original Japanese. Because Japanese honorifics contain nuances that English honorifics lack, it is our policy at Del Rey not to translate them. Here, instead, is a guide to some of the honorifics you may encounter in Del Rey Manga.

**-san:** This is the most common honorific and is equivalent to Mr., Miss, Ms., or Mrs. It is the all-purpose honorific and can be used in any situation where politeness is required.

**-sama:** This is one level higher than "-san" and is used to confer great respect.

**-dono:** This comes from the word "tono," which means "lord." It is an even higher level than "-sama" and confers utmost respect.

**-kun:** This suffix is used at the end of boys' names to express familiarity or endearment. It is also sometimes used by men among friends, or when addressing someone younger or of a lower station.

**-chan:** This is used to express endearment, mostly toward girls. It is also used for little boys, pets, and even among lovers. It gives a sense of childish cuteness.

**Bozu:** This is an informal way to refer to a boy, similar to the English terms "kid" and "squirt."

**Sempai/**
**Senpai:** This title suggests that the addressee is one's senior in a group or organization. It is most often used in a school setting, where underclassmen refer to their upperclassmen as "sempai." It can also be used in the workplace, such as when a newer employee addresses an employee who has seniority in the company.

**Kohai:** This is the opposite of "sempai" and is used toward underclassmen in school or newcomers in the workplace. It connotes that the addressee is of a lower station.

**Sensei:** Literally meaning "one who has come before," this title is used for teachers, doctors, or masters of any profession or art.

**-[blank]:** This is usually forgotten in these lists, but it is perhaps the most significant difference between Japanese and English. The lack of honorific means that the speaker has permission to address the person in a very intimate way. Usually, only family, spouses, or very close friends have this kind of per-mission. Known as *yobisute,* it can be gratifying when some-one who has earned the intimacy starts to call one by one's name without an honorific. But when that intimacy hasn't been earned, it can be very insulting.

Koji Kumeta

# SAYONARA, ZETSUBOU-SENSEI 2

## The Power of Negative Thinking

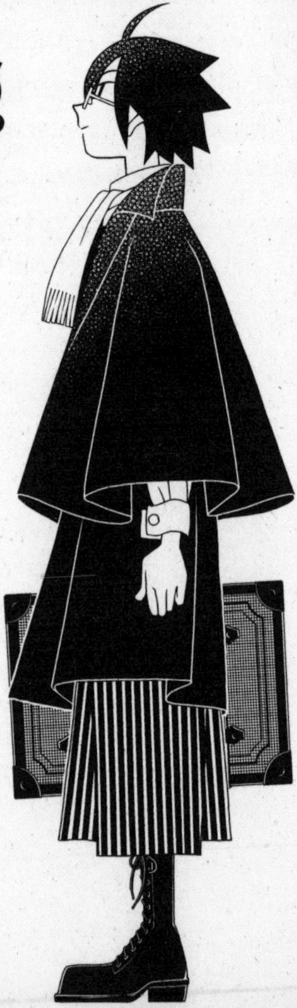

# Contents

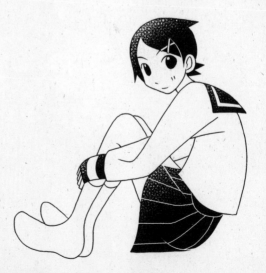

# Cast of Characters

## ATTENDANCE LIST
### CLASS 2-F

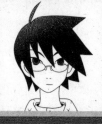

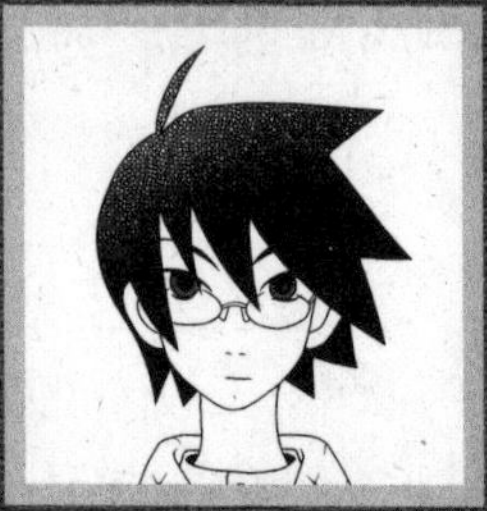

**TEACHER-IN-CHARGE
NOZOMU ITOSHIKI
SUPER-NEGATIVE MAN**

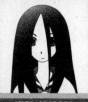

**KIRI KOMORI
HIKIKOMORI GIRL**

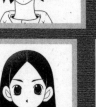

**CHIRI KITSU
METHODICAL AND PRECISE GIRL**

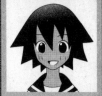

**TARO MARIA SEKIUTSU
ILLEGAL IMMIGRANT, REFUGEE GIRL**

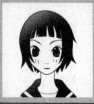

**MATOI TSUNETSUKI
SUPER-LOVE-OBSESSED
STALKER GIRL**

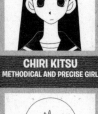

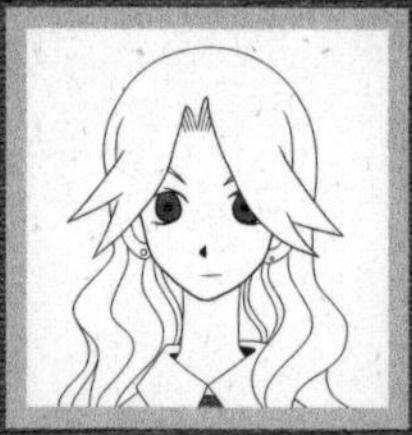

**KAERE KIMURA
(ALSO KAEDE)
BILINGUAL GIRL**

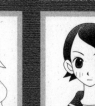

**KAFUKA FUURA
SUPER-POSITIVE GIRL**

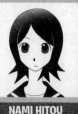

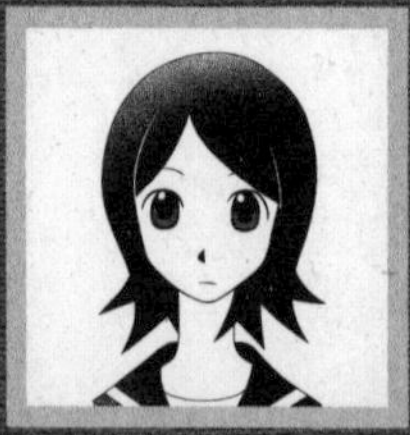

**NAMI HITOU
ORDINARY GIRL**

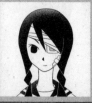

**ABIRU KOBUSHI
TAIL FETISH GIRL; THOUGHT TO BE
VICTIM OF DOMESTIC VIOLENCE**

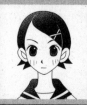

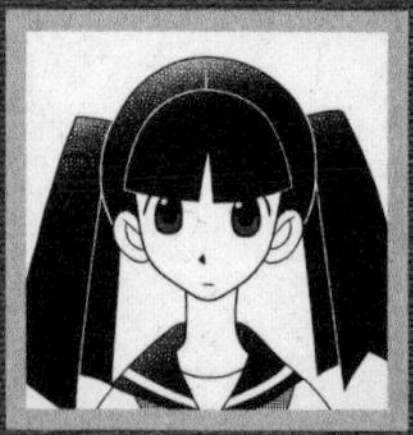

**MERU OTONASHI
POISON EMAIL GIRL**

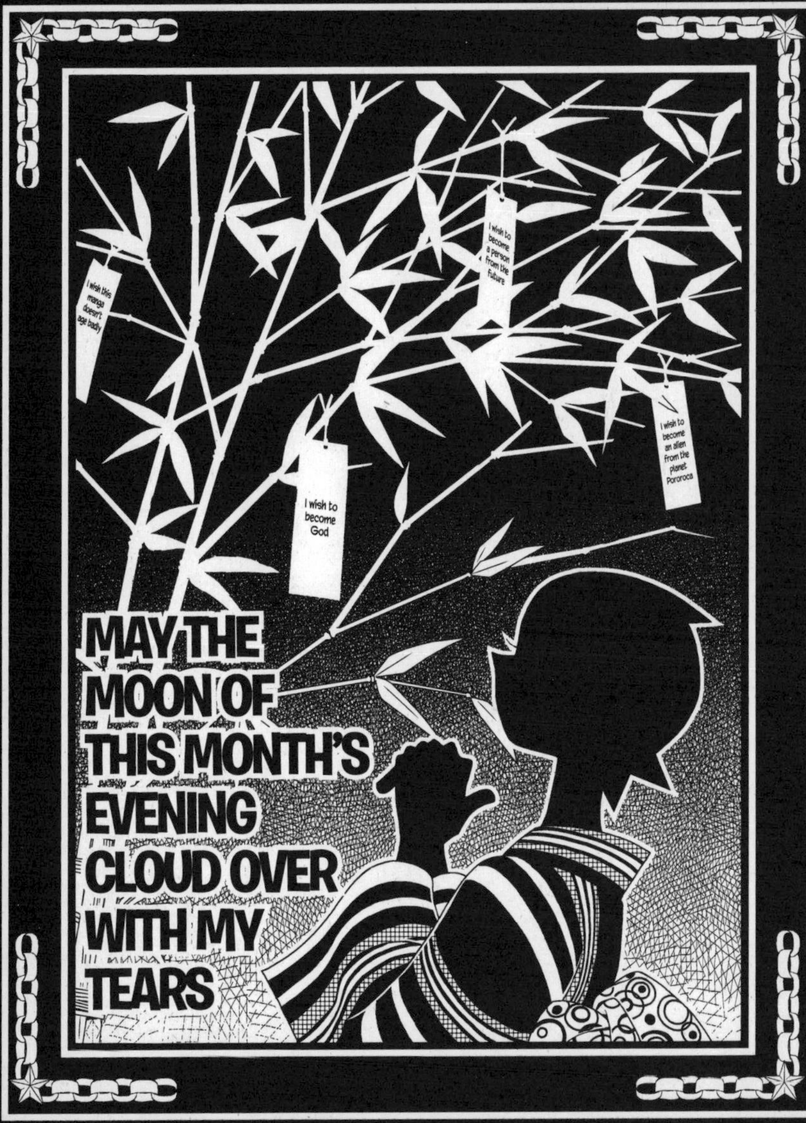
I wish to become an alien from the planet Pororoca
I wish to become a person from the future
I wish to become God
I wish this manga doesn't age badly
MAY THE MOON OF THIS MONTH'S EVENING CLOUD OVER WITH MY TEARS

# CHAPTER 11

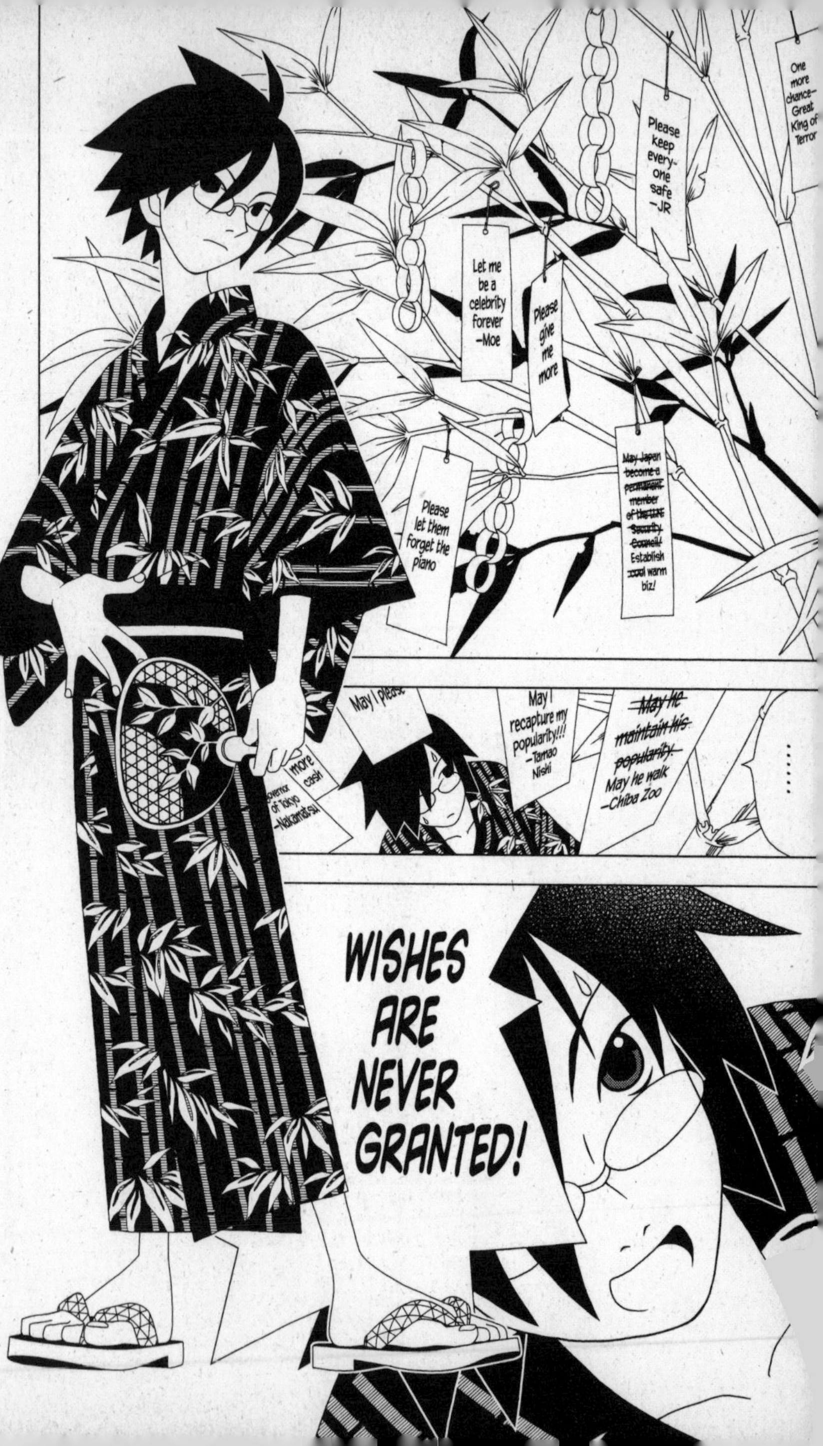
One more chance— Great King of Terror
Please keep everyone safe —JR
Let me be a celebrity forever —Moe
Please give me more
May Japan become a permanent member of the UN Security Council! Establish cool warm biz!
Please let them forget the piano
......
May he maintain his popularity. May he walk —Chiba Zoo
May I recapture my popularity!!! —Tamao Nishi
May I please
more cash
Governor of Tokyo —Nakamitsu
WISHES ARE NEVER GRANTED!

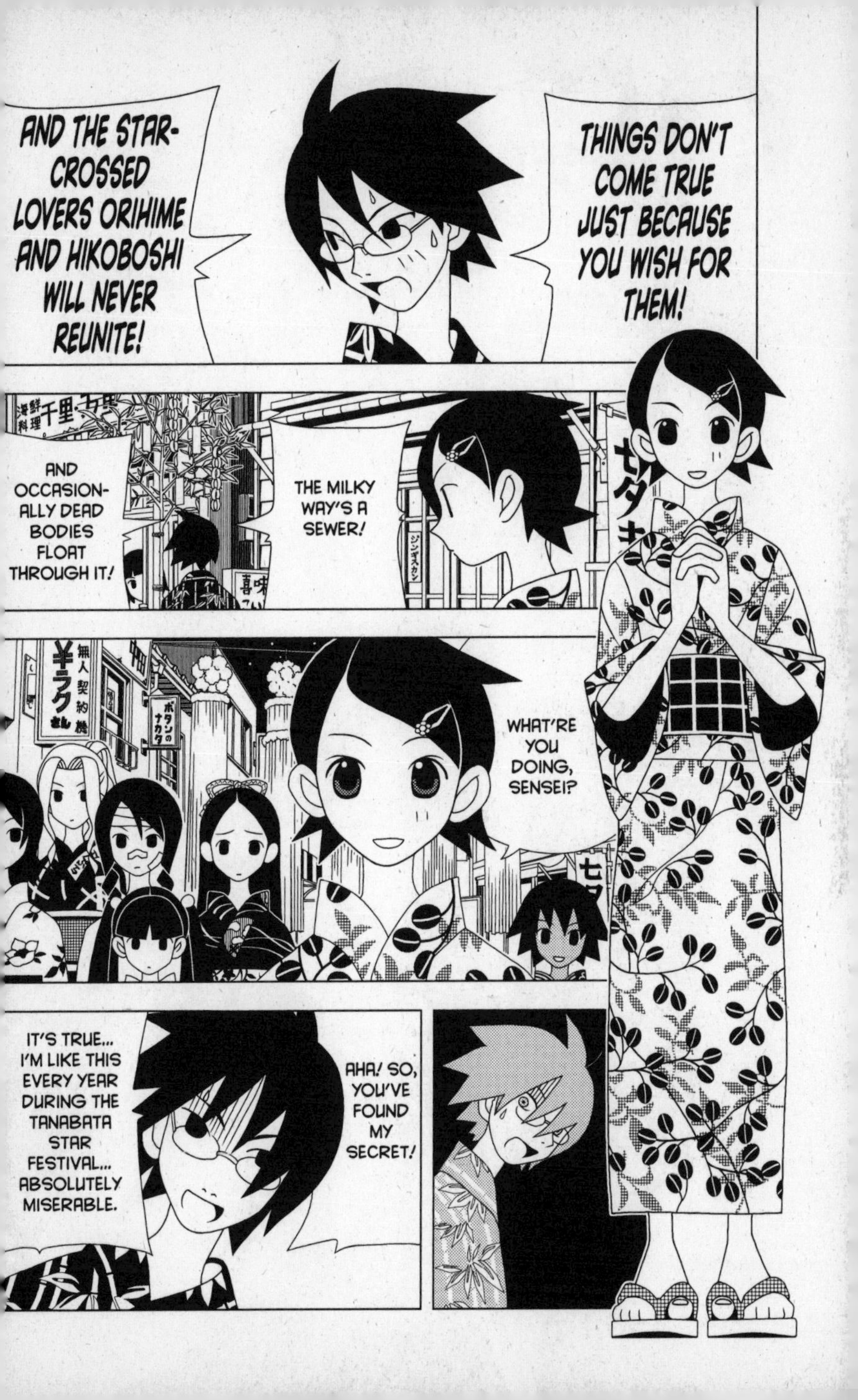
THINGS DON'T COME TRUE JUST BECAUSE YOU WISH FOR THEM!
AND THE STAR-CROSSED LOVERS ORIHIME AND HIKOBOSHI WILL NEVER REUNITE!
THE MILKY WAY'S A SEWER!
AND OCCASION-ALLY DEAD BODIES FLOAT THROUGH IT!
WHAT'RE YOU DOING, SENSEI?
AHA! SO, YOU'VE FOUND MY SECRET!
IT'S TRUE... I'M LIKE THIS EVERY YEAR DURING THE TANABATA STAR FESTIVAL... ABSOLUTELY MISERABLE.

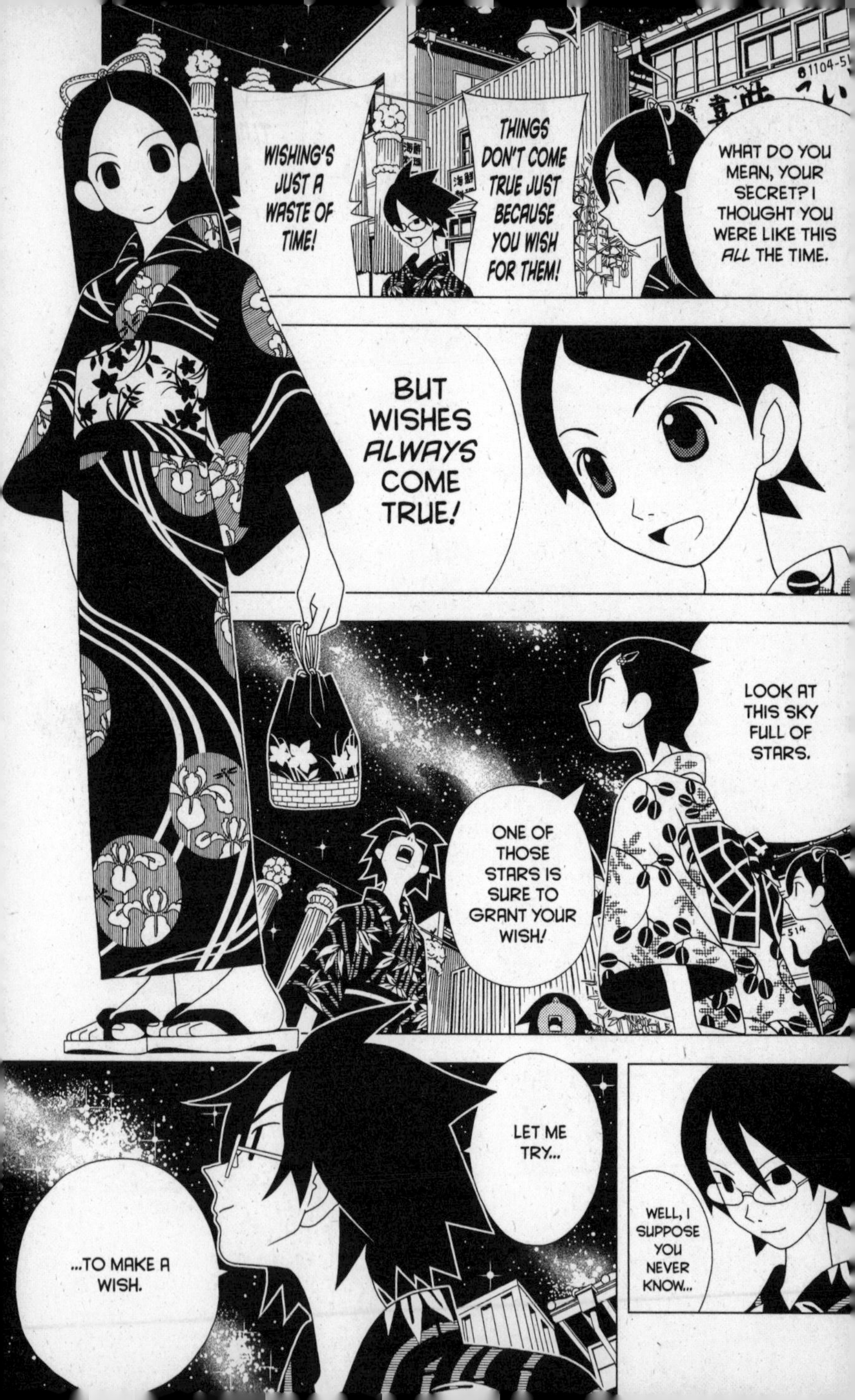
WHAT DO YOU MEAN, YOUR SECRET? I THOUGHT YOU WERE LIKE THIS *ALL* THE TIME.
THINGS DON'T COME TRUE JUST BECAUSE YOU WISH FOR THEM!
WISHING'S JUST A WASTE OF TIME!
BUT WISHES *ALWAYS* COME TRUE!
LOOK AT THIS SKY FULL OF STARS.
ONE OF THOSE STARS IS SURE TO GRANT YOUR WISH!
WELL, I SUPPOSE YOU NEVER KNOW...
LET ME TRY...
...TO MAKE A WISH.

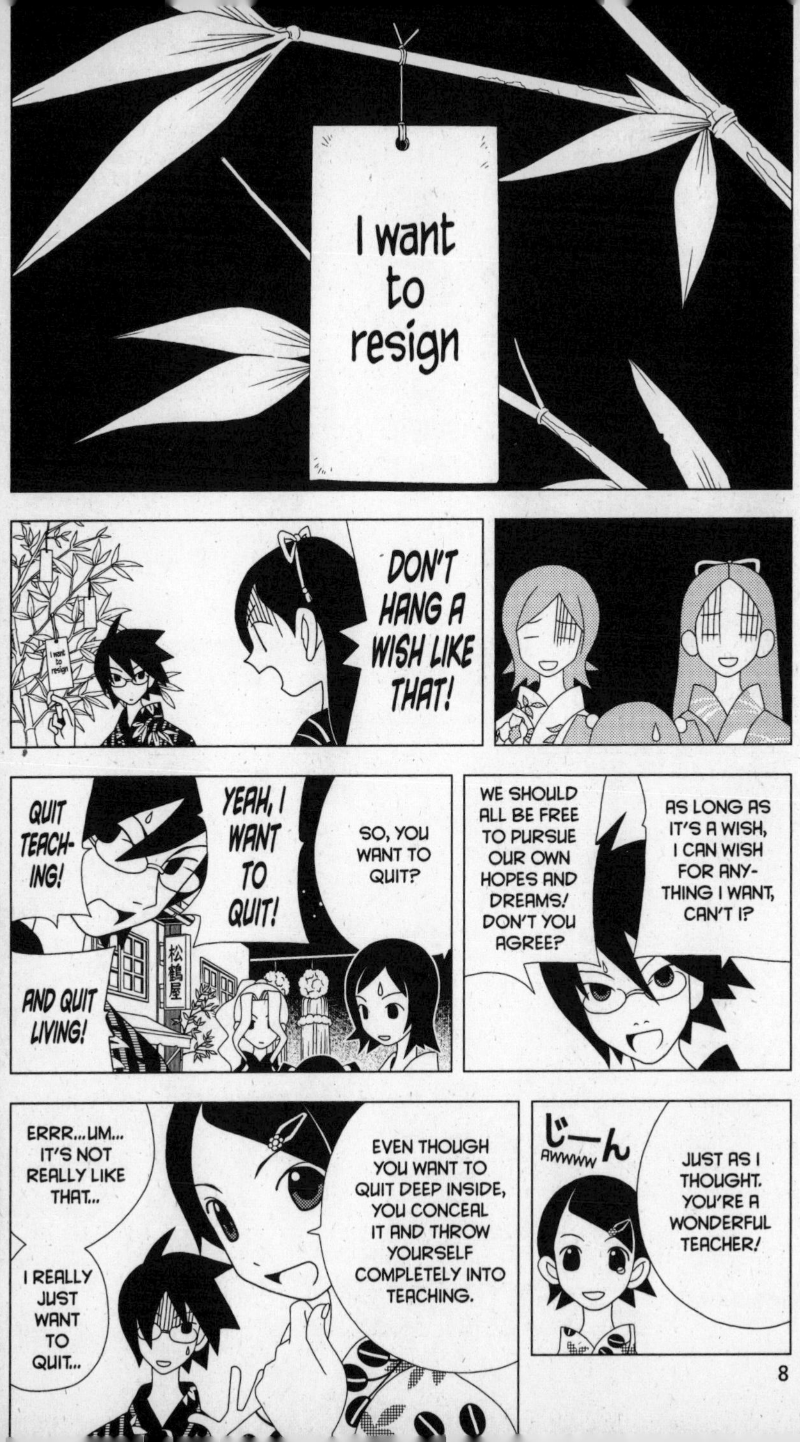
I want to resign
DON'T HANG A WISH LIKE THAT!
AS LONG AS IT'S A WISH, I CAN WISH FOR ANY-THING I WANT, CAN'T I?
WE SHOULD ALL BE FREE TO PURSUE OUR OWN HOPES AND DREAMS! DON'T YOU AGREE?
SO, YOU WANT TO QUIT?
YEAH, I WANT TO QUIT!
QUIT TEACH-ING!
松鶴屋
AND QUIT LIVING!
じーん
AWWWWW
JUST AS I THOUGHT. YOU'RE A WONDERFUL TEACHER!
EVEN THOUGH YOU WANT TO QUIT DEEP INSIDE, YOU CONCEAL IT AND THROW YOURSELF COMPLETELY INTO TEACHING.
ERRR...UM... IT'S NOT REALLY LIKE THAT...
I REALLY JUST WANT TO QUIT...

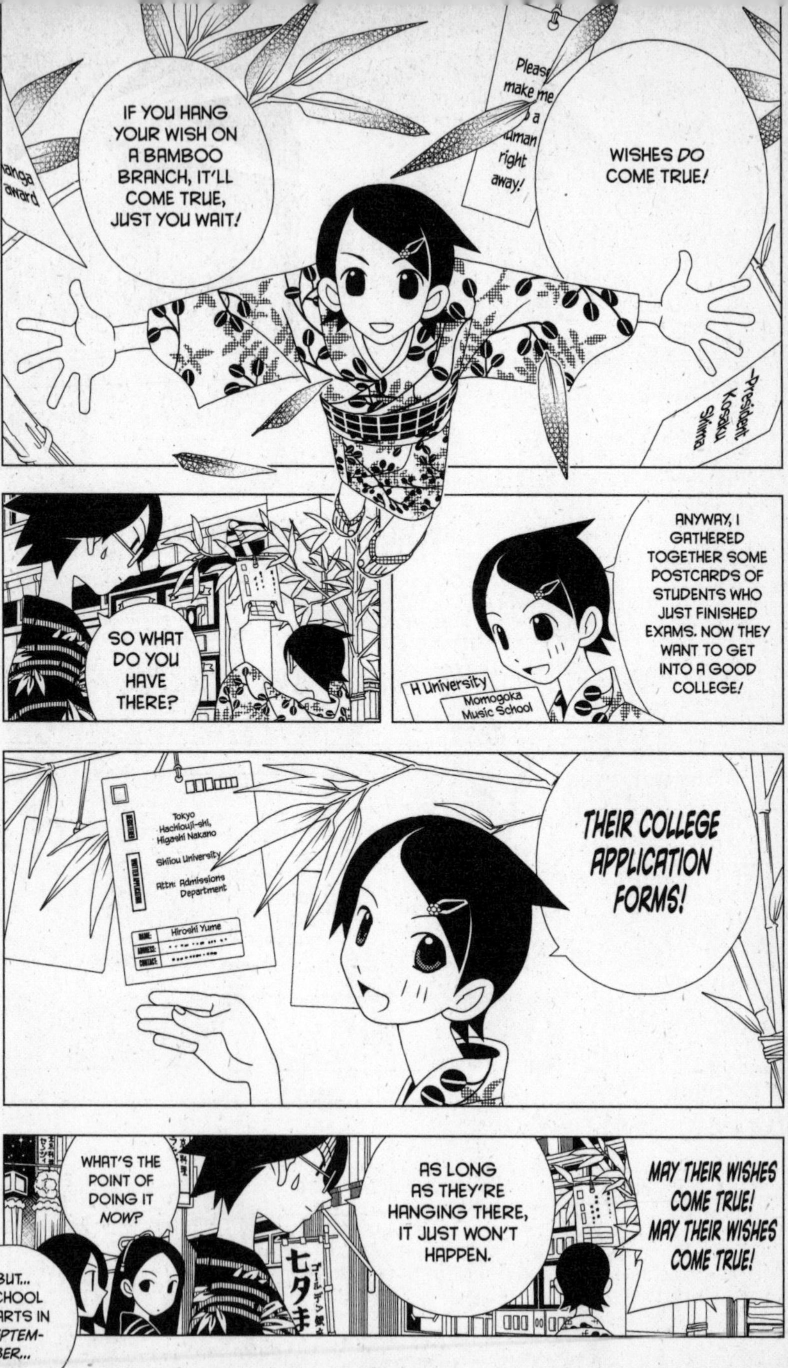
WISHES DO COME TRUE!
Please make me a
right away!
IF YOU HANG YOUR WISH ON A BAMBOO BRANCH, IT'LL COME TRUE, JUST YOU WAIT!
award
-President Kosaku Shima
ANYWAY, I GATHERED TOGETHER SOME POSTCARDS OF STUDENTS WHO JUST FINISHED EXAMS. NOW THEY WANT TO GET INTO A GOOD COLLEGE!
H University
Momogoka Music School
SO WHAT DO YOU HAVE THERE?
THEIR COLLEGE APPLICATION FORMS!
Tokyo Hachiouji-shi, Higashi Nakano
Shiiou University
Attn: Admissions Department
Hiroshi Yume
MAY THEIR WISHES COME TRUE! MAY THEIR WISHES COME TRUE!
AS LONG AS THEY'RE HANGING THERE, IT JUST WON'T HAPPEN.
WHAT'S THE POINT OF DOING IT NOW?
BUT... SCHOOL STARTS IN SEPTEMBER...

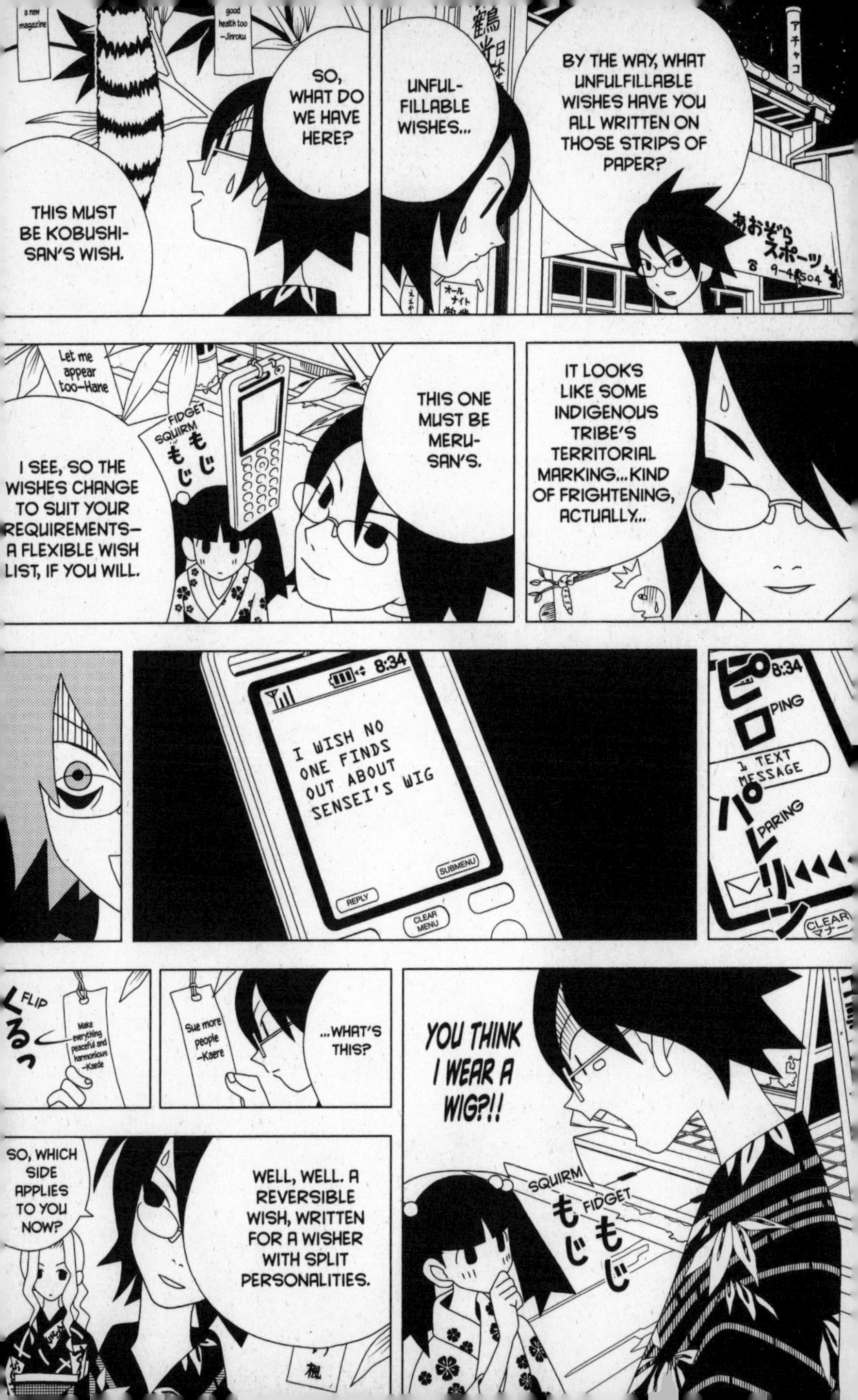

BY THE WAY, WHAT UNFULFILLABLE WISHES HAVE YOU ALL WRITTEN ON THOSE STRIPS OF PAPER?
アチャコ
あおぞらスポーツ
☎ 9-4504
UNFUL-FILLABLE WISHES...
good health too —Jinroku
a new magazine
SO, WHAT DO WE HAVE HERE?
THIS MUST BE KOBUSHI-SAN'S WISH.
IT LOOKS LIKE SOME INDIGENOUS TRIBE'S TERRITORIAL MARKING...KIND OF FRIGHTENING, ACTUALLY...
THIS ONE MUST BE MERU-SAN'S.
Let me appear too—Hane
FIDGET SQUIRM
もじもじ
I SEE, SO THE WISHES CHANGE TO SUIT YOUR REQUIREMENTS—A FLEXIBLE WISH LIST, IF YOU WILL.
8:34
ピロ PING
1 TEXT MESSAGE
パレリ PARING
CLEAR マナー
8:34
I WISH NO ONE FINDS OUT ABOUT SENSEI'S WIG
SUBMENU
REPLY
CLEAR MENU
YOU THINK I WEAR A WIG?!!
SQUIRM FIDGET
もじもじ
Sue more people —Kaere
...WHAT'S THIS?
FLIP くるっ
Make everything peaceful and harmonious —Kaede
WELL, WELL. A REVERSIBLE WISH, WRITTEN FOR A WISHER WITH SPLIT PERSONALITIES.
SO, WHICH SIDE APPLIES TO YOU NOW?

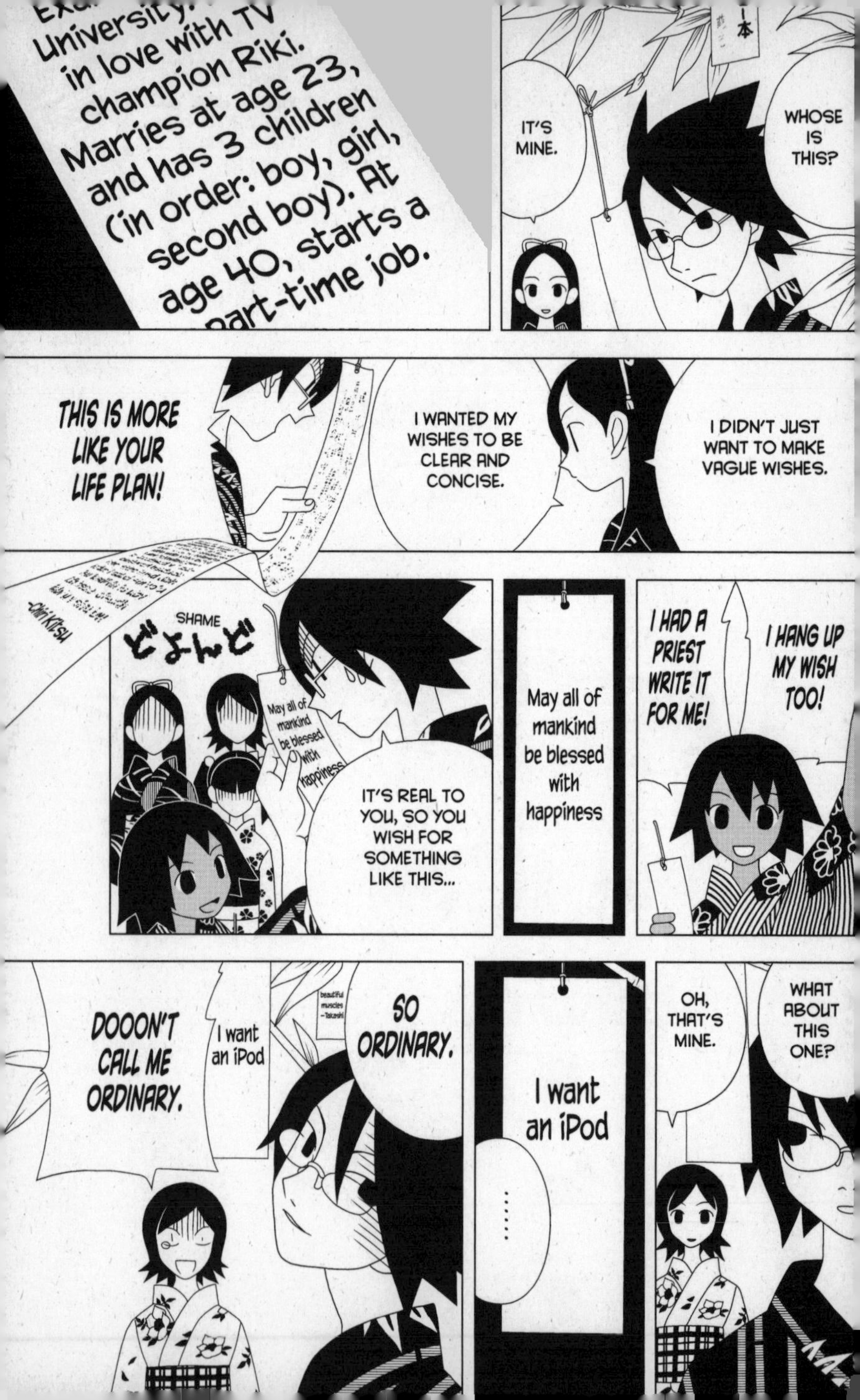
WHOSE IS THIS?
IT'S MINE.
University.
in love with TV champion Riki.
Marries at age 23, and has 3 children (in order: boy, girl, second boy). At age 40, starts a part-time job.
I DIDN'T JUST WANT TO MAKE VAGUE WISHES.
I WANTED MY WISHES TO BE CLEAR AND CONCISE.
THIS IS MORE LIKE YOUR LIFE PLAN!
I HANG UP MY WISH TOO!
I HAD A PRIEST WRITE IT FOR ME!
May all of mankind be blessed with happiness
May all of mankind be blessed with happiness
IT'S REAL TO YOU, SO YOU WISH FOR SOMETHING LIKE THIS...
SHAME
どよんど
WHAT ABOUT THIS ONE?
OH, THAT'S MINE.
I want an iPod
......
SO ORDINARY.
beautiful muscles —Takeshi
I want an iPod
DOOON'T CALL ME ORDINARY.

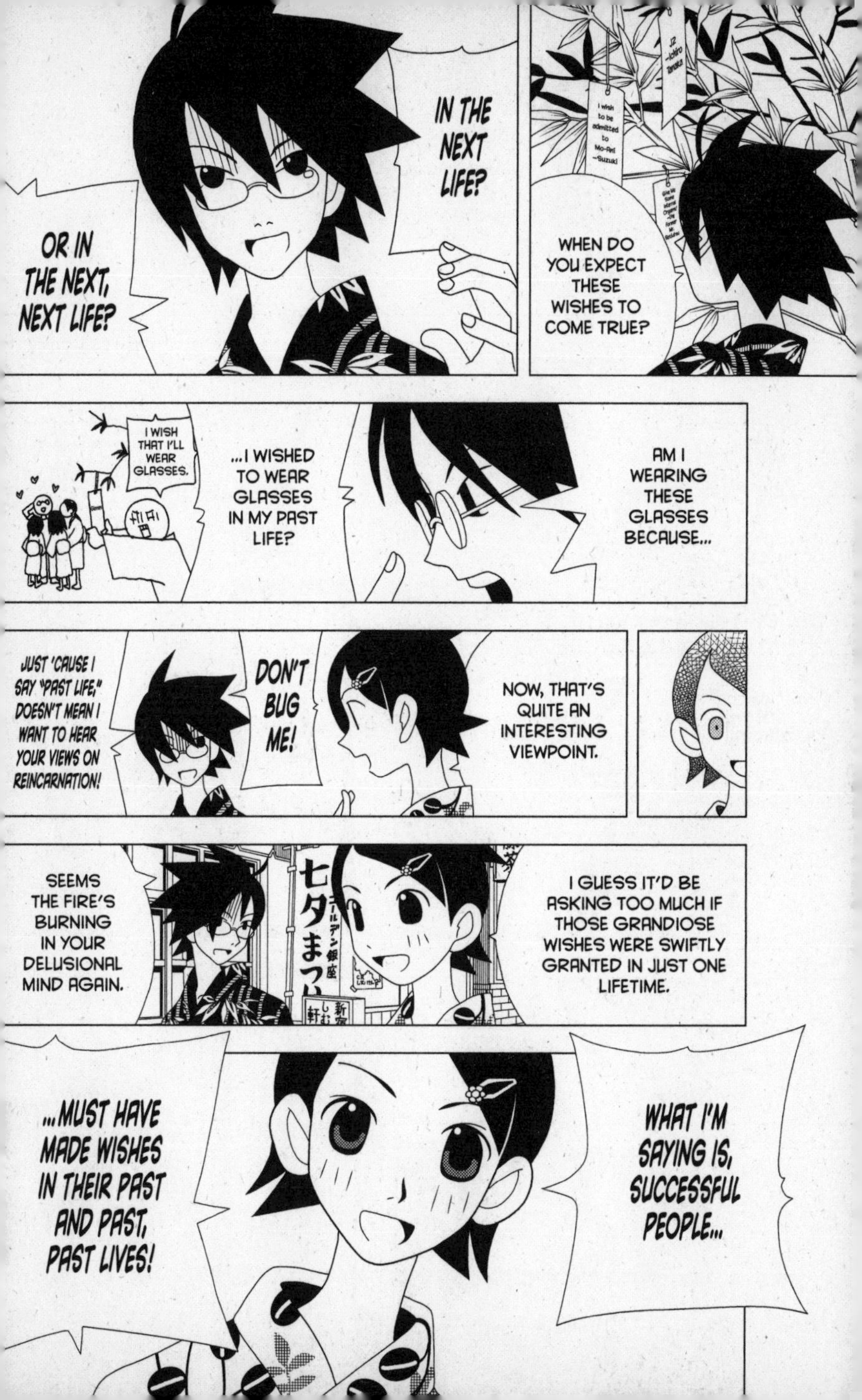
J2 —Ichiro Tanaka
I wish to be admitted to Mo-Ani —Suzuki
WHEN DO YOU EXPECT THESE WISHES TO COME TRUE?
IN THE NEXT LIFE?
OR IN THE NEXT, NEXT LIFE?
AM I WEARING THESE GLASSES BECAUSE...
...I WISHED TO WEAR GLASSES IN MY PAST LIFE?
I WISH THAT I'LL WEAR GLASSES.
NOW, THAT'S QUITE AN INTERESTING VIEWPOINT.
DON'T BUG ME!
JUST 'CAUSE I SAY "PAST LIFE," DOESN'T MEAN I WANT TO HEAR YOUR VIEWS ON REINCARNATION!
I GUESS IT'D BE ASKING TOO MUCH IF THOSE GRANDIOSE WISHES WERE SWIFTLY GRANTED IN JUST ONE LIFETIME.
七夕まつり
SEEMS THE FIRE'S BURNING IN YOUR DELUSIONAL MIND AGAIN.
WHAT I'M SAYING IS, SUCCESSFUL PEOPLE...
...MUST HAVE MADE WISHES IN THEIR PAST AND PAST, PAST LIVES!

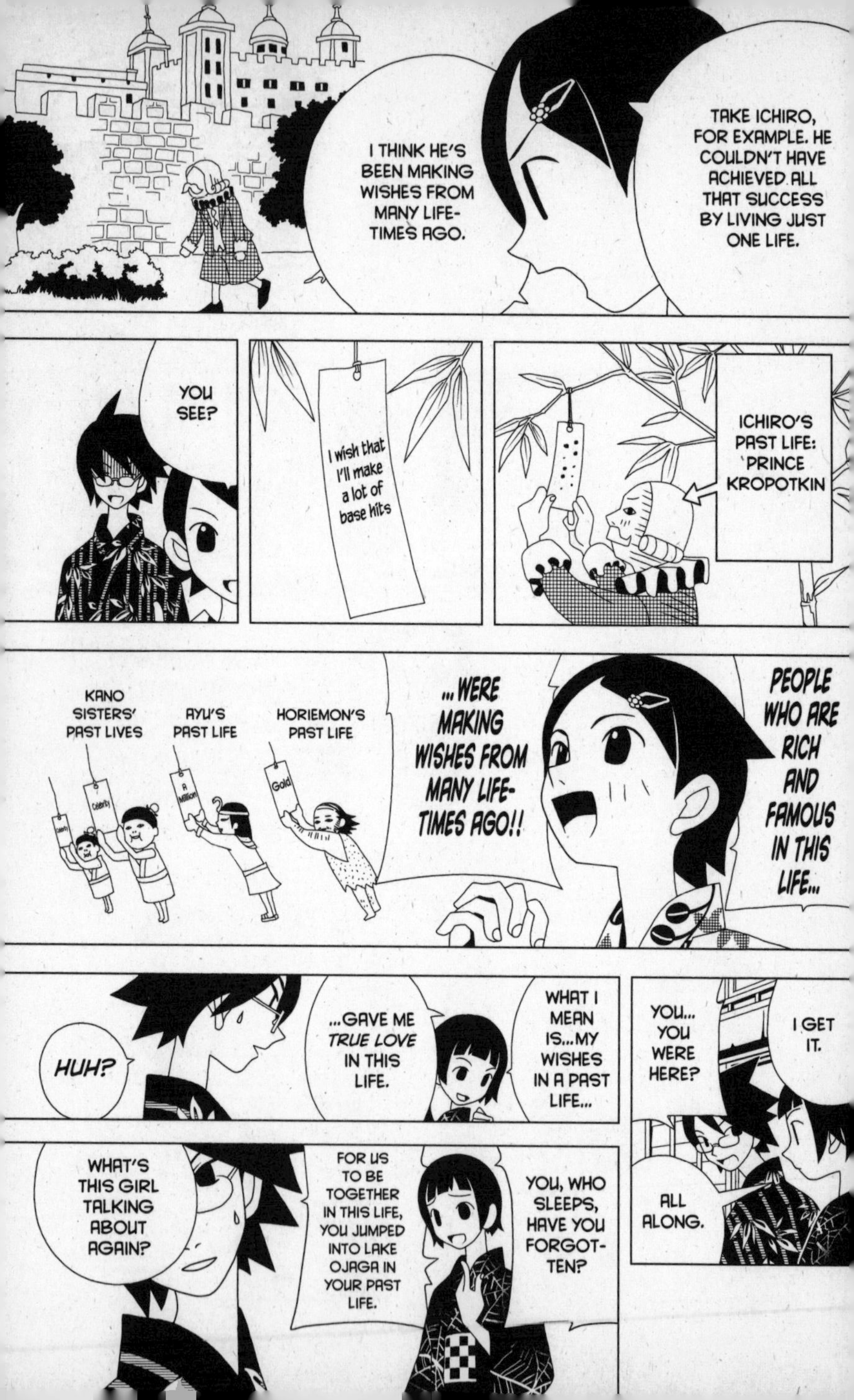
TAKE ICHIRO, FOR EXAMPLE. HE COULDN'T HAVE ACHIEVED ALL THAT SUCCESS BY LIVING JUST ONE LIFE.
I THINK HE'S BEEN MAKING WISHES FROM MANY LIFE-TIMES AGO.
ICHIRO'S PAST LIFE: PRINCE KROPOTKIN
I wish that I'll make a lot of base hits
YOU SEE?
PEOPLE WHO ARE RICH AND FAMOUS IN THIS LIFE...
...WERE MAKING WISHES FROM MANY LIFE-TIMES AGO!!
HORIEMON'S PAST LIFE
Gold
AYU'S PAST LIFE
A Million
KANO SISTERS' PAST LIVES
Celebrity
Celebrity
I GET IT.
YOU... YOU WERE HERE?
ALL ALONG.
WHAT I MEAN IS...MY WISHES IN A PAST LIFE...
...GAVE ME TRUE LOVE IN THIS LIFE.
HUH?
YOU, WHO SLEEPS, HAVE YOU FORGOT-TEN?
FOR US TO BE TOGETHER IN THIS LIFE, YOU JUMPED INTO LAKE OJAGA IN YOUR PAST LIFE.
WHAT'S THIS GIRL TALKING ABOUT AGAIN?

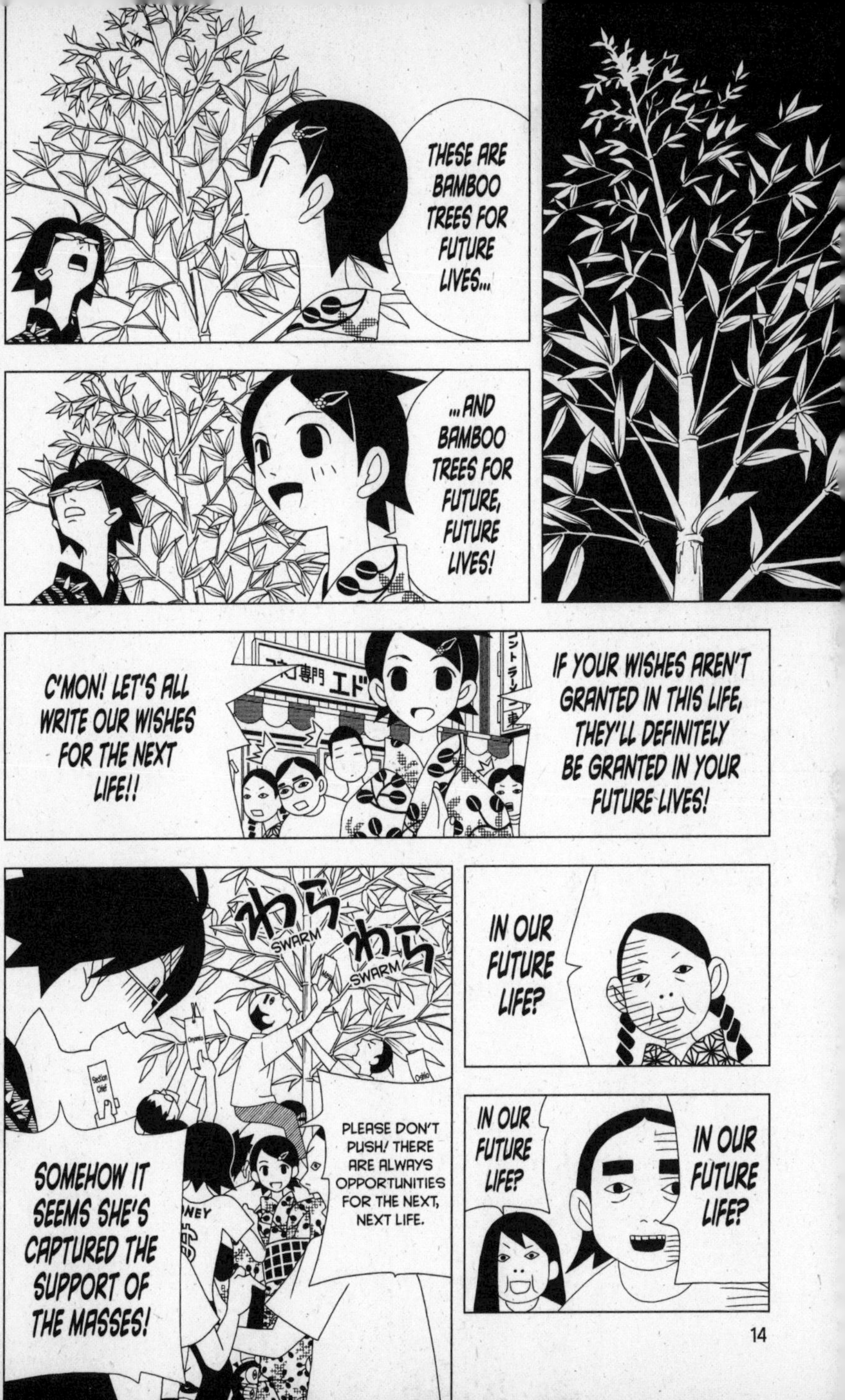
THESE ARE BAMBOO TREES FOR FUTURE LIVES...
...AND BAMBOO TREES FOR FUTURE, FUTURE LIVES!
IF YOUR WISHES AREN'T GRANTED IN THIS LIFE, THEY'LL DEFINITELY BE GRANTED IN YOUR FUTURE LIVES!
C'MON! LET'S ALL WRITE OUR WISHES FOR THE NEXT LIFE!!
IN OUR FUTURE LIFE?
IN OUR FUTURE LIFE?
IN OUR FUTURE LIFE?
わら
SWARM
わら
SWARM
PLEASE DON'T PUSH! THERE ARE ALWAYS OPPORTUNITIES FOR THE NEXT, NEXT LIFE.
SOMEHOW IT SEEMS SHE'S CAPTURED THE SUPPORT OF THE MASSES!

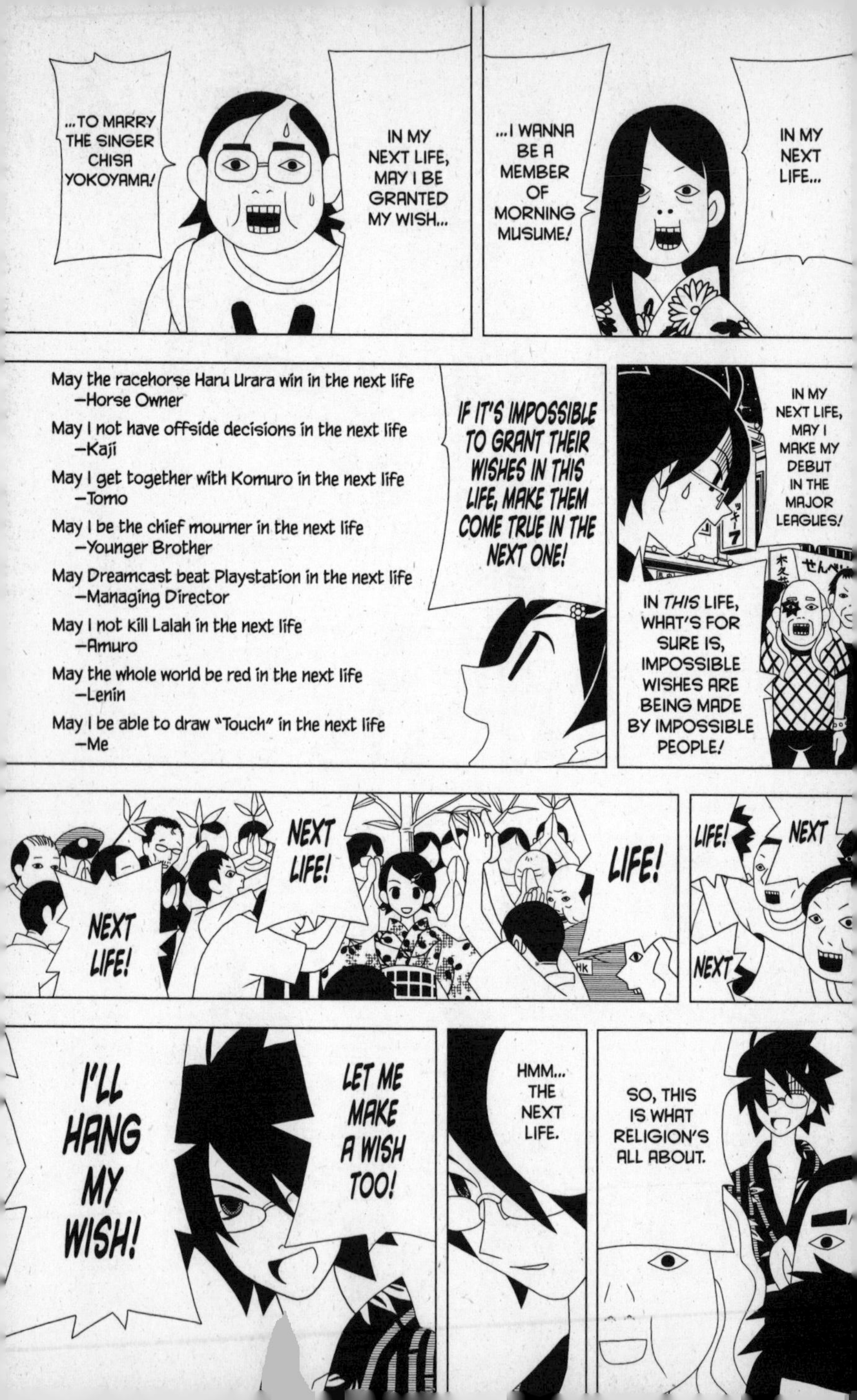
IN MY NEXT LIFE...
...I WANNA BE A MEMBER OF MORNING MUSUME!
IN MY NEXT LIFE, MAY I BE GRANTED MY WISH...
...TO MARRY THE SINGER CHISA YOKOYAMA!
IN MY NEXT LIFE, MAY I MAKE MY DEBUT IN THE MAJOR LEAGUES!
IN *THIS* LIFE, WHAT'S FOR SURE IS, IMPOSSIBLE WISHES ARE BEING MADE BY IMPOSSIBLE PEOPLE!
IF IT'S IMPOSSIBLE TO GRANT THEIR WISHES IN THIS LIFE, MAKE THEM COME TRUE IN THE NEXT ONE!
May the racehorse Haru Urara win in the next life —Horse Owner
May I not have offside decisions in the next life —Kaji
May I get together with Komuro in the next life —Tomo
May I be the chief mourner in the next life —Younger Brother
May Dreamcast beat Playstation in the next life —Managing Director
May I not kill Lalah in the next life —Amuro
May the whole world be red in the next life —Lenin
May I be able to draw "Touch" in the next life —Me
NEXT
LIFE!
NEXT
LIFE!
NEXT LIFE!
NEXT LIFE!
SO, THIS IS WHAT RELIGION'S ALL ABOUT.
HMM... THE NEXT LIFE.
LET ME MAKE A WISH TOO!
I'LL HANG MY WISH!

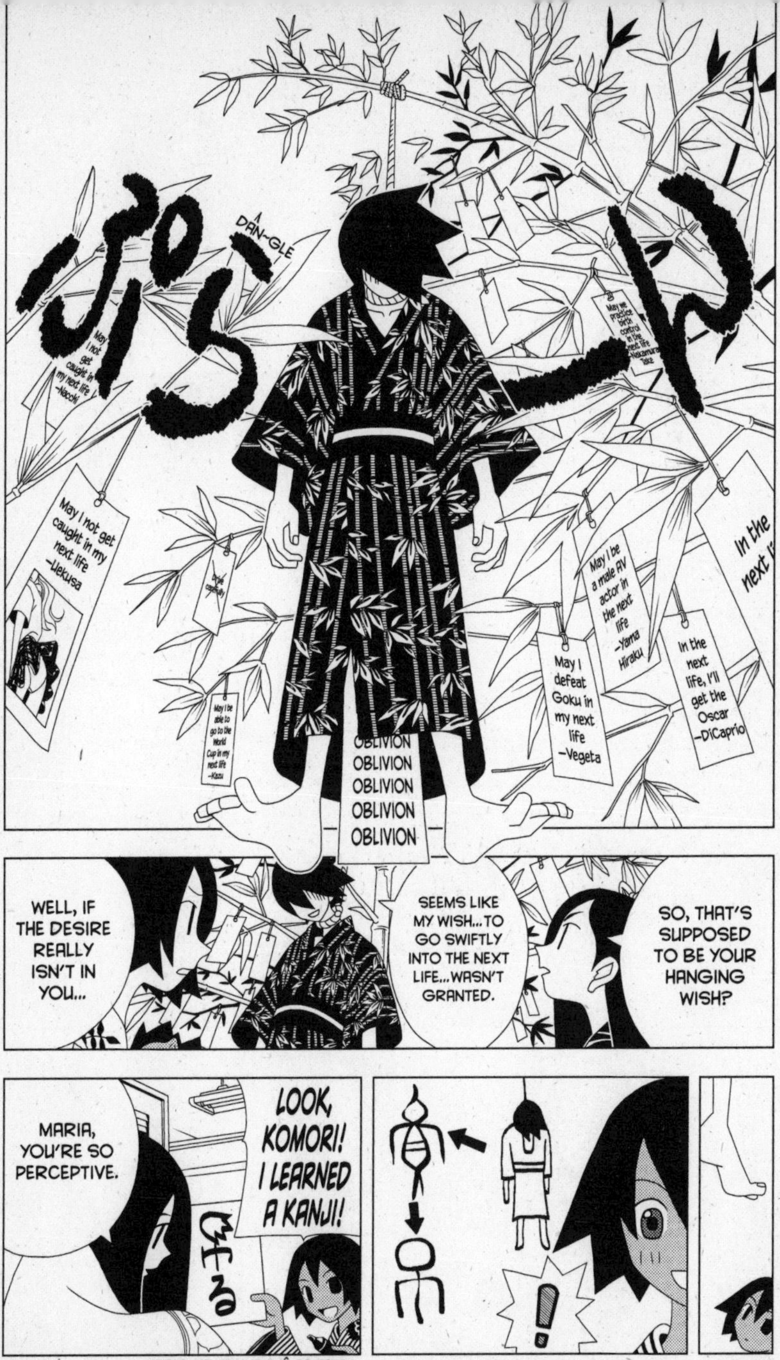

ぶらーん
DAN-GLE
In the next li
In the next life, I'll get the Oscar —DiCaprio
May I be a male AV actor in the next life —Yama Hiraku
May we practice birth control in the next life —Nakamura Take
May I defeat Goku in my next life —Vegeta
OBLIVION OBLIVION OBLIVION OBLIVION OBLIVION
May I be able to go to the World Cup in my next life —Kazu
Drive carefully
May I not get caught in my next life —Naochi
May I not get caught in my next life —Uekusa
SO, THAT'S SUPPOSED TO BE YOUR HANGING WISH?
SEEMS LIKE MY WISH...TO GO SWIFTLY INTO THE NEXT LIFE...WASN'T GRANTED.
WELL, IF THE DESIRE REALLY ISN'T IN YOU...
!
LOOK, KOMORI! I LEARNED A KANJI!
MARIA, YOU'RE SO PERCEPTIVE.


*NOTE: THE KANJI IS *CHÔ* OR *TSURU*, MEANING "TO HANG."

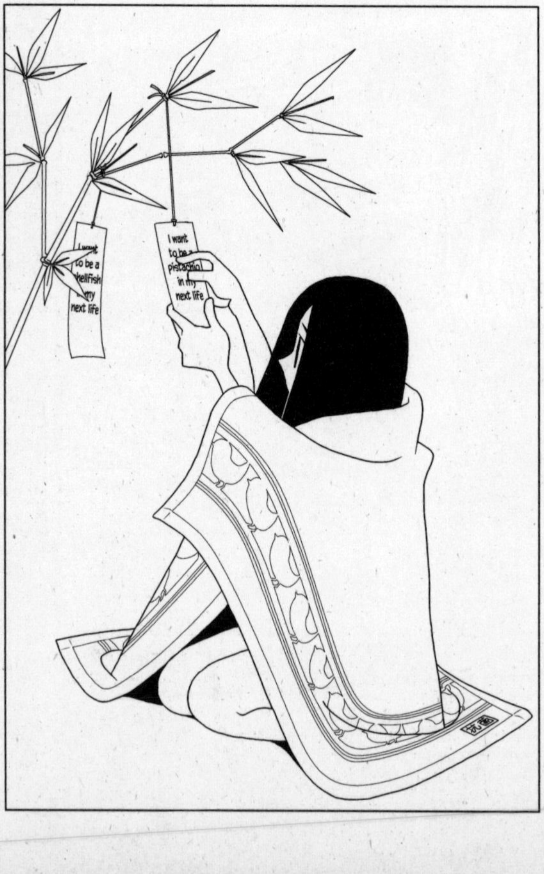

I want to be a pistachio in my next life
to be a
hellfish
next life

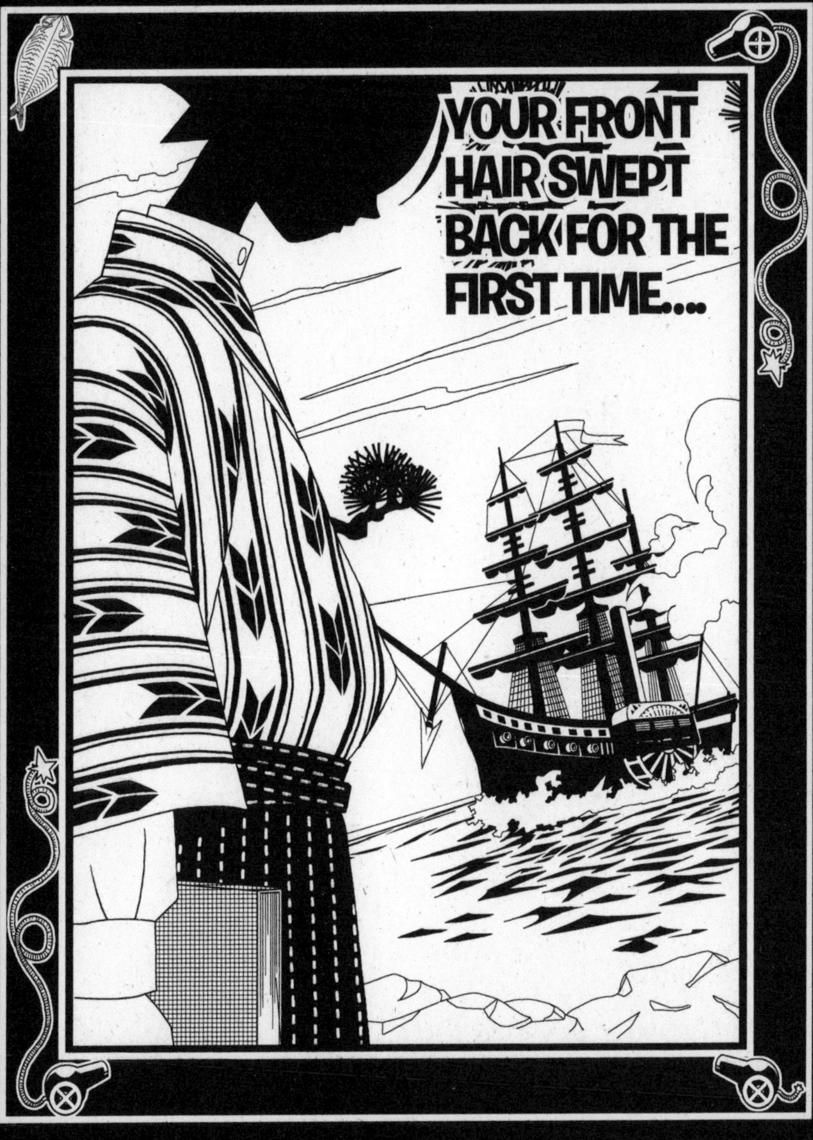
YOUR FRONT HAIR SWEPT BACK FOR THE FIRST TIME....

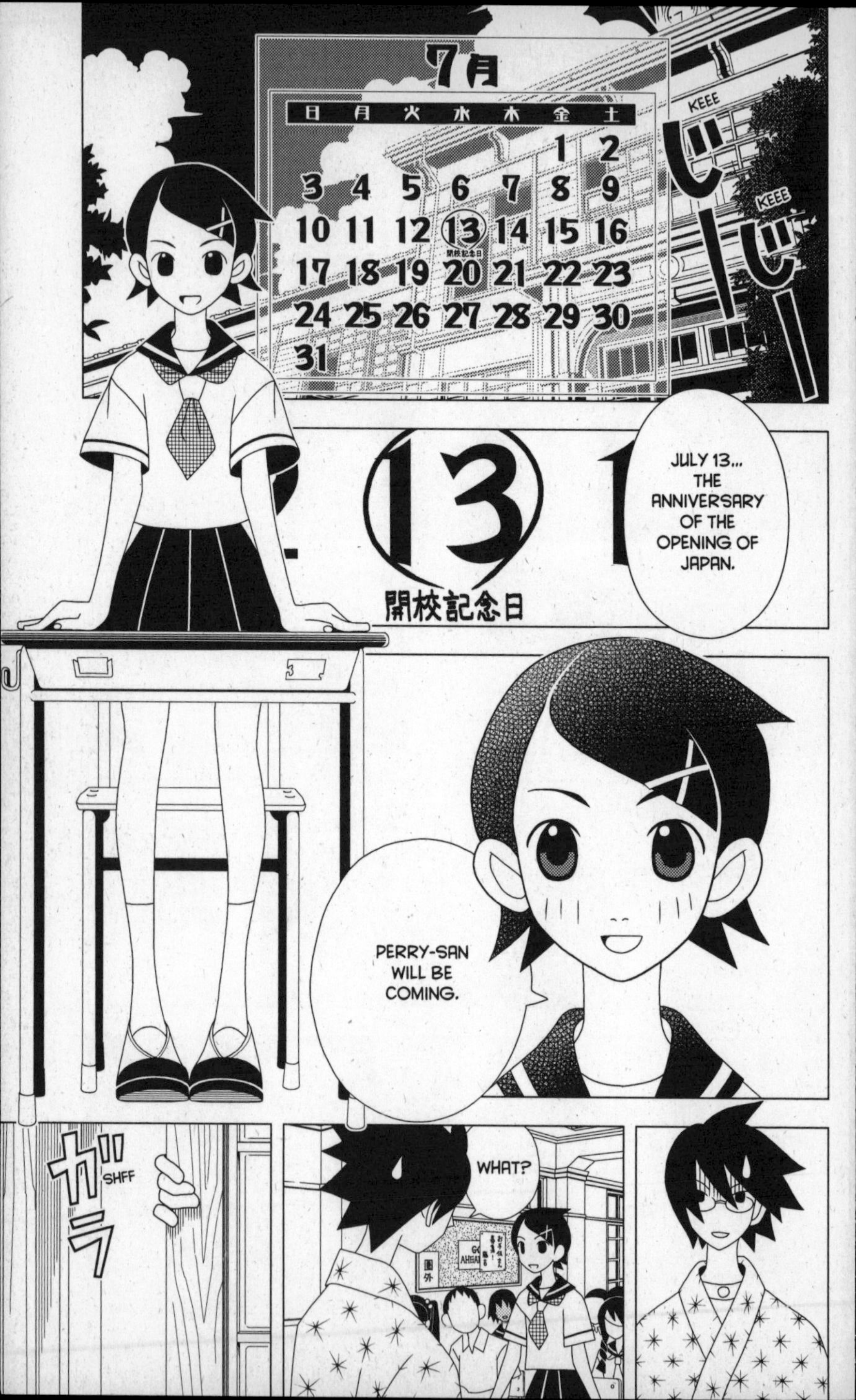
7月
日 月 火 水 木 金 土
1 2
3 4 5 6 7 8 9
10 11 12 13 14 15 16
開校記念日
17 18 19 20 21 22 23
24 25 26 27 28 29 30
31
じじー
KEEE
じー
KEEE
13
開校記念日
JULY 13... THE ANNIVERSARY OF THE OPENING OF JAPAN.
PERRY-SAN WILL BE COMING.
WHAT?
ガラ
SHFF

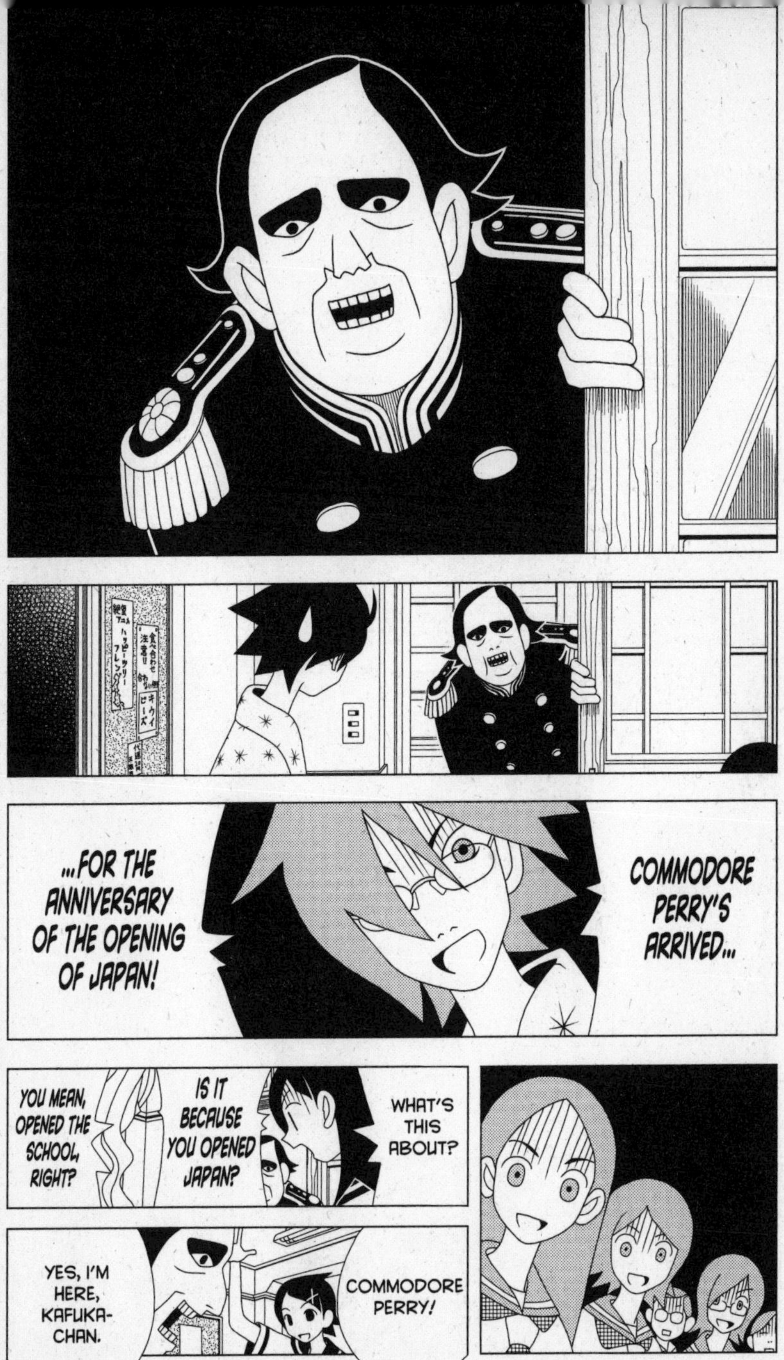
COMMODORE PERRY'S ARRIVED...
...FOR THE ANNIVERSARY OF THE OPENING OF JAPAN!
WHAT'S THIS ABOUT?
IS IT BECAUSE YOU OPENED JAPAN?
YOU MEAN, OPENED THE SCHOOL, RIGHT?
COMMODORE PERRY!
YES, I'M HERE, KAFUKA-CHAN.

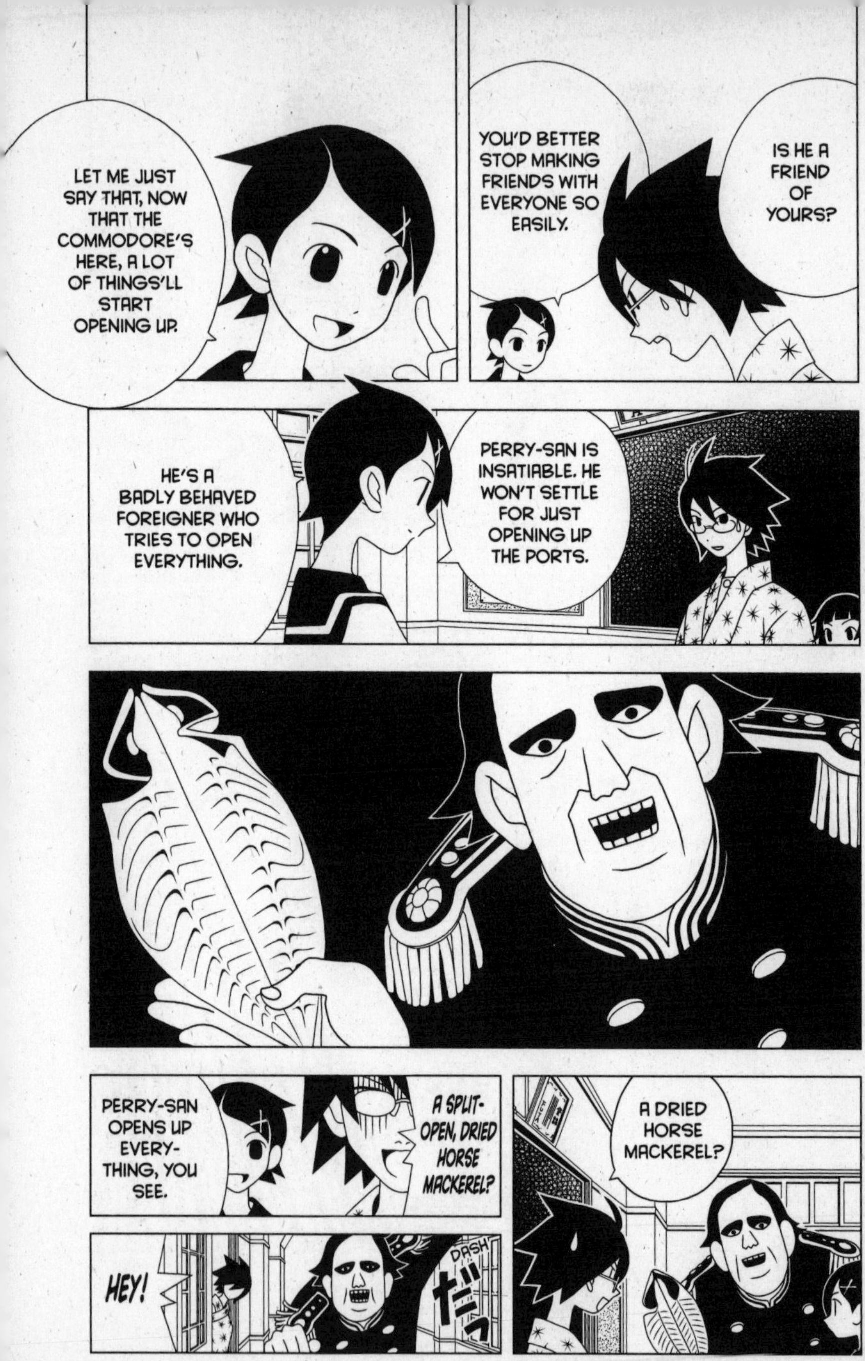
IS HE A FRIEND OF YOURS?
YOU'D BETTER STOP MAKING FRIENDS WITH EVERYONE SO EASILY.
LET ME JUST SAY THAT, NOW THAT THE COMMODORE'S HERE, A LOT OF THINGS'LL START OPENING UP.
PERRY-SAN IS INSATIABLE. HE WON'T SETTLE FOR JUST OPENING UP THE PORTS.
HE'S A BADLY BEHAVED FOREIGNER WHO TRIES TO OPEN EVERYTHING.
A DRIED HORSE MACKEREL?
A SPLIT-OPEN, DRIED HORSE MACKEREL?
PERRY-SAN OPENS UP EVERY-THING, YOU SEE.
DASH
だっ
HEY!

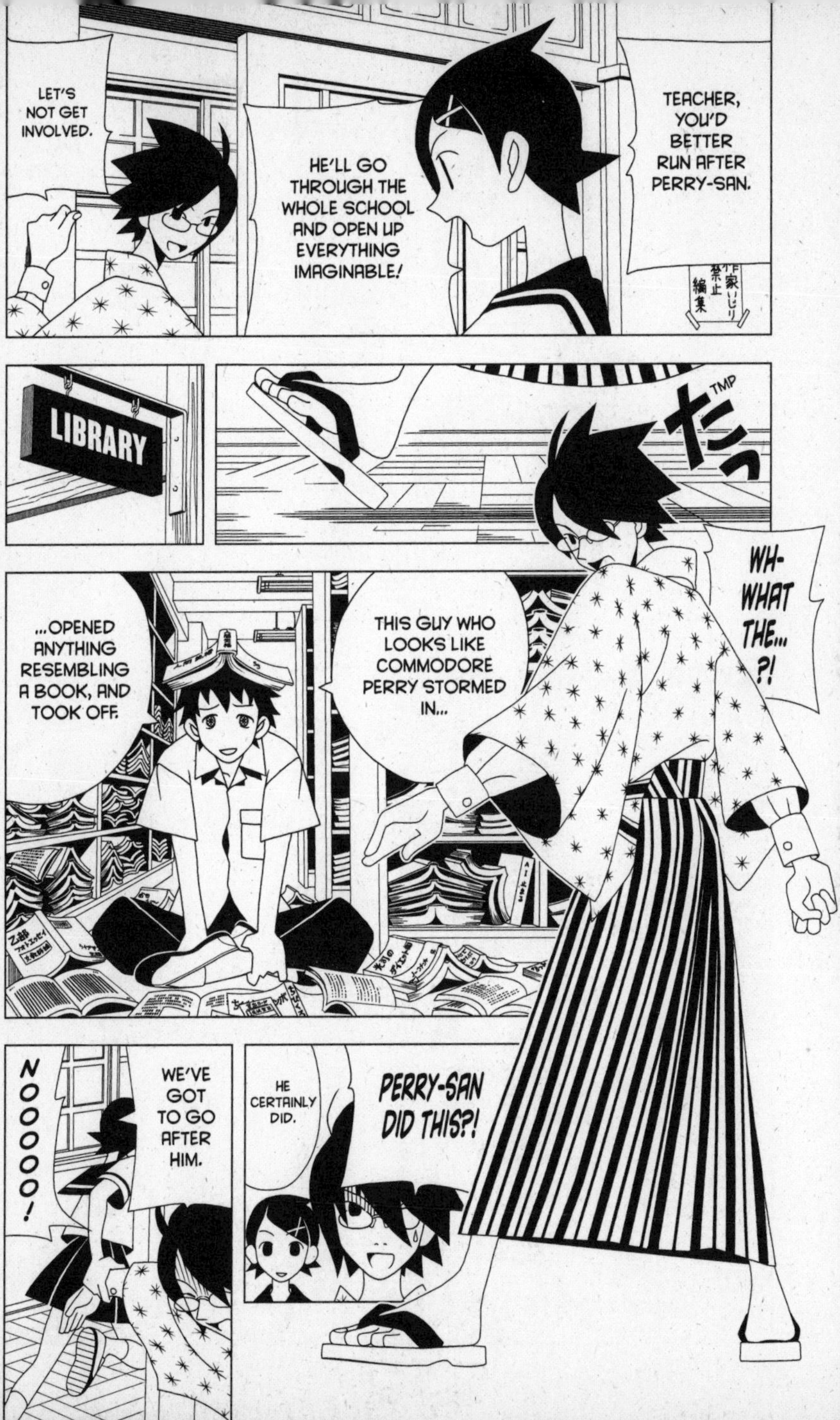
TEACHER, YOU'D BETTER RUN AFTER PERRY-SAN.
作家いじり禁止 編集
HE'LL GO THROUGH THE WHOLE SCHOOL AND OPEN UP EVERYTHING IMAGINABLE!
LET'S NOT GET INVOLVED.
TMP
たっ
LIBRARY
WH-WHAT THE...?!
THIS GUY WHO LOOKS LIKE COMMODORE PERRY STORMED IN...
...OPENED ANYTHING RESEMBLING A BOOK, AND TOOK OFF.
PERRY-SAN DID THIS?!
HE CERTAINLY DID.
WE'VE GOT TO GO AFTER HIM.
NOOOOOO!

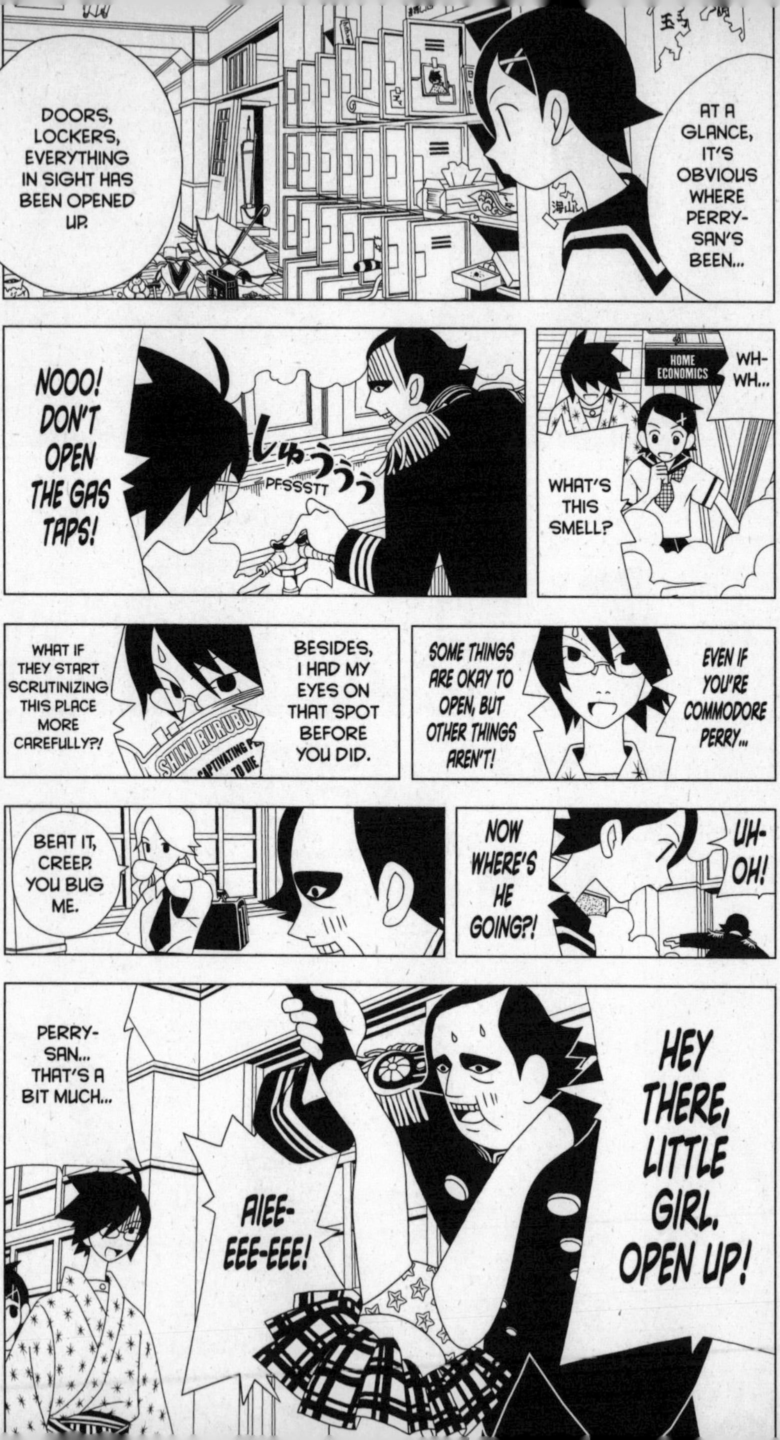
AT A GLANCE, IT'S OBVIOUS WHERE PERRY-SAN'S BEEN...
DOORS, LOCKERS, EVERYTHING IN SIGHT HAS BEEN OPENED UP.
HOME ECONOMICS
WH-WH...
WHAT'S THIS SMELL?
しゅううう
PFSSSTT
NOOO! DON'T OPEN THE GAS TAPS!
EVEN IF YOU'RE COMMODORE PERRY...
SOME THINGS ARE OKAY TO OPEN, BUT OTHER THINGS AREN'T!
BESIDES, I HAD MY EYES ON THAT SPOT BEFORE YOU DID.
WHAT IF THEY START SCRUTINIZING THIS PLACE MORE CAREFULLY?!
SHINI RURUBU
UH-OH!
NOW WHERE'S HE GOING?!
BEAT IT, CREEP. YOU BUG ME.
HEY THERE, LITTLE GIRL, OPEN UP!
AIEE-EEE-EEE!
PERRY-SAN... THAT'S A BIT MUCH...

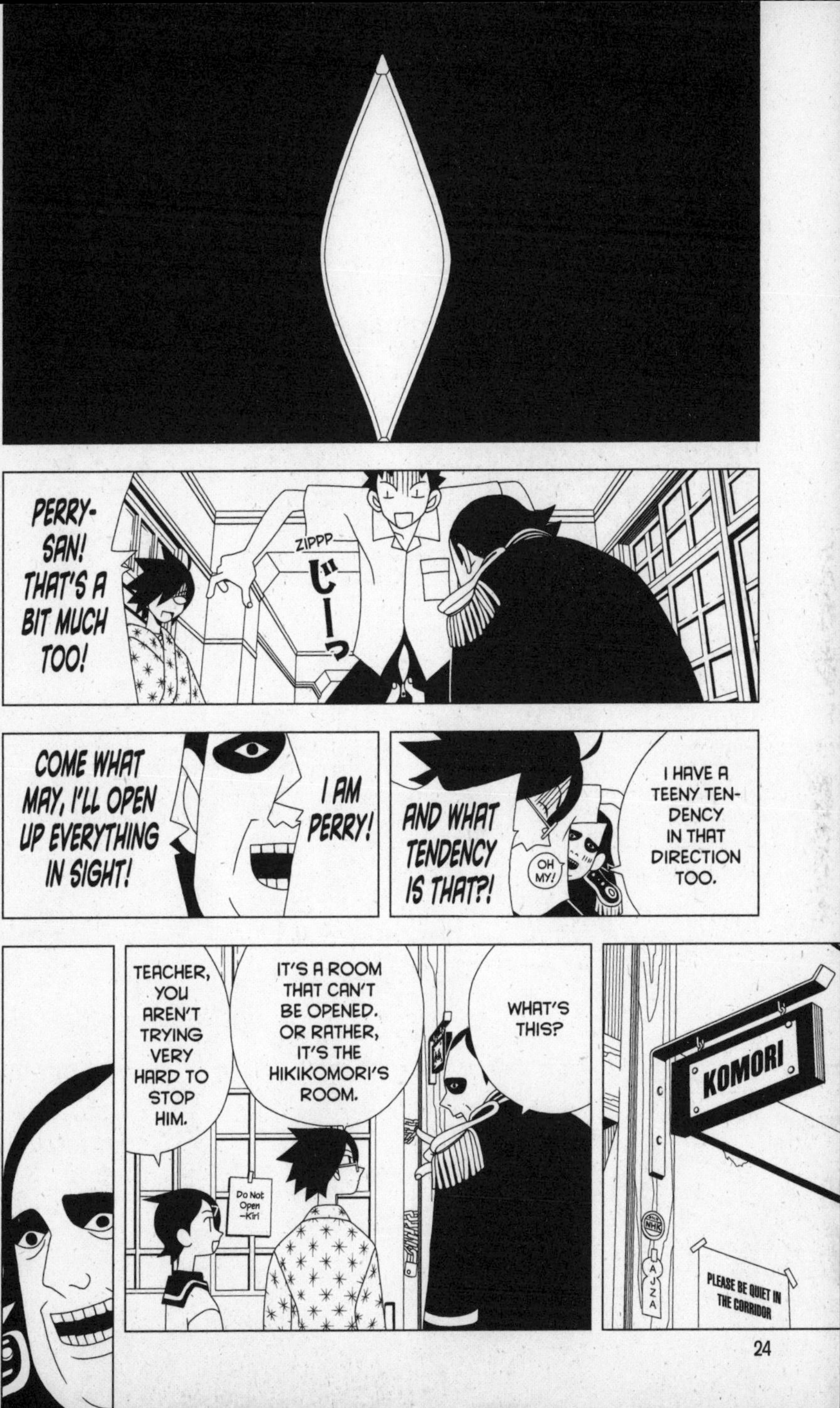
PERRY-SAN! THAT'S A BIT MUCH TOO!
ZIPPP
I HAVE A TEENY TENDENCY IN THAT DIRECTION TOO.
AND WHAT TENDENCY IS THAT?!
OH MY!
I AM PERRY!
COME WHAT MAY, I'LL OPEN UP EVERYTHING IN SIGHT!
KOMORI
NHK
AJZA
PLEASE BE QUIET IN THE CORRIDOR
WHAT'S THIS?
IT'S A ROOM THAT CAN'T BE OPENED. OR RATHER, IT'S THE HIKIKOMORI'S ROOM.
TEACHER, YOU AREN'T TRYING VERY HARD TO STOP HIM.
Do Not Open —Kiri

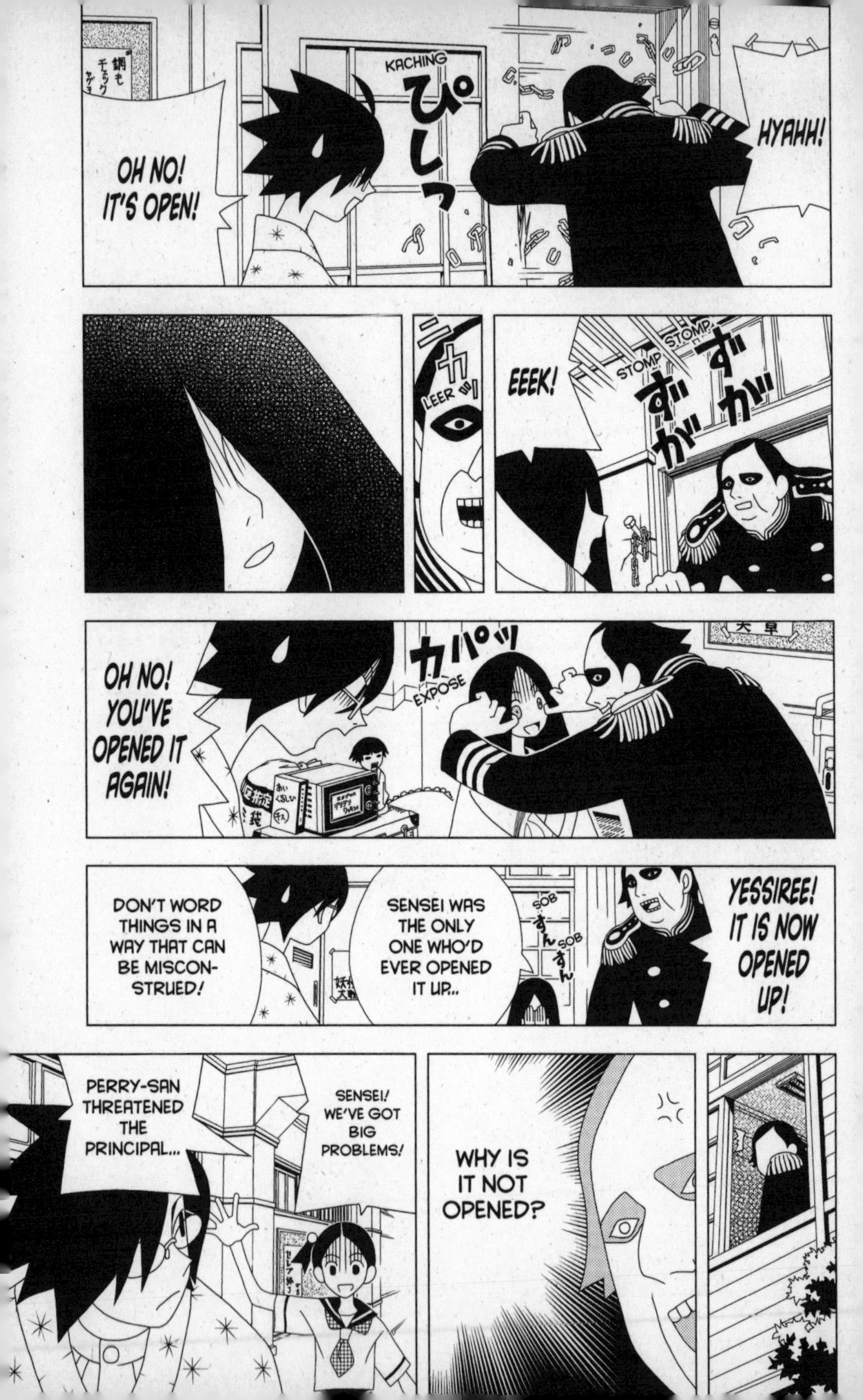
HYAHH!
KACHING
ぴしっ
OH NO! IT'S OPEN!
STOMP STOMP
ずかずか
EEEK!
ニカッ
LEER
カパッ
EXPOSE
OH NO! YOU'VE OPENED IT AGAIN!
YESSIREE! IT IS NOW OPENED UP!
SOB
ずん
SOB
ずん
SENSEI WAS THE ONLY ONE WHO'D EVER OPENED IT UP...
DON'T WORD THINGS IN A WAY THAT CAN BE MISCON-STRUED!
WHY IS IT NOT OPENED?
SENSEI! WE'VE GOT BIG PROBLEMS!
PERRY-SAN THREATENED THE PRINCIPAL...

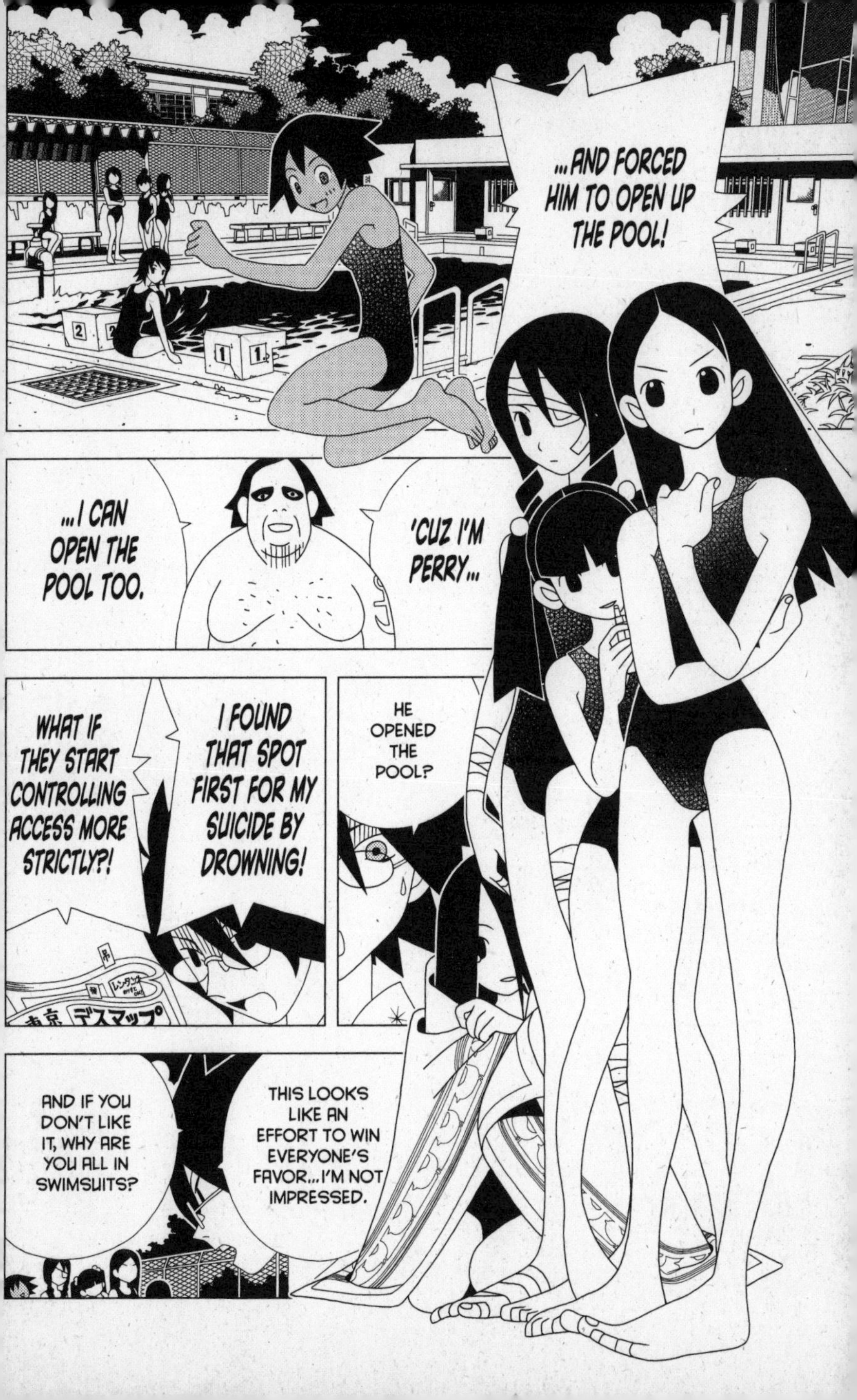

...AND FORCED HIM TO OPEN UP THE POOL!
'CUZ I'M PERRY...
...I CAN OPEN THE POOL TOO.
HE OPENED THE POOL?
I FOUND THAT SPOT FIRST FOR MY SUICIDE BY DROWNING!
WHAT IF THEY START CONTROLLING ACCESS MORE STRICTLY?!
東京 デスマップ
THIS LOOKS LIKE AN EFFORT TO WIN EVERYONE'S FAVOR...I'M NOT IMPRESSED.
AND IF YOU DON'T LIKE IT, WHY ARE YOU ALL IN SWIMSUITS?

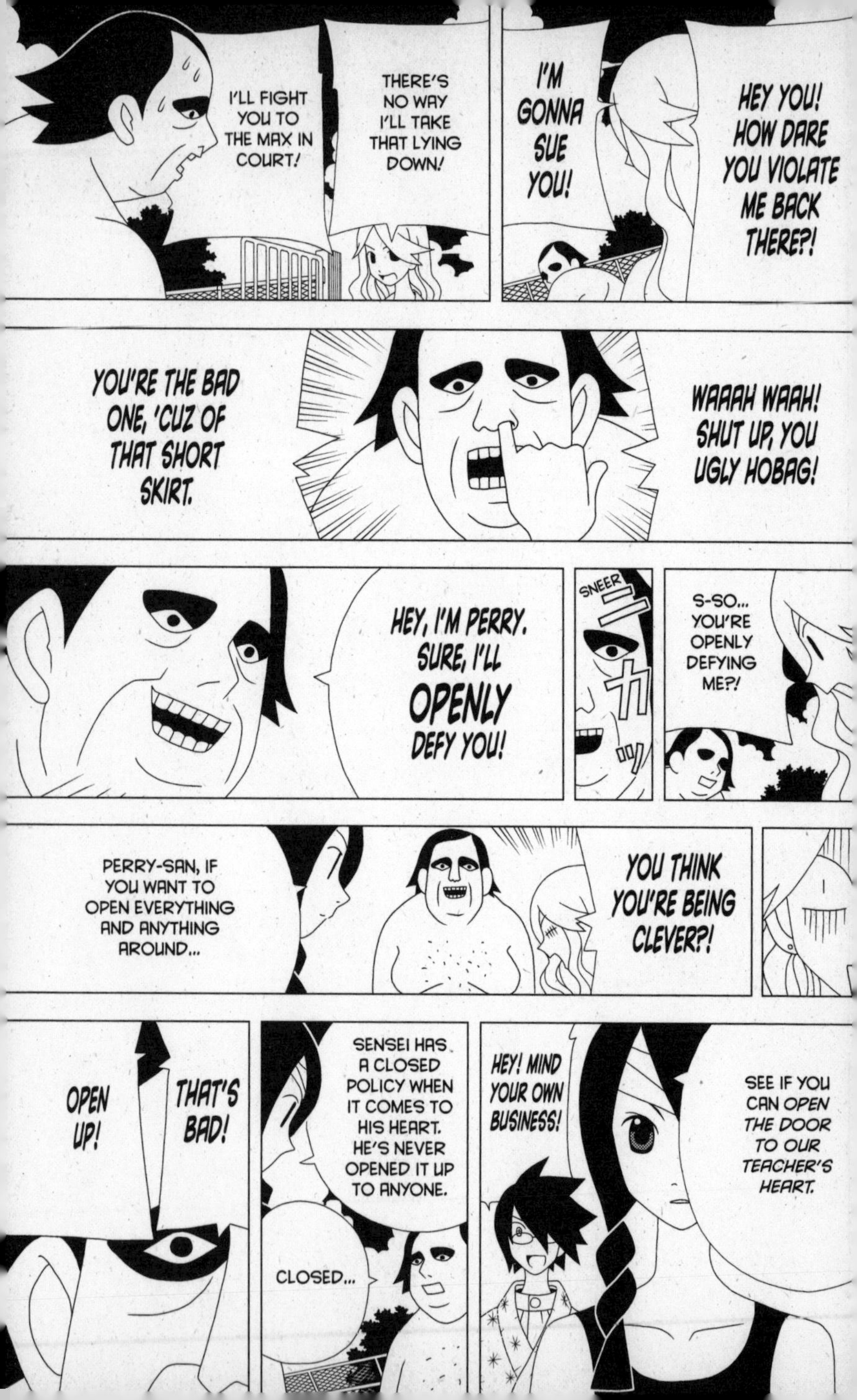
HEY YOU! HOW DARE YOU VIOLATE ME BACK THERE?!
I'M GONNA SUE YOU!
THERE'S NO WAY I'LL TAKE THAT LYING DOWN!
I'LL FIGHT YOU TO THE MAX IN COURT!
WAAAH WAAH! SHUT UP, YOU UGLY HOBAG!
YOU'RE THE BAD ONE, 'CUZ OF THAT SHORT SKIRT.
S-SO... YOU'RE OPENLY DEFYING ME?!
SNEER
HEY, I'M PERRY. SURE, I'LL OPENLY DEFY YOU!
YOU THINK YOU'RE BEING CLEVER?!
PERRY-SAN, IF YOU WANT TO OPEN EVERYTHING AND ANYTHING AROUND...
SEE IF YOU CAN OPEN THE DOOR TO OUR TEACHER'S HEART.
HEY! MIND YOUR OWN BUSINESS!
SENSEI HAS A CLOSED POLICY WHEN IT COMES TO HIS HEART. HE'S NEVER OPENED IT UP TO ANYONE.
CLOSED...
THAT'S BAD!
OPEN UP!

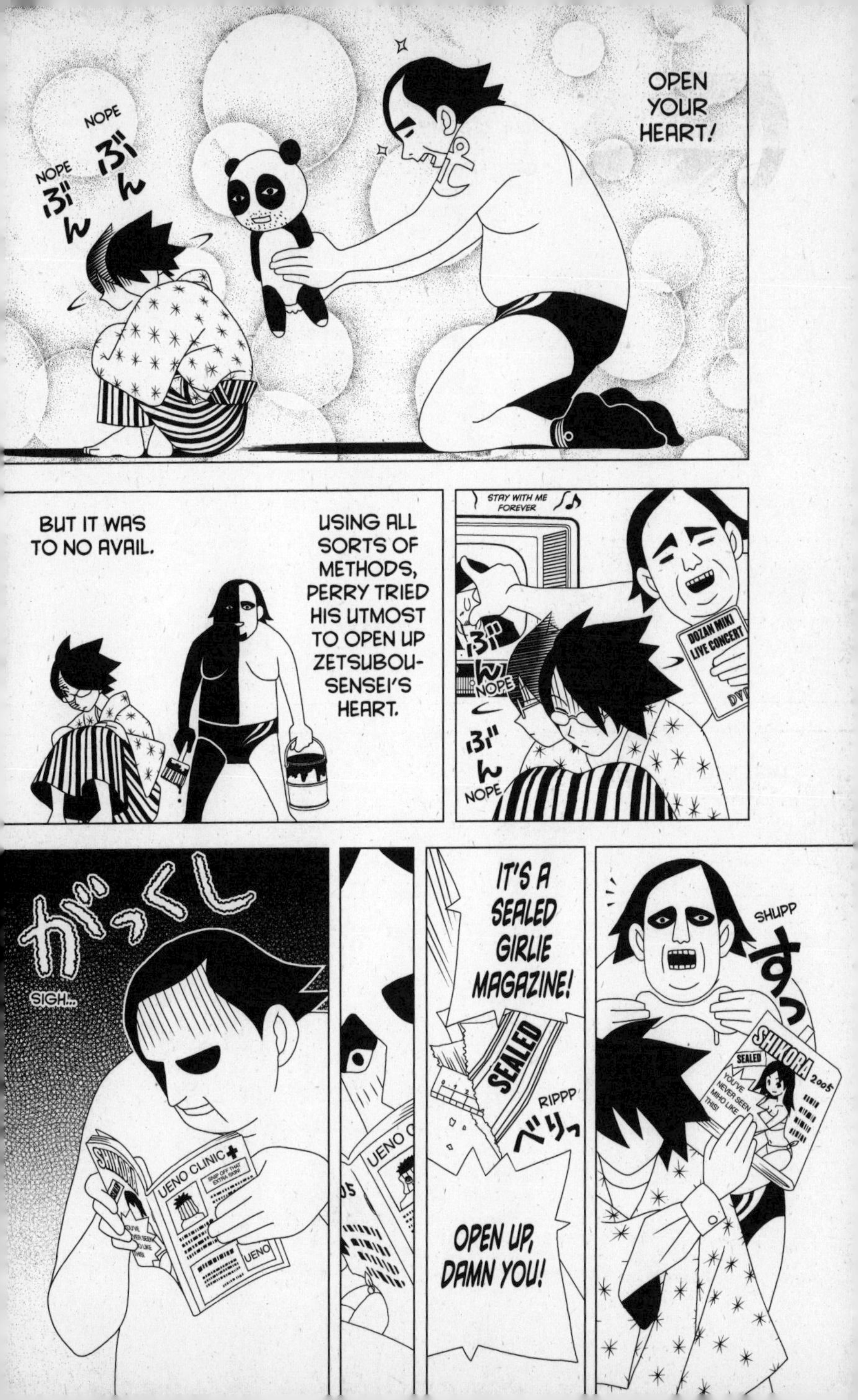
OPEN YOUR HEART!
ぶん NOPE
ぶん NOPE
STAY WITH ME FOREVER
DOZAN MIKI LIVE CONCERT DVD
ぶん NOPE
ぶん NOPE
USING ALL SORTS OF METHODS, PERRY TRIED HIS UTMOST TO OPEN UP ZETSUBOU-SENSEI'S HEART.
BUT IT WAS TO NO AVAIL.
すっ SHUPP
SHIKORA 2005
SEALED
YOU'VE NEVER SEEN MIHO LIKE THIS!
IT'S A SEALED GIRLIE MAGAZINE!
SEALED
べりっ RIPPP
OPEN UP, DAMN YOU!
がっくし
SIGH...
UENO CLINIC
SKIP OFF THAT EXTRA SKIN!
UENO

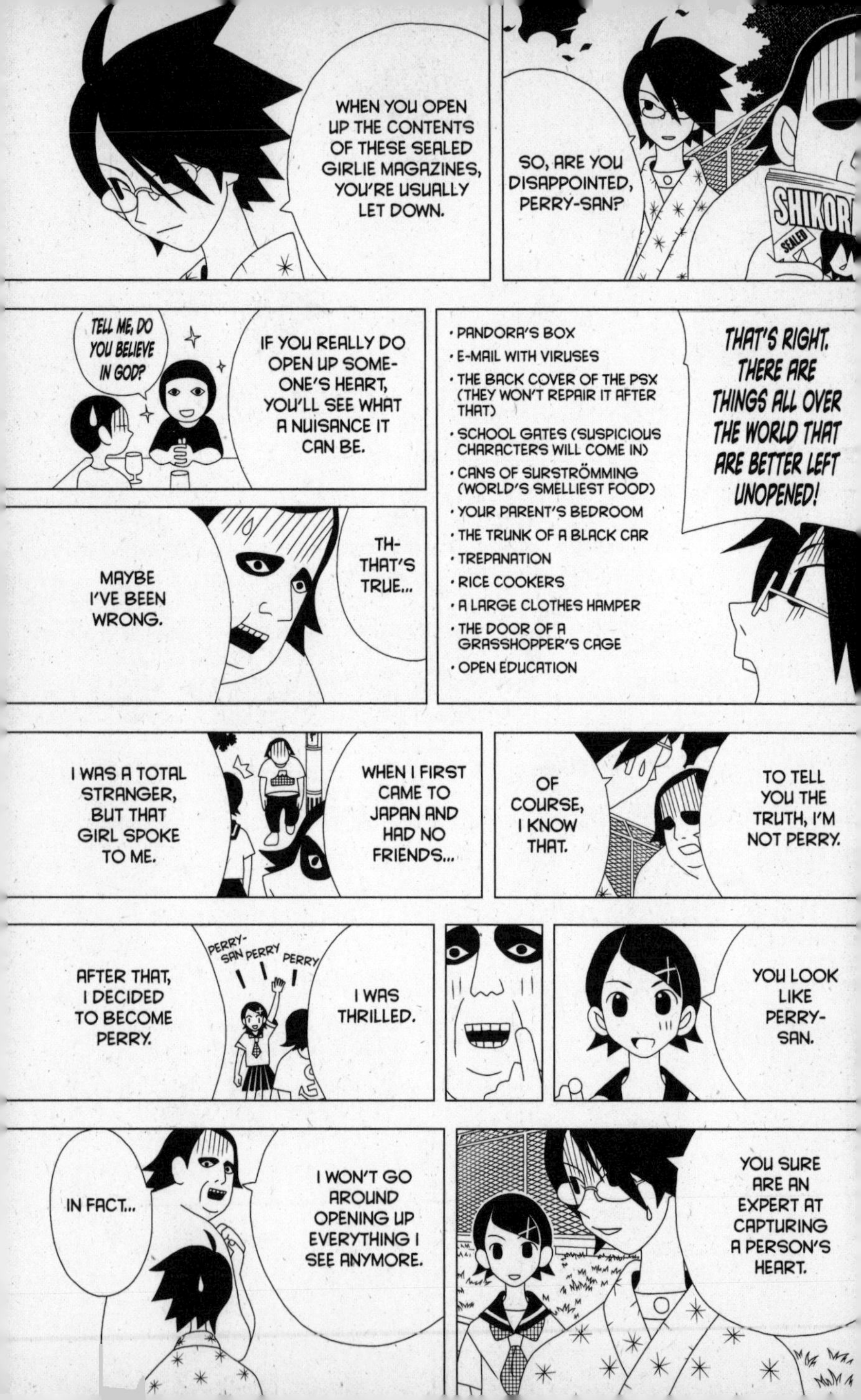
SO, ARE YOU DISAPPOINTED, PERRY-SAN?
SHIKOR
SEALED
WHEN YOU OPEN UP THE CONTENTS OF THESE SEALED GIRLIE MAGAZINES, YOU'RE USUALLY LET DOWN.
THAT'S RIGHT. THERE ARE THINGS ALL OVER THE WORLD THAT ARE BETTER LEFT UNOPENED!
• PANDORA'S BOX
• E-MAIL WITH VIRUSES
• THE BACK COVER OF THE PSX (THEY WON'T REPAIR IT AFTER THAT)
• SCHOOL GATES (SUSPICIOUS CHARACTERS WILL COME IN)
• CANS OF SURSTRÖMMING (WORLD'S SMELLIEST FOOD)
• YOUR PARENT'S BEDROOM
• THE TRUNK OF A BLACK CAR
• TREPANATION
• RICE COOKERS
• A LARGE CLOTHES HAMPER
• THE DOOR OF A GRASSHOPPER'S CAGE
• OPEN EDUCATION
IF YOU REALLY DO OPEN UP SOME-ONE'S HEART, YOU'LL SEE WHAT A NUISANCE IT CAN BE.
TELL ME, DO YOU BELIEVE IN GOD?
TH- THAT'S TRUE...
MAYBE I'VE BEEN WRONG.
TO TELL YOU THE TRUTH, I'M NOT PERRY.
OF COURSE, I KNOW THAT.
WHEN I FIRST CAME TO JAPAN AND HAD NO FRIENDS...
I WAS A TOTAL STRANGER, BUT THAT GIRL SPOKE TO ME.
YOU LOOK LIKE PERRY-SAN.
I WAS THRILLED.
PERRY
PERRY
PERRY-SAN
AFTER THAT, I DECIDED TO BECOME PERRY.
YOU SURE ARE AN EXPERT AT CAPTURING A PERSON'S HEART.
I WON'T GO AROUND OPENING UP EVERYTHING I SEE ANYMORE.
IN FACT...

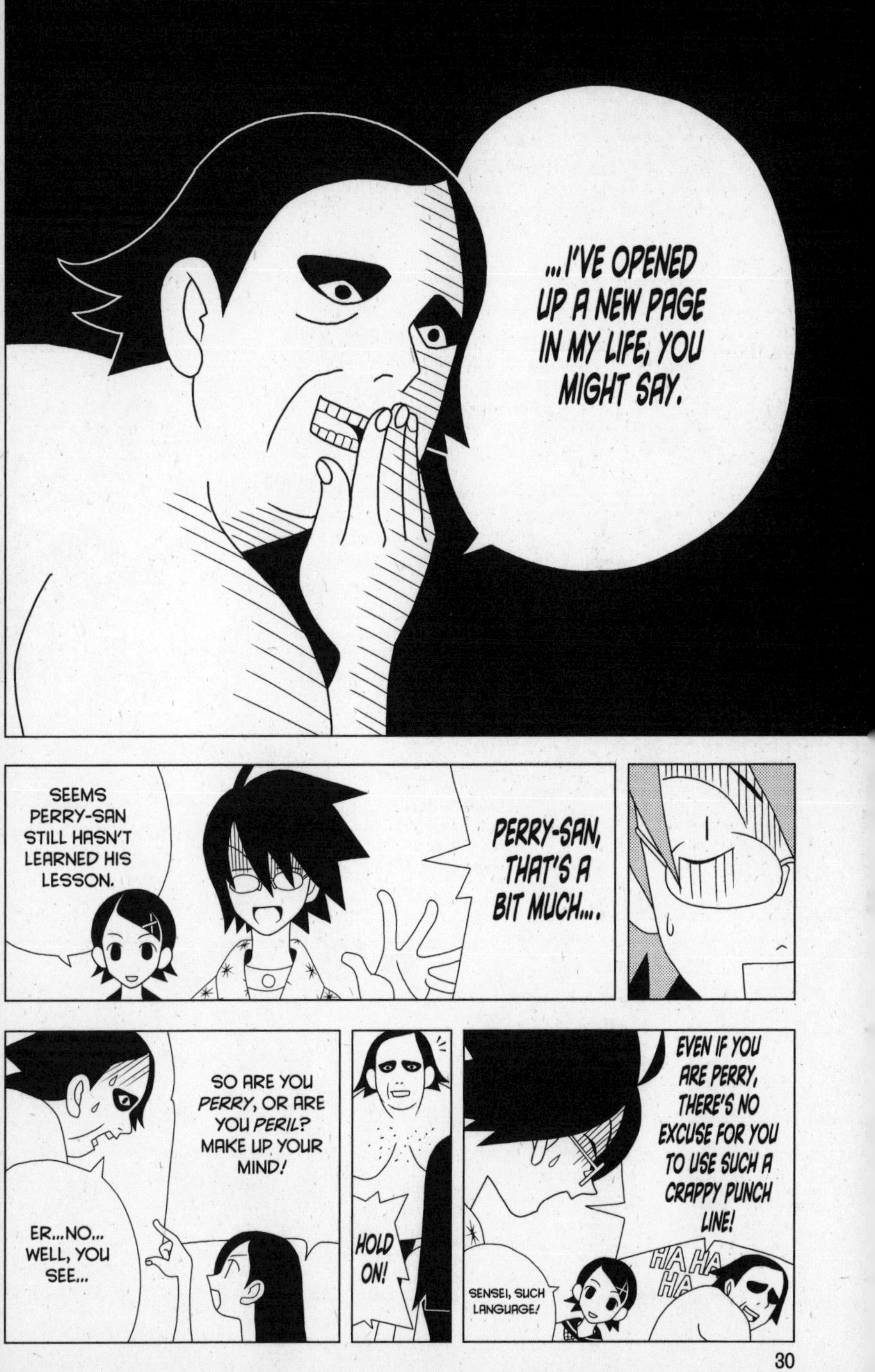
...I'VE OPENED UP A NEW PAGE IN MY LIFE, YOU MIGHT SAY.
PERRY-SAN, THAT'S A BIT MUCH....
SEEMS PERRY-SAN STILL HASN'T LEARNED HIS LESSON.
EVEN IF YOU ARE PERRY, THERE'S NO EXCUSE FOR YOU TO USE SUCH A CRAPPY PUNCH LINE!
HA HA HA
SENSEI, SUCH LANGUAGE!
HOLD ON!
SO ARE YOU *PERRY*, OR ARE YOU *PERIL*? MAKE UP YOUR MIND!
ER...NO... WELL, YOU SEE...

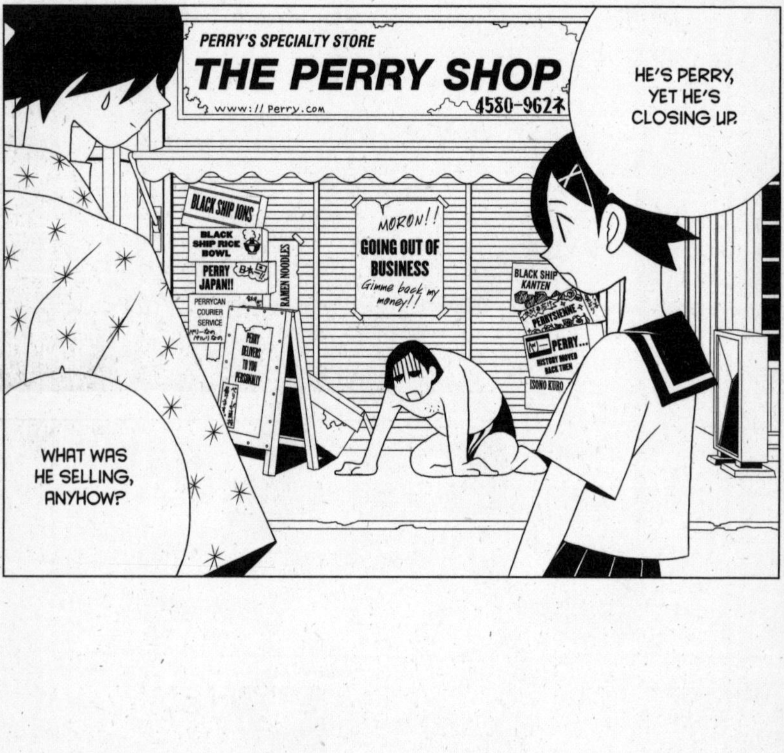
HE'S PERRY, YET HE'S CLOSING UP.
PERRY'S SPECIALTY STORE
THE PERRY SHOP
www://Perry.com
4580-962ネ
MORON!!
GOING OUT OF BUSINESS
Gimme back my money!!
BLACK SHIP KANTEN
PERRYSIENNE
PERRY...
HISTORY MOVED BACK THEN
ISONO KURO
BLACK SHIP IONS
BLACK SHIP RICE BOWL
PERRY JAPAN!!
RAMEN NOODLES
PERRYCAN COURIER SERVICE
PERRY DELIVERS TO YOU PERSONALLY
WHAT WAS HE SELLING, ANYHOW?

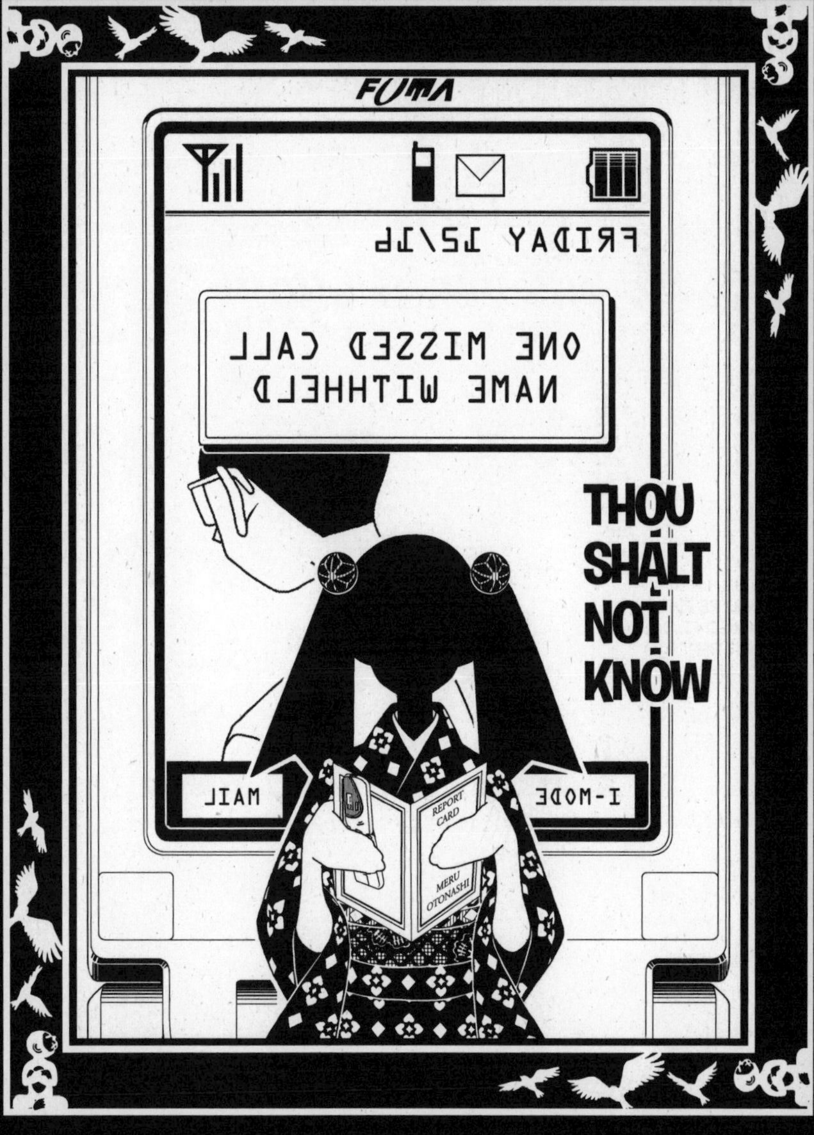
FUMA
FRIDAY 12/16
ONE MISSED CALL
NAME WITHHELD
MAIL
I-MODE
REPORT CARD
MERU OTONASHI
THOU SHALT NOT KNOW

# CHAPTER 13

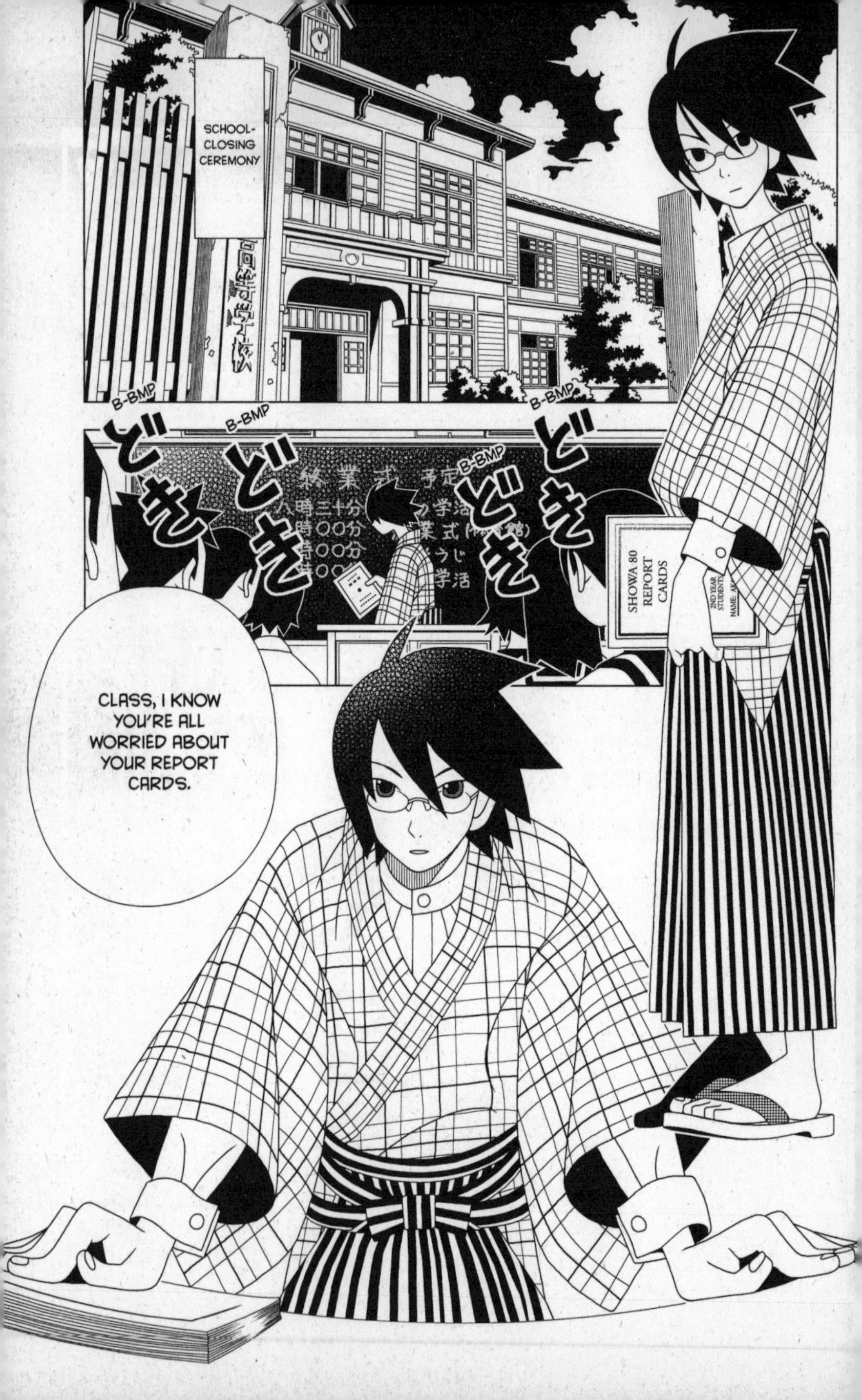
SCHOOL-CLOSING CEREMONY
B-BMP
どき
B-BMP
どき
B-BMP
どき
B-BMP
どき
SHOWA 80 REPORT CARDS
CLASS, I KNOW YOU'RE ALL WORRIED ABOUT YOUR REPORT CARDS.

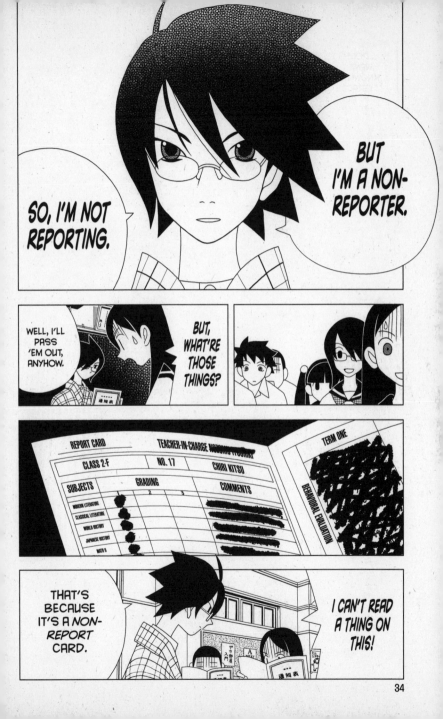

SO, I'M NOT REPORTING.

BUT I'M A NON-REPORTER.

WELL, I'LL PASS 'EM OUT, ANYHOW.

BUT, WHAT'RE THOSE THINGS?

| REPORT CARD | | TEACHER-IN-CHARGE NOZOMU ITOSHIKI | | |
|---|---|---|---|---|
| CLASS 2-F | | NO. 17 | CHIRI KITSU | |
| SUBJECTS | GRADING | | COMMENTS | |
| | 1 | 2 | 3 | |
| MODERN LITERATURE | | | | |
| CLASSICAL LITERATURE | | | | |
| WORLD HISTORY | | | | |
| JAPANESE HISTORY | | | | |
| MATH II | | | | |

TERM ONE

BEHAVIORAL EVALUATION

THAT'S BECAUSE IT'S A NON-REPORT CARD.

I CAN'T READ A THING ON THIS!

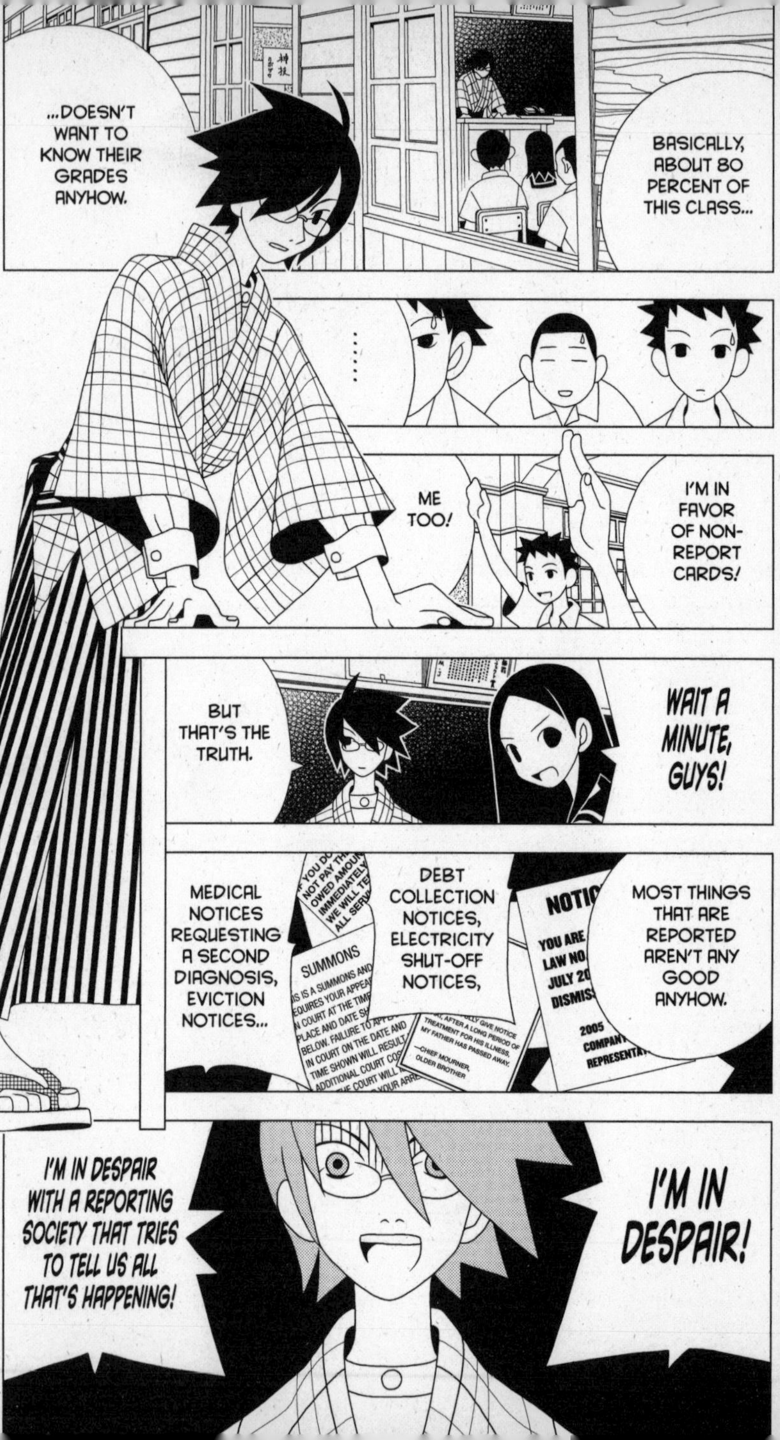
BASICALLY, ABOUT 80 PERCENT OF THIS CLASS...
...DOESN'T WANT TO KNOW THEIR GRADES ANYHOW.
......
I'M IN FAVOR OF NON-REPORT CARDS!
ME TOO!
WAIT A MINUTE, GUYS!
BUT THAT'S THE TRUTH.
MOST THINGS THAT ARE REPORTED AREN'T ANY GOOD ANYHOW.
DEBT COLLECTION NOTICES, ELECTRICITY SHUT-OFF NOTICES,
MEDICAL NOTICES REQUESTING A SECOND DIAGNOSIS, EVICTION NOTICES...
SUMMONS
—CHIEF MOURNER, OLDER BROTHER
I'M IN DESPAIR!
I'M IN DESPAIR WITH A REPORTING SOCIETY THAT TRIES TO TELL US ALL THAT'S HAPPENING!

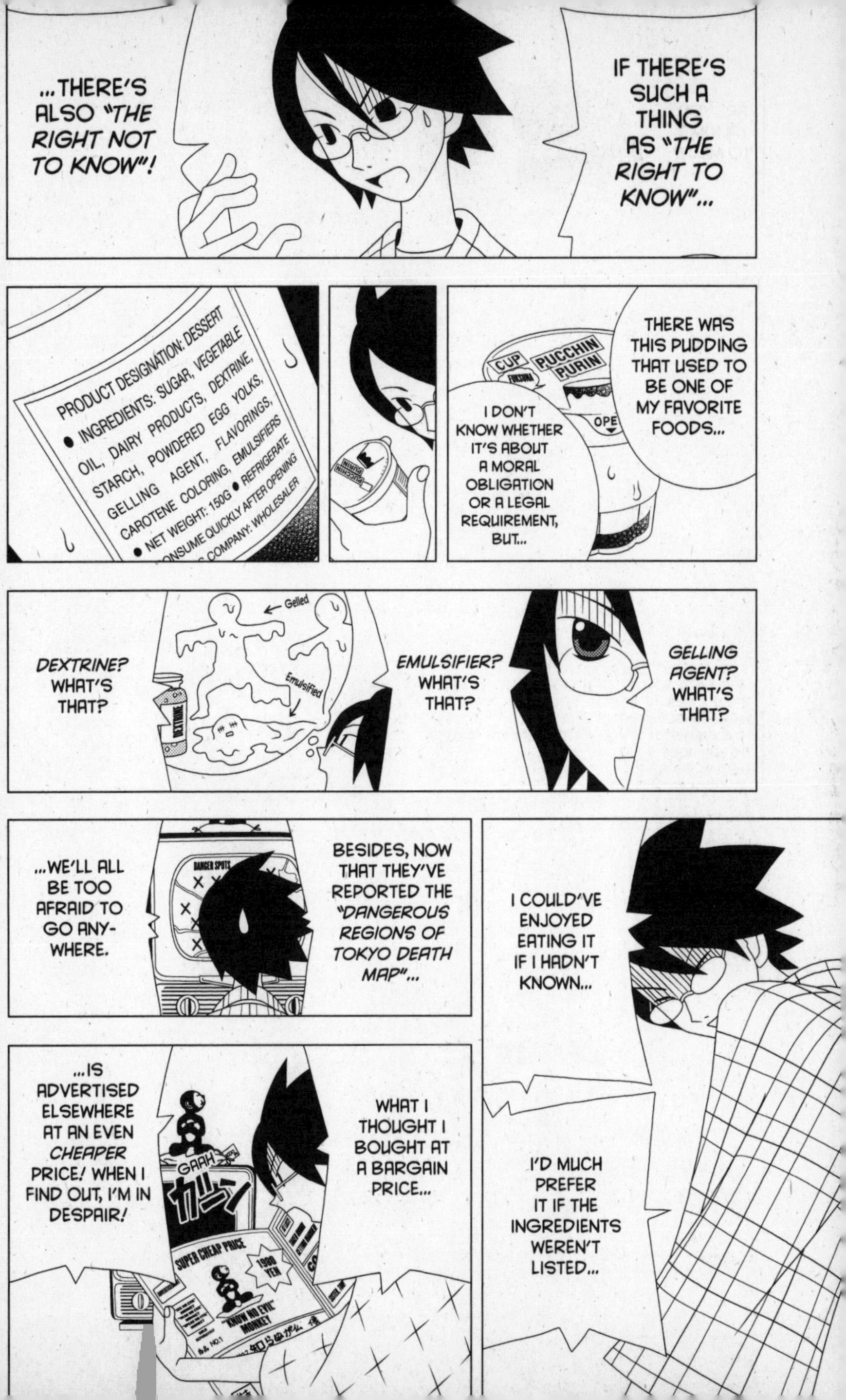
IF THERE'S SUCH A THING AS *"THE RIGHT TO KNOW"*...
...THERE'S ALSO *"THE RIGHT NOT TO KNOW"*!
THERE WAS THIS PUDDING THAT USED TO BE ONE OF MY FAVORITE FOODS...
CUP
PUCCHIN PURIN
I DON'T KNOW WHETHER IT'S ABOUT A MORAL OBLIGATION OR A LEGAL REQUIREMENT, BUT...
PRODUCT DESIGNATION: DESSERT
● INGREDIENTS: SUGAR, VEGETABLE OIL, DAIRY PRODUCTS, DEXTRINE, STARCH, POWDERED EGG YOLKS, GELLING AGENT, FLAVORINGS, CAROTENE COLORING, EMULSIFIERS
● NET WEIGHT: 150G ● REFRIGERATE
CONSUME QUICKLY AFTER OPENING
COMPANY: WHOLESALER
*GELLING AGENT?* WHAT'S THAT?
*EMULSIFIER?* WHAT'S THAT?
Gelled
Emulsified
DEXTRINE
*DEXTRINE?* WHAT'S THAT?
I COULD'VE ENJOYED EATING IT IF I HADN'T KNOWN...
I'D MUCH PREFER IT IF THE INGREDIENTS WEREN'T LISTED...
BESIDES, NOW THAT THEY'VE REPORTED THE *"DANGEROUS REGIONS OF TOKYO DEATH MAP"*...
DANGER SPOTS
...WE'LL ALL BE TOO AFRAID TO GO ANY-WHERE.
WHAT I THOUGHT I BOUGHT AT A BARGAIN PRICE...
...IS ADVERTISED ELSEWHERE AT AN EVEN *CHEAPER* PRICE! WHEN I FIND OUT, I'M IN *DESPAIR!*
GAAH
SUPER CHEAP PRICE
1980 YEN
"KNOW NO EVIL" MONKEY

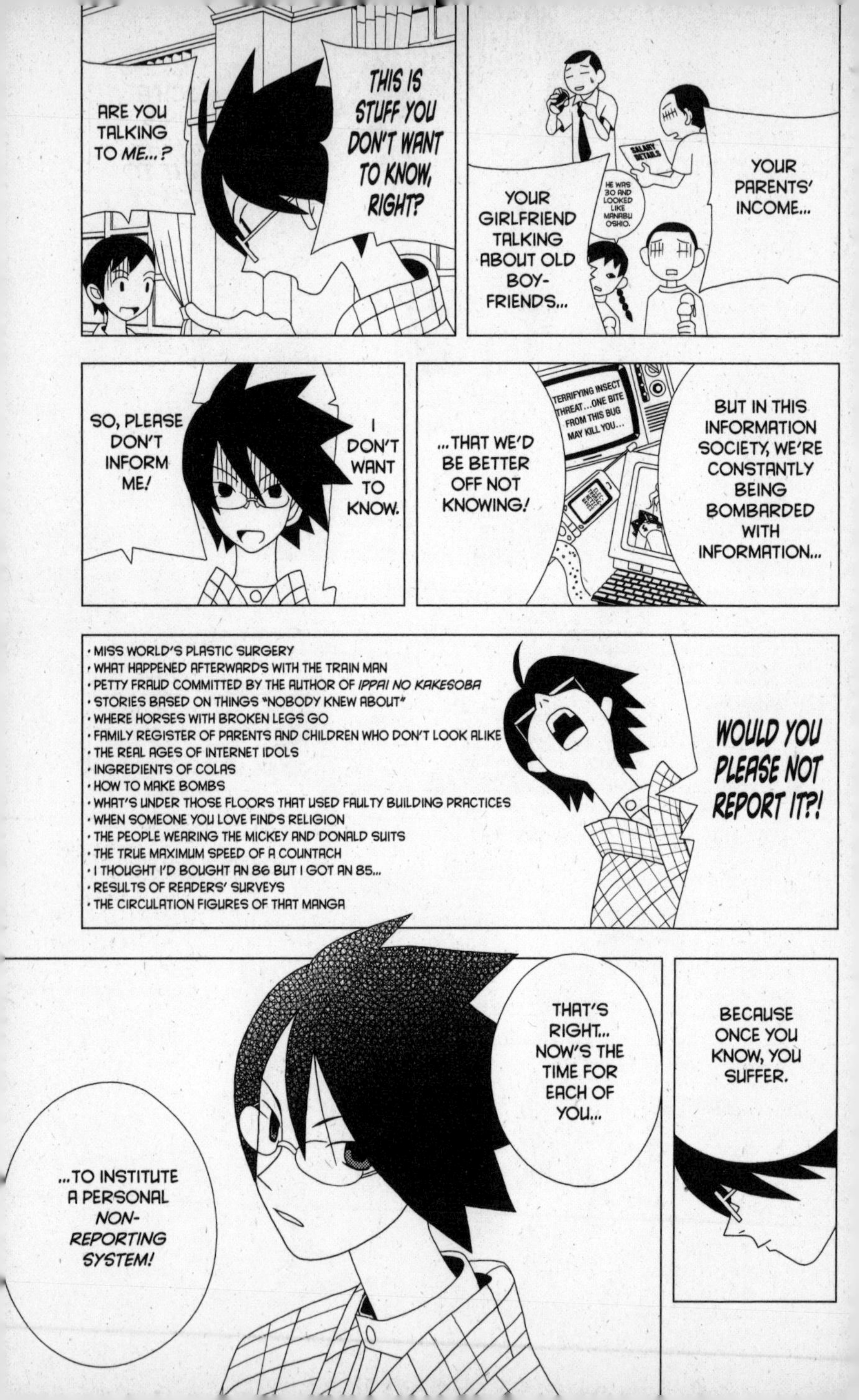
YOUR PARENTS' INCOME...
SALARY DETAILS
HE WAS 30 AND LOOKED LIKE MANABU OSHIO.
YOUR GIRLFRIEND TALKING ABOUT OLD BOY-FRIENDS...
THIS IS STUFF YOU DON'T WANT TO KNOW, RIGHT?
ARE YOU TALKING TO *ME*...?
BUT IN THIS INFORMATION SOCIETY, WE'RE CONSTANTLY BEING BOMBARDED WITH INFORMATION...
TERRIFYING INSECT THREAT...ONE BITE FROM THIS BUG MAY KILL YOU...
...THAT WE'D BE BETTER OFF NOT KNOWING!
I DON'T WANT TO KNOW.
SO, PLEASE DON'T INFORM ME!
WOULD YOU PLEASE NOT REPORT IT?!
• MISS WORLD'S PLASTIC SURGERY
• WHAT HAPPENED AFTERWARDS WITH THE TRAIN MAN
• PETTY FRAUD COMMITTED BY THE AUTHOR OF *IPPAI NO KAKESOBA*
• STORIES BASED ON THINGS "NOBODY KNEW ABOUT"
• WHERE HORSES WITH BROKEN LEGS GO
• FAMILY REGISTER OF PARENTS AND CHILDREN WHO DON'T LOOK ALIKE
• THE REAL AGES OF INTERNET IDOLS
• INGREDIENTS OF COLAS
• HOW TO MAKE BOMBS
• WHAT'S UNDER THOSE FLOORS THAT USED FAULTY BUILDING PRACTICES
• WHEN SOMEONE YOU LOVE FINDS RELIGION
• THE PEOPLE WEARING THE MICKEY AND DONALD SUITS
• THE TRUE MAXIMUM SPEED OF A COUNTACH
• I THOUGHT I'D BOUGHT AN 86 BUT I GOT AN 85...
• RESULTS OF READERS' SURVEYS
• THE CIRCULATION FIGURES OF THAT MANGA
BECAUSE ONCE YOU KNOW, YOU SUFFER.
THAT'S RIGHT... NOW'S THE TIME FOR EACH OF YOU...
...TO INSTITUTE A PERSONAL *NON-REPORTING* SYSTEM!

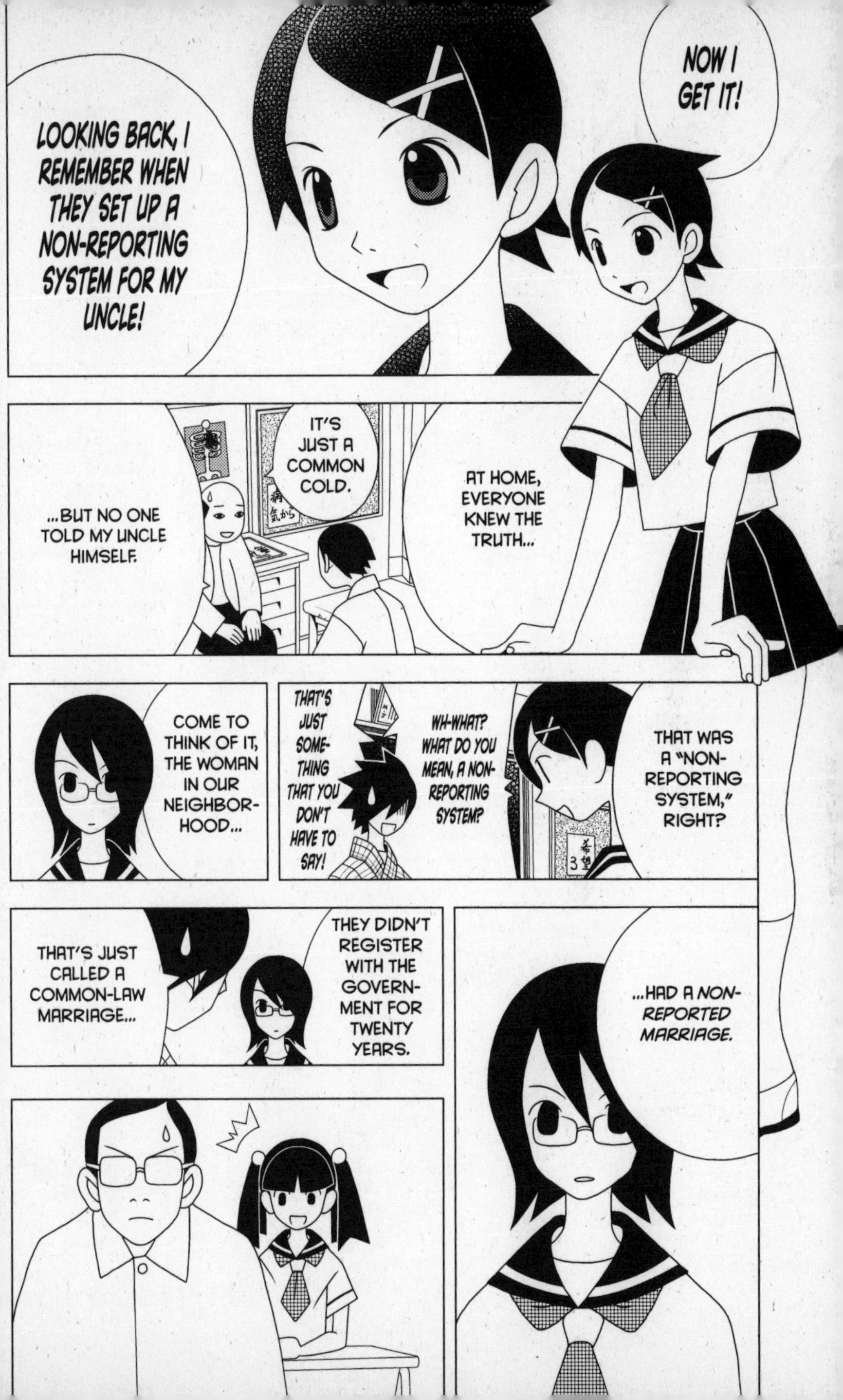
NOW I GET IT!
LOOKING BACK, I REMEMBER WHEN THEY SET UP A NON-REPORTING SYSTEM FOR MY UNCLE!
AT HOME, EVERYONE KNEW THE TRUTH...
IT'S JUST A COMMON COLD.
...BUT NO ONE TOLD MY UNCLE HIMSELF.
THAT WAS A "NON-REPORTING SYSTEM," RIGHT?
WH-WHAT? WHAT DO YOU MEAN, A NON-REPORTING SYSTEM?
THAT'S JUST SOMETHING THAT YOU DON'T HAVE TO SAY!
COME TO THINK OF IT, THE WOMAN IN OUR NEIGHBORHOOD...
...HAD A *NON-REPORTED MARRIAGE.*
THEY DIDN'T REGISTER WITH THE GOVERNMENT FOR TWENTY YEARS.
THAT'S JUST CALLED A COMMON-LAW MARRIAGE...

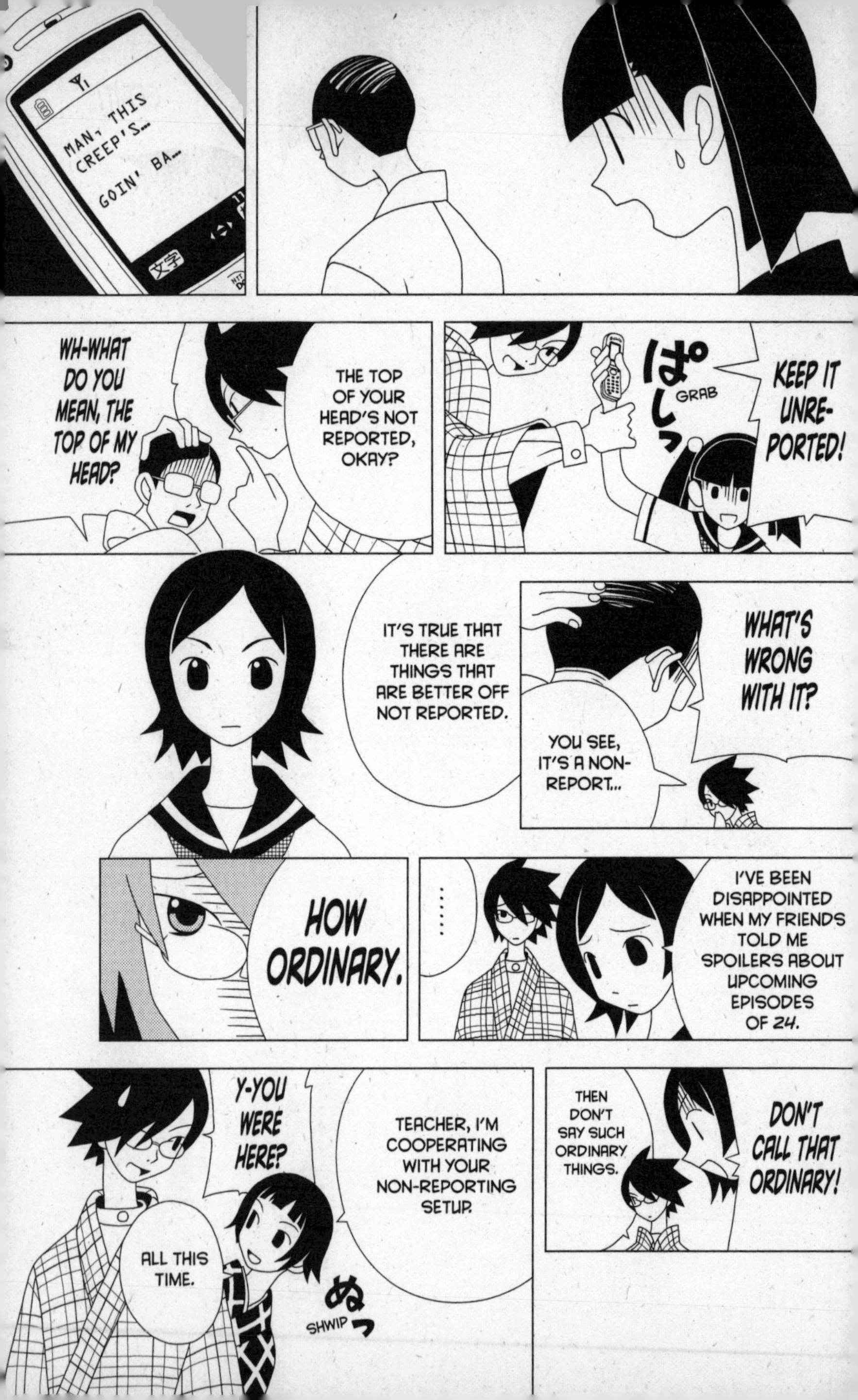
MAN, THIS CREEP'S...
GOIN' BA...
文字
KEEP IT UNREPORTED!
ぱしっ
GRAB
THE TOP OF YOUR HEAD'S NOT REPORTED, OKAY?
WH-WHAT DO YOU MEAN, THE TOP OF MY HEAD?
WHAT'S WRONG WITH IT?
YOU SEE, IT'S A NON-REPORT...
IT'S TRUE THAT THERE ARE THINGS THAT ARE BETTER OFF NOT REPORTED.
I'VE BEEN DISAPPOINTED WHEN MY FRIENDS TOLD ME SPOILERS ABOUT UPCOMING EPISODES OF 24.
......
HOW ORDINARY.
DON'T CALL THAT ORDINARY!
THEN DON'T SAY SUCH ORDINARY THINGS.
TEACHER, I'M COOPERATING WITH YOUR NON-REPORTING SETUP.
ぬっ
SHWIP
Y-YOU WERE HERE?
ALL THIS TIME.

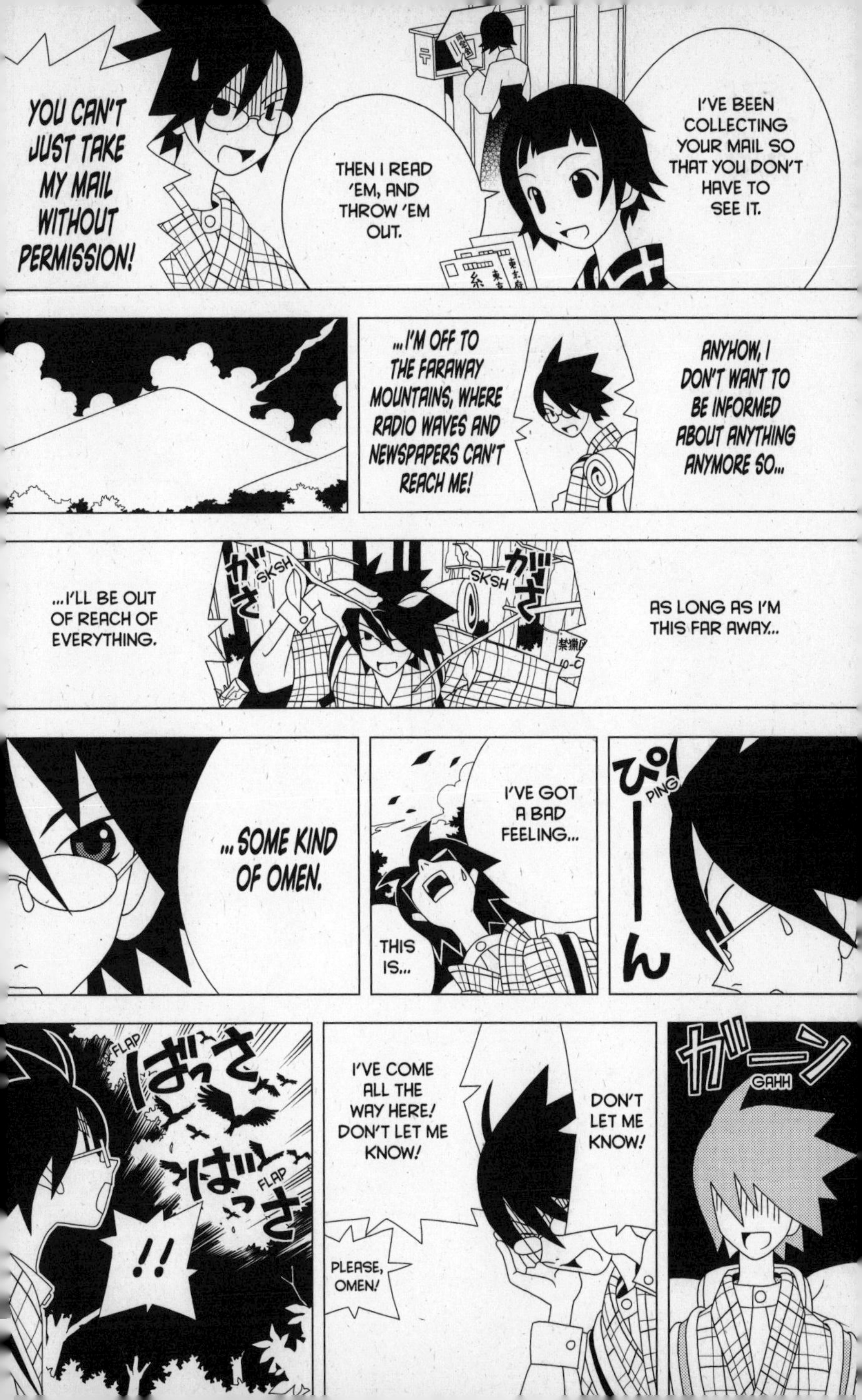
I'VE BEEN COLLECTING YOUR MAIL SO THAT YOU DON'T HAVE TO SEE IT.
THEN I READ 'EM, AND THROW 'EM OUT.
YOU CAN'T JUST TAKE MY MAIL WITHOUT PERMISSION!
ANYHOW, I DON'T WANT TO BE INFORMED ABOUT ANYTHING ANYMORE SO...
...I'M OFF TO THE FARAWAY MOUNTAINS, WHERE RADIO WAVES AND NEWSPAPERS CAN'T REACH ME!
AS LONG AS I'M THIS FAR AWAY...
がさ SKSH
がさ SKSH
...I'LL BE OUT OF REACH OF EVERYTHING.
ぴーーん PING
I'VE GOT A BAD FEELING...
THIS IS...
...SOME KIND OF OMEN.
ガーン GAHH
DON'T LET ME KNOW!
I'VE COME ALL THE WAY HERE! DON'T LET ME KNOW!
PLEASE, OMEN!
ばっさ FLAP
ばっさ FLAP
!!

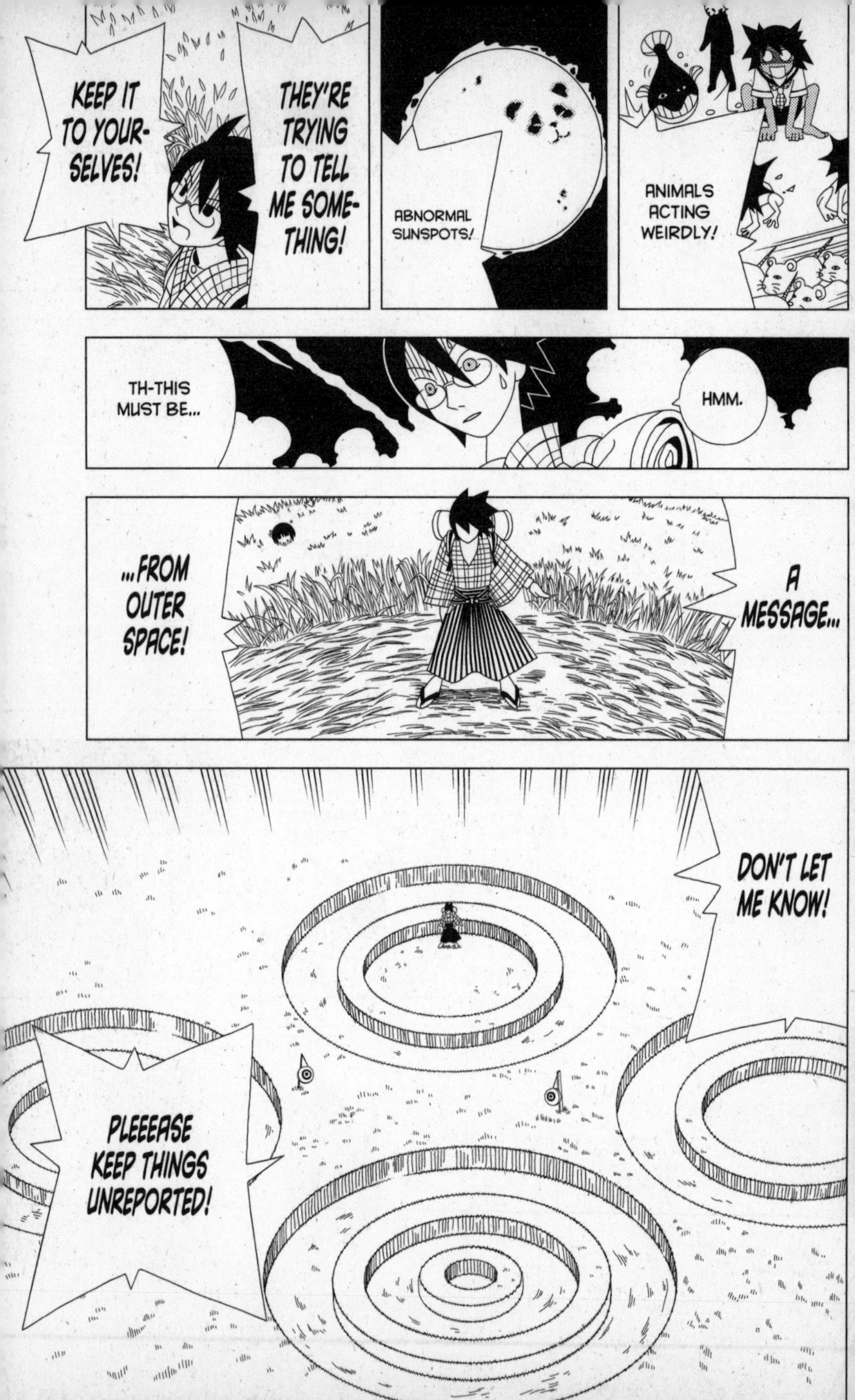

ANIMALS ACTING WEIRDLY!
ABNORMAL SUNSPOTS!
THEY'RE TRYING TO TELL ME SOME-THING!
KEEP IT TO YOUR-SELVES!
HMM.
TH-THIS MUST BE...
A MESSAGE...
...FROM OUTER SPACE!
DON'T LET ME KNOW!
PLEEEASE KEEP THINGS UNREPORTED!

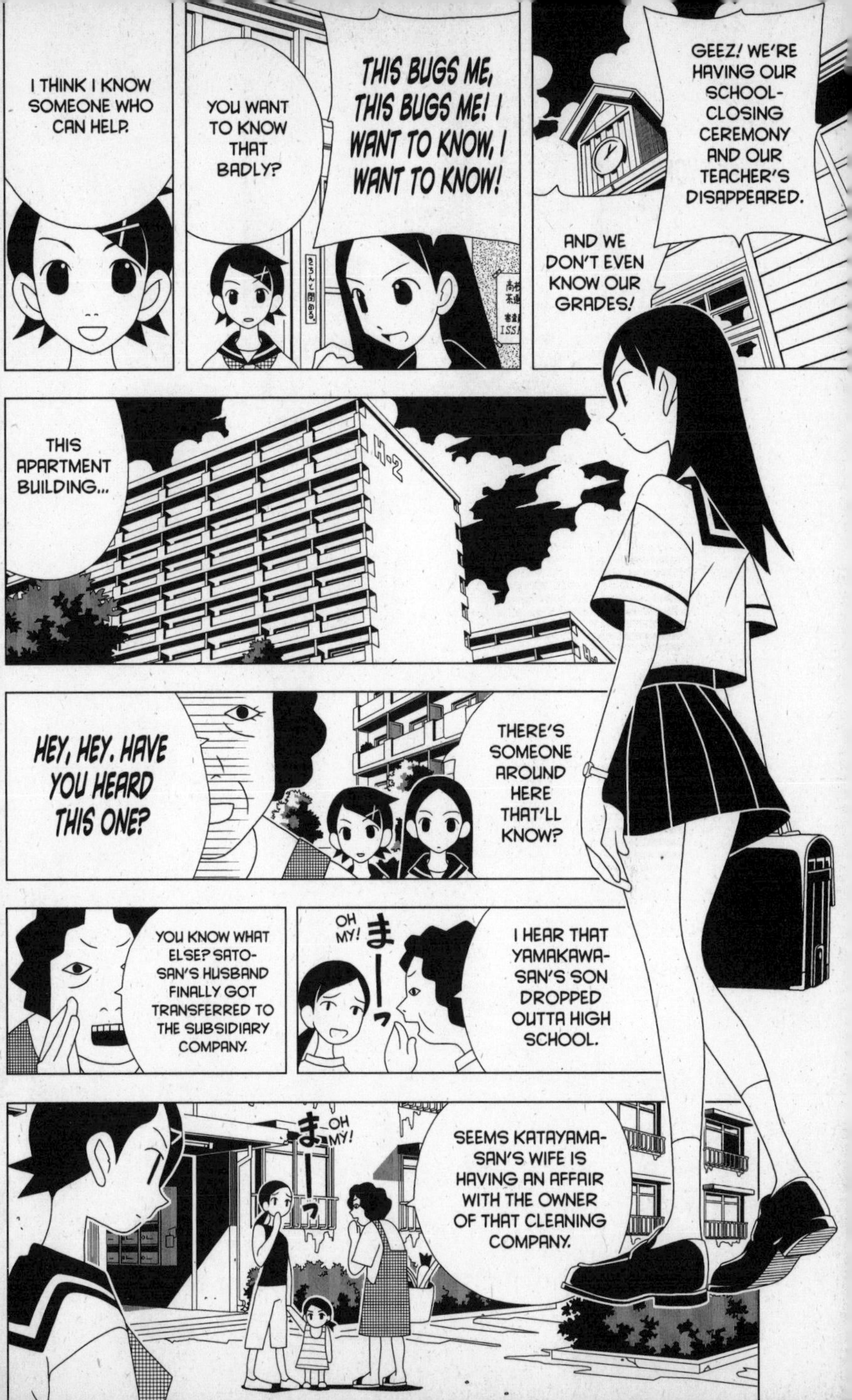
GEEZ! WE'RE HAVING OUR SCHOOL-CLOSING CEREMONY AND OUR TEACHER'S DISAPPEARED.
AND WE DON'T EVEN KNOW OUR GRADES!
THIS BUGS ME, THIS BUGS ME! I WANT TO KNOW, I WANT TO KNOW!
YOU WANT TO KNOW THAT BADLY?
I THINK I KNOW SOMEONE WHO CAN HELP.
THIS APARTMENT BUILDING...
THERE'S SOMEONE AROUND HERE THAT'LL KNOW?
HEY, HEY. HAVE YOU HEARD THIS ONE?
I HEAR THAT YAMAKAWA-SAN'S SON DROPPED OUTTA HIGH SCHOOL.
OH MY!
まーっ
YOU KNOW WHAT ELSE? SATO-SAN'S HUSBAND FINALLY GOT TRANSFERRED TO THE SUBSIDIARY COMPANY.
SEEMS KATAYAMA-SAN'S WIFE IS HAVING AN AFFAIR WITH THE OWNER OF THAT CLEANING COMPANY.
まーっ
OH MY!

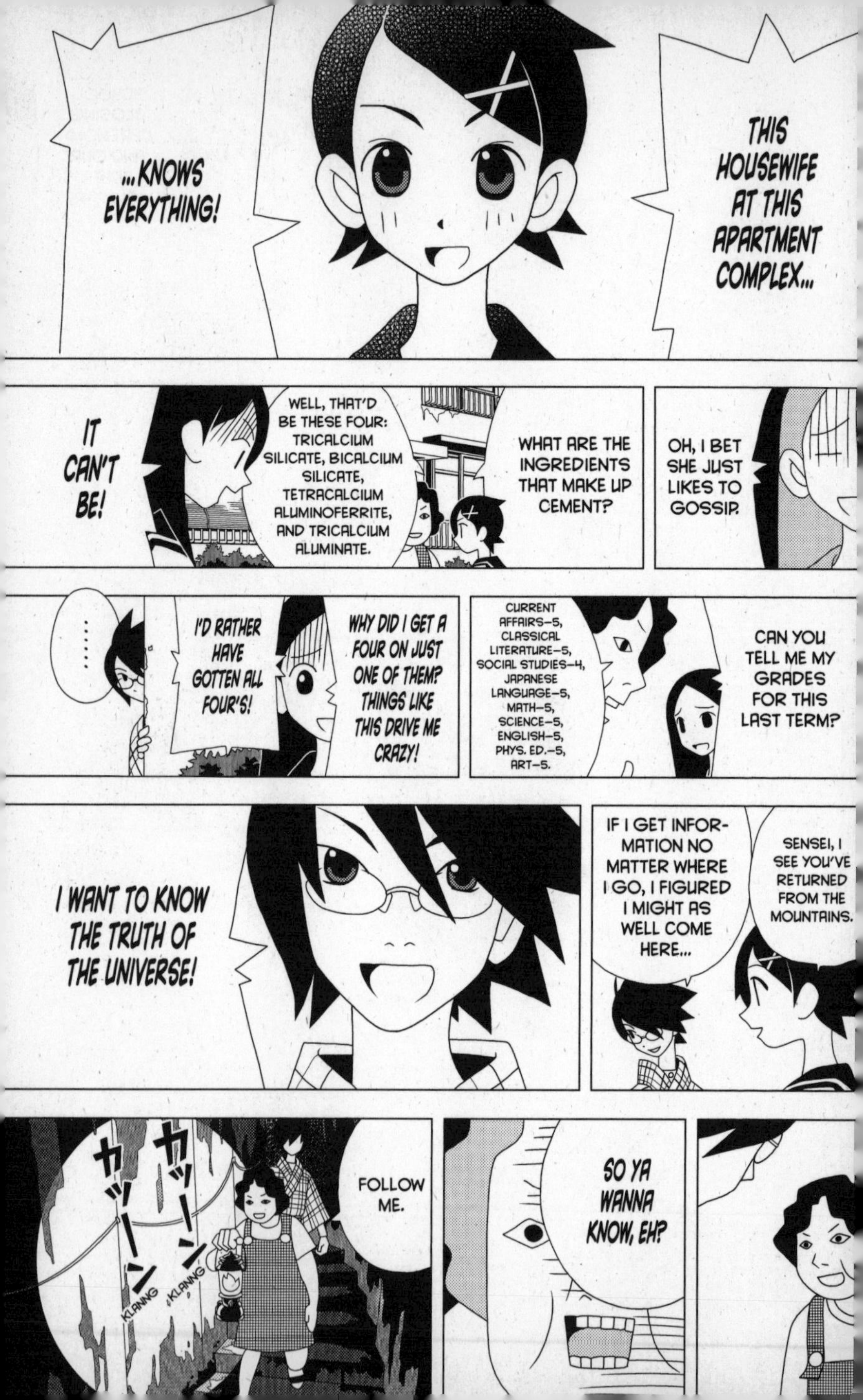
THIS HOUSEWIFE AT THIS APARTMENT COMPLEX...
...KNOWS EVERYTHING!
OH, I BET SHE JUST LIKES TO GOSSIP.
WHAT ARE THE INGREDIENTS THAT MAKE UP CEMENT?
WELL, THAT'D BE THESE FOUR: TRICALCIUM SILICATE, BICALCIUM SILICATE, TETRACALCIUM ALUMINOFERRITE, AND TRICALCIUM ALUMINATE.
IT CAN'T BE!
CAN YOU TELL ME MY GRADES FOR THIS LAST TERM?
CURRENT AFFAIRS–5, CLASSICAL LITERATURE–5, SOCIAL STUDIES–4, JAPANESE LANGUAGE–5, MATH–5, SCIENCE–5, ENGLISH–5, PHYS. ED.–5, ART–5.
WHY DID I GET A FOUR ON JUST ONE OF THEM? THINGS LIKE THIS DRIVE ME CRAZY!
I'D RATHER HAVE GOTTEN ALL FOUR'S!
......
SENSEI, I SEE YOU'VE RETURNED FROM THE MOUNTAINS.
IF I GET INFORMATION NO MATTER WHERE I GO, I FIGURED I MIGHT AS WELL COME HERE...
I WANT TO KNOW THE TRUTH OF THE UNIVERSE!
SO YA WANNA KNOW, EH?
FOLLOW ME.
KLANNG
KLANNG

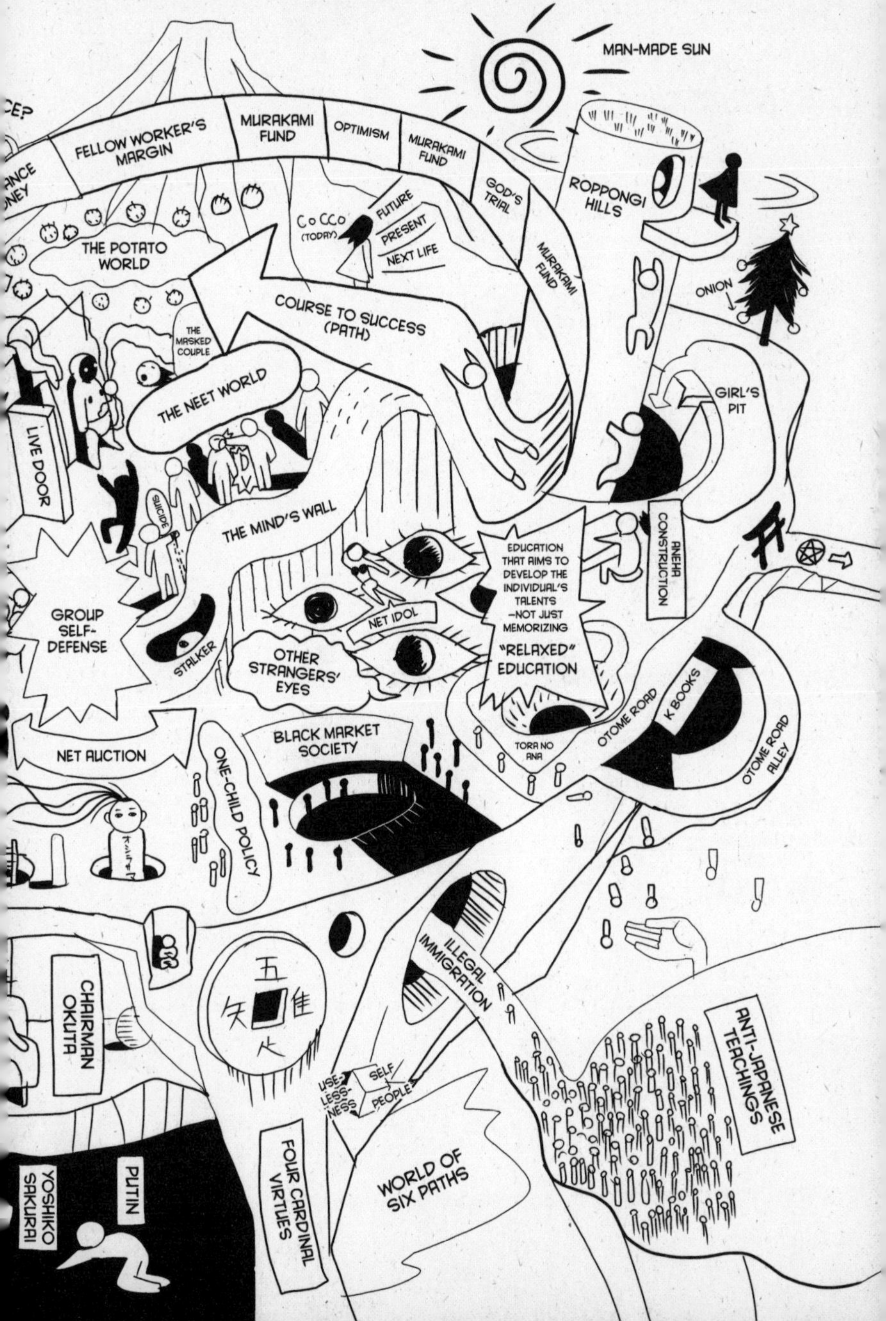

MAN-MADE SUN
ROPPONGI HILLS
GOD'S TRIAL
MURAKAMI FUND
OPTIMISM
MURAKAMI FUND
FELLOW WORKER'S MARGIN
COCCO (TODAY)
FUTURE
PRESENT
NEXT LIFE
THE POTATO WORLD
MURAKAMI FUND
ONION
COURSE TO SUCCESS (PATH)
THE MASKED COUPLE
GIRL'S PIT
THE NEET WORLD
LIVE DOOR
SUICIDE
THE MIND'S WALL
ANEHA CONSTRUCTION
EDUCATION THAT AIMS TO DEVELOP THE INDIVIDUAL'S TALENTS —NOT JUST MEMORIZING
"RELAXED" EDUCATION
NET IDOL
GROUP SELF-DEFENSE
STALKER
OTHER STRANGERS' EYES
K BOOKS
OTOME ROAD
OTOME ROAD ALLEY
TORA NO ANA
BLACK MARKET SOCIETY
NET AUCTION
ONE-CHILD POLICY
ILLEGAL IMMIGRATION
五
矢
隹
CHAIRMAN OKUTA
ANTI-JAPANESE TEACHINGS
USE-LESS-NESS
SELF
PEOPLE
FOUR CARDINAL VIRTUES
WORLD OF SIX PATHS
PUTIN
YOSHIKO SAKURAI

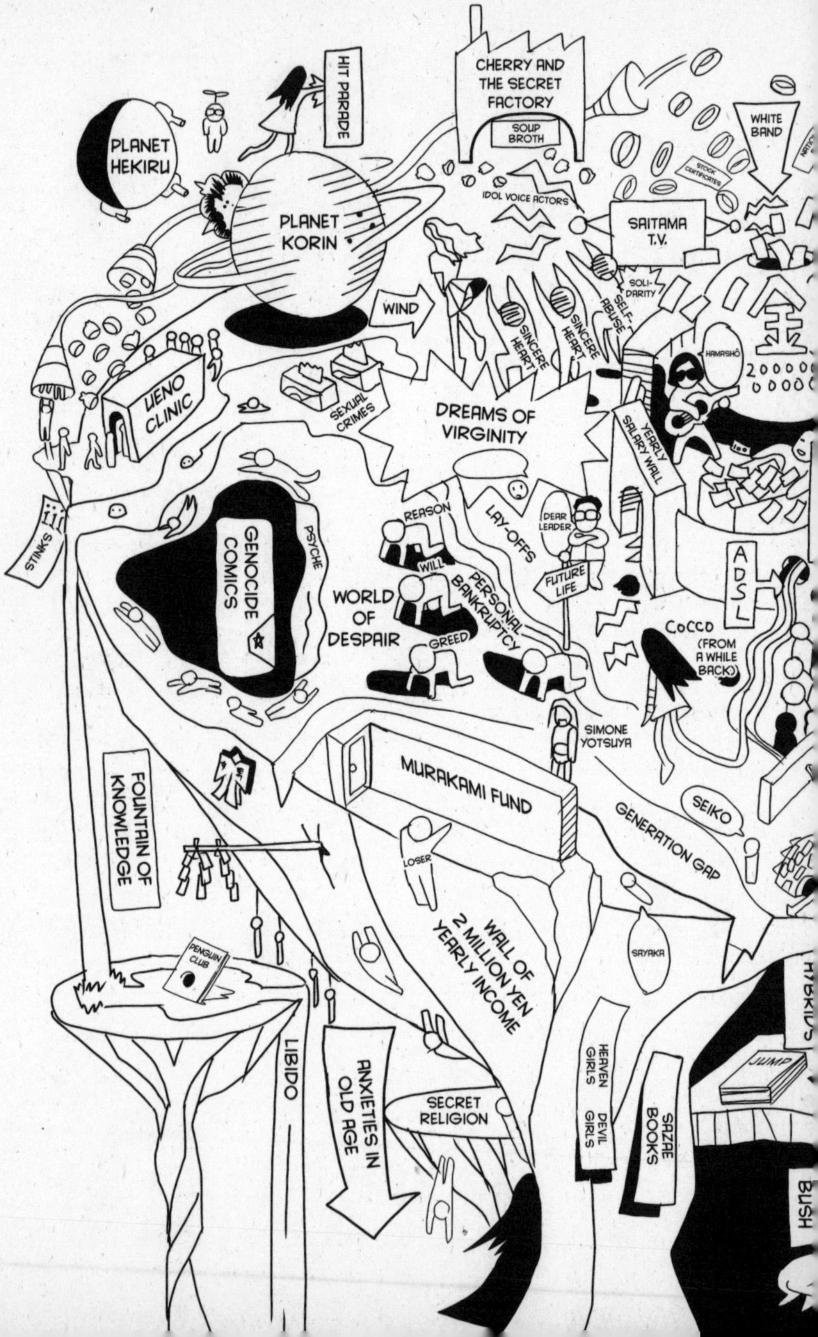

HIT PARADE
CHERRY AND THE SECRET FACTORY
SOUP BROTH
WHITE BAND
STOCK CERTIFICATES
PLANET HEKIRU
PLANET KORIN
IDOL VOICE ACTORS
SAITAMA T.V.
SOLI-DARITY
SELF-ABUSE
SINCERE HEART
SINCERE HEART
WIND
HAMASHŌ
20000 0000
UENO CLINIC
SEXUAL CRIMES
DREAMS OF VIRGINITY
YEARLY SALARY WALL
STINKS
GENOCIDE COMICS
PSYCHE
REASON
LAY-OFFS
DEAR LEADER
WILL
PERSONAL BANKRUPTCY
FUTURE LIFE
ADSL
WORLD OF DESPAIR
GREED
COCCO (FROM A WHILE BACK)
SIMONE YOTSUYA
MURAKAMI FUND
FOUNTAIN OF KNOWLEDGE
SEIKO
GENERATION GAP
LOSER
WALL OF 2 MILLION YEN YEARLY INCOME
SAYAKA
PENGUIN CLUB
HYBRIDS
LIBIDO
ANXIETIES IN OLD AGE
HEAVEN GIRLS
DEVIL GIRLS
SAZAE BOOKS
JUMP
SECRET RELIGION
BUSH

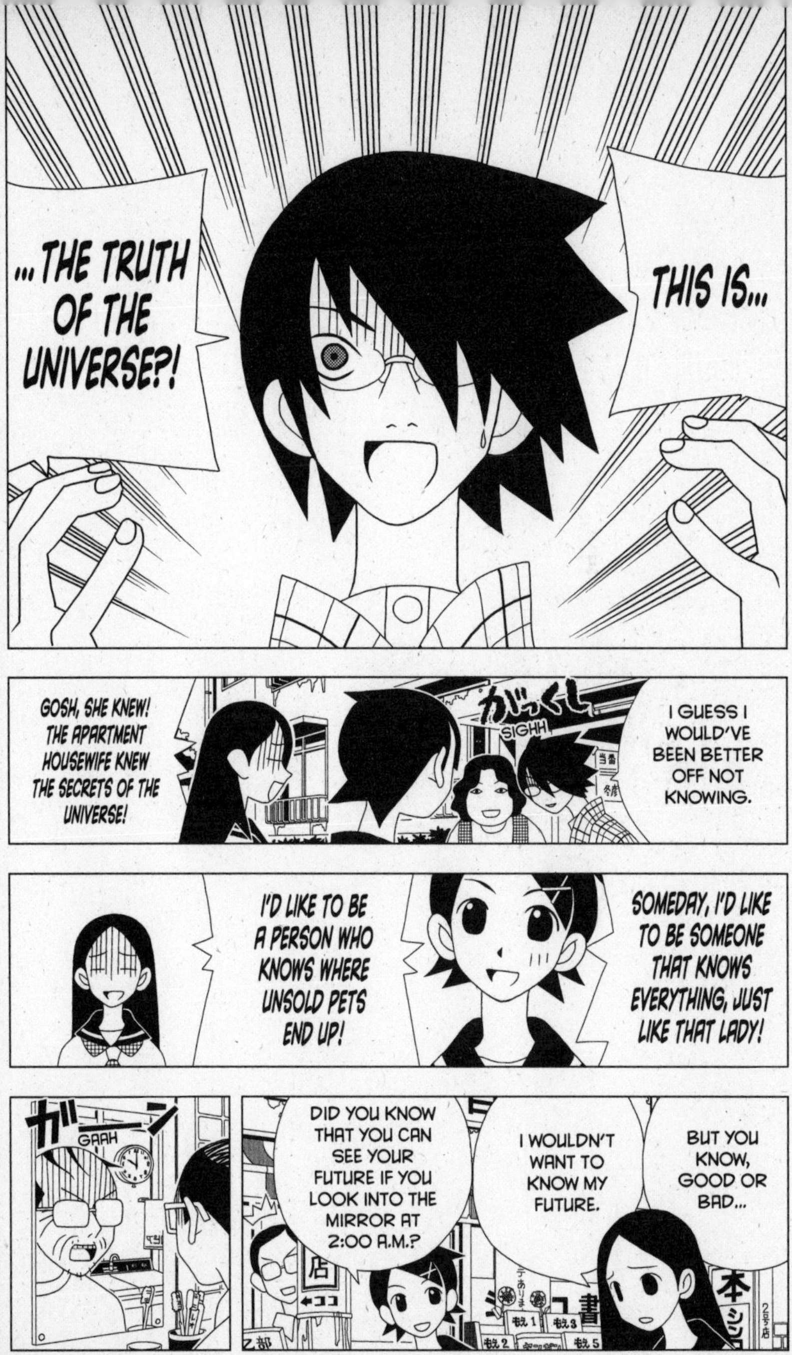
THIS IS...
...THE TRUTH OF THE UNIVERSE?!
I GUESS I WOULD'VE BEEN BETTER OFF NOT KNOWING.
がっくし
SIGHH
GOSH, SHE KNEW! THE APARTMENT HOUSEWIFE KNEW THE SECRETS OF THE UNIVERSE!
SOMEDAY, I'D LIKE TO BE SOMEONE THAT KNOWS EVERYTHING, JUST LIKE THAT LADY!
I'D LIKE TO BE A PERSON WHO KNOWS WHERE UNSOLD PETS END UP!
BUT YOU KNOW, GOOD OR BAD...
I WOULDN'T WANT TO KNOW MY FUTURE.
DID YOU KNOW THAT YOU CAN SEE YOUR FUTURE IF YOU LOOK INTO THE MIRROR AT 2:00 A.M.?
ガーン
GAAH

YOU WOULDN'T WANT TO KNOW WHERE UNSOLD MANGA LEFTOVERS END UP....

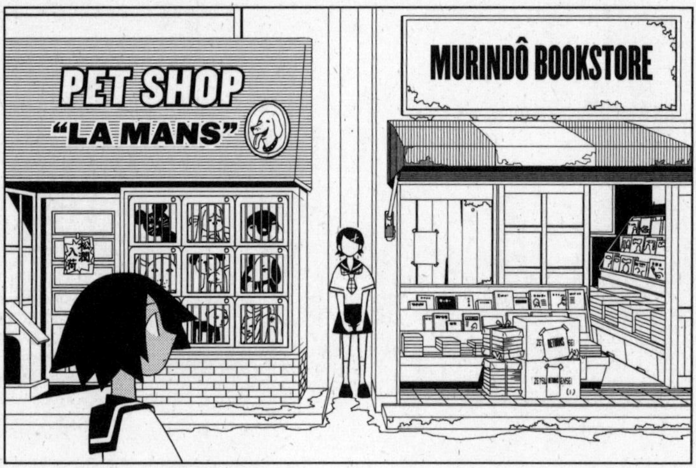
PET SHOP
"LA MANS"
MURINDÔ BOOKSTORE
WISH PEOPLE'D BUY FROM THEM.

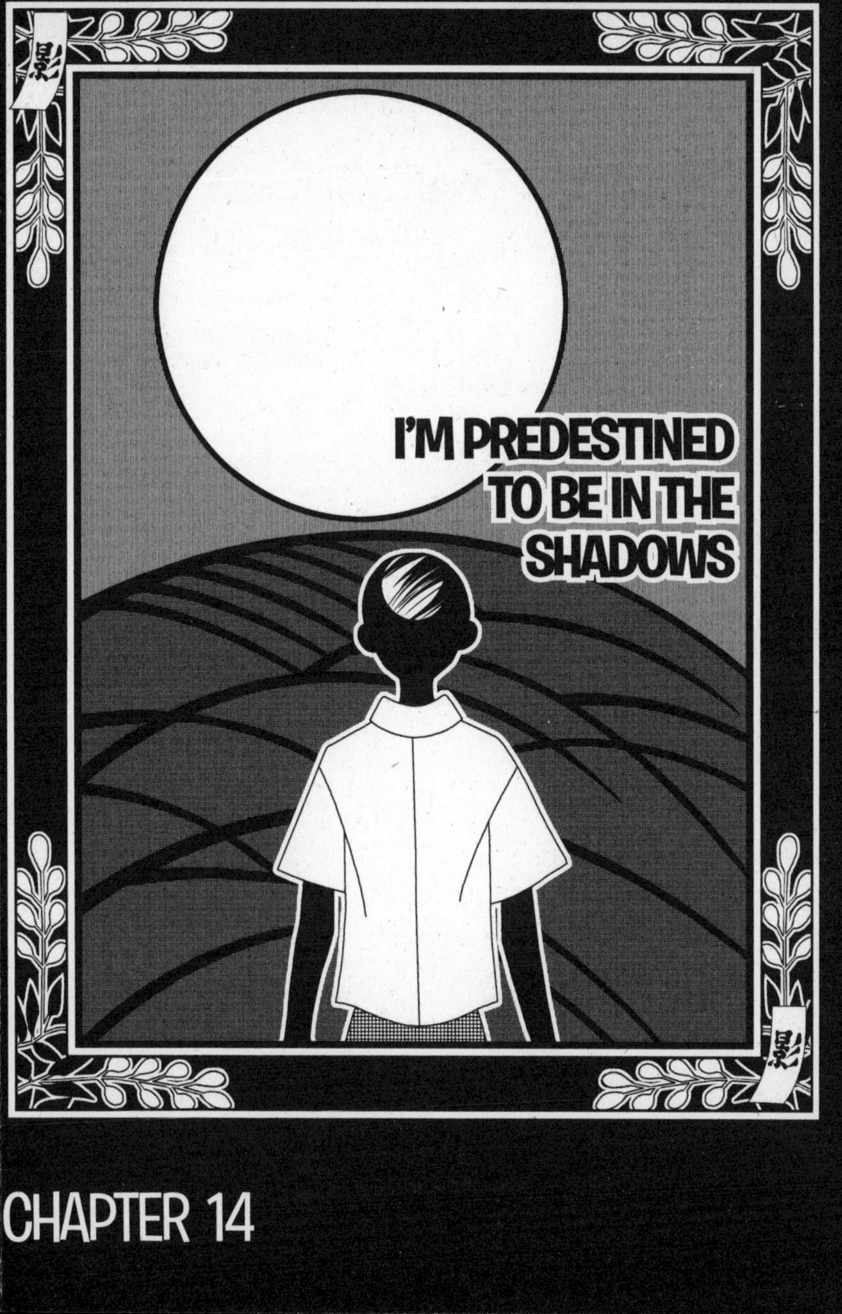
影
I'M PREDESTINED TO BE IN THE SHADOWS
影

# CHAPTER 14

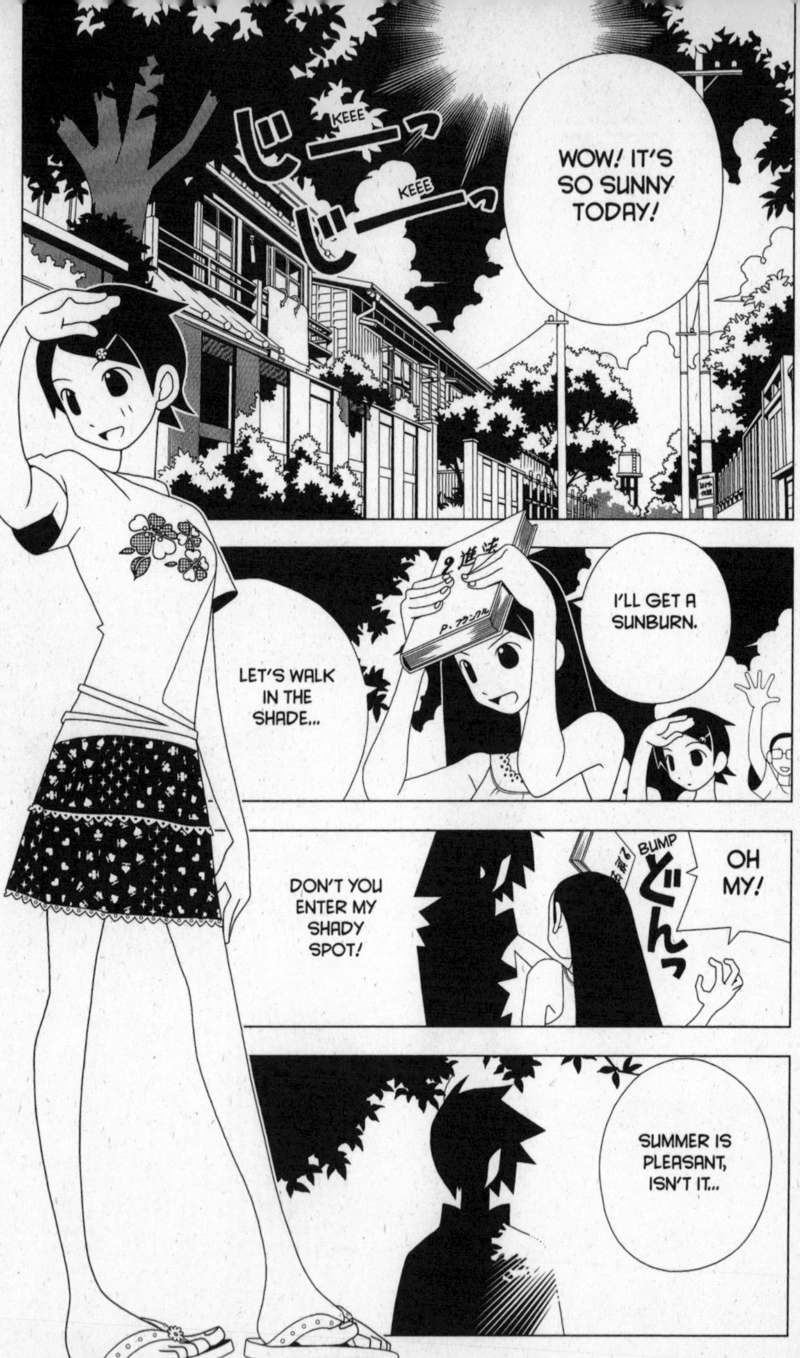
WOW! IT'S SO SUNNY TODAY!
KEEE
KEEE
I'LL GET A SUNBURN.
LET'S WALK IN THE SHADE...
OH MY!
BUMP
DON'T YOU ENTER MY SHADY SPOT!
SUMMER IS PLEASANT, ISN'T IT...

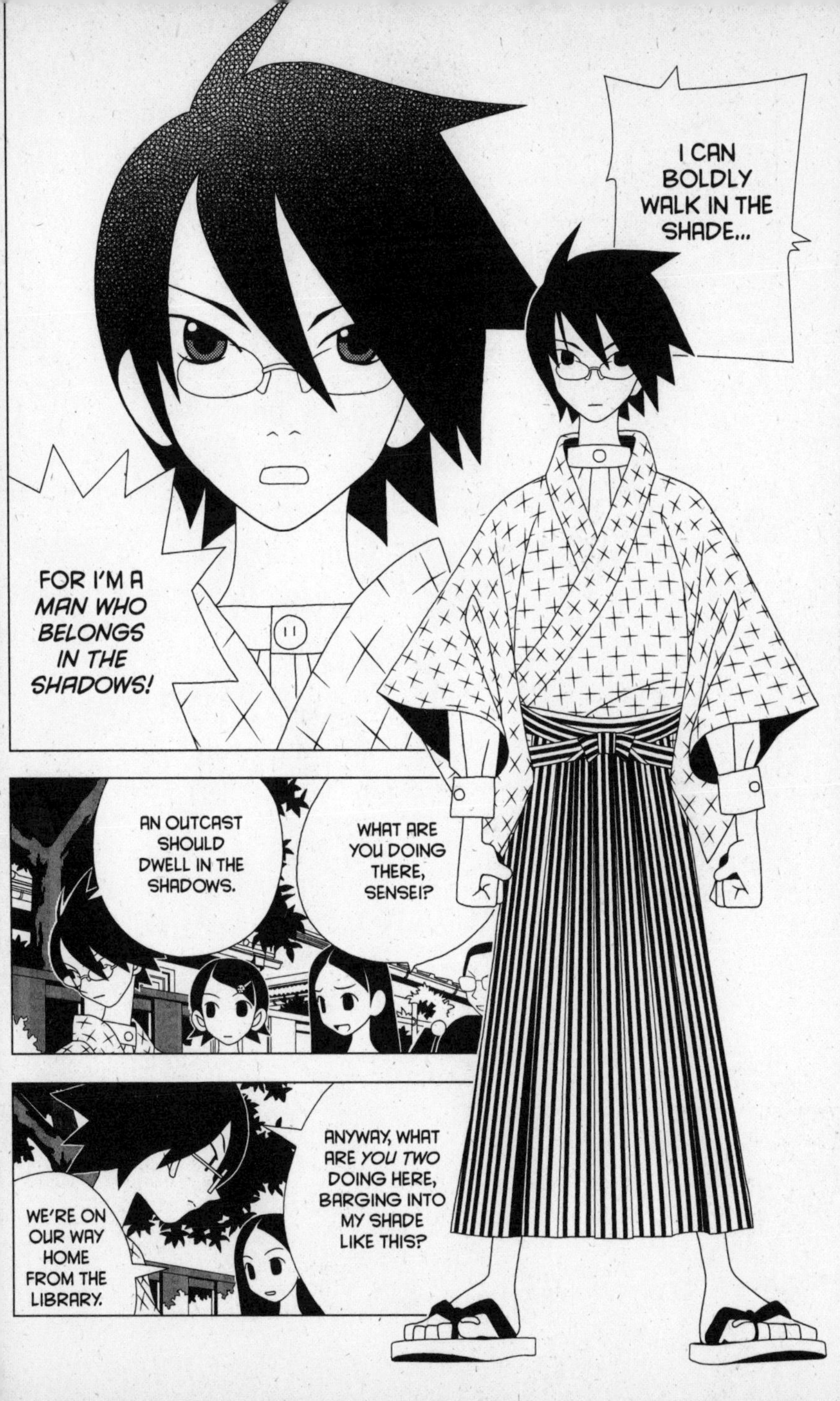
I CAN BOLDLY WALK IN THE SHADE...
FOR I'M A *MAN WHO* BELONGS *IN THE SHADOWS!*
WHAT ARE YOU DOING THERE, SENSEI?
AN OUTCAST SHOULD DWELL IN THE SHADOWS.
ANYWAY, WHAT ARE *YOU TWO* DOING HERE, BARGING INTO MY SHADE LIKE THIS?
WE'RE ON OUR WAY HOME FROM THE LIBRARY.

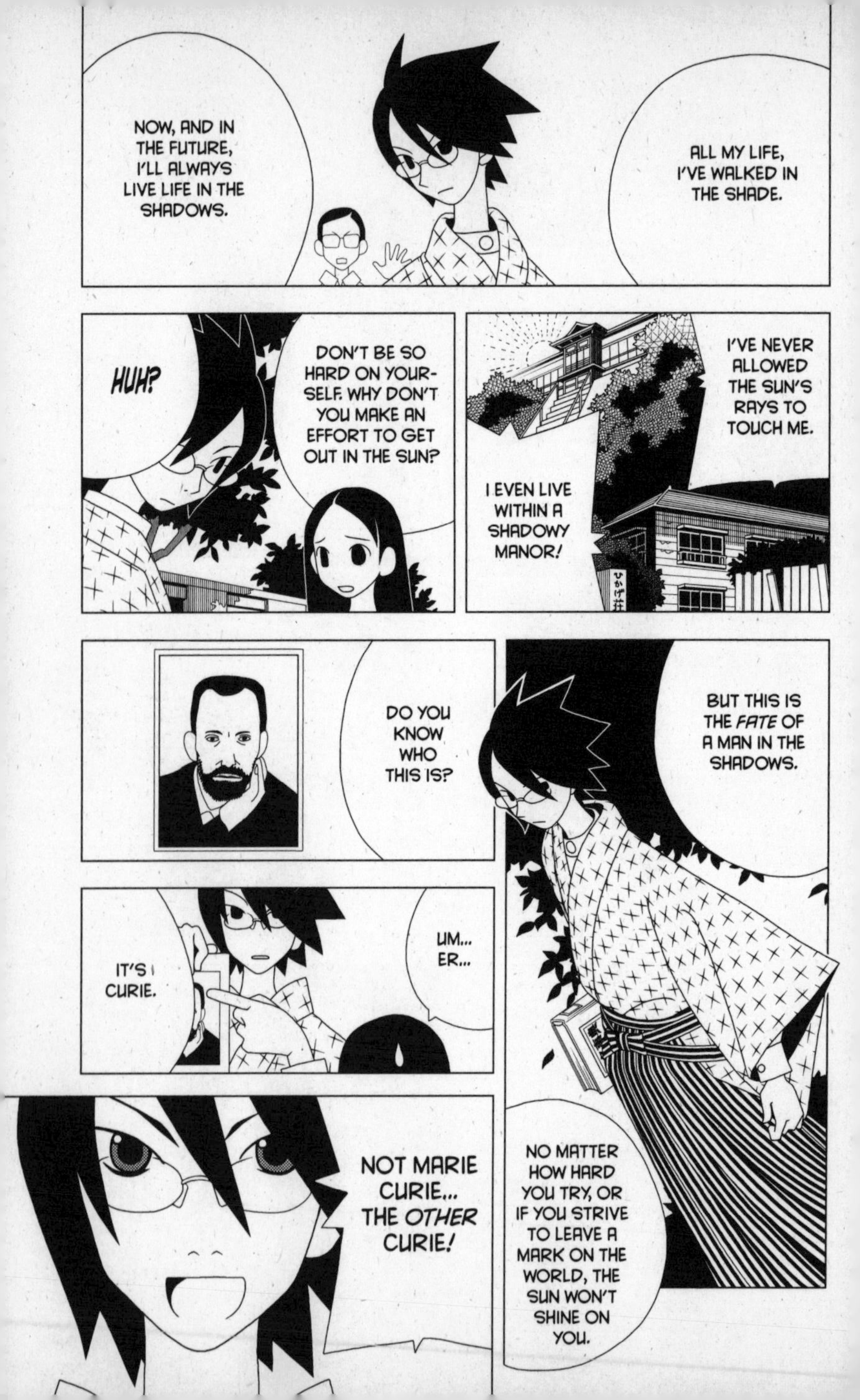
ALL MY LIFE, I'VE WALKED IN THE SHADE.
NOW, AND IN THE FUTURE, I'LL ALWAYS LIVE LIFE IN THE SHADOWS.
I'VE NEVER ALLOWED THE SUN'S RAYS TO TOUCH ME.
I EVEN LIVE WITHIN A SHADOWY MANOR!
ひかげ荘
DON'T BE SO HARD ON YOURSELF. WHY DON'T YOU MAKE AN EFFORT TO GET OUT IN THE SUN?
HUH?
BUT THIS IS THE *FATE* OF A MAN IN THE SHADOWS.
NO MATTER HOW HARD YOU TRY, OR IF YOU STRIVE TO LEAVE A MARK ON THE WORLD, THE SUN WON'T SHINE ON YOU.
DO YOU KNOW WHO THIS IS?
UM... ER...
IT'S CURIE.
NOT MARIE CURIE... THE *OTHER* CURIE!

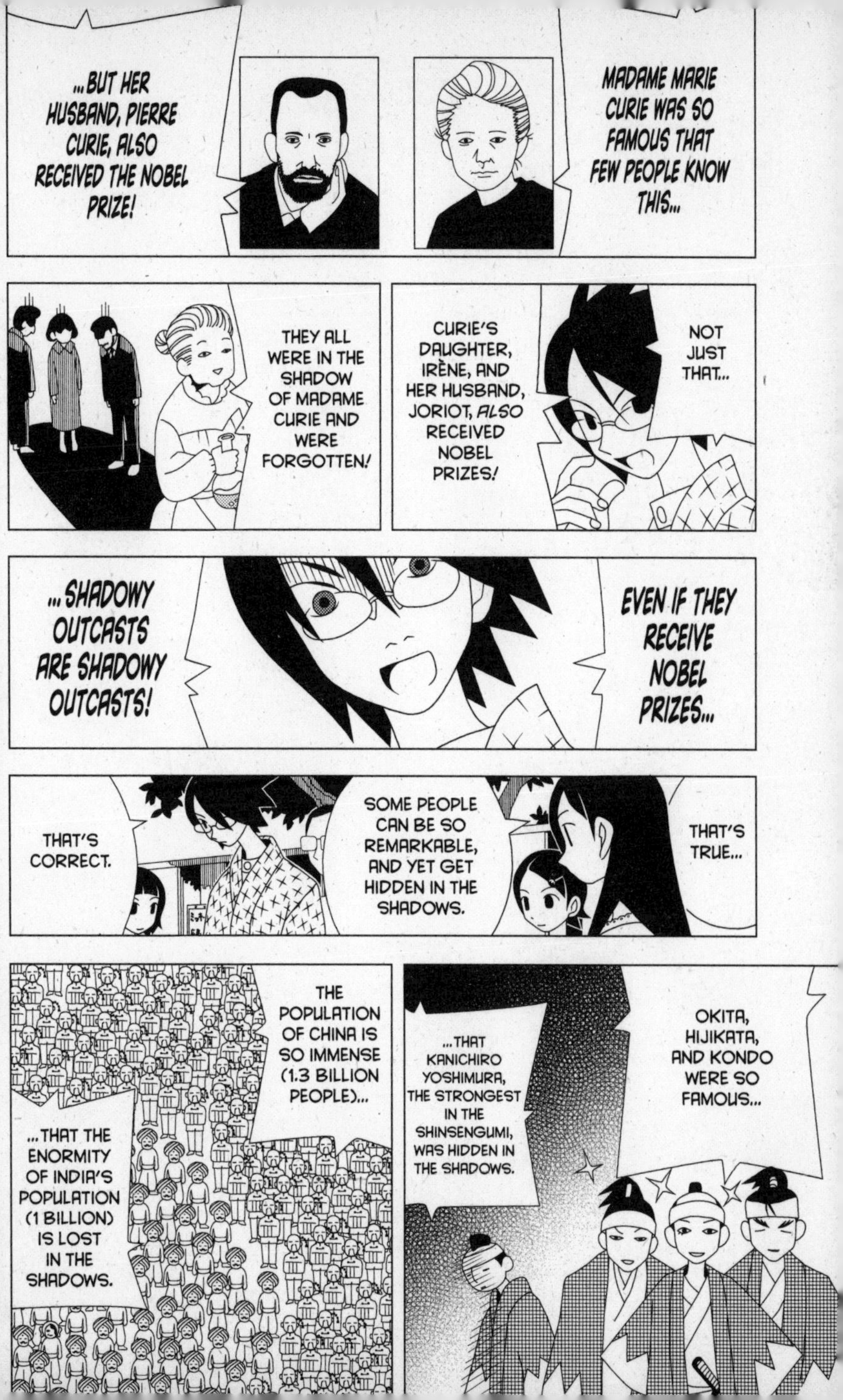
MADAME MARIE CURIE WAS SO FAMOUS THAT FEW PEOPLE KNOW THIS...
...BUT HER HUSBAND, PIERRE CURIE, ALSO RECEIVED THE NOBEL PRIZE!
NOT JUST THAT...
CURIE'S DAUGHTER, IRÈNE, AND HER HUSBAND, JORIOT, *ALSO* RECEIVED NOBEL PRIZES!
THEY ALL WERE IN THE SHADOW OF MADAME CURIE AND WERE FORGOTTEN!
EVEN IF THEY RECEIVE NOBEL PRIZES...
...SHADOWY OUTCASTS ARE SHADOWY OUTCASTS!
THAT'S TRUE...
SOME PEOPLE CAN BE SO REMARKABLE, AND YET GET HIDDEN IN THE SHADOWS.
THAT'S CORRECT.
OKITA, HIJIKATA, AND KONDO WERE SO FAMOUS...
...THAT KANICHIRO YOSHIMURA, THE STRONGEST IN THE SHINSENGUMI, WAS HIDDEN IN THE SHADOWS.
THE POPULATION OF CHINA IS SO IMMENSE (1.3 BILLION PEOPLE)...
...THAT THE ENORMITY OF INDIA'S POPULATION (1 BILLION) IS LOST IN THE SHADOWS.

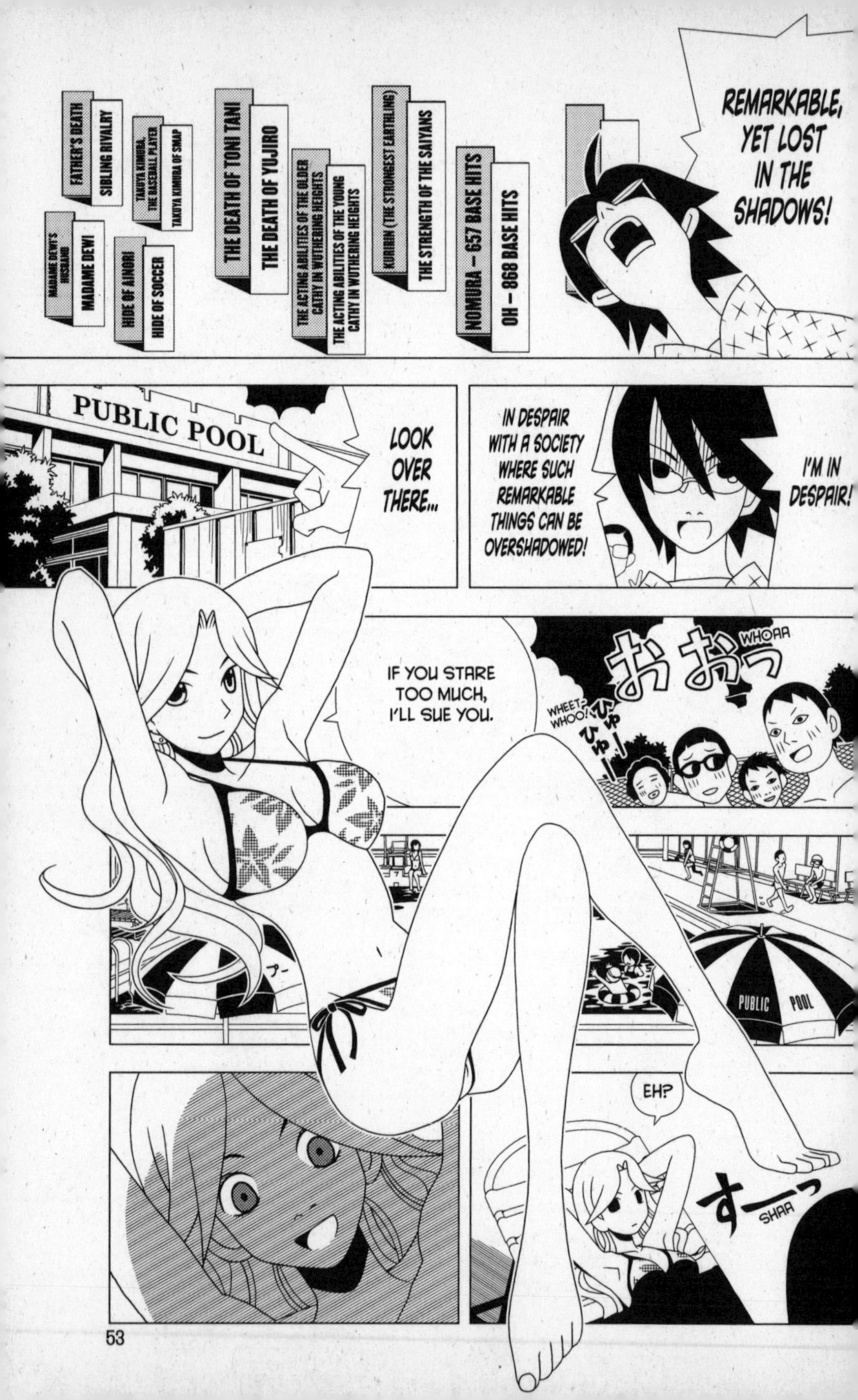

REMARKABLE, YET LOST IN THE SHADOWS!
NOMURA – 657 BASE HITS
OH – 868 BASE HITS
KURIRIN (THE STRONGEST EARTHLING)
THE STRENGTH OF THE SAIYANS
THE ACTING ABILITIES OF THE OLDER CATHY IN WUTHERING HEIGHTS
THE ACTING ABILITIES OF THE YOUNG CATHY IN WUTHERING HEIGHTS
THE DEATH OF TONI TANI
THE DEATH OF YUJIRO
TAKUYA KIMURA, THE BASEBALL PLAYER
TAKUYA KIMURA OF SMAP
HIDE OF AINORI
HIDE OF SOCCER
FATHER'S DEATH
SIBLING RIVALRY
MADAME DEWI'S HUSBAND
MADAME DEWI
I'M IN DESPAIR!
IN DESPAIR WITH A SOCIETY WHERE SUCH REMARKABLE THINGS CAN BE OVERSHADOWED!
PUBLIC POOL
LOOK OVER THERE...
おおっ WHOAA
ひゅーひゅー WHEET-WHOO!
IF YOU STARE TOO MUCH, I'LL SUE YOU.
PUBLIC POOL
EH?
すーっ SHAA

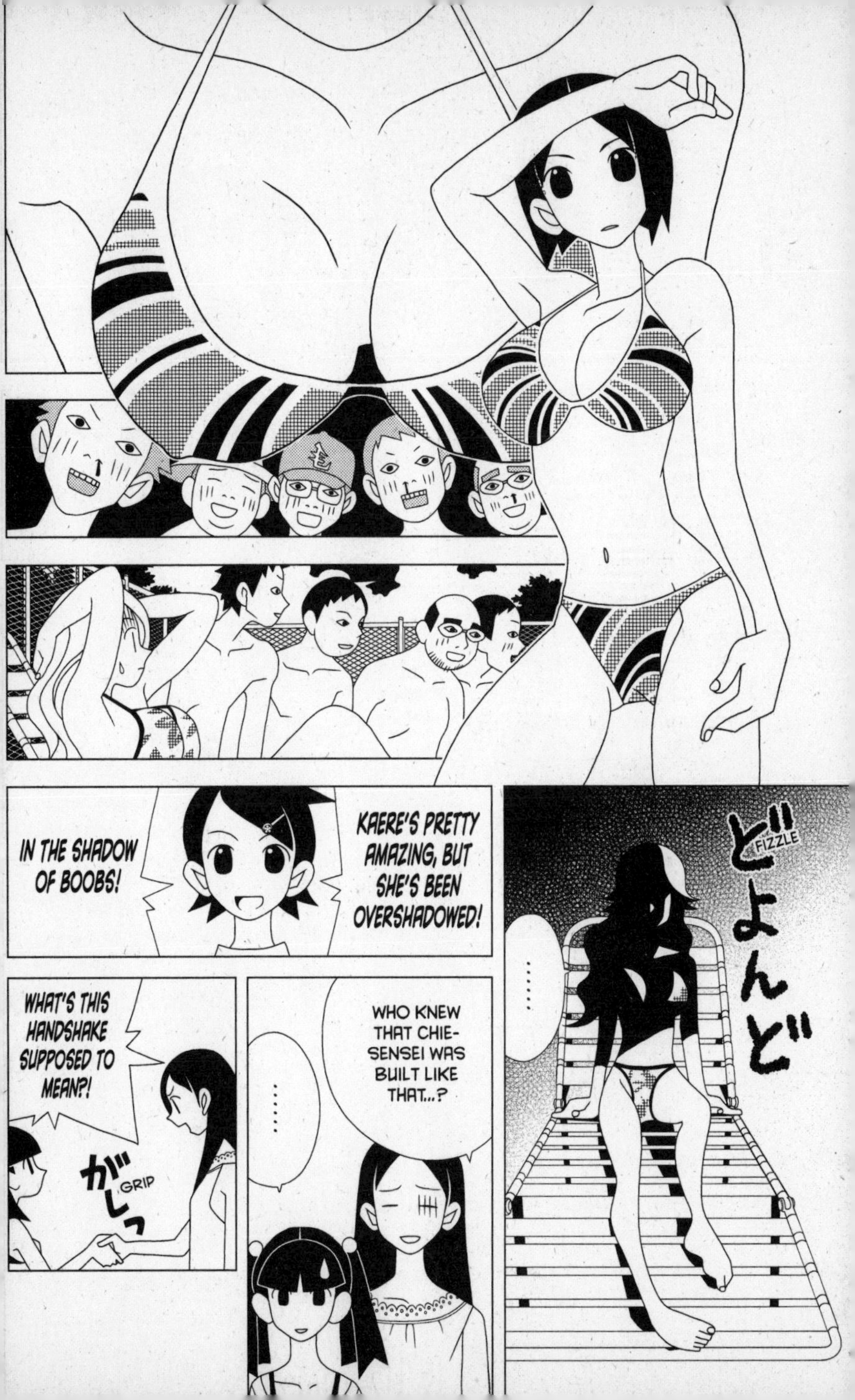
どよんど
FIZZLE
......
KAERE'S PRETTY AMAZING, BUT SHE'S BEEN OVERSHADOWED!
IN THE SHADOW OF BOOBS!
WHO KNEW THAT CHIE-SENSEI WAS BUILT LIKE THAT...?
......
WHAT'S THIS HANDSHAKE SUPPOSED TO MEAN?!
がしっ
GRIP

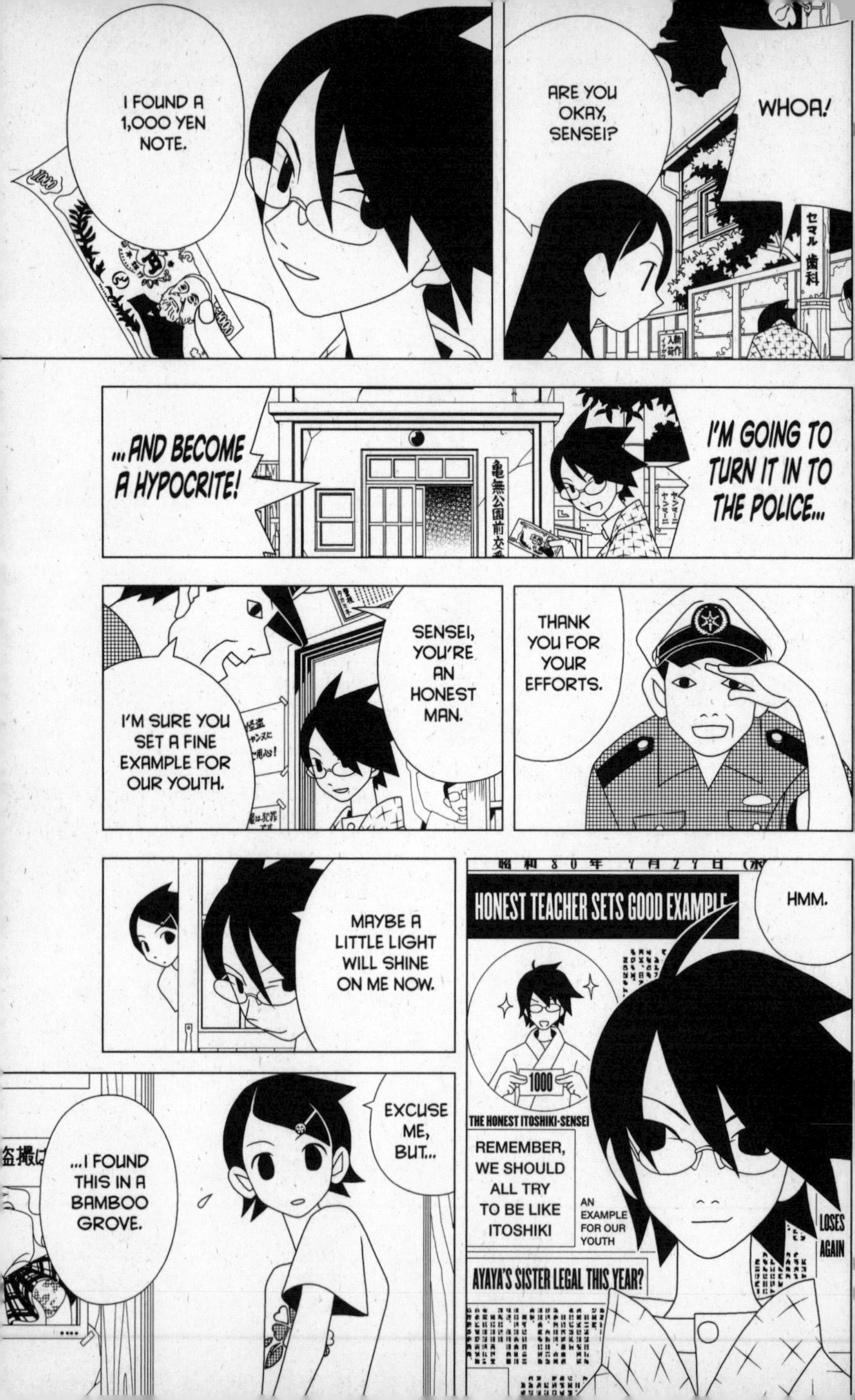
WHOA!
ARE YOU OKAY, SENSEI?
セマル 歯科
I FOUND A 1,000 YEN NOTE.
I'M GOING TO TURN IT IN TO THE POLICE...
...AND BECOME A HYPOCRITE!
THANK YOU FOR YOUR EFFORTS.
SENSEI, YOU'RE AN HONEST MAN.
I'M SURE YOU SET A FINE EXAMPLE FOR OUR YOUTH.
HMM.
HONEST TEACHER SETS GOOD EXAMPLE
THE HONEST ITOSHIKI-SENSEI
REMEMBER, WE SHOULD ALL TRY TO BE LIKE ITOSHIKI
AN EXAMPLE FOR OUR YOUTH
LOSES AGAIN
AYAYA'S SISTER LEGAL THIS YEAR?
MAYBE A LITTLE LIGHT WILL SHINE ON ME NOW.
EXCUSE ME, BUT...
...I FOUND THIS IN A BAMBOO GROVE.

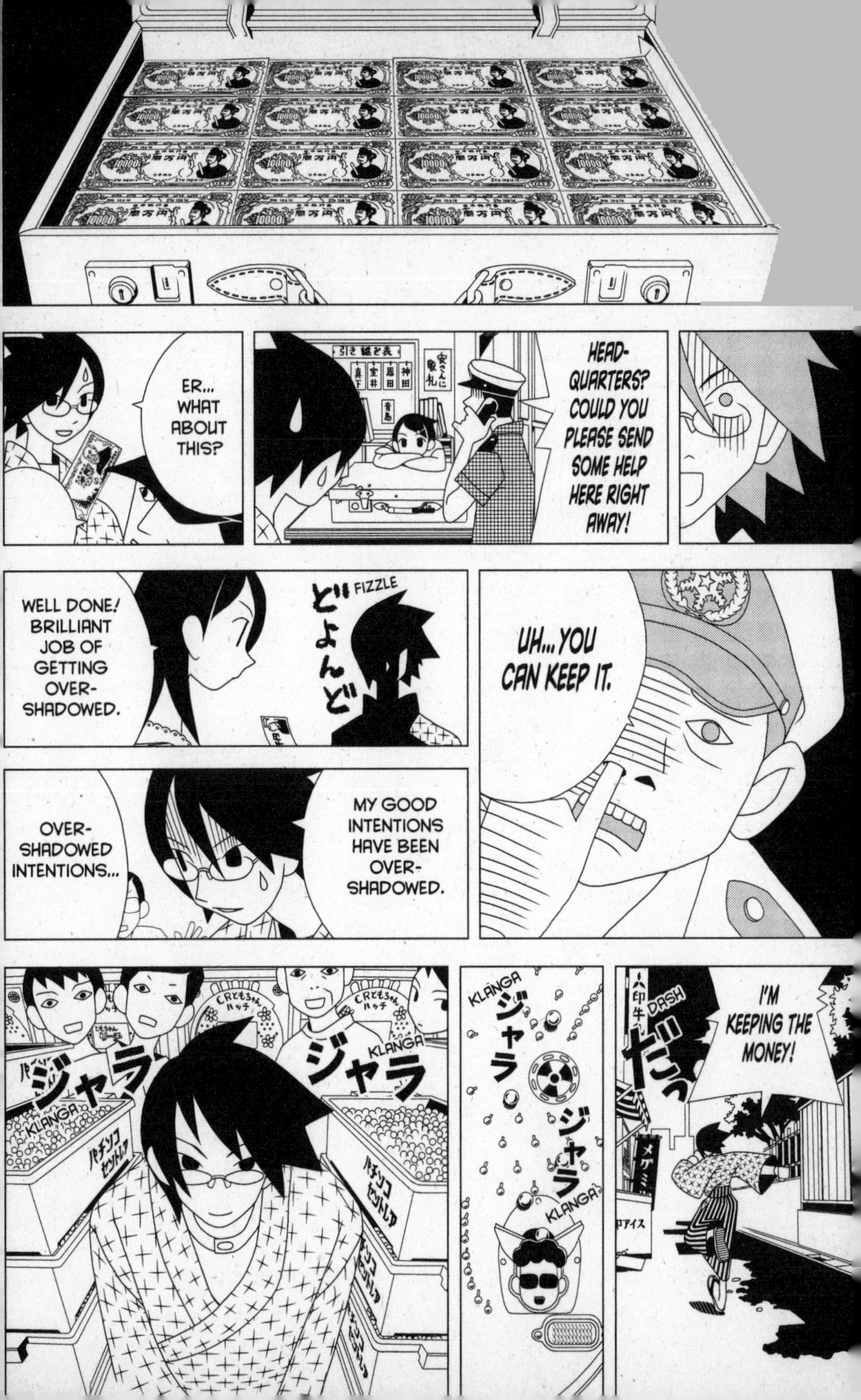

HEAD-QUARTERS? COULD YOU PLEASE SEND SOME HELP HERE RIGHT AWAY!
ER... WHAT ABOUT THIS?
UH...YOU CAN KEEP IT.
どよんど FIZZLE
WELL DONE! BRILLIANT JOB OF GETTING OVER-SHADOWED.
MY GOOD INTENTIONS HAVE BEEN OVER-SHADOWED.
OVER-SHADOWED INTENTIONS...
だっ DASH
I'M KEEPING THE MONEY!
ジャラ KLANGA
ジャラ KLANGA
ジャラ KLANGA
ジャラ KLANGA

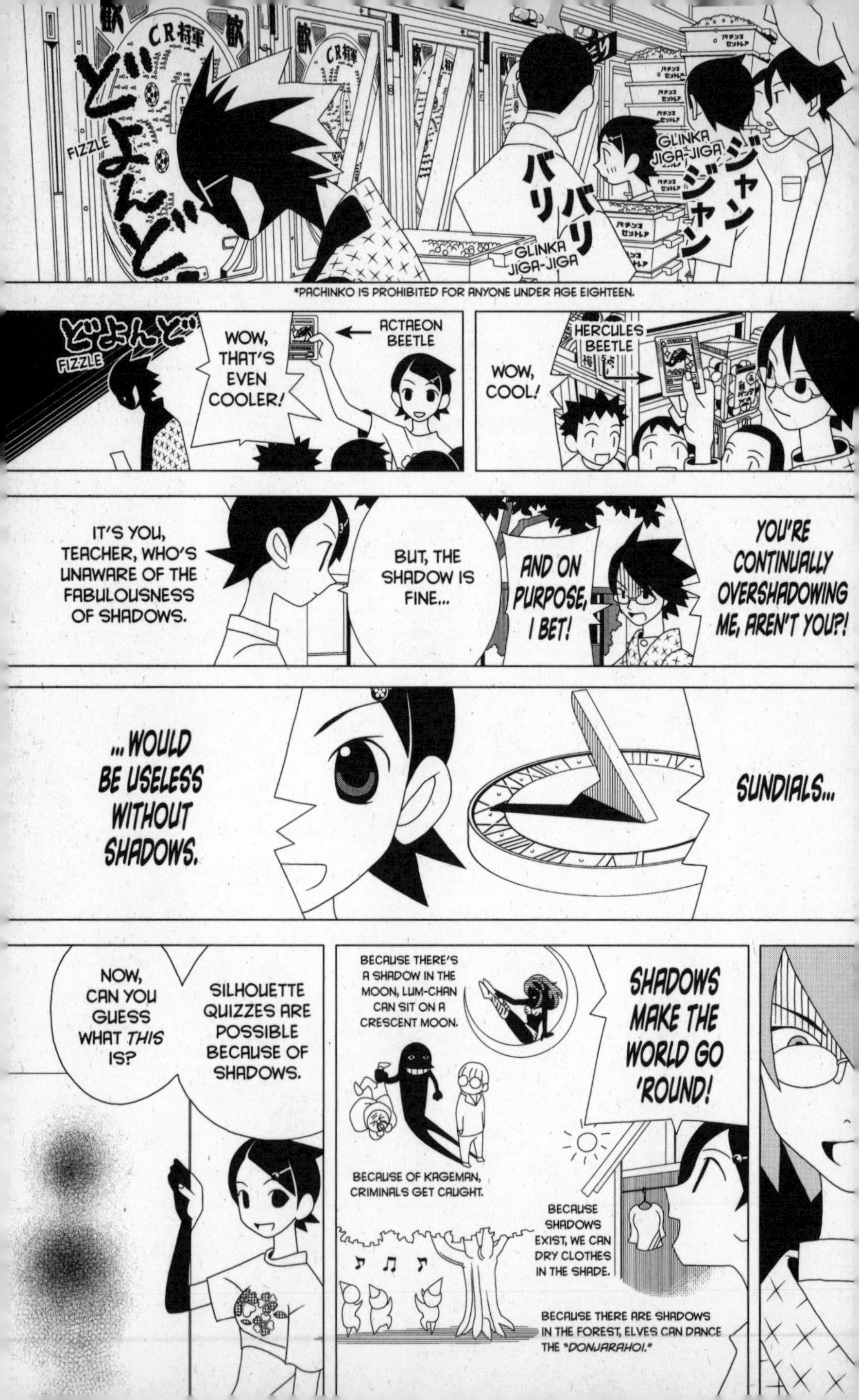
ジャンジャン
GLINKA JIGA-JIGA
バリバリ
GLINKA JIGA-JIGA
どよんど
FIZZLE
*PACHINKO IS PROHIBITED FOR ANYONE UNDER AGE EIGHTEEN.
WOW, COOL!
HERCULES BEETLE
ACTAEON BEETLE
WOW, THAT'S EVEN COOLER!
どよんど
FIZZLE
YOU'RE CONTINUALLY OVERSHADOWING ME, AREN'T YOU?!
AND ON PURPOSE, I BET!
BUT, THE SHADOW IS FINE...
IT'S YOU, TEACHER, WHO'S UNAWARE OF THE FABULOUSNESS OF SHADOWS.
SUNDIALS...
...WOULD BE USELESS WITHOUT SHADOWS.
SHADOWS MAKE THE WORLD GO 'ROUND!
BECAUSE THERE'S A SHADOW IN THE MOON, LUM-CHAN CAN SIT ON A CRESCENT MOON.
BECAUSE OF KAGEMAN, CRIMINALS GET CAUGHT.
BECAUSE SHADOWS EXIST, WE CAN DRY CLOTHES IN THE SHADE.
BECAUSE THERE ARE SHADOWS IN THE FOREST, ELVES CAN DANCE THE "DONJARAHOI."
SILHOUETTE QUIZZES ARE POSSIBLE BECAUSE OF SHADOWS.
NOW, CAN YOU GUESS WHAT THIS IS?

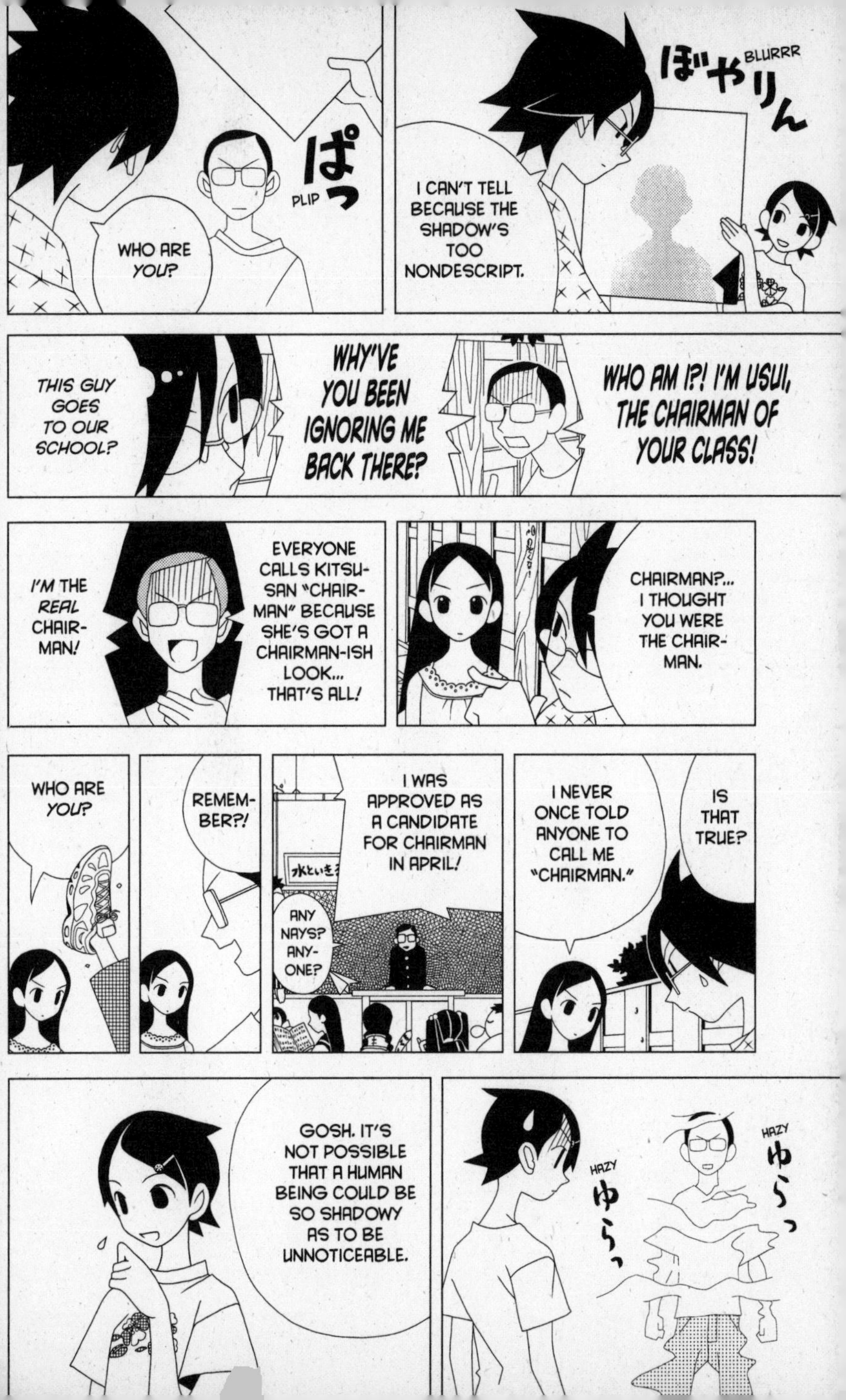
ぼやりん
BLURRR
I CAN'T TELL BECAUSE THE SHADOW'S TOO NONDESCRIPT.
ぱっ
PLIP
WHO ARE YOU?
WHO AM I?! I'M USUI, THE CHAIRMAN OF YOUR CLASS!
WHY'VE YOU BEEN IGNORING ME BACK THERE?
THIS GUY GOES TO OUR SCHOOL?
CHAIRMAN?... I THOUGHT YOU WERE THE CHAIRMAN.
EVERYONE CALLS KITSU-SAN "CHAIRMAN" BECAUSE SHE'S GOT A CHAIRMAN-ISH LOOK... THAT'S ALL!
I'M THE REAL CHAIRMAN!
IS THAT TRUE?
I NEVER ONCE TOLD ANYONE TO CALL ME "CHAIRMAN."
I WAS APPROVED AS A CANDIDATE FOR CHAIRMAN IN APRIL!
ANY NAYS? ANYONE?
REMEMBER?!
WHO ARE YOU?
ゆらっ
HAZY
ゆらっ
HAZY
GOSH. IT'S NOT POSSIBLE THAT A HUMAN BEING COULD BE SO SHADOWY AS TO BE UNNOTICEABLE.

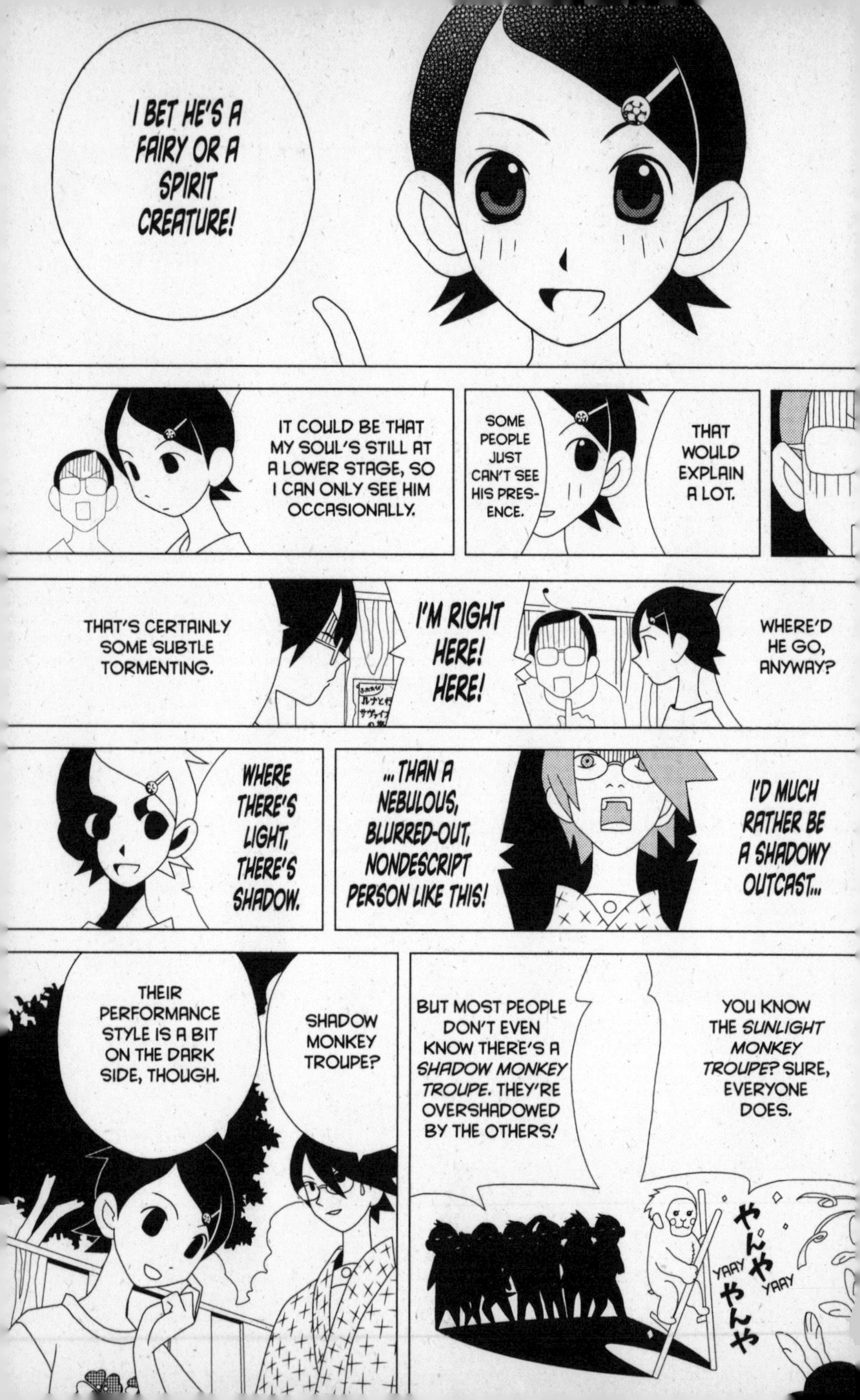
I BET HE'S A FAIRY OR A SPIRIT CREATURE!
THAT WOULD EXPLAIN A LOT.
SOME PEOPLE JUST CAN'T SEE HIS PRES-ENCE.
IT COULD BE THAT MY SOUL'S STILL AT A LOWER STAGE, SO I CAN ONLY SEE HIM OCCASIONALLY.
WHERE'D HE GO, ANYWAY?
I'M RIGHT HERE! HERE!
THAT'S CERTAINLY SOME SUBTLE TORMENTING.
I'D MUCH RATHER BE A SHADOWY OUTCAST...
...THAN A NEBULOUS, BLURRED-OUT, NONDESCRIPT PERSON LIKE THIS!
WHERE THERE'S LIGHT, THERE'S SHADOW.
YOU KNOW THE *SUNLIGHT MONKEY TROUPE*? SURE, EVERYONE DOES.
BUT MOST PEOPLE DON'T EVEN KNOW THERE'S A *SHADOW MONKEY TROUPE*. THEY'RE OVERSHADOWED BY THE OTHERS!
やんや YAAY
やんや YAAY
SHADOW MONKEY TROUPE?
THEIR PERFORMANCE STYLE IS A BIT ON THE DARK SIDE, THOUGH.

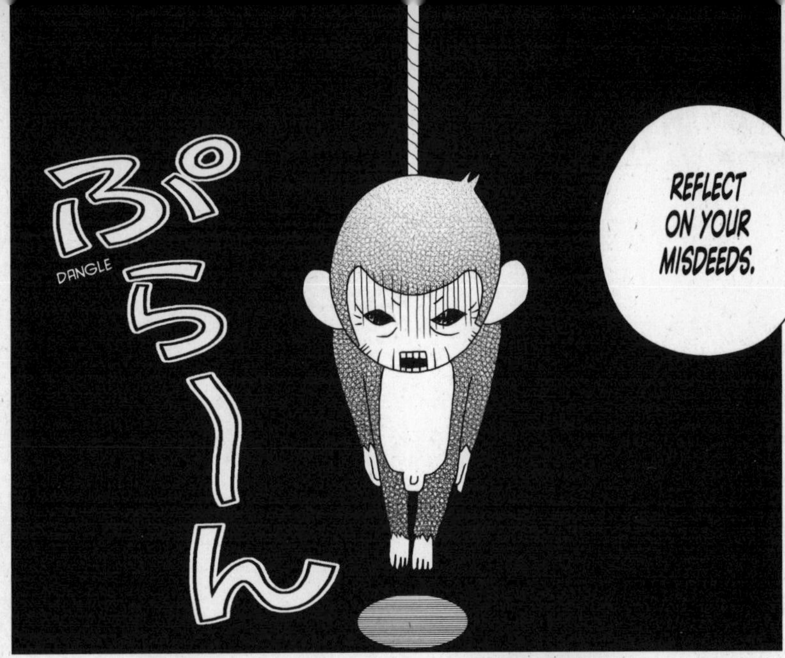
REFLECT ON YOUR MISDEEDS.
ぷらーん
DANGLE

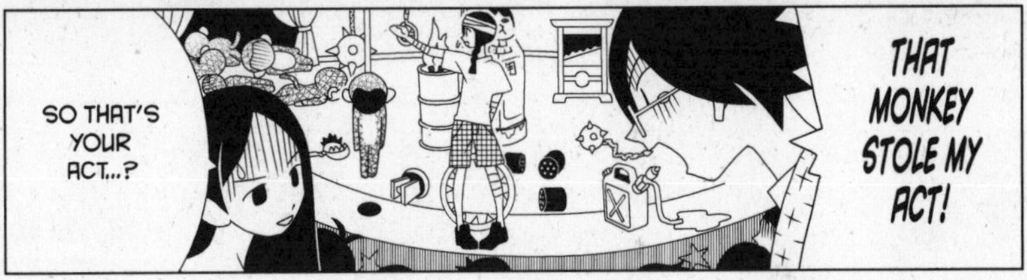
THAT MONKEY STOLE MY ACT!
SO THAT'S YOUR ACT...?

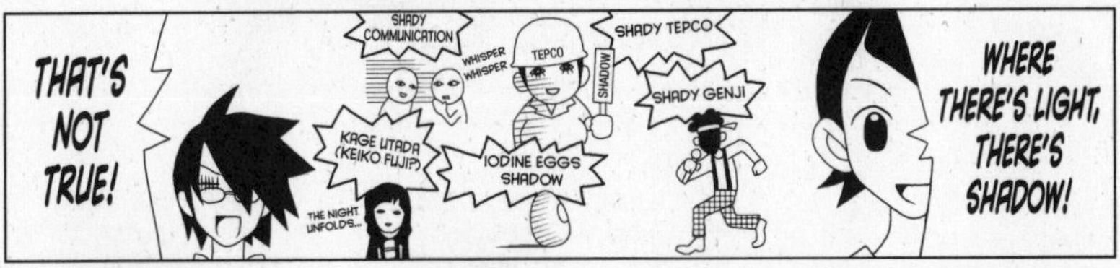
WHERE THERE'S LIGHT, THERE'S SHADOW!
SHADY TEPCO
SHADY GENJI
SHADOW
TEPCO
WHISPER WHISPER
SHADY COMMUNICATION
IODINE EGGS SHADOW
KAGE UTADA (KEIKO FUJI?)
THE NIGHT UNFOLDS...
THAT'S NOT TRUE!

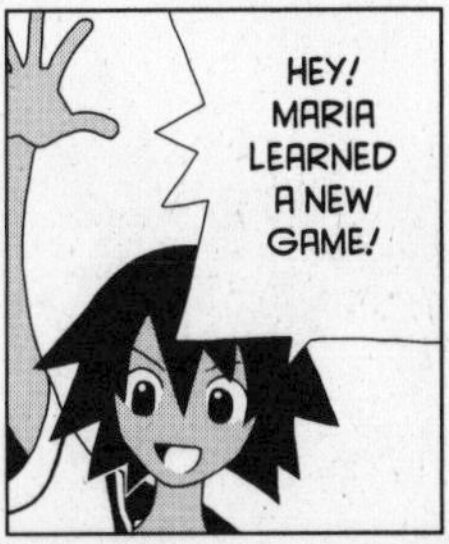
HEY! MARIA LEARNED A NEW GAME!

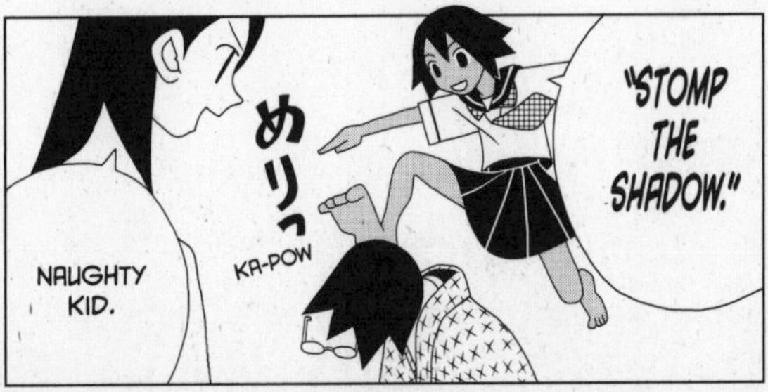
"STOMP THE SHADOW."
めりっ
KA-POW
NAUGHTY KID.

ATTENDANCE LIST
CLASS 2-F

ATTENDANCE NO. 3

**KAGERO USUI**

CHAIRMAN

LACKING BOTH HAIR AND PRESENCE

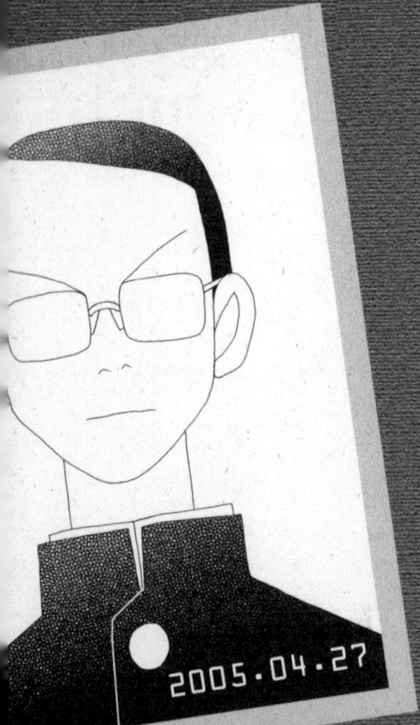
2005.04.27

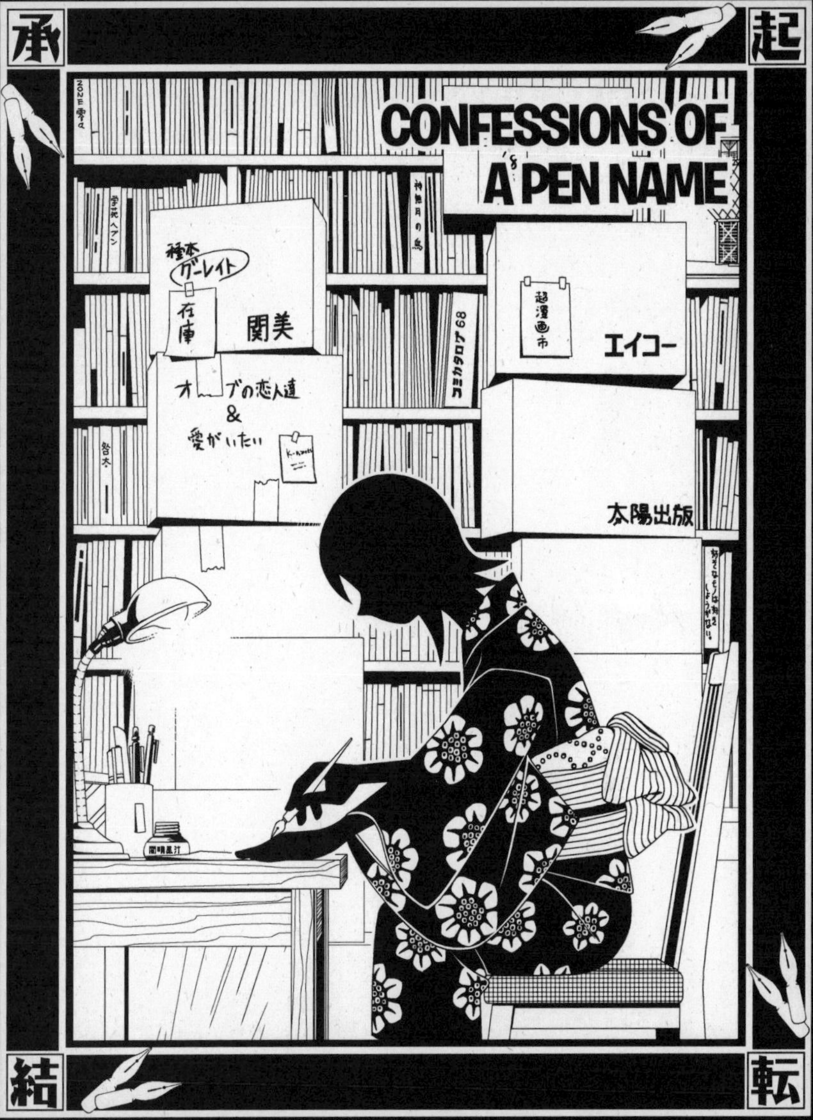
起
承
転
結
CONFESSIONS OF
A PEN NAME
神無月の鳥
グーレイト
在庫
関美
オーブの恋人道
&
愛がいたい
コミカタログ68
超漫画市
エイコー
太陽出版

# CHAPTER 15

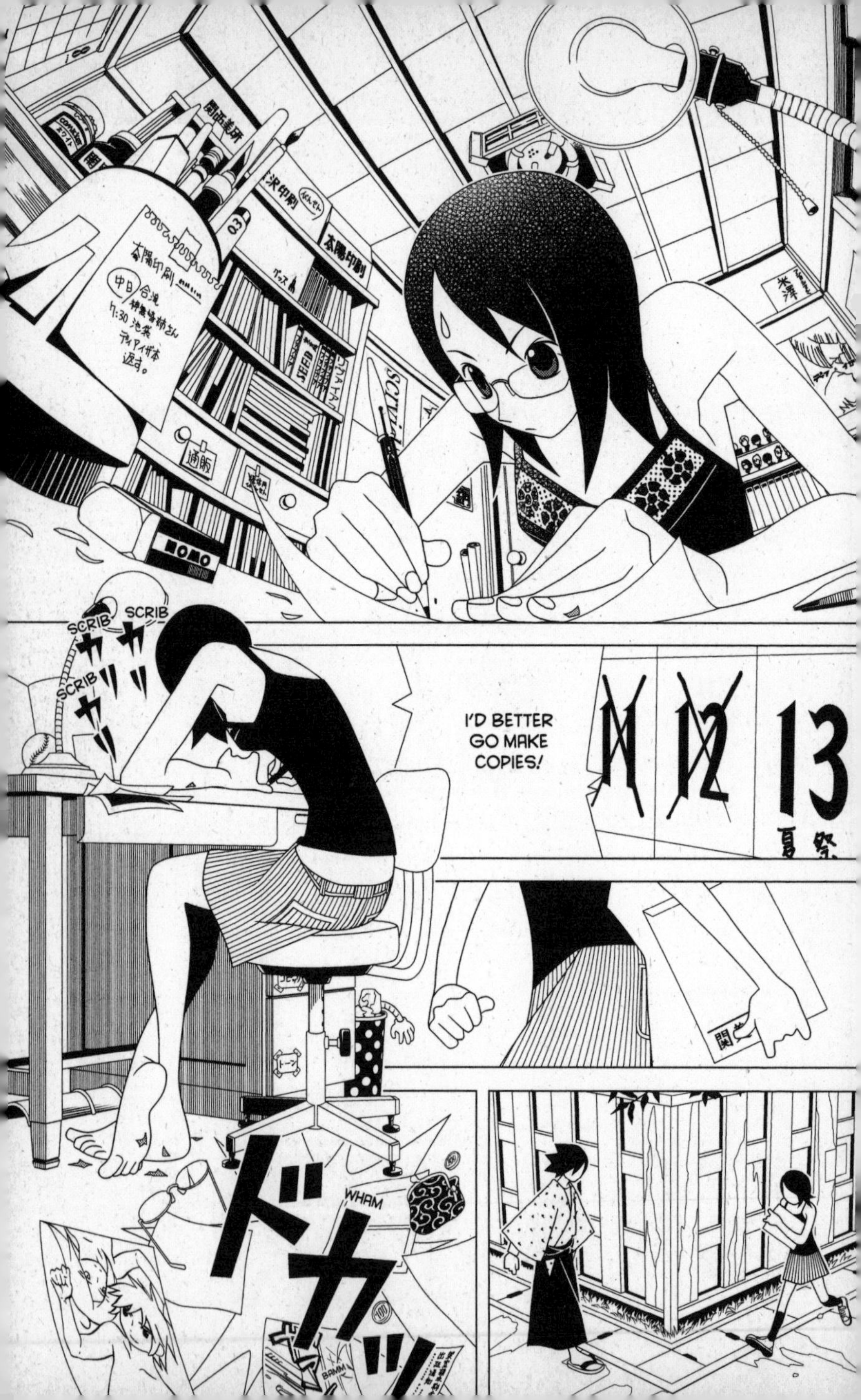

I'D BETTER GO MAKE COPIES!
SCRIB
SCRIB
SCRIB
WHAM
BAMM

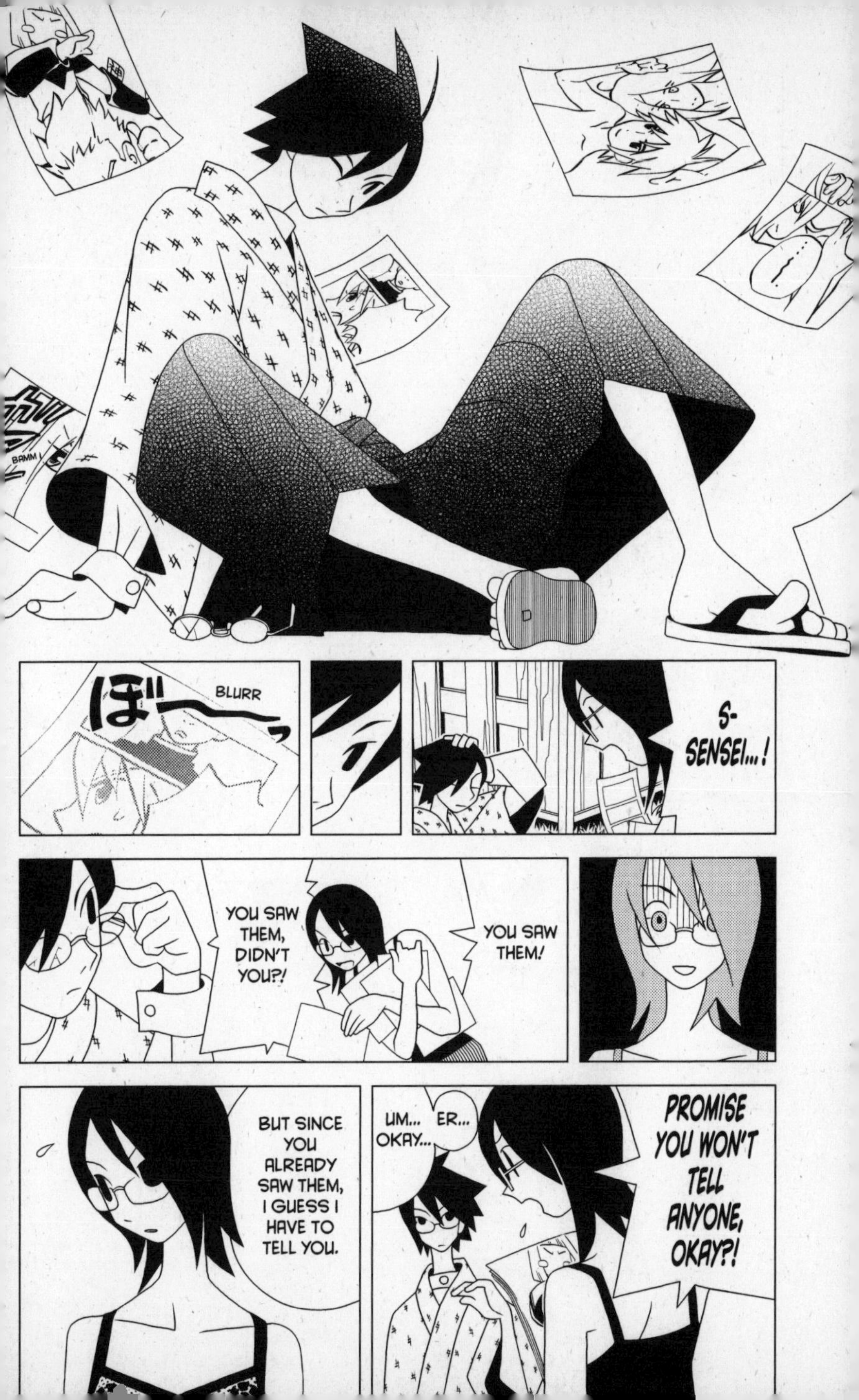
BAMM
S-SENSEI...!
ぼ～～っ
BLURR
YOU SAW THEM!
YOU SAW THEM, DIDN'T YOU?!
PROMISE YOU WON'T TELL ANYONE, OKAY?!
UM... ER... OKAY...
BUT SINCE YOU ALREADY SAW THEM, I GUESS I HAVE TO TELL YOU.

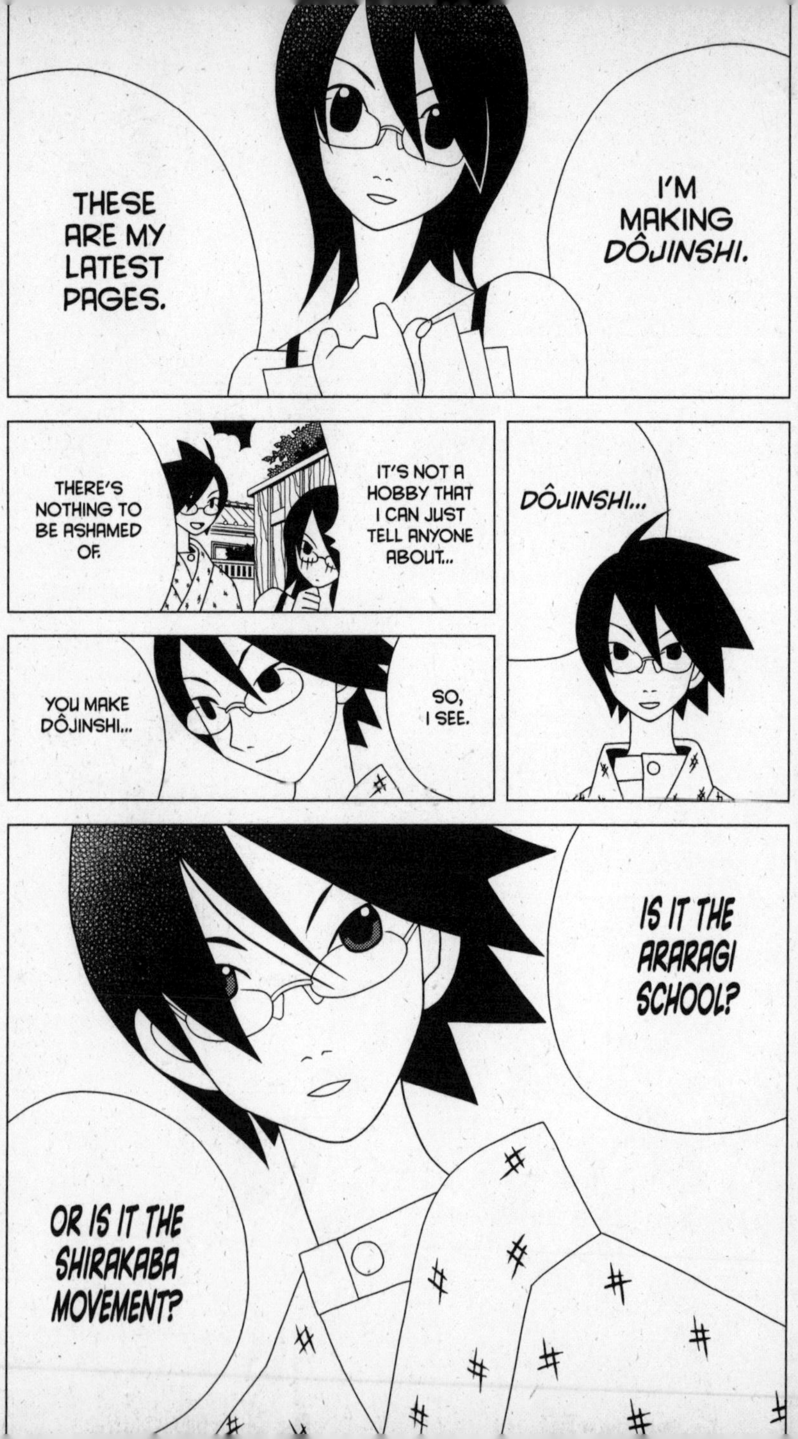
I'M MAKING DÔJINSHI.
THESE ARE MY LATEST PAGES.
DÔJINSHI...
IT'S NOT A HOBBY THAT I CAN JUST TELL ANYONE ABOUT...
THERE'S NOTHING TO BE ASHAMED OF.
SO, I SEE.
YOU MAKE DÔJINSHI...
IS IT THE ARARAGI SCHOOL?
OR IS IT THE SHIRAKABA MOVEMENT?

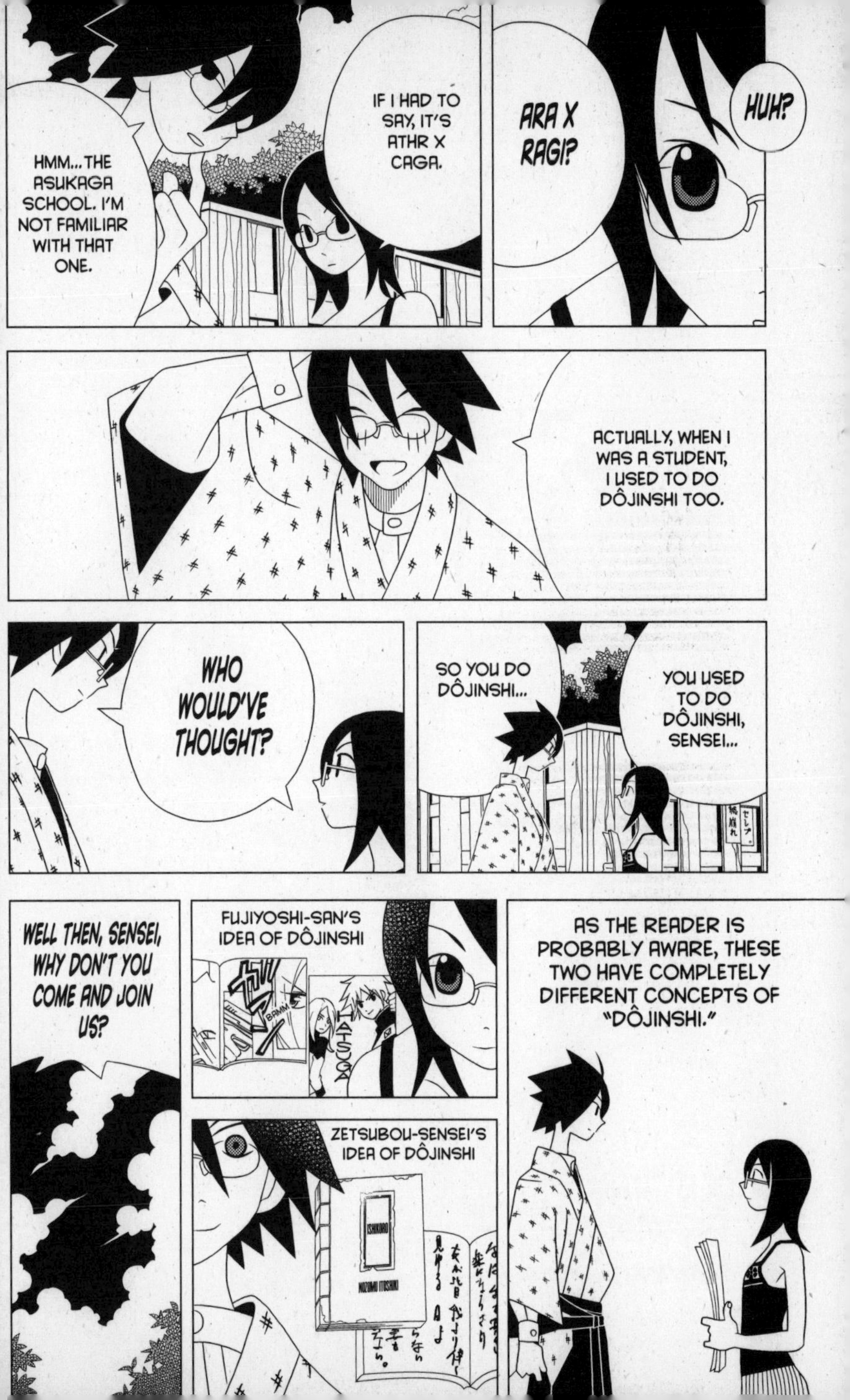
HUH?
ARA X RAGI?
IF I HAD TO SAY, IT'S ATHR X CAGA.
HMM... THE ASUKAGA SCHOOL. I'M NOT FAMILIAR WITH THAT ONE.
ACTUALLY, WHEN I WAS A STUDENT, I USED TO DO DÔJINSHI TOO.
YOU USED TO DO DÔJINSHI, SENSEI...
SO YOU DO DÔJINSHI...
WHO WOULD'VE THOUGHT?
AS THE READER IS PROBABLY AWARE, THESE TWO HAVE COMPLETELY DIFFERENT CONCEPTS OF "DÔJINSHI."
FUJIYOSHI-SAN'S IDEA OF DÔJINSHI
BAMM
HATSUGA
ZETSUBOU-SENSEI'S IDEA OF DÔJINSHI
ISHIKORO
NOZOMU ITOSHIKI
WELL THEN, SENSEI, WHY DON'T YOU COME AND JOIN US?

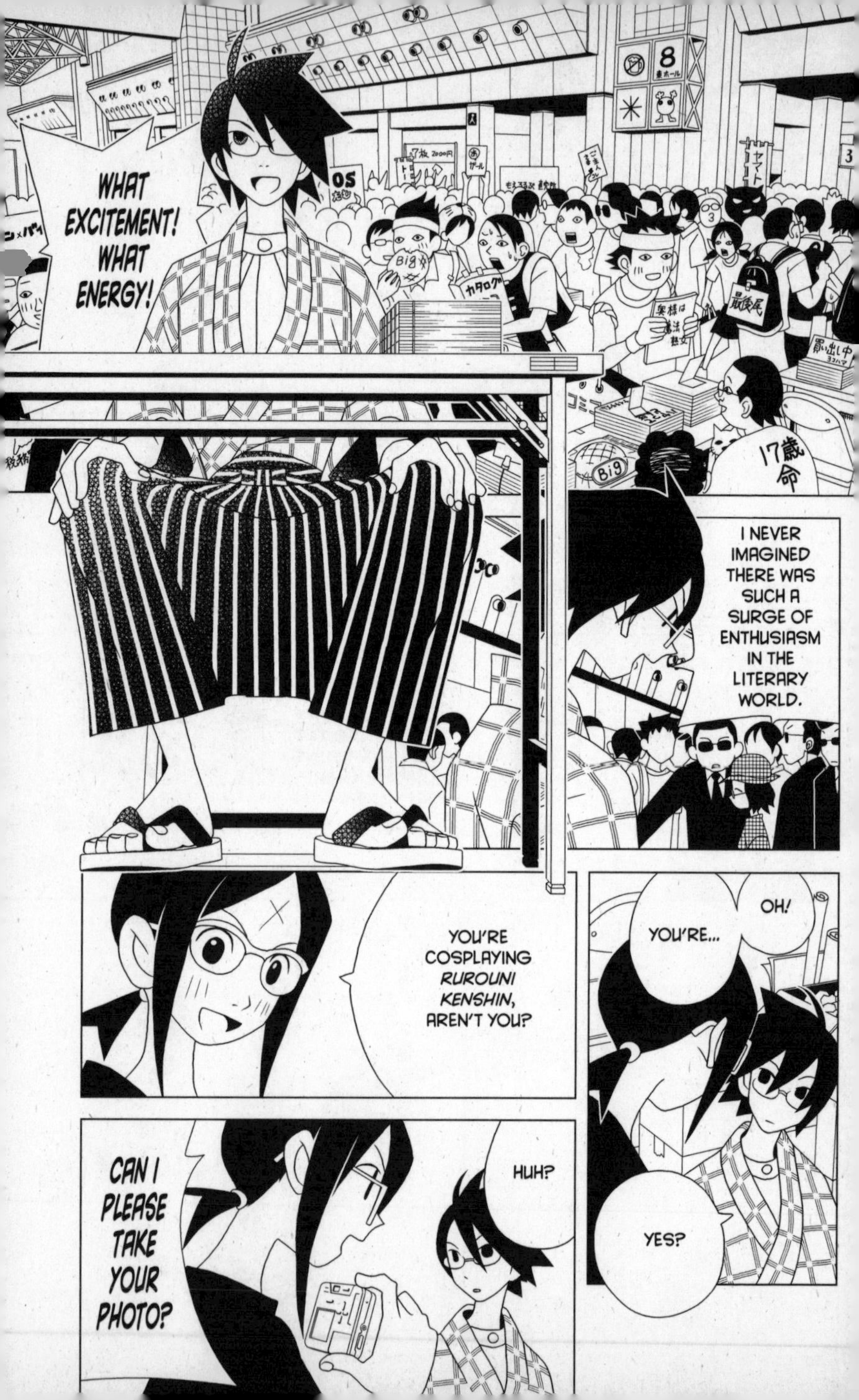
WHAT EXCITEMENT! WHAT ENERGY!
最後尾
17歳命
I NEVER IMAGINED THERE WAS SUCH A SURGE OF ENTHUSIASM IN THE LITERARY WORLD.
OH!
YOU'RE...
YES?
YOU'RE COSPLAYING *RUROUNI KENSHIN*, AREN'T YOU?
CAN I PLEASE TAKE YOUR PHOTO?
HUH?

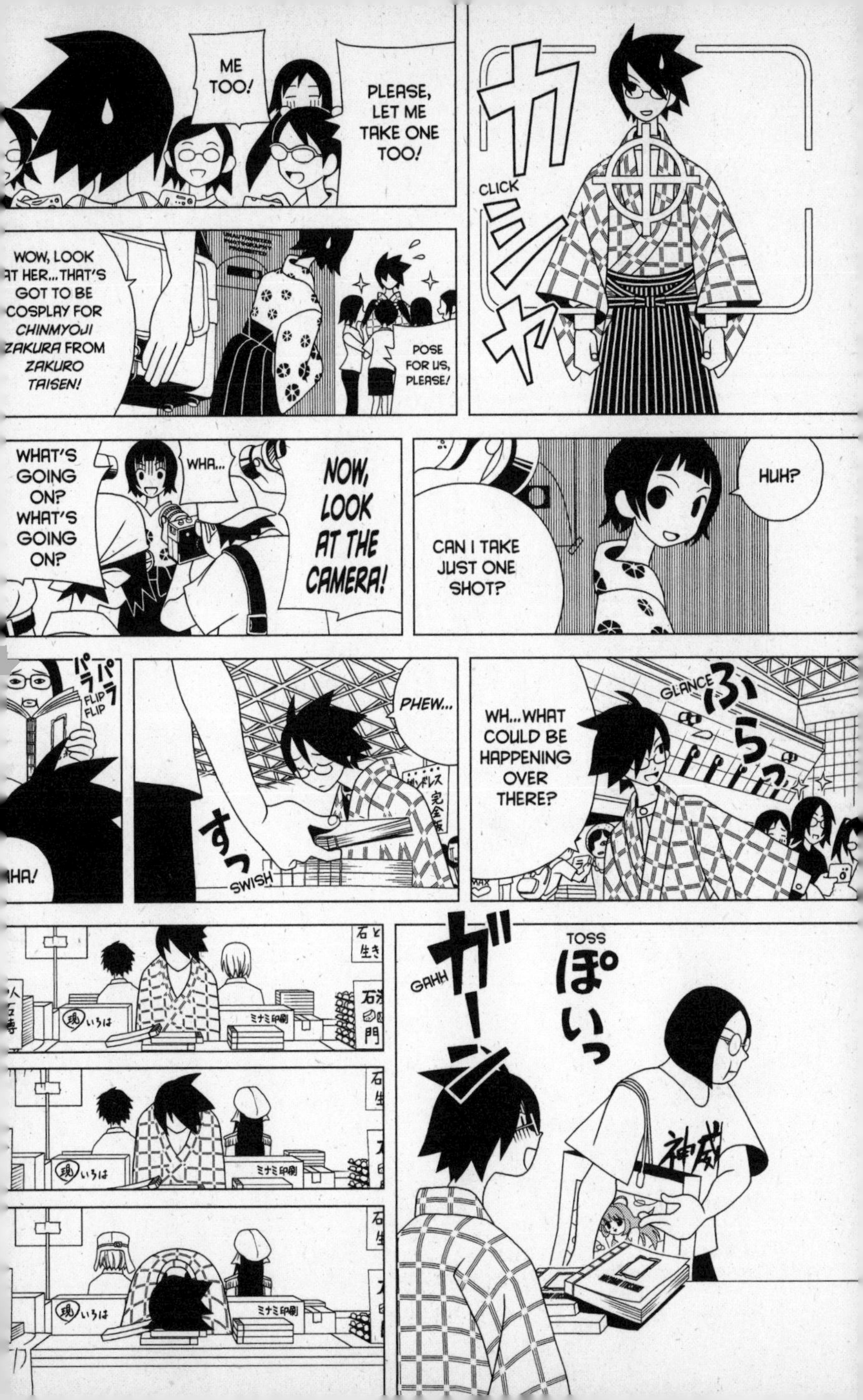
カシャ
CLICK
PLEASE, LET ME TAKE ONE TOO!
ME TOO!
POSE FOR US, PLEASE!
WOW, LOOK AT HER...THAT'S GOT TO BE COSPLAY FOR CHINMYOJI ZAKURA FROM ZAKURO TAISEN!
HUH?
CAN I TAKE JUST ONE SHOT?
NOW, LOOK AT THE CAMERA!
WHA...
WHAT'S GOING ON? WHAT'S GOING ON?
ふらっ
GLANCE
WH...WHAT COULD BE HAPPENING OVER THERE?
PHEW...
すっ
SWISH
パラパラ
FLIP FLIP
HA!
ガーン
GAHH
ぽいっ
TOSS
いろは
ミナミ印刷
いろは
ミナミ印刷
いろは
ミナミ印刷

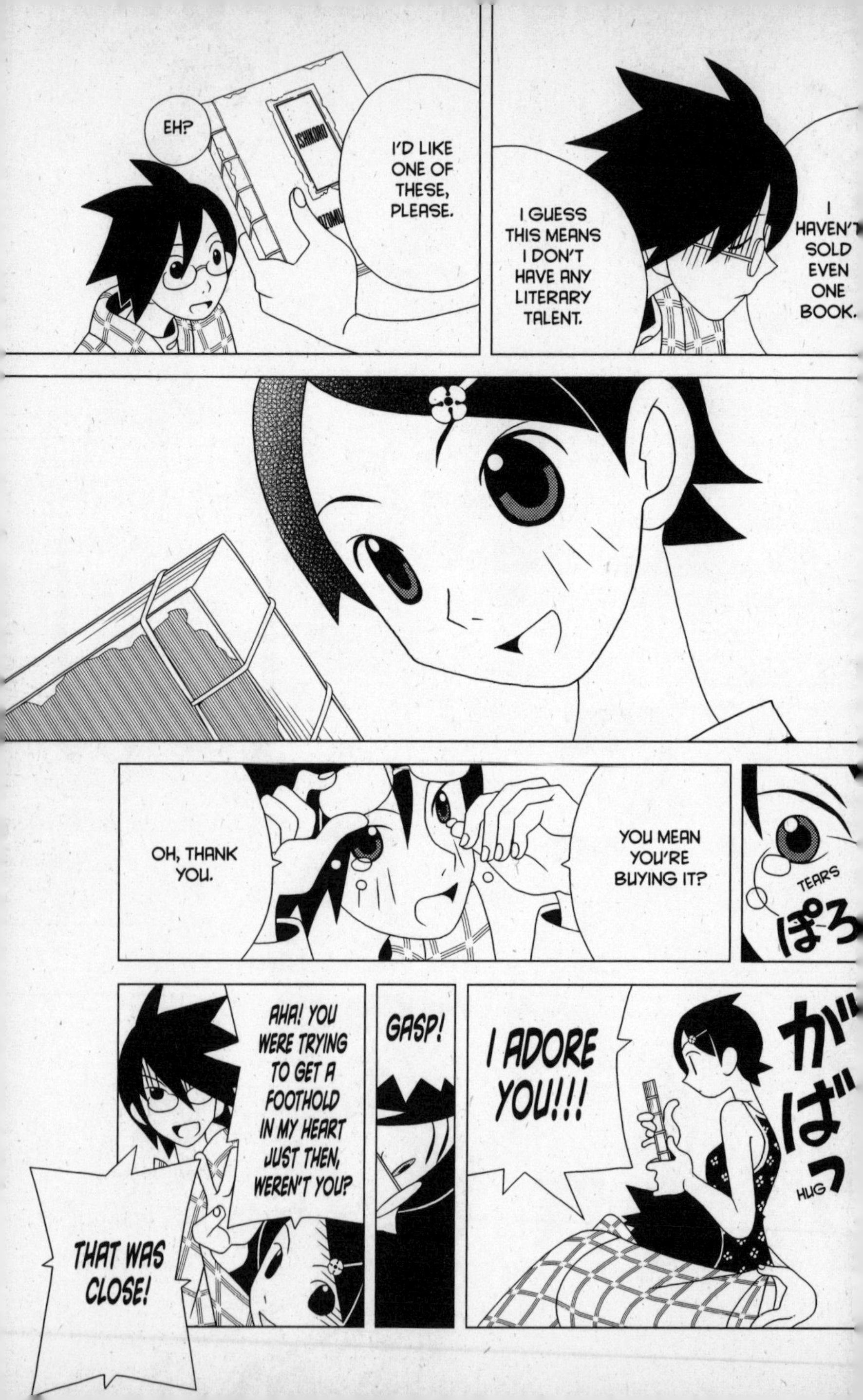
I HAVEN'T SOLD EVEN ONE BOOK.
I GUESS THIS MEANS I DON'T HAVE ANY LITERARY TALENT.
ISHIKORO
I'D LIKE ONE OF THESE, PLEASE.
EH?
ぽろ
TEARS
YOU MEAN YOU'RE BUYING IT?
OH, THANK YOU.
がばっ
HUG
I ADORE YOU!!!
GASP!
AHA! YOU WERE TRYING TO GET A FOOTHOLD IN MY HEART JUST THEN, WEREN'T YOU?
THAT WAS CLOSE!

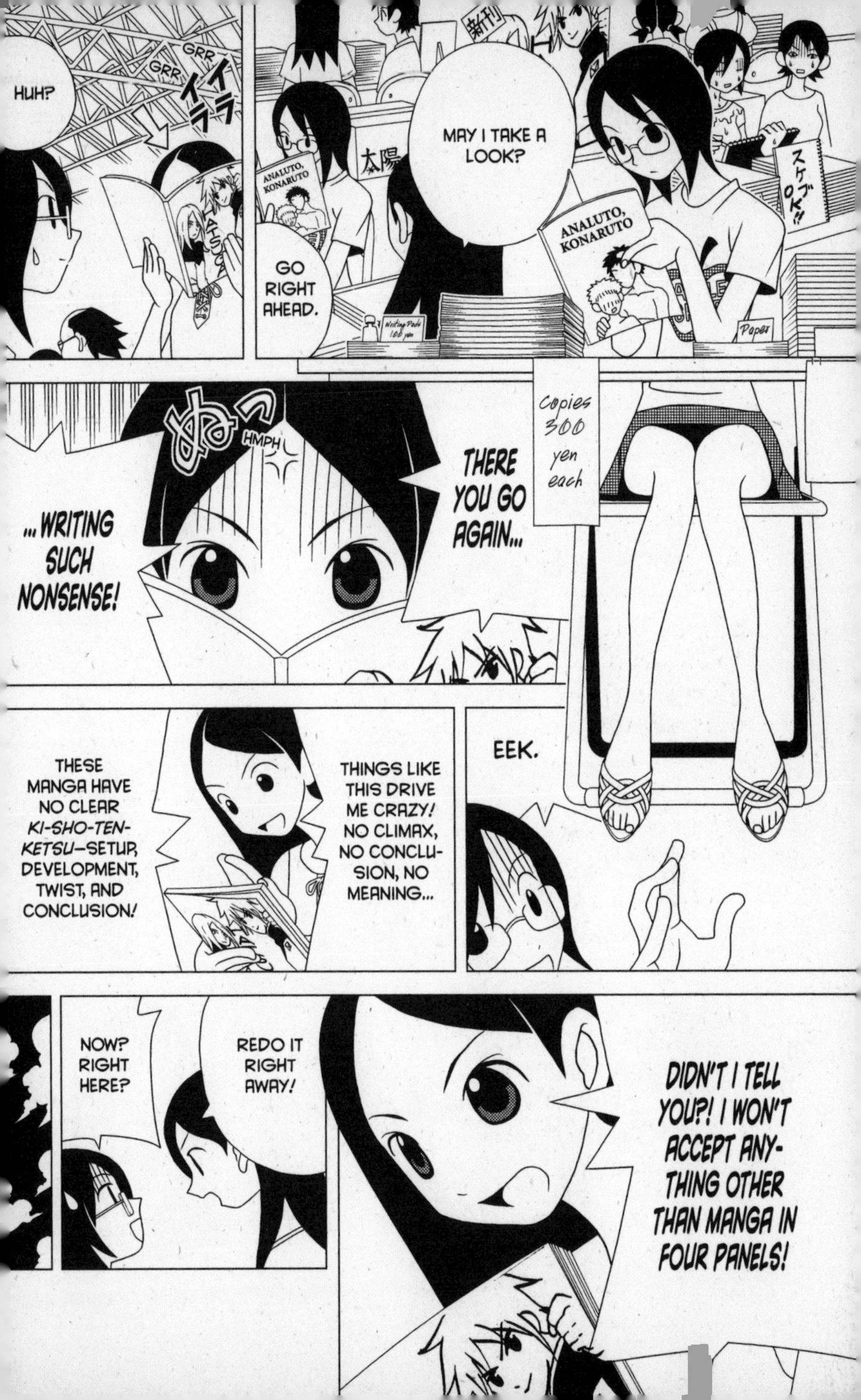
新刊
スケブOK!!
ANALUTO, KONARUTO
MAY I TAKE A LOOK?
Papers
Writing Pads 100 yen
太陽
ANALUTO, KONARUTO
GO RIGHT AHEAD.
GRR イラ
GRR イラ
HUH?
Copies 300 yen each
THERE YOU GO AGAIN...
ぬっ HMPH
...WRITING SUCH NONSENSE!
EEK.
THINGS LIKE THIS DRIVE ME CRAZY! NO CLIMAX, NO CONCLUSION, NO MEANING...
THESE MANGA HAVE NO CLEAR KI-SHO-TEN-KETSU—SETUP, DEVELOPMENT, TWIST, AND CONCLUSION!
DIDN'T I TELL YOU?! I WON'T ACCEPT ANYTHING OTHER THAN MANGA IN FOUR PANELS!
REDO IT RIGHT AWAY!
NOW? RIGHT HERE?

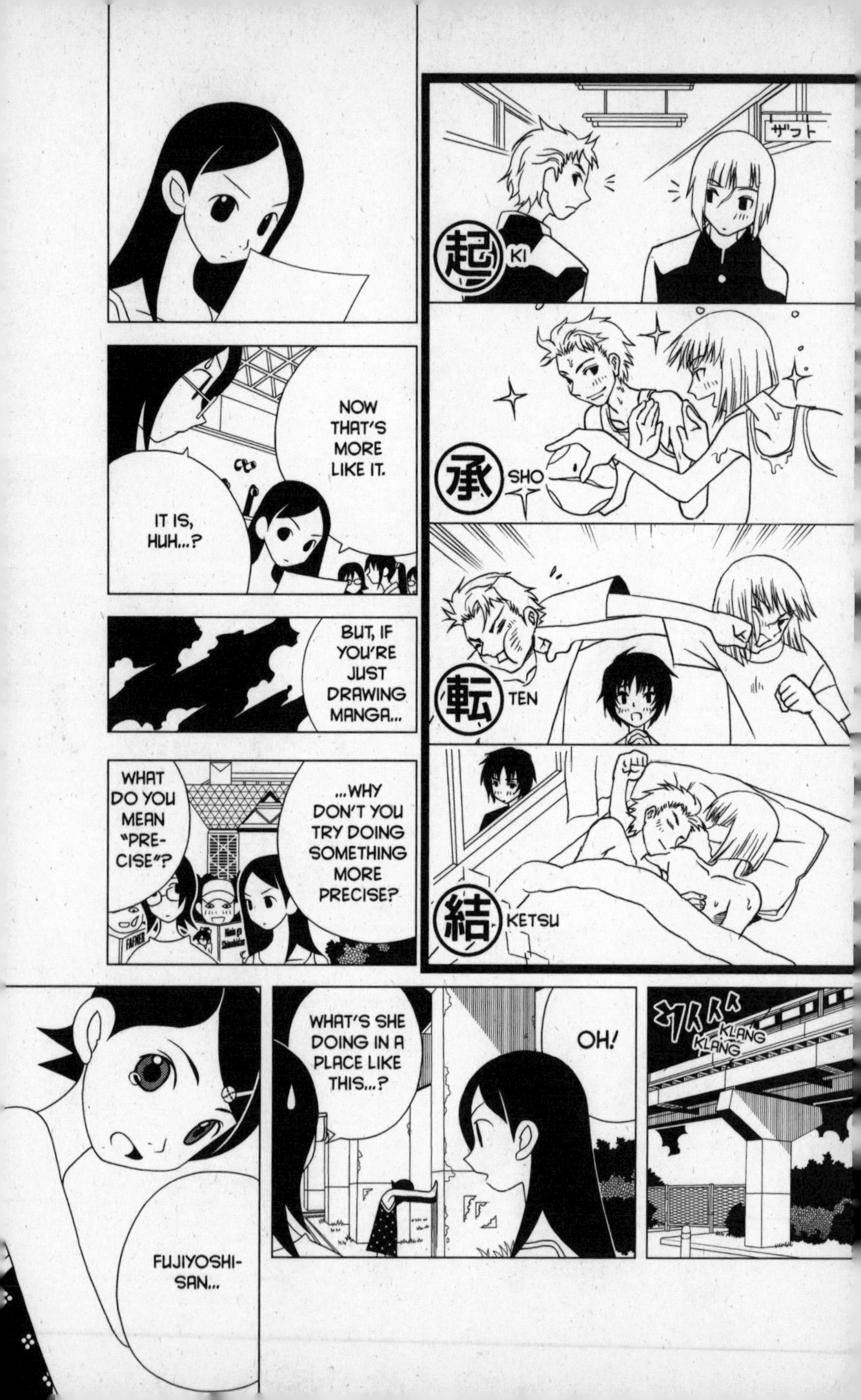
ザフト
起
KI
承
SHO
転
TEN
結
KETSU
NOW THAT'S MORE LIKE IT.
IT IS, HUH...?
BUT, IF YOU'RE JUST DRAWING MANGA...
...WHY DON'T YOU TRY DOING SOMETHING MORE PRECISE?
WHAT DO YOU MEAN "PRE-CISE"?
KLANG KLANG
OH!
WHAT'S SHE DOING IN A PLACE LIKE THIS...?
FUJIYOSHI-SAN...

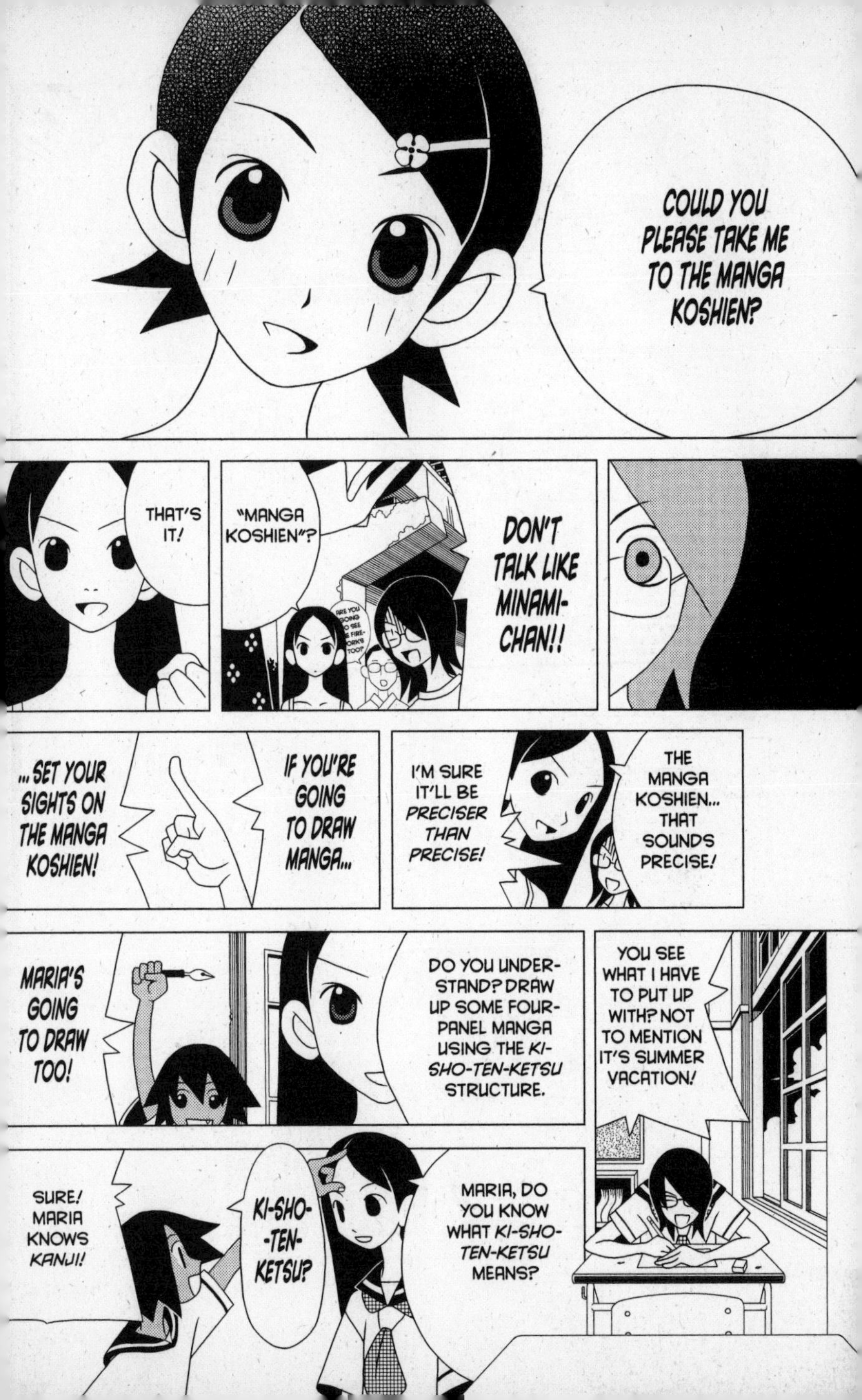
COULD YOU PLEASE TAKE ME TO THE MANGA KOSHIEN?
DON'T TALK LIKE MINAMI-CHAN!!
"MANGA KOSHIEN"?
THAT'S IT!
THE MANGA KOSHIEN... THAT SOUNDS PRECISE!
I'M SURE IT'LL BE *PRECISER* THAN *PRECISE!*
IF YOU'RE GOING TO DRAW MANGA...
...SET YOUR SIGHTS ON THE MANGA KOSHIEN!
YOU SEE WHAT I HAVE TO PUT UP WITH? NOT TO MENTION IT'S SUMMER VACATION!
DO YOU UNDERSTAND? DRAW UP SOME FOUR-PANEL MANGA USING THE *KI-SHO-TEN-KETSU* STRUCTURE.
MARIA'S GOING TO DRAW TOO!
MARIA, DO YOU KNOW WHAT *KI-SHO-TEN-KETSU* MEANS?
KI-SHO-TEN-KETSU?
SURE! MARIA KNOWS *KANJI!*

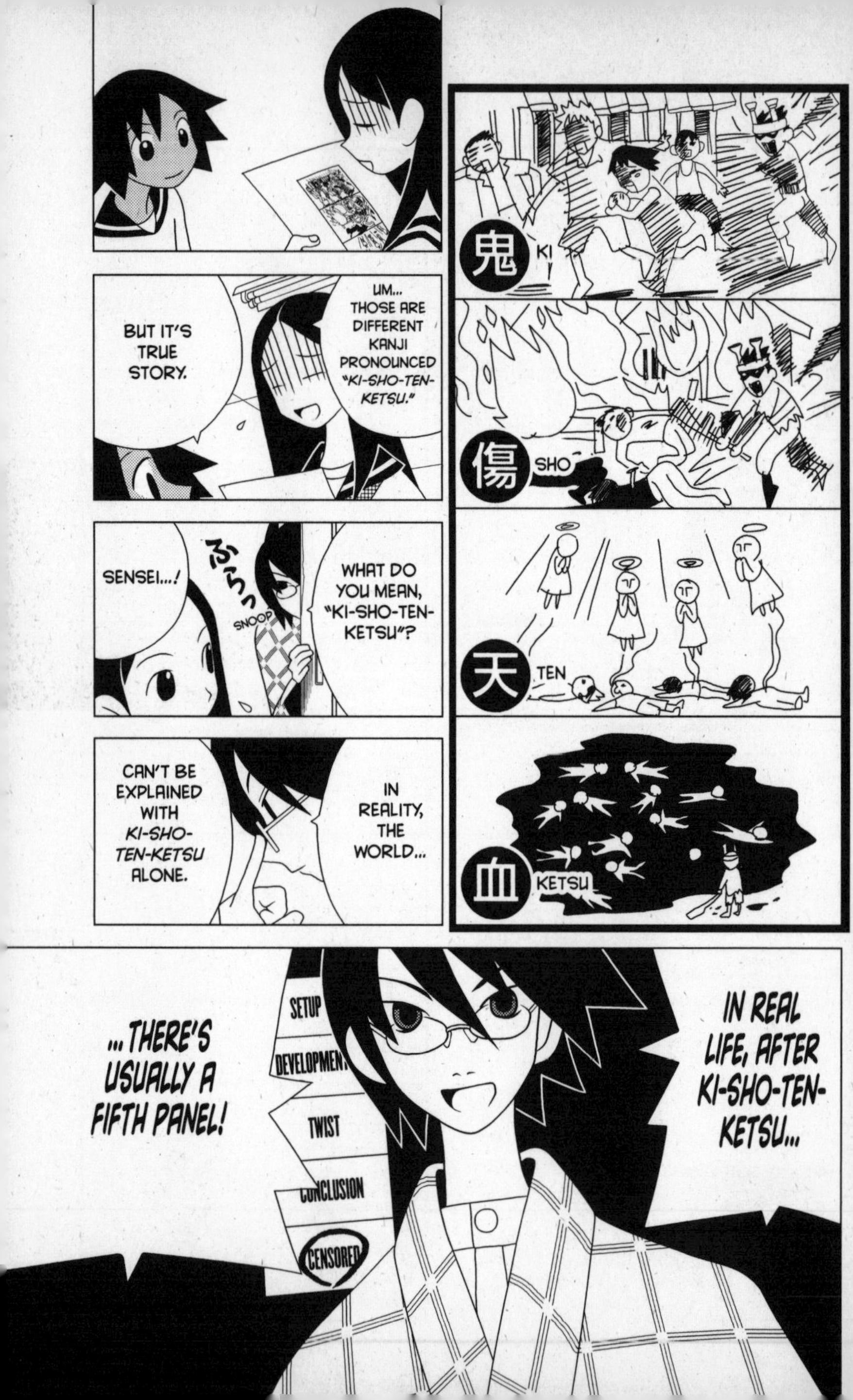

鬼
KI
傷
SHO
天
TEN
血
KETSU
UM... THOSE ARE DIFFERENT KANJI PRONOUNCED "KI-SHO-TEN-KETSU."
BUT IT'S TRUE STORY.
WHAT DO YOU MEAN, "KI-SHO-TEN-KETSU"?
ふらっ
SNOOP
SENSEI...!
IN REALITY, THE WORLD...
CAN'T BE EXPLAINED WITH KI-SHO-TEN-KETSU ALONE.
IN REAL LIFE, AFTER KI-SHO-TEN-KETSU...
SETUP
DEVELOPMENT
TWIST
CONCLUSION
CENSORED
...THERE'S USUALLY A FIFTH PANEL!

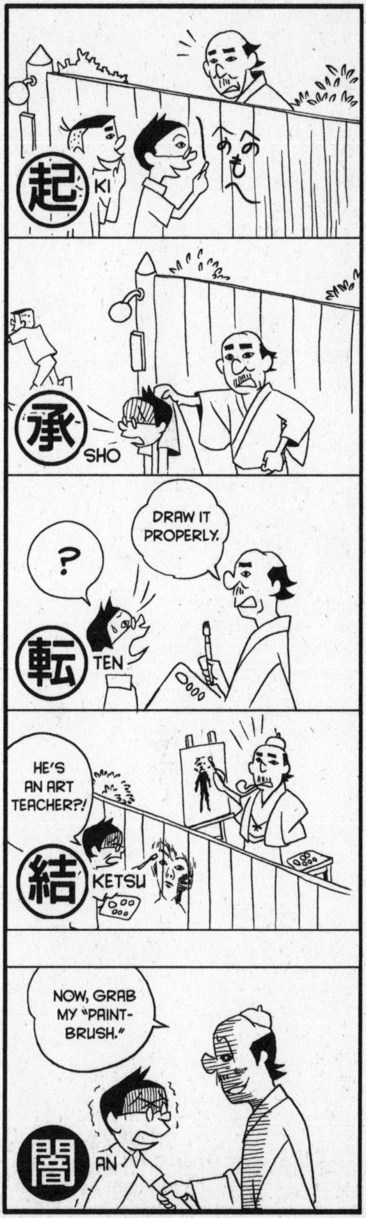
起
KI
承
SHO
DRAW IT PROPERLY.
?
転
TEN
HE'S AN ART TEACHER?!
結
KETSU
NOW, GRAB MY "PAINT-BRUSH."
闇
AN

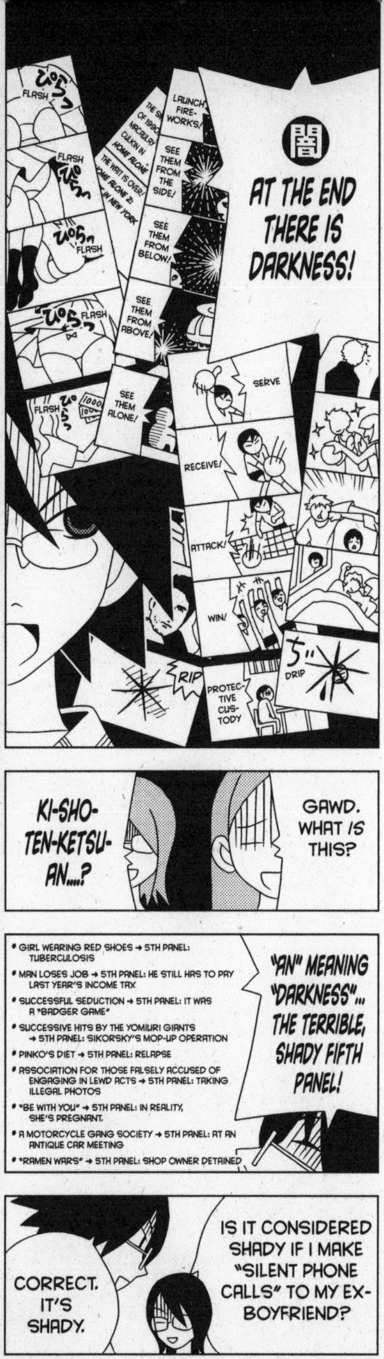
闇
AT THE END THERE IS DARKNESS!
LAUNCH FIRE-WORKS!
SEE THEM FROM THE SIDE!
SEE THEM FROM BELOW!
SEE THEM FROM ABOVE!
SEE THEM ALONE!
MACAULAY CULKIN IN HOME ALONE
THE WAIT IS OVER!
IN NEW YORK
FLASH
FLASH
FLASH
FLASH
FLASH
SERVE
RECEIVE!
ATTACK!
WIN!
RIP
PROTEC-TIVE CUS-TODY
DRIP
GAWD. WHAT IS THIS?
KI-SHO-TEN-KETSU-AN....?
"AN" MEANING "DARKNESS"... THE TERRIBLE, SHADY FIFTH PANEL!
• GIRL WEARING RED SHOES → 5TH PANEL: TUBERCULOSIS
• MAN LOSES JOB → 5TH PANEL: HE STILL HAS TO PAY LAST YEAR'S INCOME TAX
• SUCCESSFUL SEDUCTION → 5TH PANEL: IT WAS A "BADGER GAME"
• SUCCESSIVE HITS BY THE YOMIURI GIANTS → 5TH PANEL: SIKORSKY'S MOP-UP OPERATION
• PINKO'S DIET → 5TH PANEL: RELAPSE
• ASSOCIATION FOR THOSE FALSELY ACCUSED OF ENGAGING IN LEWD ACTS → 5TH PANEL: TAKING ILLEGAL PHOTOS
• "BE WITH YOU" → 5TH PANEL: IN REALITY, SHE'S PREGNANT.
• A MOTORCYCLE GANG SOCIETY → 5TH PANEL: AT AN ANTIQUE CAR MEETING
• "RAMEN WARS" → 5TH PANEL: SHOP OWNER DETAINED
IS IT CONSIDERED SHADY IF I MAKE "SILENT PHONE CALLS" TO MY EX-BOYFRIEND?
CORRECT. IT'S SHADY.

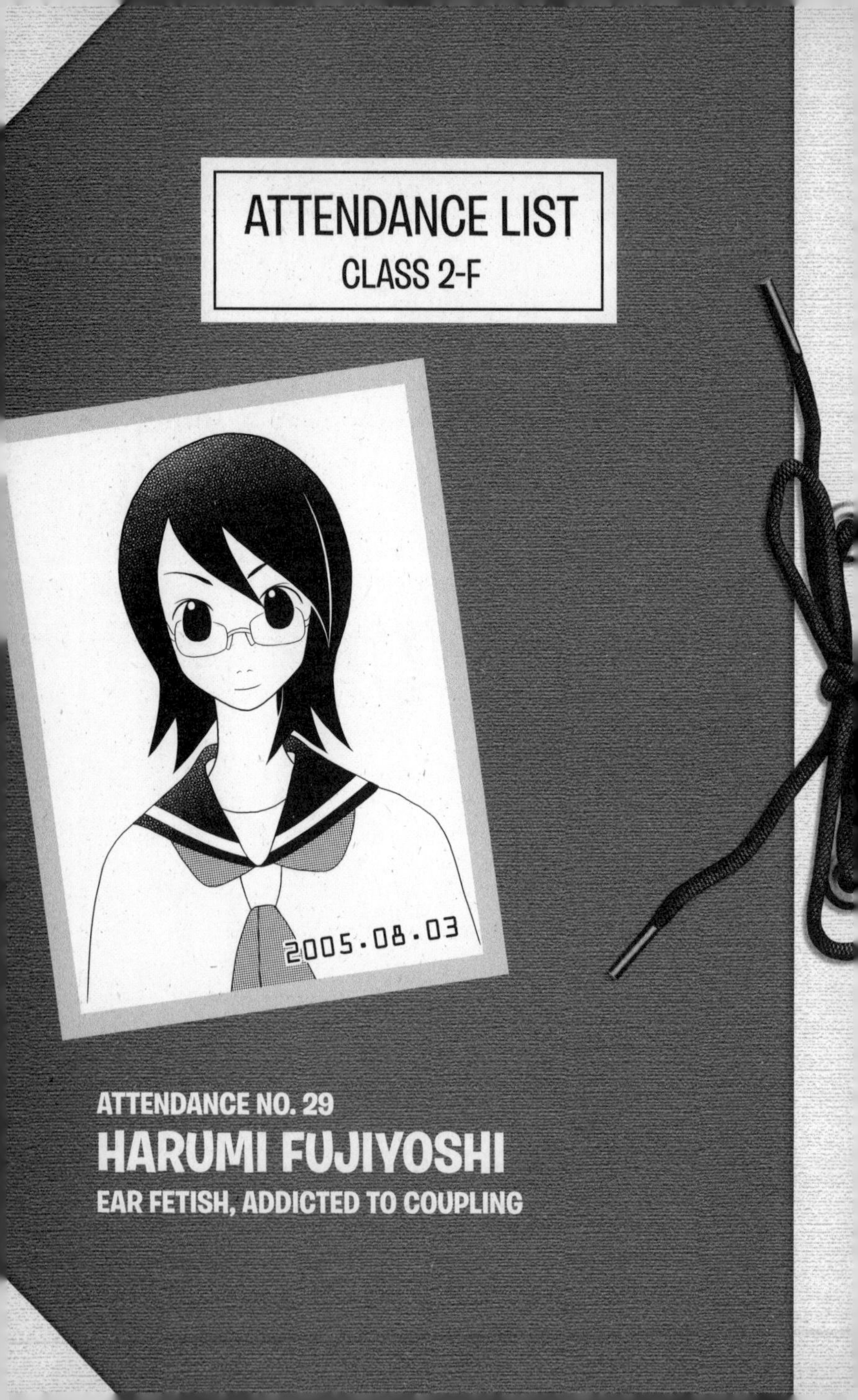
ATTENDANCE LIST
CLASS 2-F
2005.08.03
ATTENDANCE NO. 29
HARUMI FUJIYOSHI
EAR FETISH, ADDICTED TO COUPLING

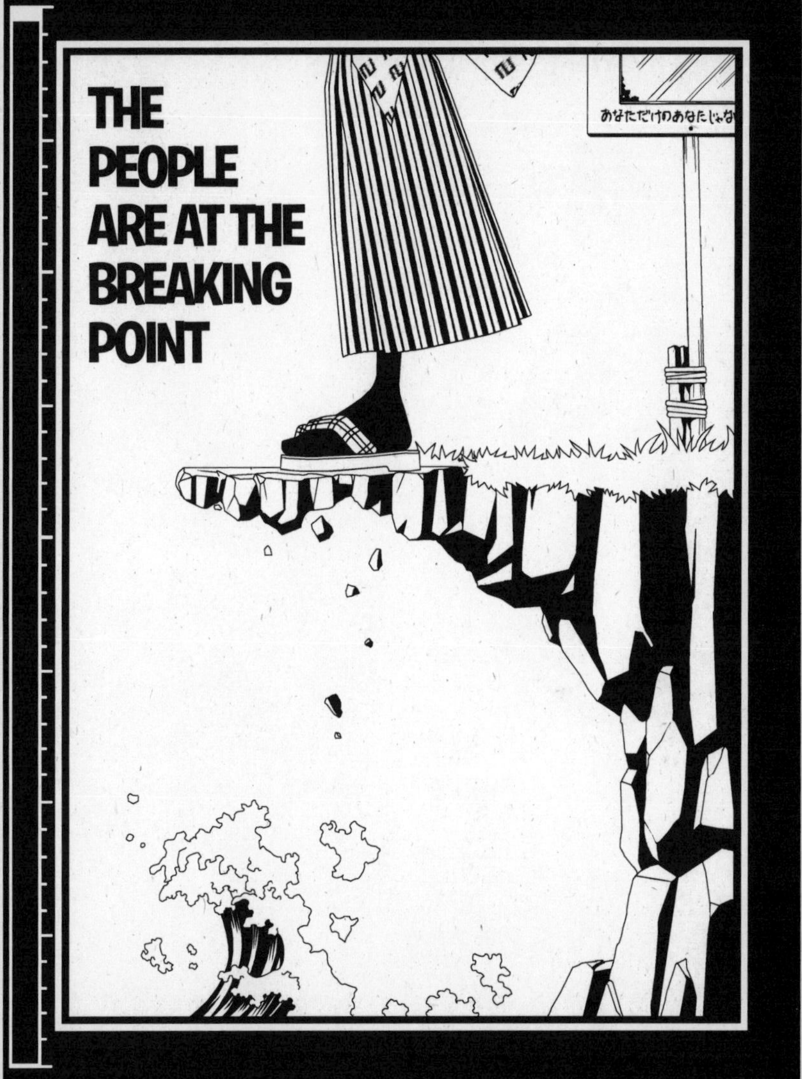
THE PEOPLE ARE AT THE BREAKING POINT
あなただけのあなたじゃな

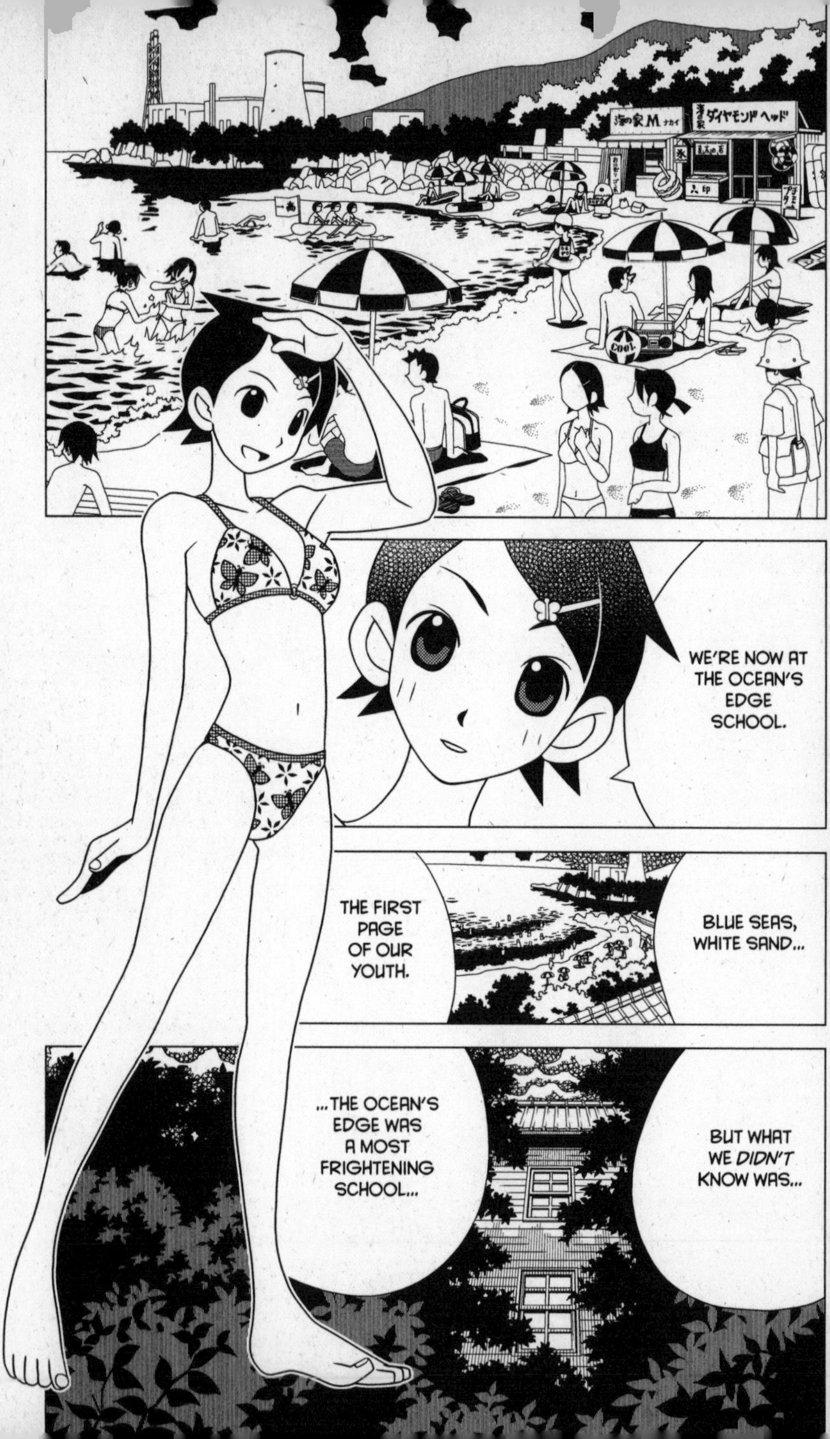
海の家M ナカイ
ダイヤモンド ヘッド
COOL
WE'RE NOW AT THE OCEAN'S EDGE SCHOOL.
BLUE SEAS, WHITE SAND...
THE FIRST PAGE OF OUR YOUTH.
BUT WHAT WE *DIDN'T* KNOW WAS...
...THE OCEAN'S EDGE WAS A MOST FRIGHTENING SCHOOL...

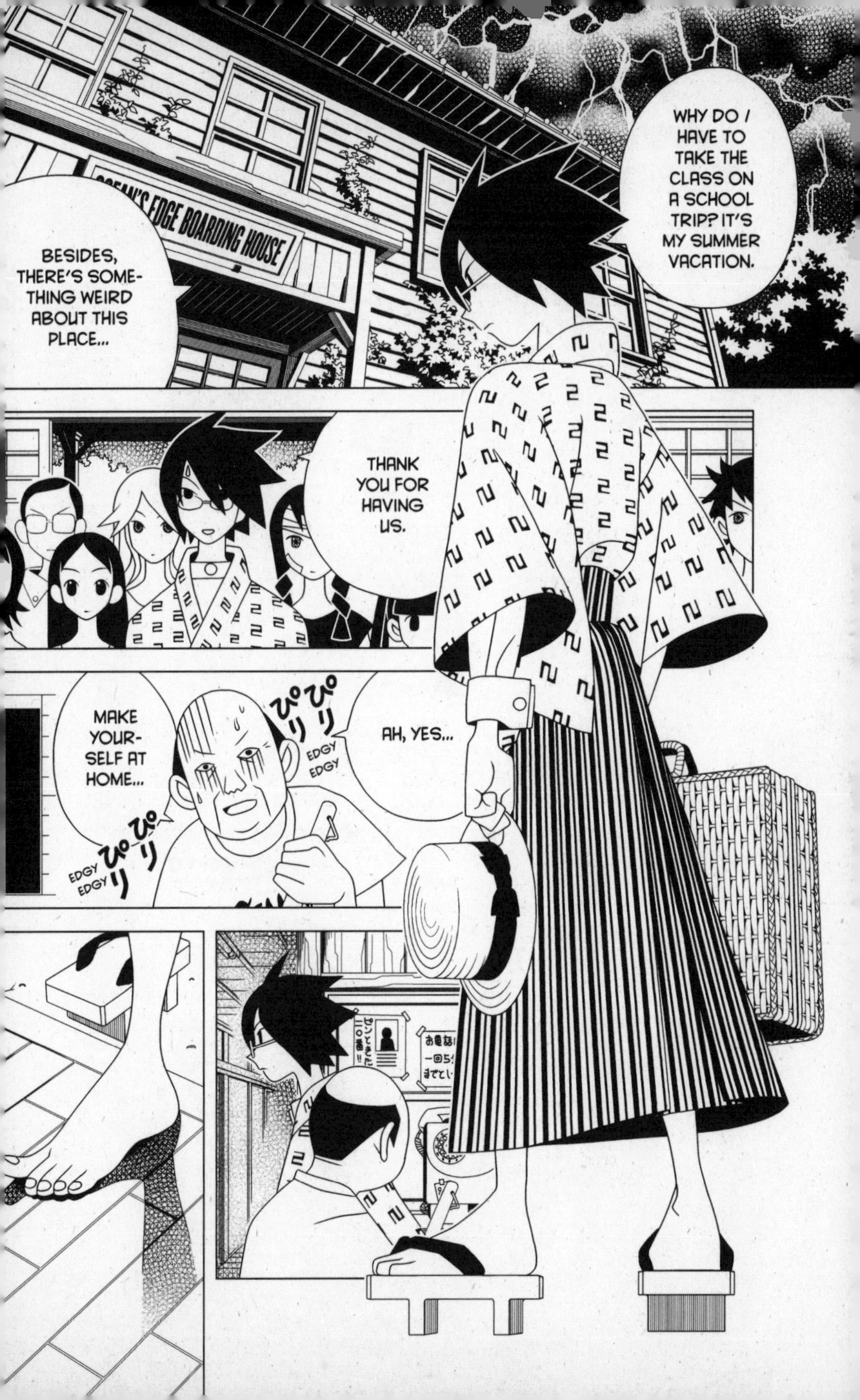
WHY DO I HAVE TO TAKE THE CLASS ON A SCHOOL TRIP? IT'S MY SUMMER VACATION.
EDGE BOARDING HOUSE
BESIDES, THERE'S SOME-THING WEIRD ABOUT THIS PLACE...
THANK YOU FOR HAVING US.
AH, YES...
ぴりぴり
EDGY EDGY
MAKE YOUR-SELF AT HOME...
ぴりぴり
EDGY EDGY

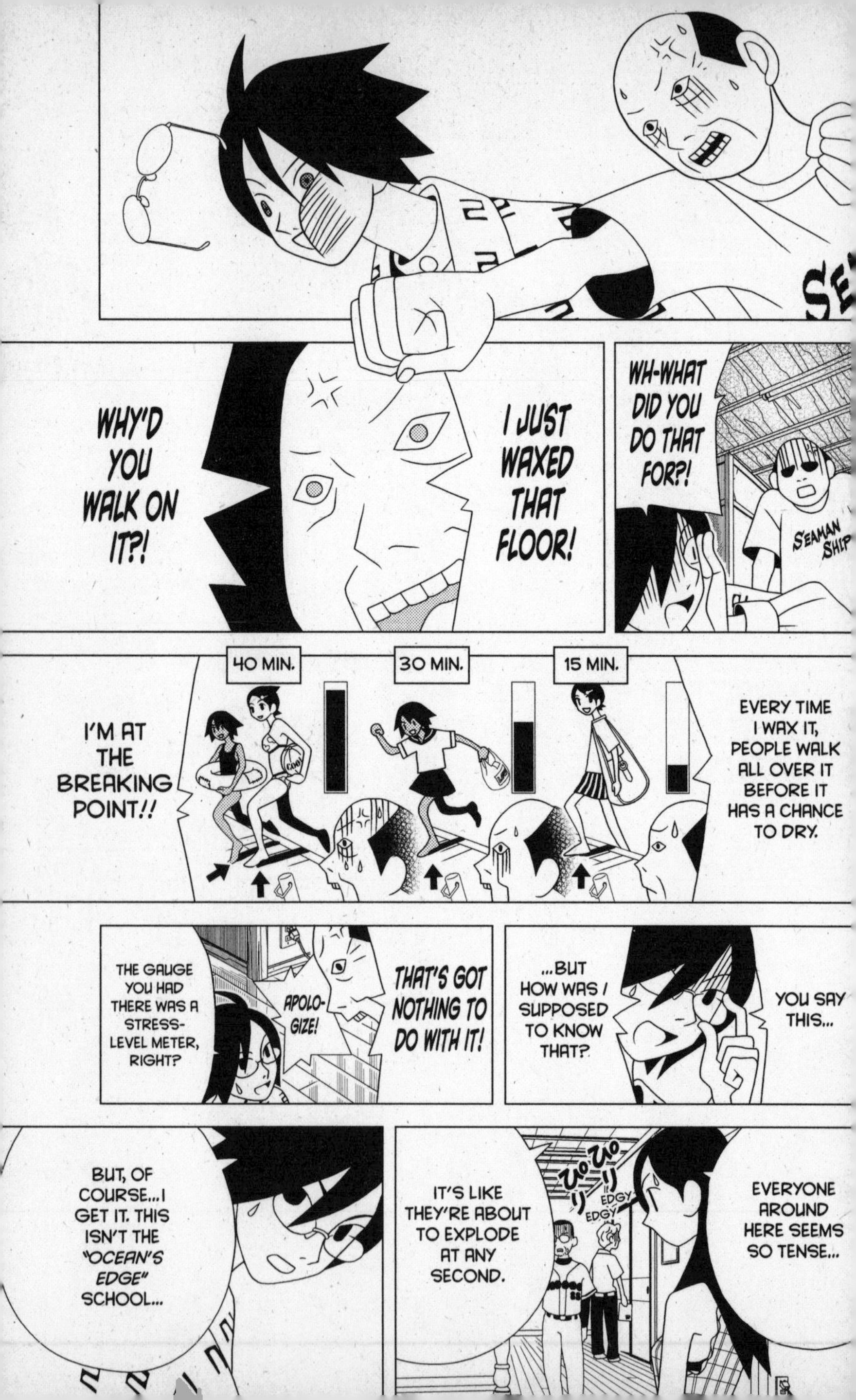
WH-WHAT DID YOU DO THAT FOR?!
SEAMAN SHIP
I JUST WAXED THAT FLOOR!
WHY'D YOU WALK ON IT?!
EVERY TIME I WAX IT, PEOPLE WALK ALL OVER IT BEFORE IT HAS A CHANCE TO DRY.
15 MIN.
30 MIN.
40 MIN.
I'M AT THE BREAKING POINT!!
YOU SAY THIS...
...BUT HOW WAS I SUPPOSED TO KNOW THAT?
THAT'S GOT NOTHING TO DO WITH IT!
APOLOGIZE!
THE GAUGE YOU HAD THERE WAS A STRESS-LEVEL METER, RIGHT?
EVERYONE AROUND HERE SEEMS SO TENSE...
ぴり ぴり
EDGY EDGY
IT'S LIKE THEY'RE ABOUT TO EXPLODE AT ANY SECOND.
BUT, OF COURSE...I GET IT. THIS ISN'T THE "OCEAN'S EDGE" SCHOOL...

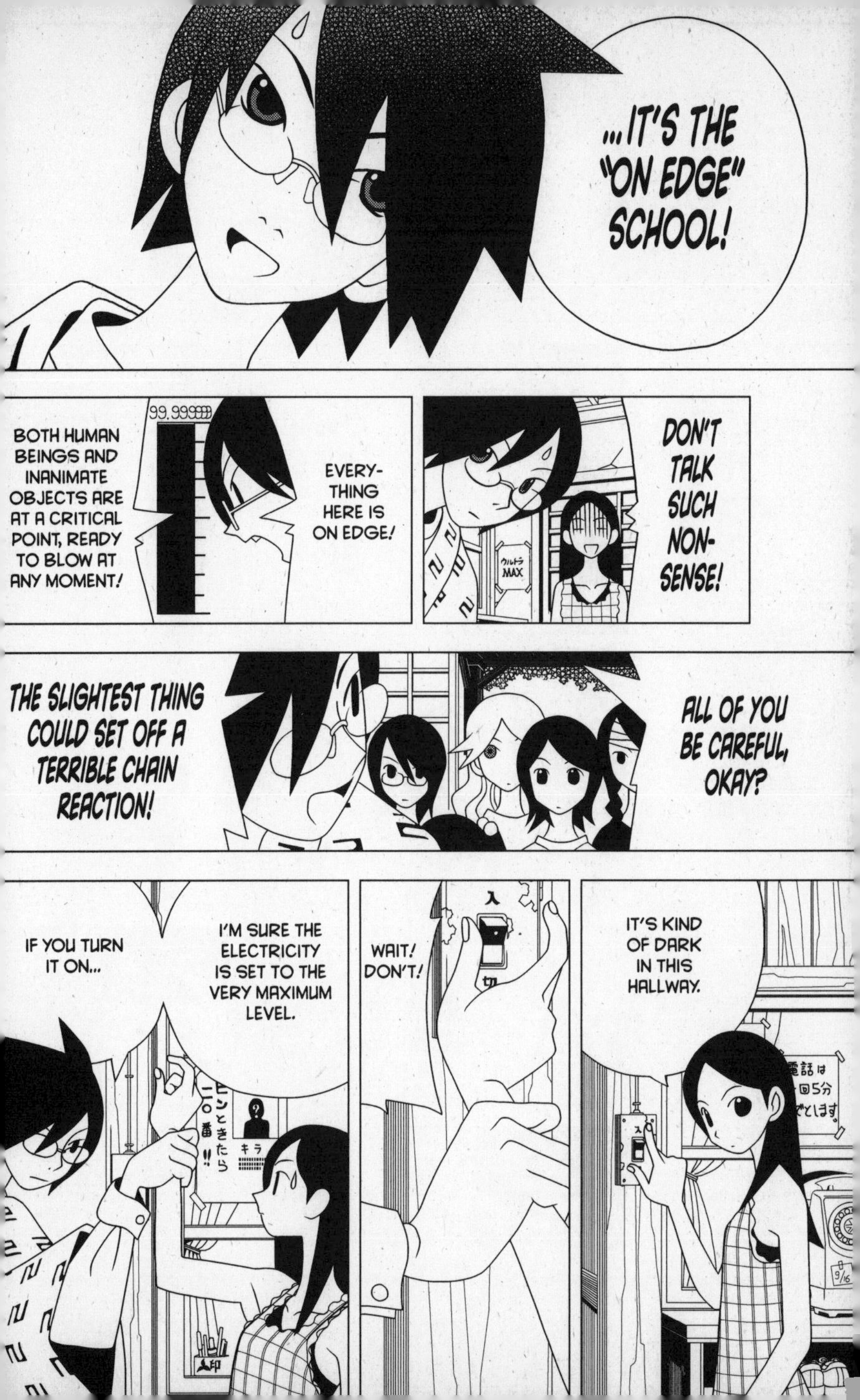
...IT'S THE "ON EDGE" SCHOOL!
DON'T TALK SUCH NON-SENSE!
ウルトラ MAX
EVERY-THING HERE IS ON EDGE!
99.99999
BOTH HUMAN BEINGS AND INANIMATE OBJECTS ARE AT A CRITICAL POINT, READY TO BLOW AT ANY MOMENT!
ALL OF YOU BE CAREFUL, OKAY?
THE SLIGHTEST THING COULD SET OFF A TERRIBLE CHAIN REACTION!
IT'S KIND OF DARK IN THIS HALLWAY.
WAIT! DON'T!
入
切
I'M SURE THE ELECTRICITY IS SET TO THE VERY MAXIMUM LEVEL.
IF YOU TURN IT ON...

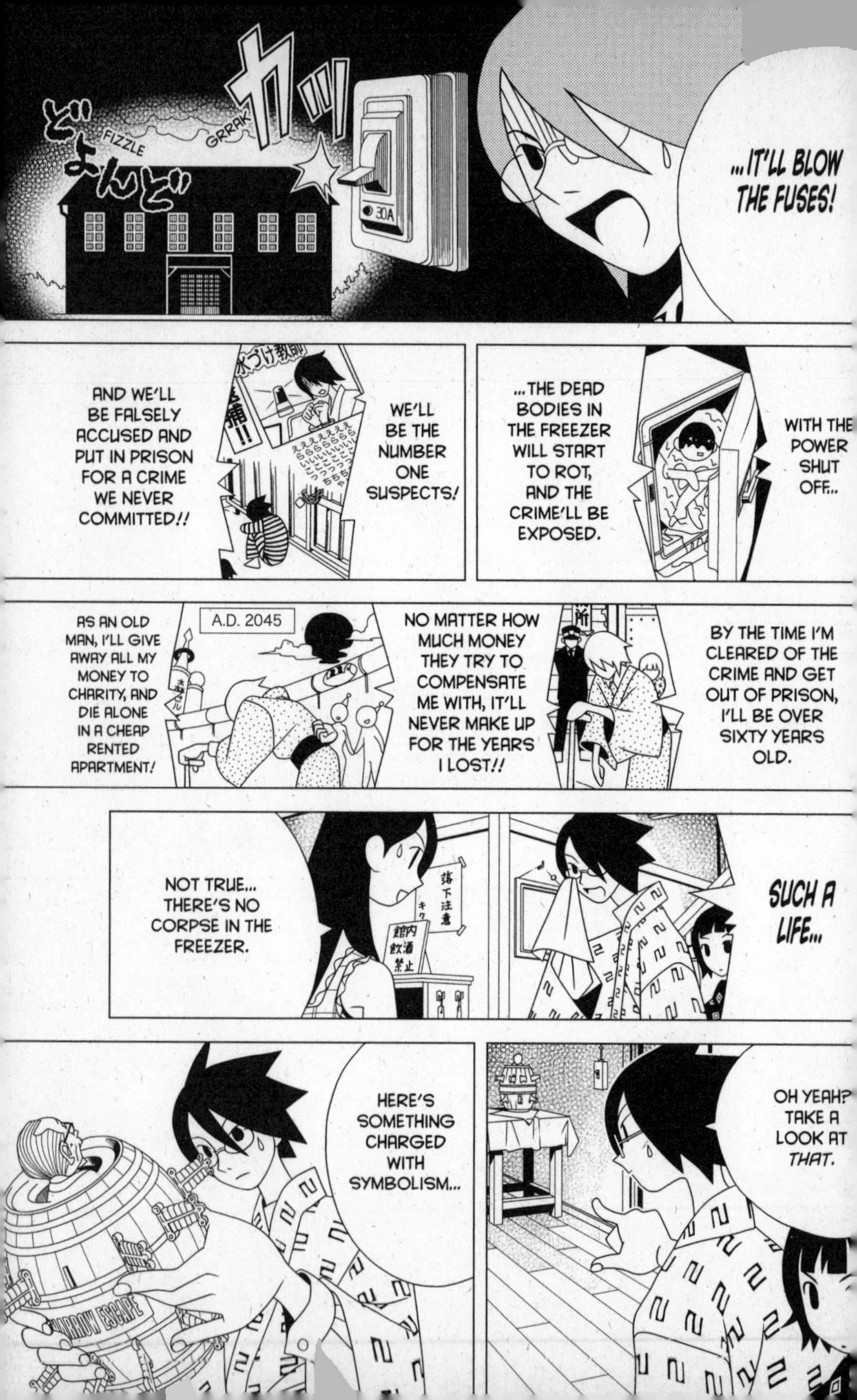
...IT'LL BLOW THE FUSES!
GRRAK
FIZZLE
30A
WITH THE POWER SHUT OFF...
...THE DEAD BODIES IN THE FREEZER WILL START TO ROT, AND THE CRIME'LL BE EXPOSED.
WE'LL BE THE NUMBER ONE SUSPECTS!
AND WE'LL BE FALSELY ACCUSED AND PUT IN PRISON FOR A CRIME WE NEVER COMMITTED!!
BY THE TIME I'M CLEARED OF THE CRIME AND GET OUT OF PRISON, I'LL BE OVER SIXTY YEARS OLD.
NO MATTER HOW MUCH MONEY THEY TRY TO COMPENSATE ME WITH, IT'LL NEVER MAKE UP FOR THE YEARS I LOST!!
A.D. 2045
AS AN OLD MAN, I'LL GIVE AWAY ALL MY MONEY TO CHARITY, AND DIE ALONE IN A CHEAP RENTED APARTMENT!
SUCH A LIFE...
落下注意
館内飲酒禁止
NOT TRUE... THERE'S NO CORPSE IN THE FREEZER.
OH YEAH? TAKE A LOOK AT *THAT*.
HERE'S SOMETHING CHARGED WITH SYMBOLISM...

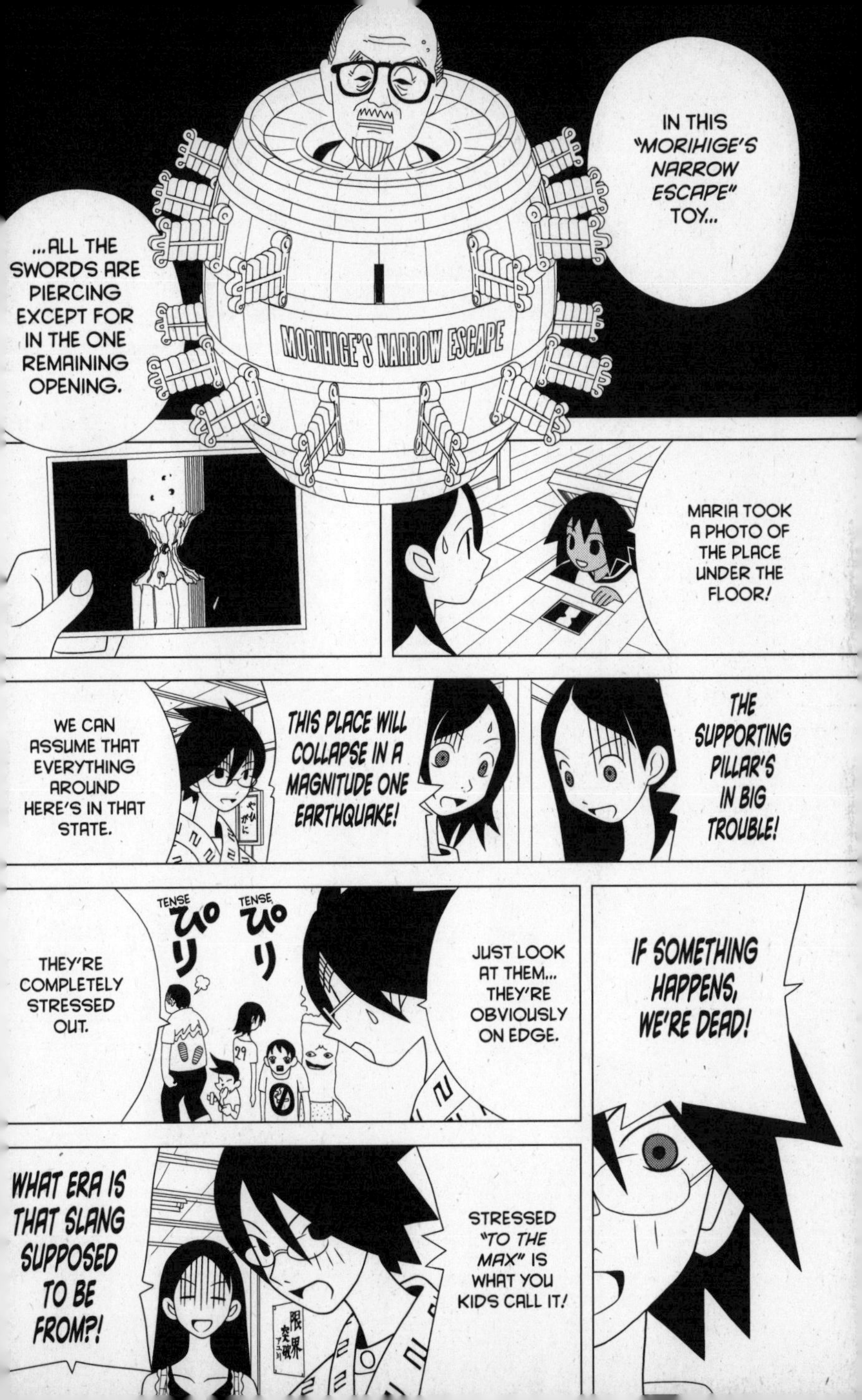
IN THIS "MORIHIGE'S NARROW ESCAPE" TOY...
MORIHIGE'S NARROW ESCAPE
...ALL THE SWORDS ARE PIERCING EXCEPT FOR IN THE ONE REMAINING OPENING.
MARIA TOOK A PHOTO OF THE PLACE UNDER THE FLOOR!
THE SUPPORTING PILLAR'S IN BIG TROUBLE!
THIS PLACE WILL COLLAPSE IN A MAGNITUDE ONE EARTHQUAKE!
WE CAN ASSUME THAT EVERYTHING AROUND HERE'S IN THAT STATE.
IF SOMETHING HAPPENS, WE'RE DEAD!
JUST LOOK AT THEM... THEY'RE OBVIOUSLY ON EDGE.
TENSE ぴり
TENSE ぴり
THEY'RE COMPLETELY STRESSED OUT.
STRESSED "TO THE MAX" IS WHAT YOU KIDS CALL IT!
WHAT ERA IS THAT SLANG SUPPOSED TO BE FROM?!

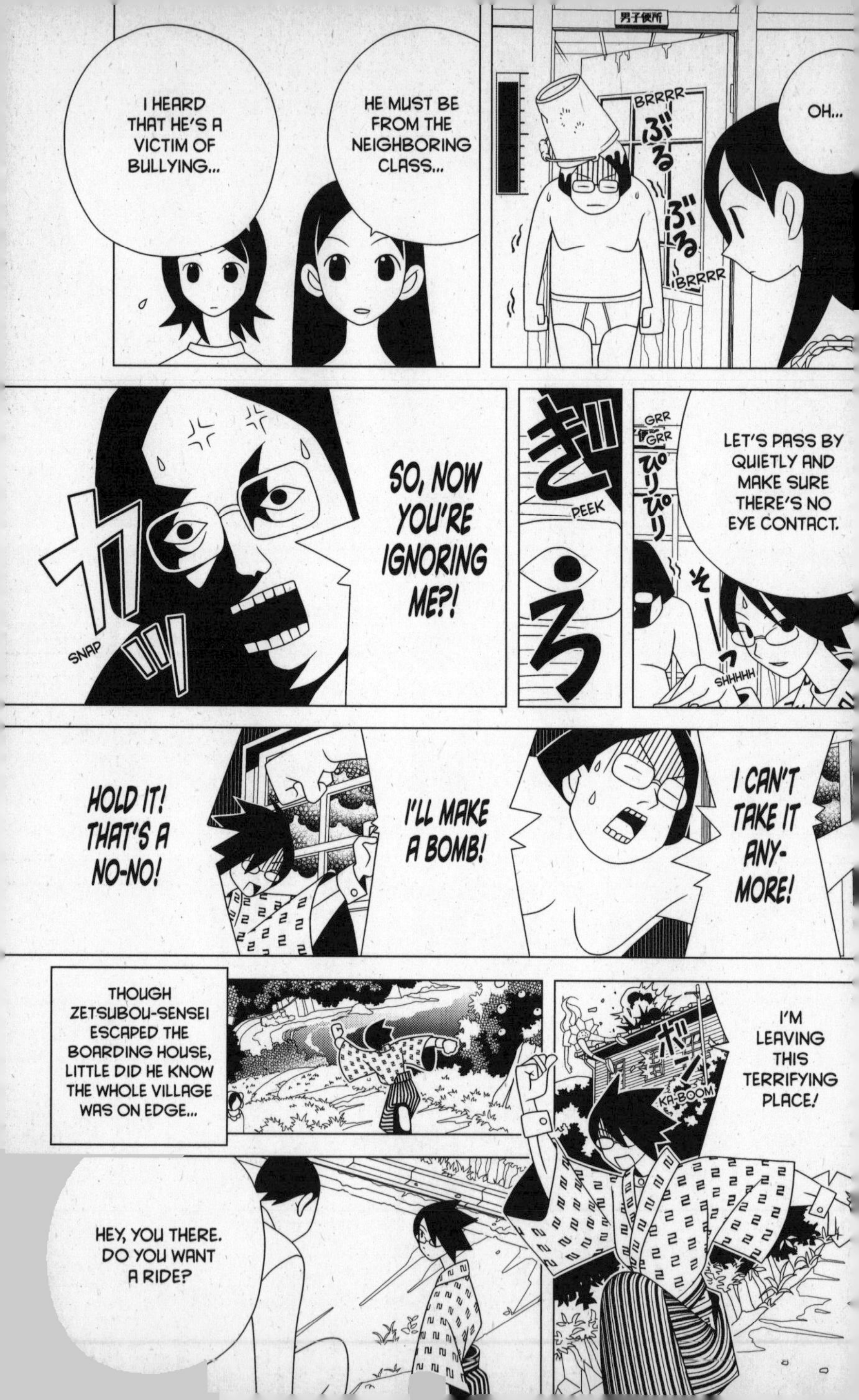
OH...
男子便所
BRRRR
ぶる
ぶる
BRRRR
HE MUST BE FROM THE NEIGHBORING CLASS...
I HEARD THAT HE'S A VICTIM OF BULLYING...
LET'S PASS BY QUIETLY AND MAKE SURE THERE'S NO EYE CONTACT.
GRR
GRR
ぴりぴり
そーっ
SHHHHH
ぎろ
PEEK
SO, NOW YOU'RE IGNORING ME?!
カッ
SNAP
I CAN'T TAKE IT ANY-MORE!
I'LL MAKE A BOMB!
HOLD IT! THAT'S A NO-NO!
I'M LEAVING THIS TERRIFYING PLACE!
ボン
KA-BOOM
THOUGH ZETSUBOU-SENSEI ESCAPED THE BOARDING HOUSE, LITTLE DID HE KNOW THE WHOLE VILLAGE WAS ON EDGE...
HEY, YOU THERE. DO YOU WANT A RIDE?

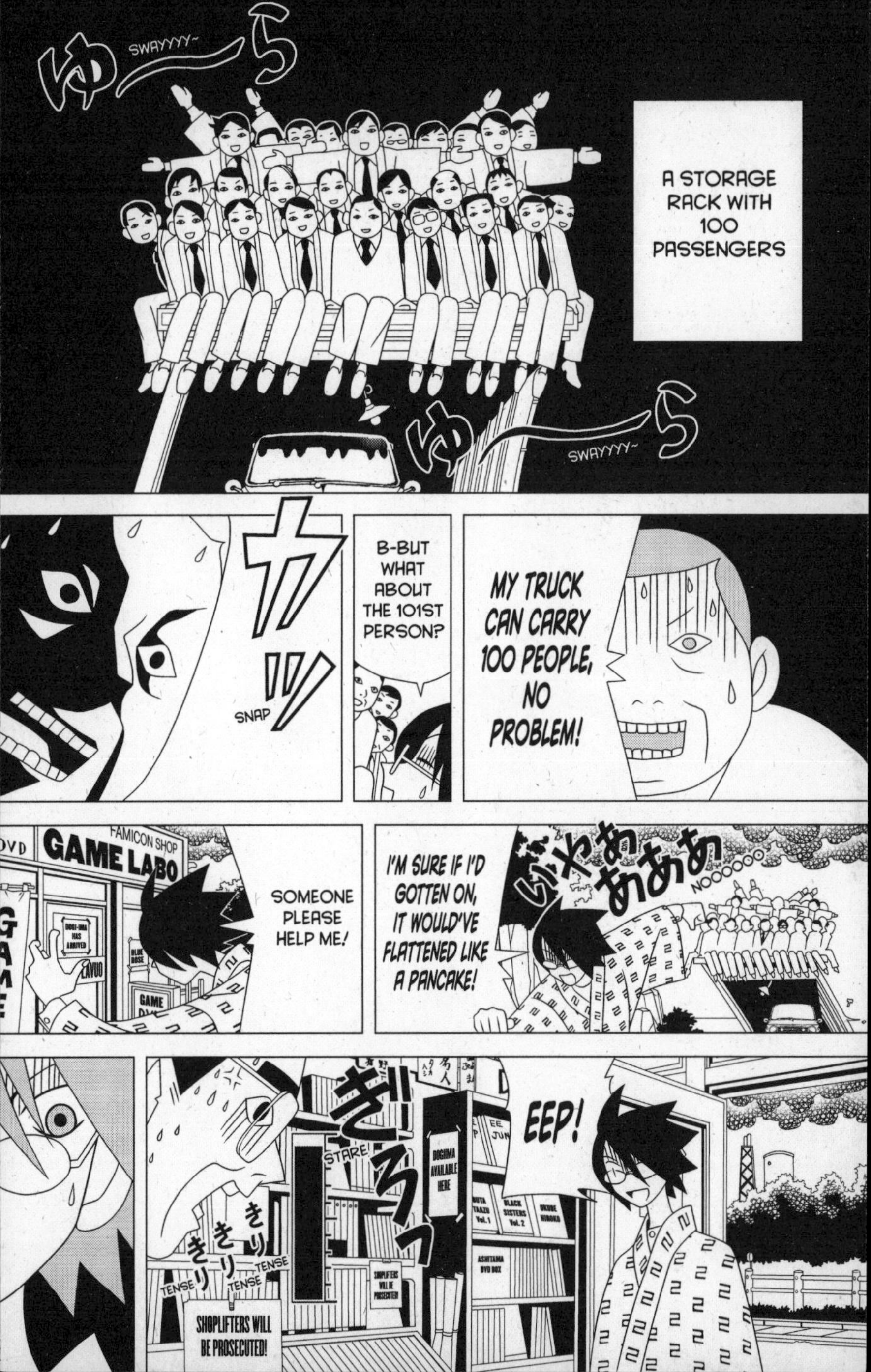
A STORAGE RACK WITH 100 PASSENGERS
ゆーら
SWAYYYY~
ゆーら
SWAYYYY~
MY TRUCK CAN CARRY 100 PEOPLE, NO PROBLEM!
B-BUT WHAT ABOUT THE 101ST PERSON?
カッ
SNAP
いやあああ
NOOOOOO
I'M SURE IF I'D GOTTEN ON, IT WOULD'VE FLATTENED LIKE A PANCAKE!
SOMEONE PLEASE HELP ME!
FAMICON SHOP
GAME LABO
DVD
DOGI-IMA HAS ARRIVED
BLUE ROSE
LAVUO
GAME DVD
EEP!
ぎろっ
STARE!
DOGIIMA AVAILABLE HERE
BLACK SISTERS Vol. 2
OKUBE HIROKA
ASHITAMA DVD BOX
SHOPLIFTERS WILL BE PROSECUTED!
きりきりきり
TENSE TENSE TENSE
SHOPLIFTERS WILL BE PROSECUTED!

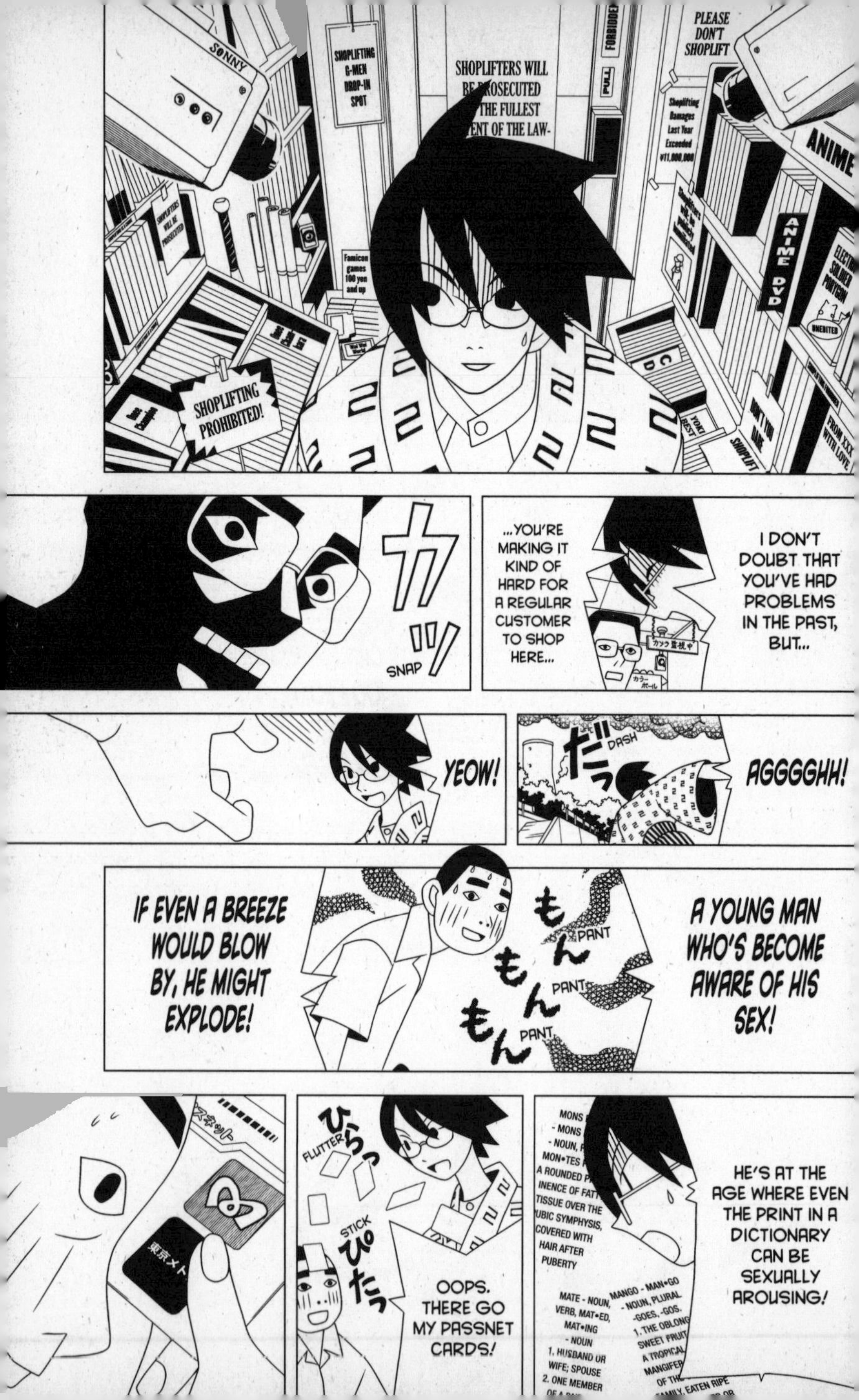
PLEASE DON'T SHOPLIFT
FORBIDDEN
PULL
SHOPLIFTERS WILL BE PROSECUTED TO THE FULLEST EXTENT OF THE LAW-
SHOPLIFTING G-MEN DROP-IN SPOT
SONNY
ANIME
Shoplifting Damages Last Year Exceeded ¥11,000,000
ANIME DVD
ELECTRIC SOLDIER PORYGON
UNEDITED
Famicom games 100 yen and up
SHOPLIFTERS WILL BE PROSECUTED
SHOPLIFTING PROHIBITED!
CD
YOKO BEST
DON'T YOU DARE SHOPLIFT
FROM XXX WITH LOVE
I DON'T DOUBT THAT YOU'VE HAD PROBLEMS IN THE PAST, BUT...
...YOU'RE MAKING IT KIND OF HARD FOR A REGULAR CUSTOMER TO SHOP HERE...
カメラ監視中
カラーボール
カッ
SNAP
AGGGGHH!
だっ
DASH
YEOW!
A YOUNG MAN WHO'S BECOME AWARE OF HIS SEX!
もん もん もん
PANT PANT PANT
IF EVEN A BREEZE WOULD BLOW BY, HE MIGHT EXPLODE!
HE'S AT THE AGE WHERE EVEN THE PRINT IN A DICTIONARY CAN BE SEXUALLY AROUSING!
MONS - MONS - NOUN, PL. MON•TES A ROUNDED PROMINENCE OF FATTY TISSUE OVER THE PUBIC SYMPHYSIS, COVERED WITH HAIR AFTER PUBERTY
MANGO - MAN•GO - NOUN, PLURAL -GOES, -GOS. 1. THE OBLONG SWEET FRUIT A TROPICAL MANGIFER OF THE FAMILY, EATEN RIPE
MATE - NOUN, VERB, MAT•ED, MAT•ING - NOUN 1. HUSBAND OR WIFE; SPOUSE 2. ONE MEMBER
ひらっ
FLUTTER
ぴたっ
STICK
OOPS. THERE GO MY PASSNET CARDS!
東京メトロ

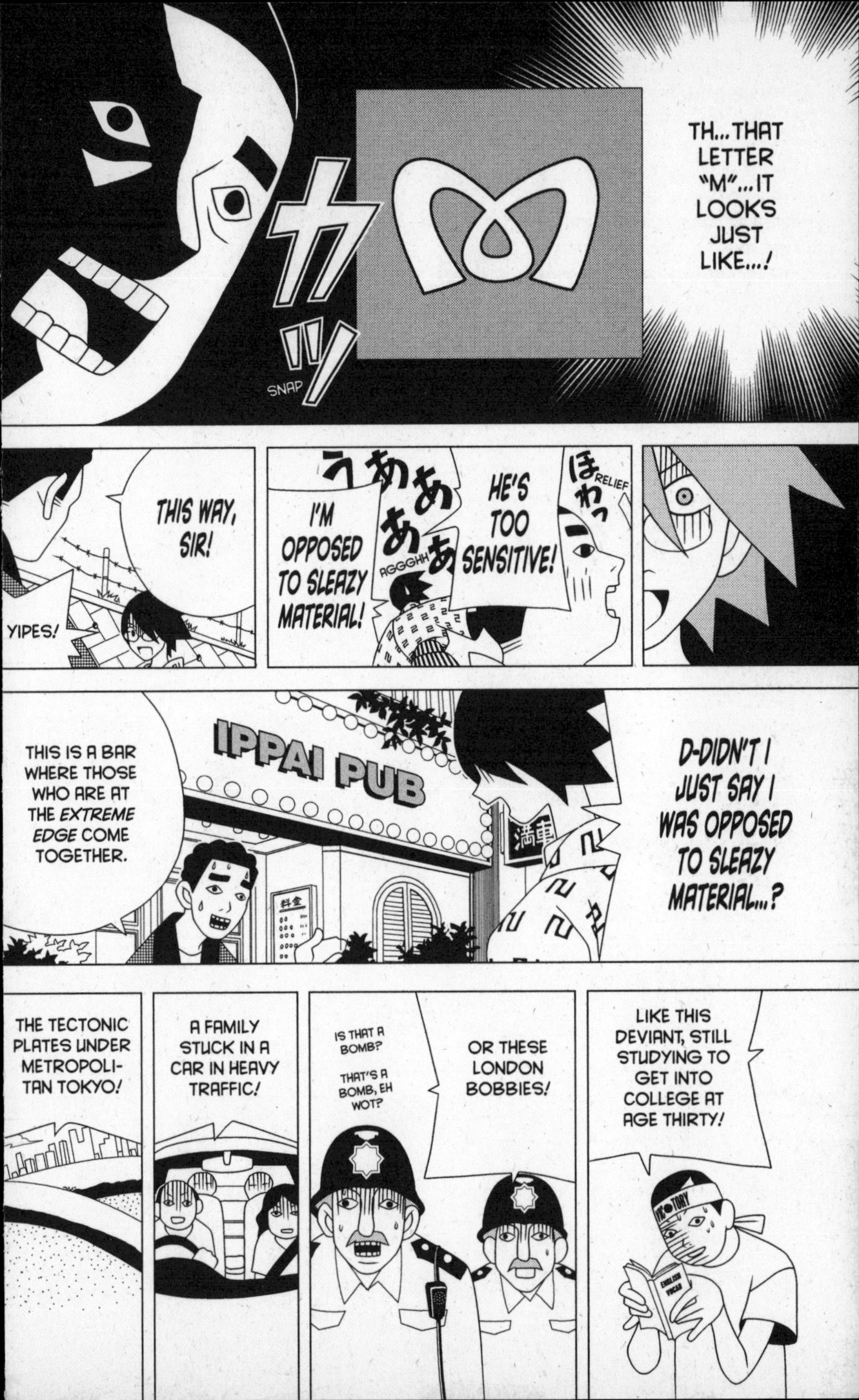
TH...THAT LETTER "M"...IT LOOKS JUST LIKE...!
カッ
SNAP
ほわっ
RELIEF
HE'S TOO SENSITIVE!
うあああああ
AGGGHH
I'M OPPOSED TO SLEAZY MATERIAL!
THIS WAY, SIR!
YIPES!
D-DIDN'T I JUST SAY I WAS OPPOSED TO SLEAZY MATERIAL...?
満車
IPPAI PUB
料金
THIS IS A BAR WHERE THOSE WHO ARE AT THE *EXTREME EDGE* COME TOGETHER.
LIKE THIS DEVIANT, STILL STUDYING TO GET INTO COLLEGE AT AGE THIRTY!
ENGLISH VOCAB
OR THESE LONDON BOBBIES!
IS THAT A BOMB?
THAT'S A BOMB, EH WOT?
A FAMILY STUCK IN A CAR IN HEAVY TRAFFIC!
THE TECTONIC PLATES UNDER METROPOLITAN TOKYO!

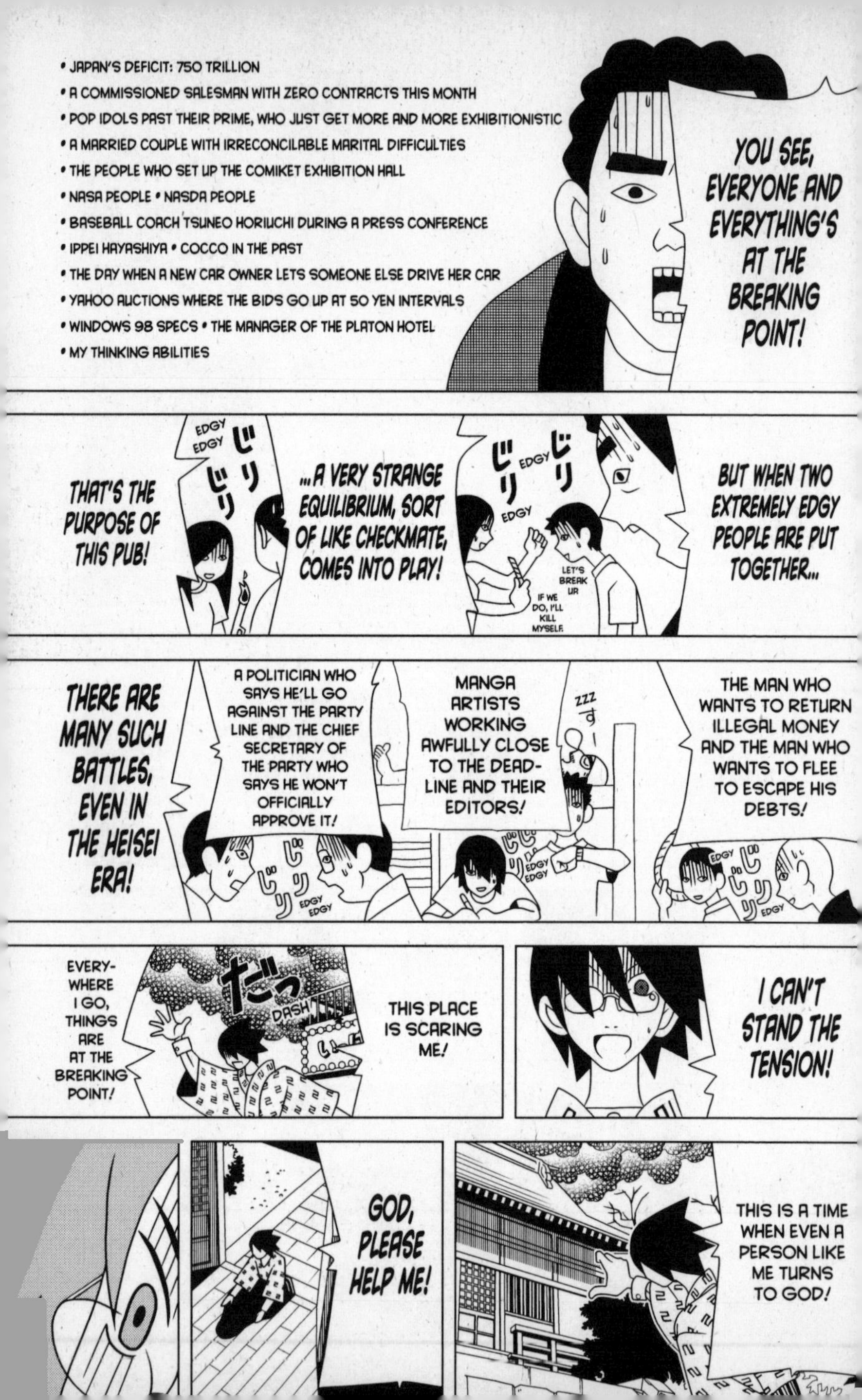
YOU SEE, EVERYONE AND EVERYTHING'S AT THE BREAKING POINT!
• JAPAN'S DEFICIT: 750 TRILLION
• A COMMISSIONED SALESMAN WITH ZERO CONTRACTS THIS MONTH
• POP IDOLS PAST THEIR PRIME, WHO JUST GET MORE AND MORE EXHIBITIONISTIC
• A MARRIED COUPLE WITH IRRECONCILABLE MARITAL DIFFICULTIES
• THE PEOPLE WHO SET UP THE COMIKET EXHIBITION HALL
• NASA PEOPLE • NASDA PEOPLE
• BASEBALL COACH TSUNEO HORIUCHI DURING A PRESS CONFERENCE
• IPPEI HAYASHIYA • COCCO IN THE PAST
• THE DAY WHEN A NEW CAR OWNER LETS SOMEONE ELSE DRIVE HER CAR
• YAHOO AUCTIONS WHERE THE BIDS GO UP AT 50 YEN INTERVALS
• WINDOWS 98 SPECS • THE MANAGER OF THE PLATON HOTEL
• MY THINKING ABILITIES
BUT WHEN TWO EXTREMELY EDGY PEOPLE ARE PUT TOGETHER...
じり EDGY じり EDGY
LET'S BREAK UP
IF WE DO, I'LL KILL MYSELF
...A VERY STRANGE EQUILIBRIUM, SORT OF LIKE CHECKMATE, COMES INTO PLAY!
EDGY EDGY じりじり
THAT'S THE PURPOSE OF THIS PUB!
THE MAN WHO WANTS TO RETURN ILLEGAL MONEY AND THE MAN WHO WANTS TO FLEE TO ESCAPE HIS DEBTS!
EDGY じりじり EDGY
ZZZ す
MANGA ARTISTS WORKING AWFULLY CLOSE TO THE DEAD-LINE AND THEIR EDITORS!
じり EDGY EDGY
A POLITICIAN WHO SAYS HE'LL GO AGAINST THE PARTY LINE AND THE CHIEF SECRETARY OF THE PARTY WHO SAYS HE WON'T OFFICIALLY APPROVE IT!
じりじり EDGY EDGY
THERE ARE MANY SUCH BATTLES, EVEN IN THE HEISEI ERA!
I CAN'T STAND THE TENSION!
THIS PLACE IS SCARING ME!
だっ DASH
EVERY-WHERE I GO, THINGS ARE AT THE BREAKING POINT!
THIS IS A TIME WHEN EVEN A PERSON LIKE ME TURNS TO GOD!
GOD, PLEASE HELP ME!

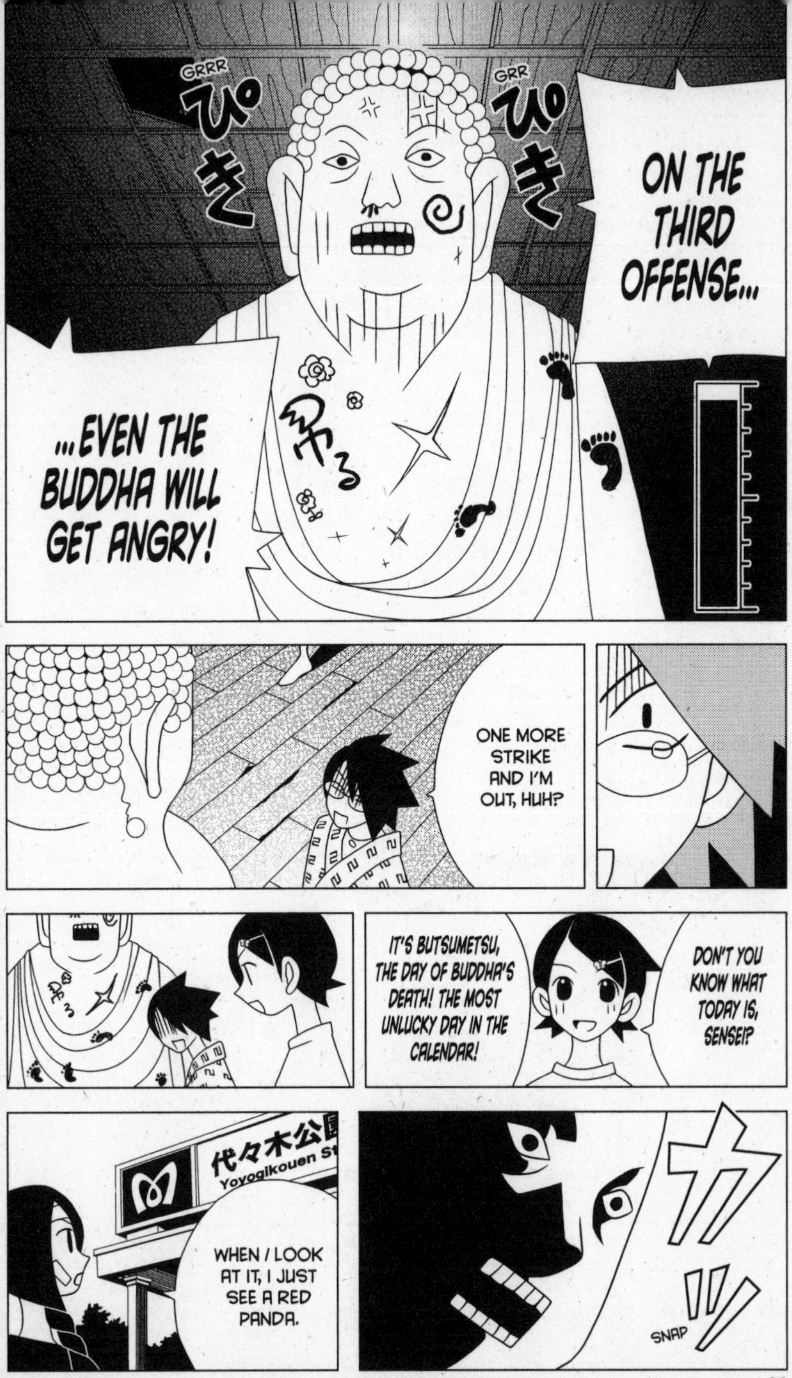
GRR
ぴき
ON THE THIRD OFFENSE...
GRRR
ぴき
...EVEN THE BUDDHA WILL GET ANGRY!
ONE MORE STRIKE AND I'M OUT, HUH?
DON'T YOU KNOW WHAT TODAY IS, SENSEI?
IT'S BUTSUMETSU, THE DAY OF BUDDHA'S DEATH! THE MOST UNLUCKY DAY IN THE CALENDAR!
カッ
SNAP
代々木公園
Yoyogikouen St
WHEN I LOOK AT IT, I JUST SEE A RED PANDA.

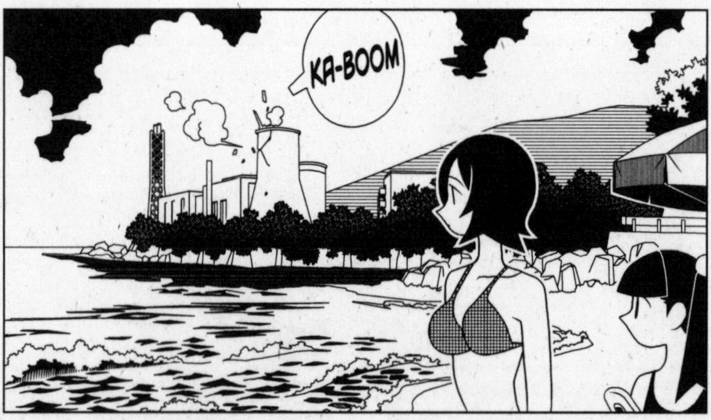
KA-BOOM

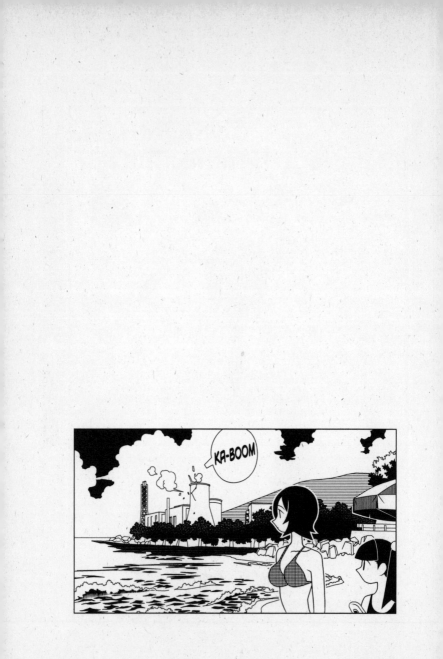

# CHAPTER 17

# SISTER-IN-LAW, I'M AN ARISTOCRAT

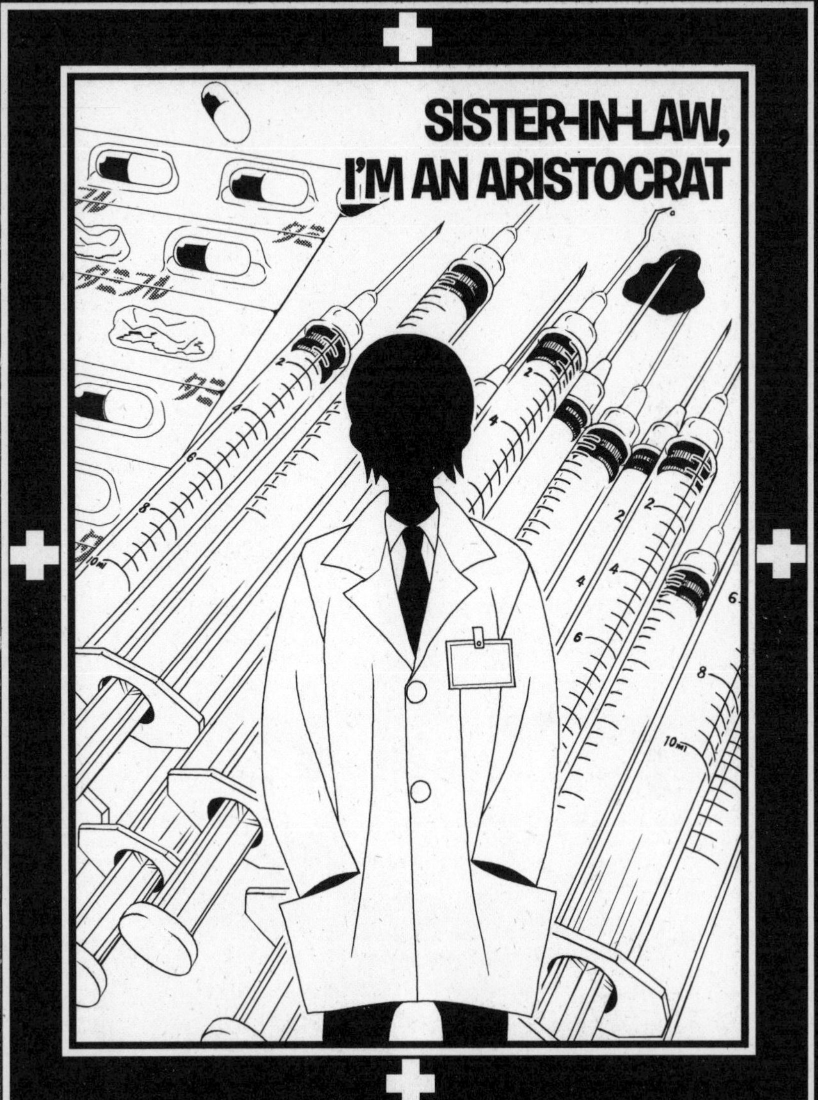

タミフル

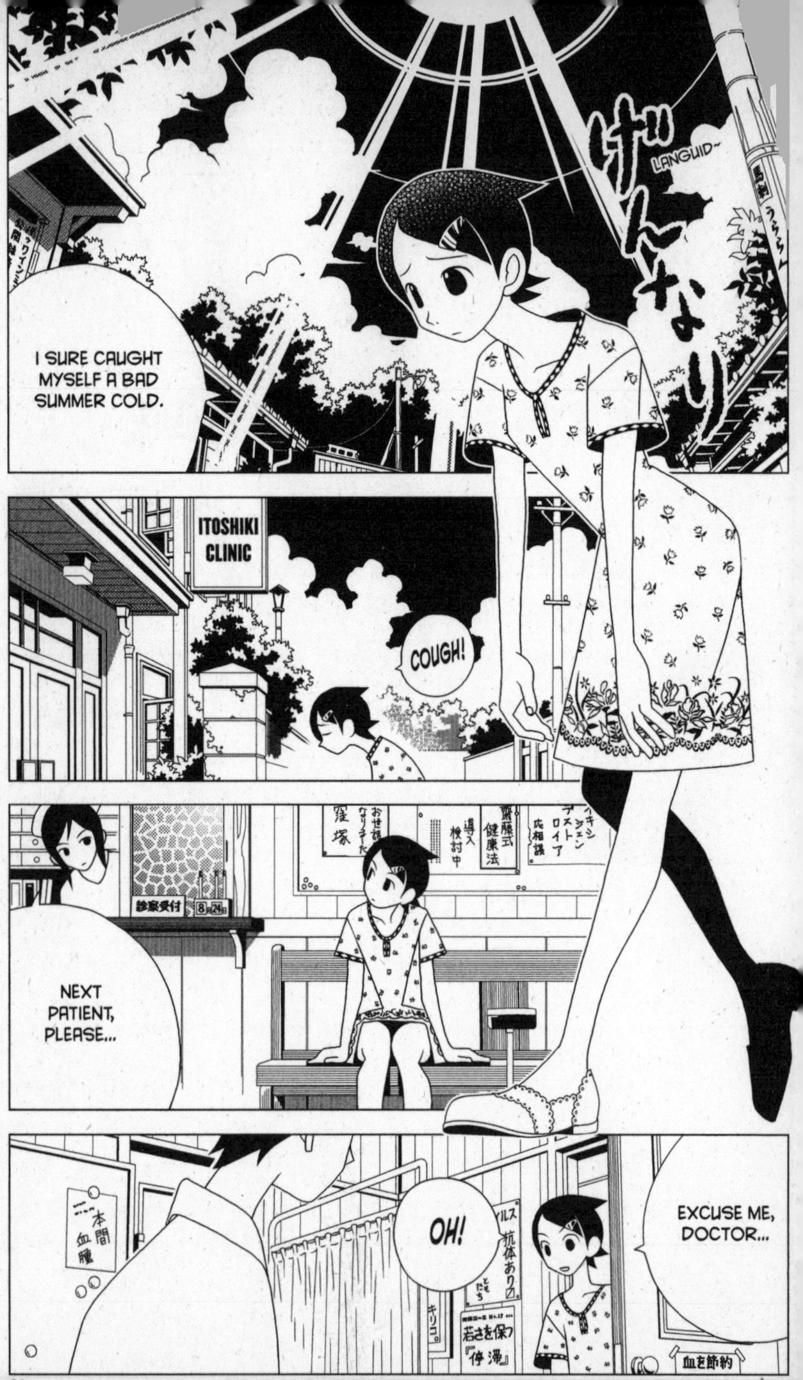
げんなり
LANGUID~
I SURE CAUGHT MYSELF A BAD SUMMER COLD.
ITOSHIKI CLINIC
COUGH!
診察受付
NEXT PATIENT, PLEASE...
EXCUSE ME, DOCTOR...
OH!
若さを保つ『停滞』
血を節約

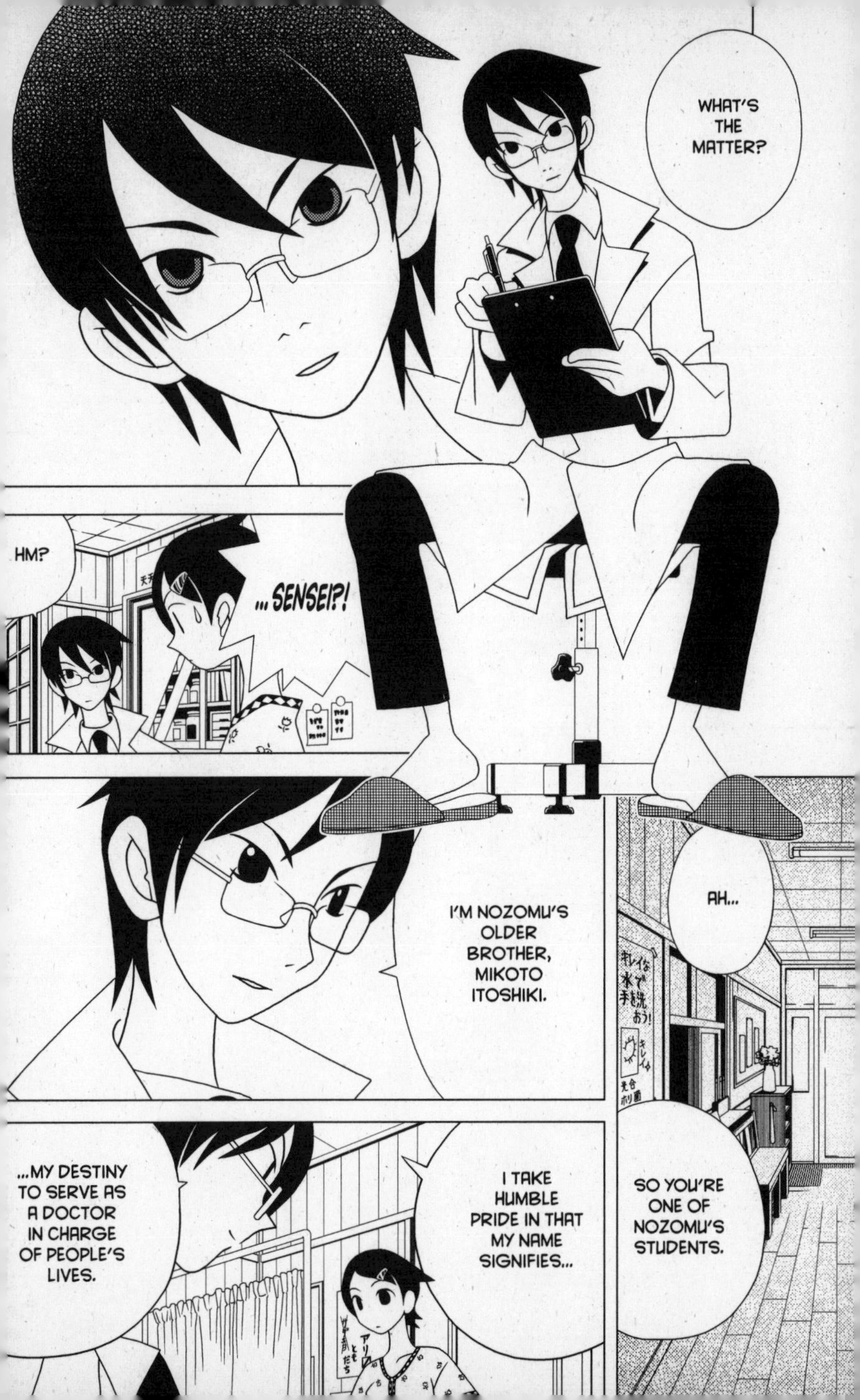
WHAT'S THE MATTER?
...SENSEI?!
HM?
AH...
SO YOU'RE ONE OF NOZOMU'S STUDENTS.
I'M NOZOMU'S OLDER BROTHER, MIKOTO ITOSHIKI.
I TAKE HUMBLE PRIDE IN THAT MY NAME SIGNIFIES...
...MY DESTINY TO SERVE AS A DOCTOR IN CHARGE OF PEOPLE'S LIVES.

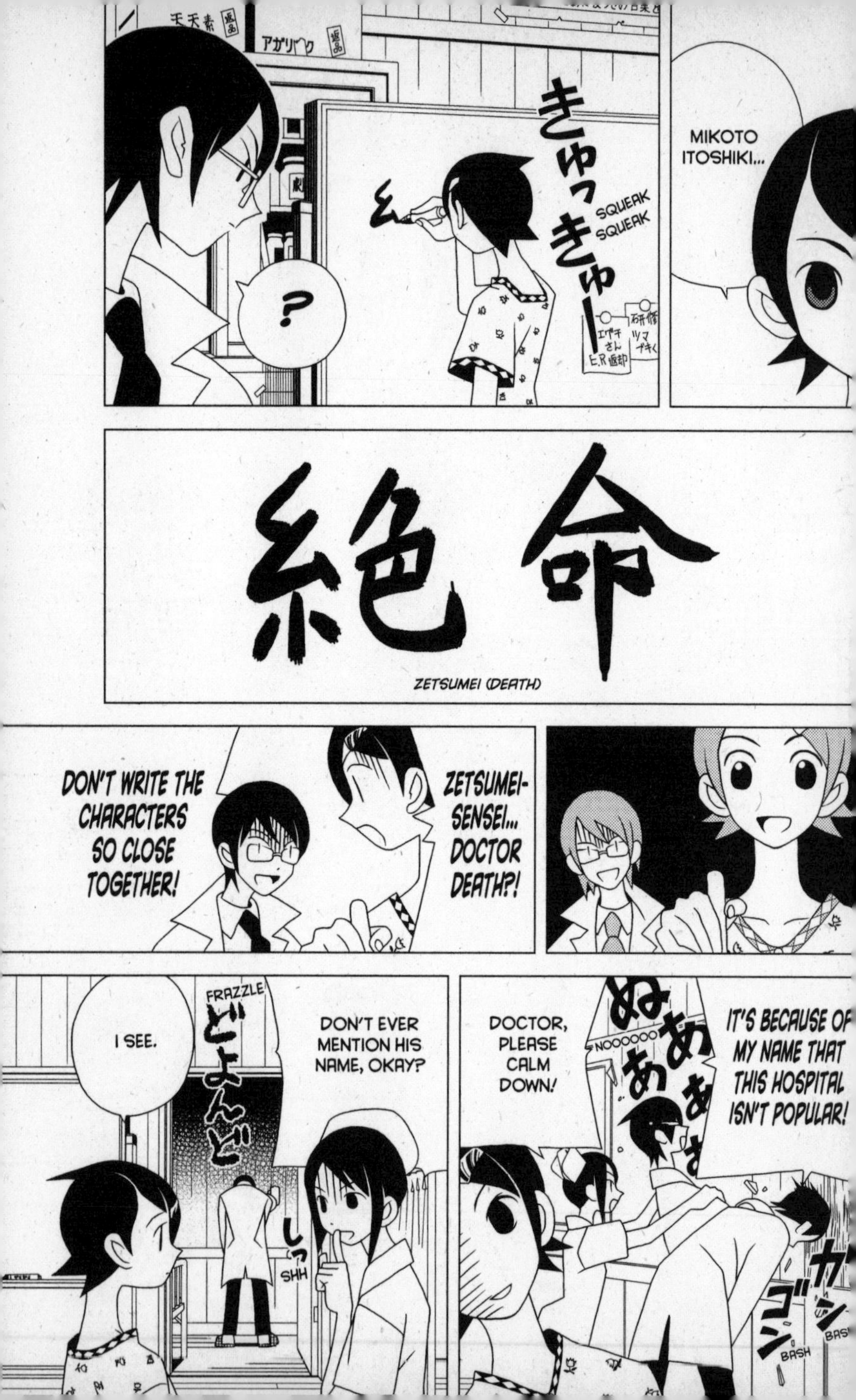

MIKOTO ITOSHIKI...
きゅっきゅー
SQUEAK SQUEAK
?
絶命
ZETSUMEI (DEATH)
ZETSUMEI-SENSEI... DOCTOR DEATH?!
DON'T WRITE THE CHARACTERS SO CLOSE TOGETHER!
IT'S BECAUSE OF MY NAME THAT THIS HOSPITAL ISN'T POPULAR!
ぬあぁぁぁ
NOOOOOO
DOCTOR, PLEASE CALM DOWN!
ガン
BASH
ゴン
BASH
DON'T EVER MENTION HIS NAME, OKAY?
しっ
SHH
どよんど
FRAZZLE
I SEE.

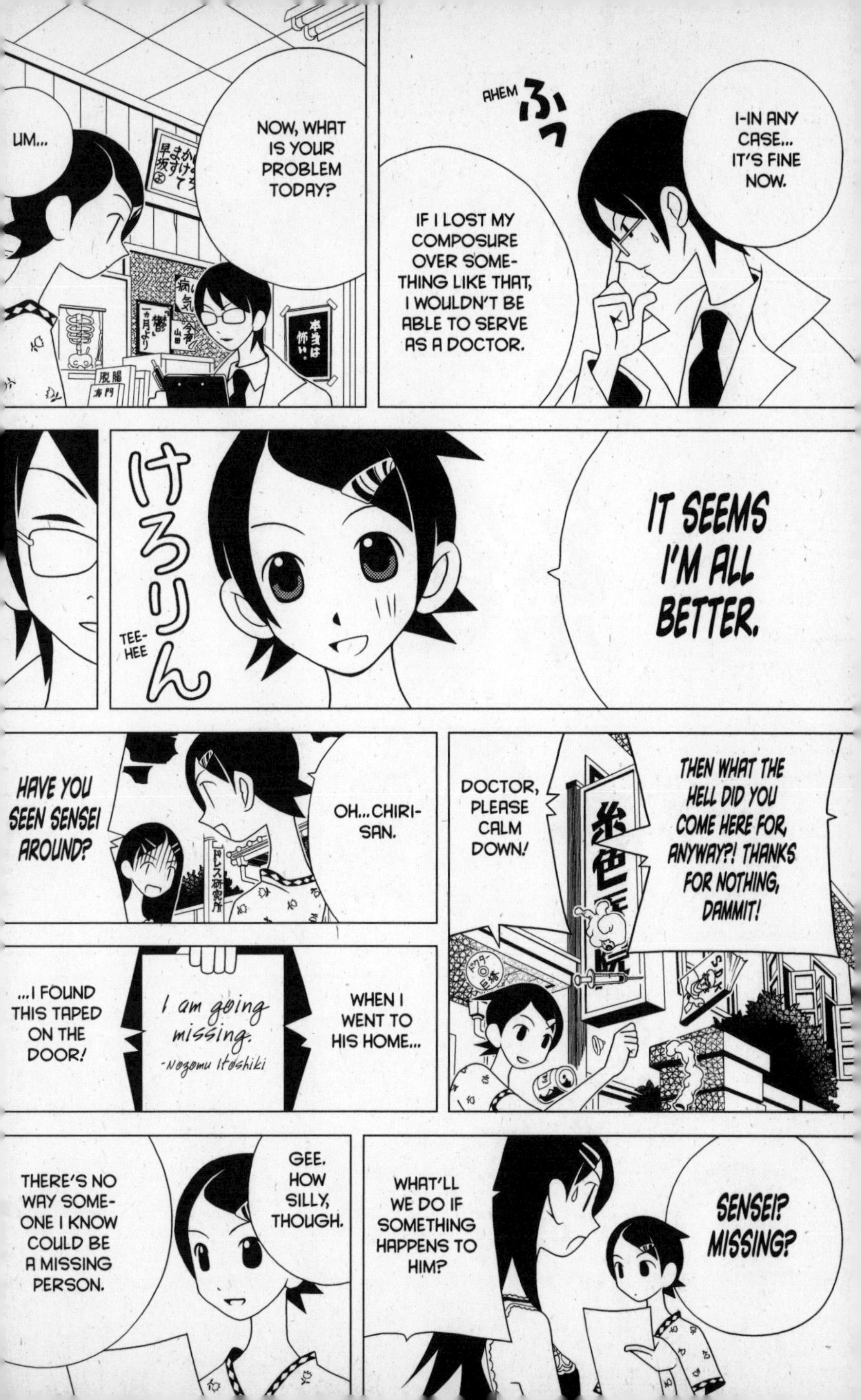
AHEM ふっ
I-IN ANY CASE... IT'S FINE NOW.
IF I LOST MY COMPOSURE OVER SOME-THING LIKE THAT, I WOULDN'T BE ABLE TO SERVE AS A DOCTOR.
NOW, WHAT IS YOUR PROBLEM TODAY?
UM...
IT SEEMS I'M ALL BETTER.
けろりん
TEE-HEE
THEN WHAT THE HELL DID YOU COME HERE FOR, ANYWAY?! THANKS FOR NOTHING, DAMMIT!
DOCTOR, PLEASE CALM DOWN!
OH...CHIRI-SAN.
HAVE YOU SEEN SENSEI AROUND?
WHEN I WENT TO HIS HOME...
I am going missing.
-Nozomu Itoshiki
...I FOUND THIS TAPED ON THE DOOR!
SENSEI? MISSING?
WHAT'LL WE DO IF SOMETHING HAPPENS TO HIM?
GEE. HOW SILLY, THOUGH.
THERE'S NO WAY SOME-ONE I KNOW COULD BE A MISSING PERSON.

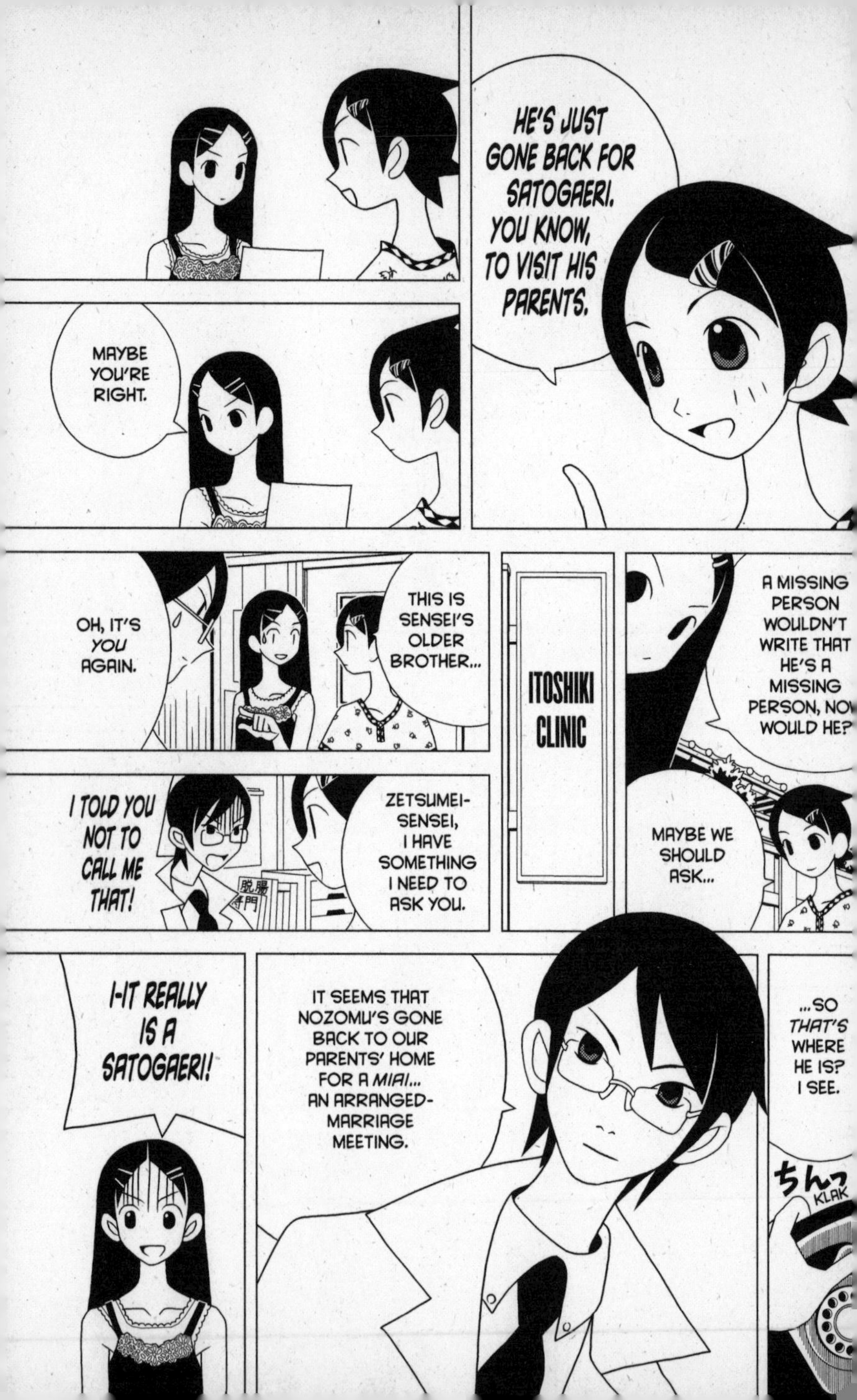
HE'S JUST GONE BACK FOR SATOGAERI. YOU KNOW, TO VISIT HIS PARENTS.
MAYBE YOU'RE RIGHT.
A MISSING PERSON WOULDN'T WRITE THAT HE'S A MISSING PERSON, NOW WOULD HE?
MAYBE WE SHOULD ASK...
ITOSHIKI CLINIC
THIS IS SENSEI'S OLDER BROTHER...
OH, IT'S *YOU* AGAIN.
ZETSUMEI-SENSEI, I HAVE SOMETHING I NEED TO ASK YOU.
脱腸専門
I TOLD YOU NOT TO CALL ME THAT!
...SO *THAT'S* WHERE HE IS? I SEE.
ちんっ
KLAK
IT SEEMS THAT NOZOMU'S GONE BACK TO OUR PARENTS' HOME FOR A *MIAI*... AN ARRANGED-MARRIAGE MEETING.
I-IT REALLY IS A SATOGAERI!

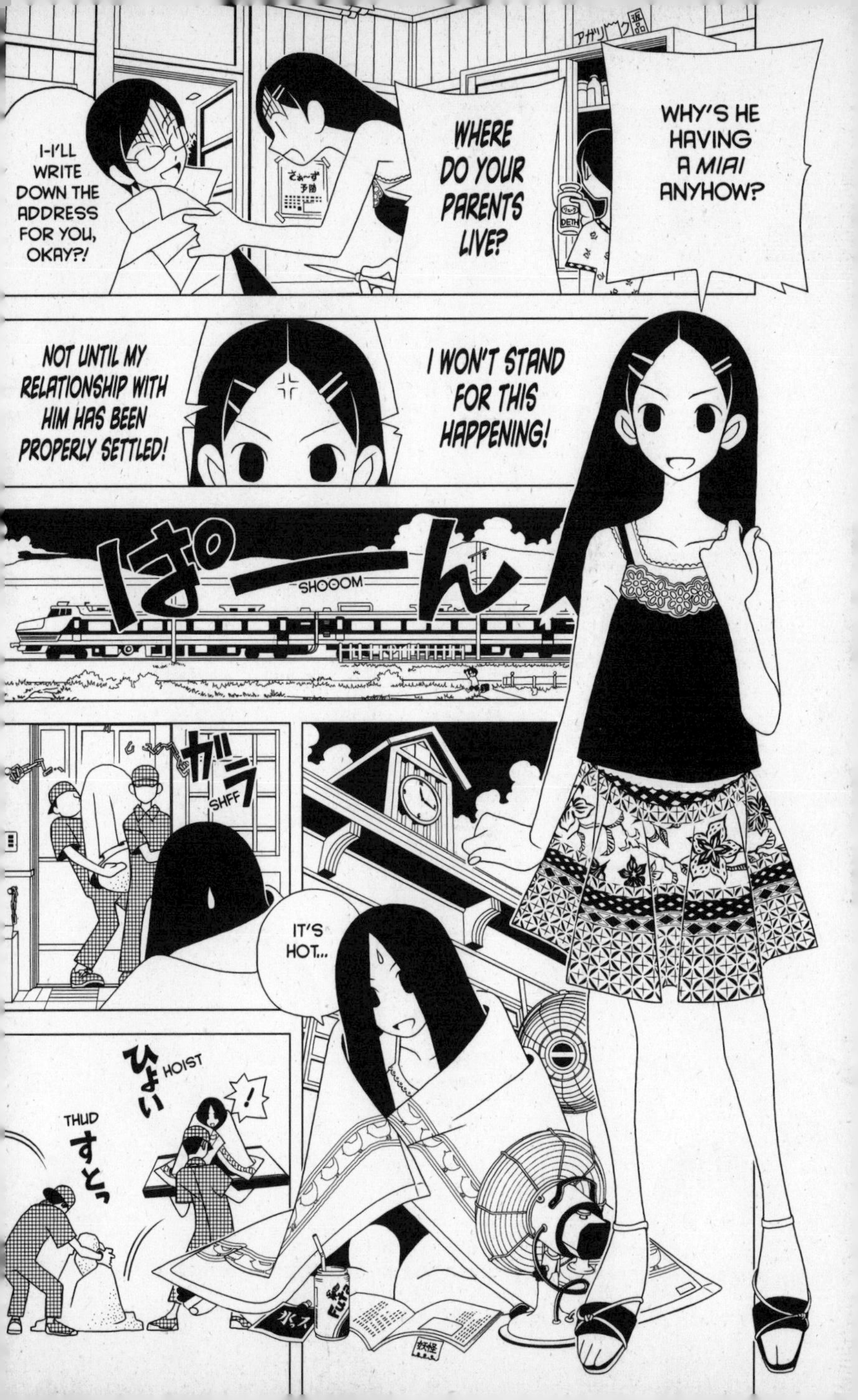
WHY'S HE HAVING A *MIAI* ANYHOW?
WHERE DO YOUR PARENTS LIVE?
I-I'LL WRITE DOWN THE ADDRESS FOR YOU, OKAY?!
I WON'T STAND FOR THIS HAPPENING!
NOT UNTIL MY RELATIONSHIP WITH HIM HAS BEEN PROPERLY SETTLED!
ぽーん
SHOOOM
ガラ
SHFF
IT'S HOT...
!
ひょい
HOIST
すとっ
THUD

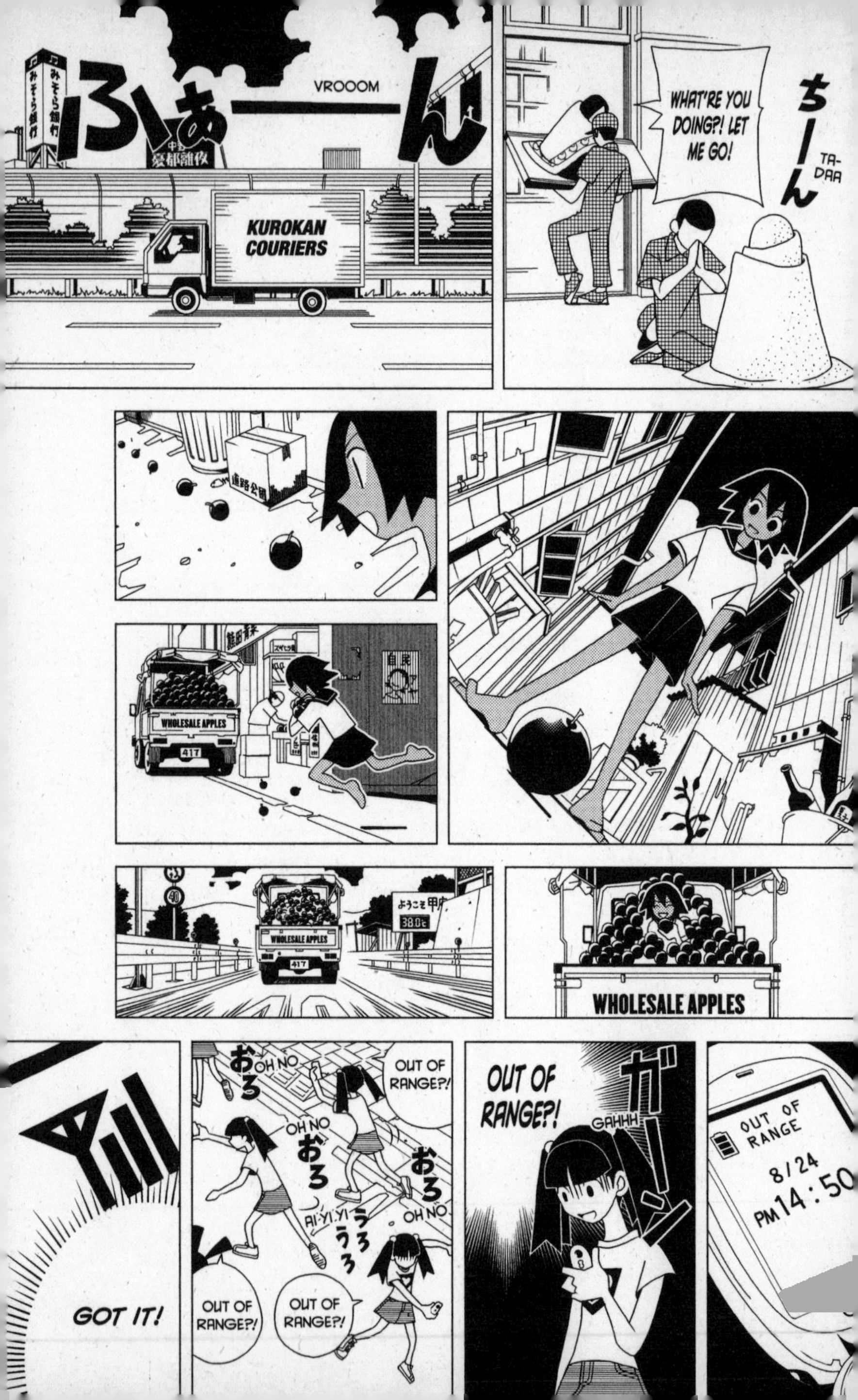
ちーん
TA-DAA
WHAT'RE YOU DOING?! LET ME GO!
ふぁーーーん
VROOOM
みそら銀行
KUROKAN COURIERS
WHOLESALE APPLES
417
ようこそ甲府
38.0℃
40
WHOLESALE APPLES
417
WHOLESALE APPLES
OUT OF RANGE
8/24
PM 14:50
ガー
GAHHH
OUT OF RANGE?!
OUT OF RANGE?!
おろ
OH NO
おろ
OH NO
おろ
OH NO
うろうろ
AI-YI-YI
OUT OF RANGE?!
OUT OF RANGE?!
GOT IT!

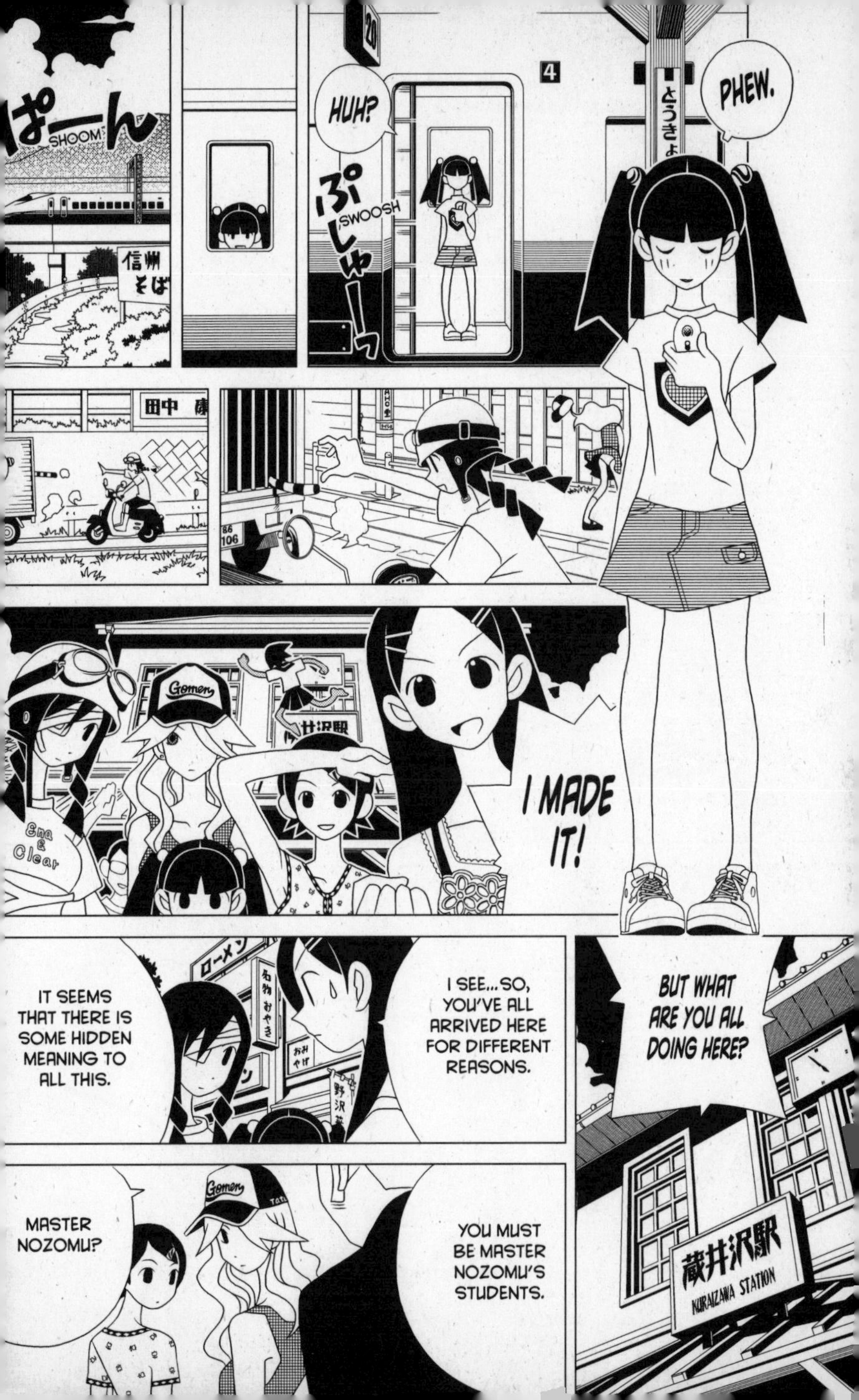

とうきょ
PHEW.
4
HUH?
ぷしゅーっ
SWOOSH
ぱーん
SHOOM
信州そば
I MADE IT!
BUT WHAT ARE YOU ALL DOING HERE?
蔵井沢駅
KURAIZAWA STATION
I SEE...SO, YOU'VE ALL ARRIVED HERE FOR DIFFERENT REASONS.
IT SEEMS THAT THERE IS SOME HIDDEN MEANING TO ALL THIS.
YOU MUST BE MASTER NOZOMU'S STUDENTS.
MASTER NOZOMU?

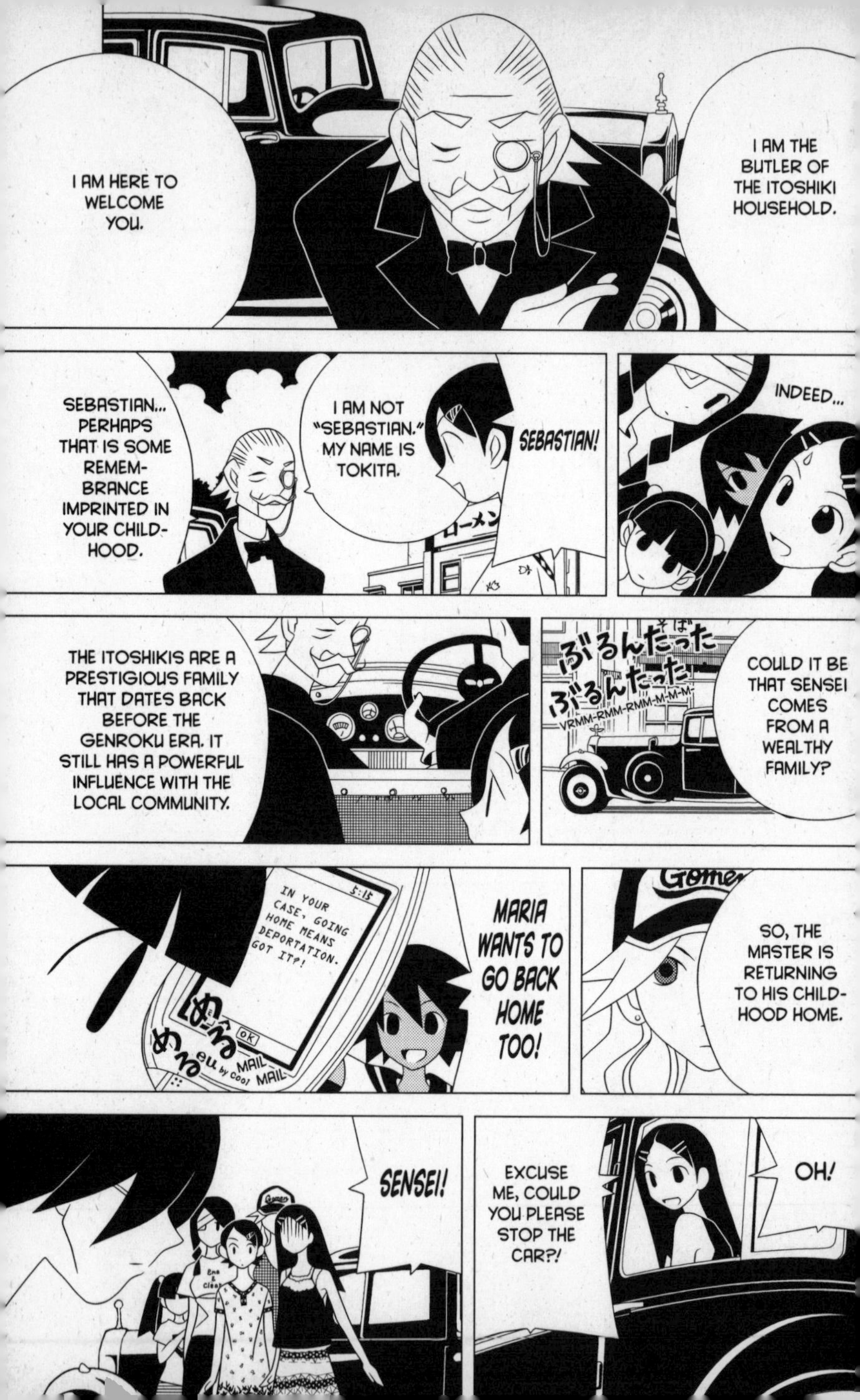
I AM THE BUTLER OF THE ITOSHIKI HOUSEHOLD.
I AM HERE TO WELCOME YOU.
INDEED...
SEBASTIAN!
I AM NOT "SEBASTIAN." MY NAME IS TOKITA.
SEBASTIAN... PERHAPS THAT IS SOME REMEMBRANCE IMPRINTED IN YOUR CHILDHOOD.
ぶるんたった ぶるんたった
VRMM-RMM-RMM-M-M-M-
COULD IT BE THAT SENSEI COMES FROM A WEALTHY FAMILY?
THE ITOSHIKIS ARE A PRESTIGIOUS FAMILY THAT DATES BACK BEFORE THE GENROKU ERA. IT STILL HAS A POWERFUL INFLUENCE WITH THE LOCAL COMMUNITY.
SO, THE MASTER IS RETURNING TO HIS CHILDHOOD HOME.
MARIA WANTS TO GO BACK HOME TOO!
5:15
IN YOUR CASE, GOING HOME MEANS DEPORTATION. GOT IT?!
OK
MAIL
OH!
EXCUSE ME, COULD YOU PLEASE STOP THE CAR?!
SENSEI!

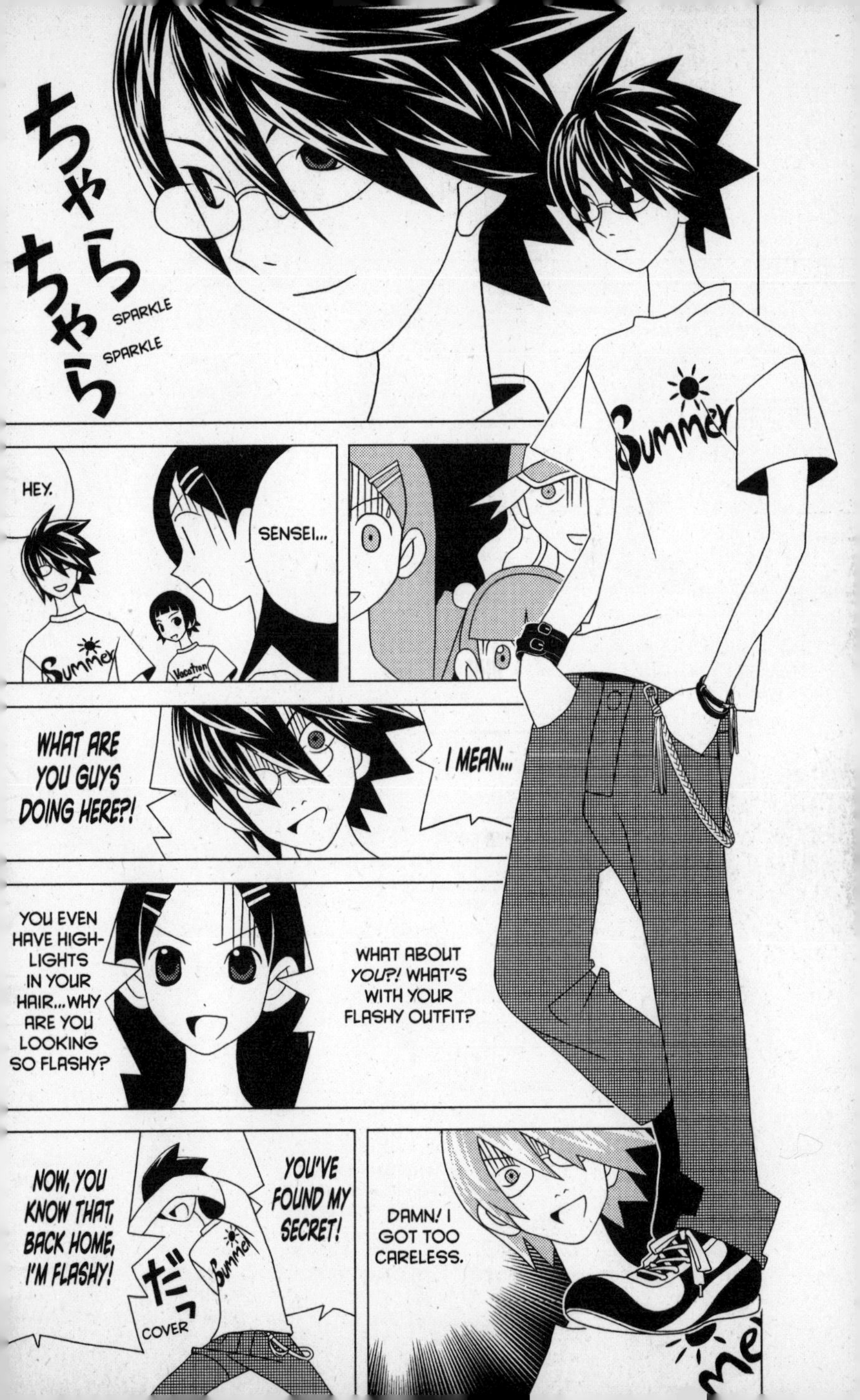
ちゃらちゃら
SPARKLE
SPARKLE
SENSEI...
HEY.
I MEAN...
WHAT ARE YOU GUYS DOING HERE?!
WHAT ABOUT *YOU?!* WHAT'S WITH YOUR FLASHY OUTFIT?
YOU EVEN HAVE HIGH-LIGHTS IN YOUR HAIR...WHY ARE YOU LOOKING SO FLASHY?
DAMN! I GOT TOO CARELESS.
YOU'VE FOUND MY SECRET!
NOW, YOU KNOW THAT, BACK HOME, I'M FLASHY!
だっ
COVER

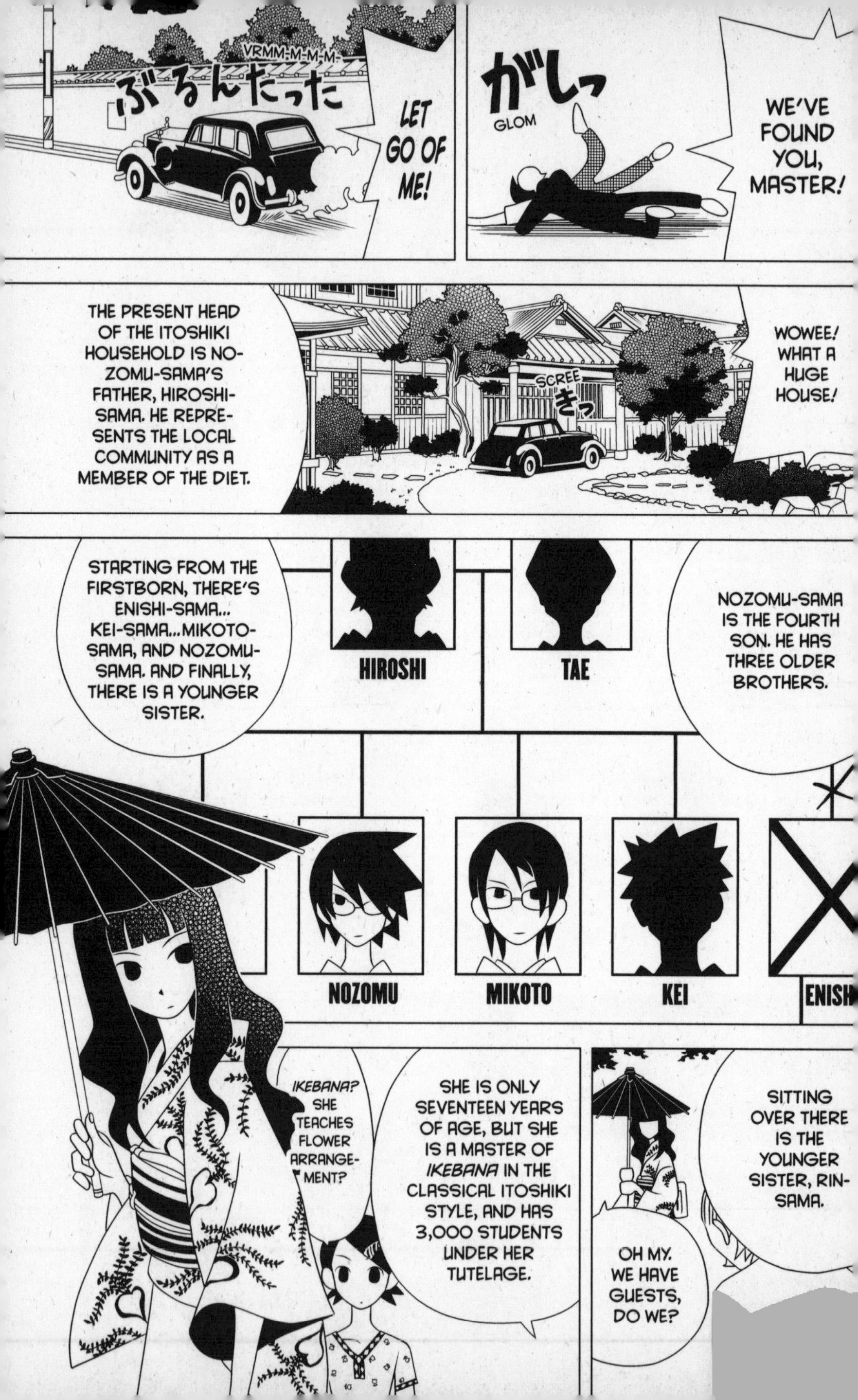
WE'VE FOUND YOU, MASTER!
がしっ
GLOM
LET GO OF ME!
ぶるんたった
VRMM-M-M-M
WOWEE! WHAT A HUGE HOUSE!
SCREE
きっ
THE PRESENT HEAD OF THE ITOSHIKI HOUSEHOLD IS NOZOMU-SAMA'S FATHER, HIROSHI-SAMA. HE REPRESENTS THE LOCAL COMMUNITY AS A MEMBER OF THE DIET.
NOZOMU-SAMA IS THE FOURTH SON. HE HAS THREE OLDER BROTHERS.
TAE
HIROSHI
STARTING FROM THE FIRSTBORN, THERE'S ENISHI-SAMA... KEI-SAMA...MIKOTO-SAMA, AND NOZOMU-SAMA. AND FINALLY, THERE IS A YOUNGER SISTER.
ENISH
KEI
MIKOTO
NOZOMU
SITTING OVER THERE IS THE YOUNGER SISTER, RIN-SAMA.
OH MY. WE HAVE GUESTS, DO WE?
SHE IS ONLY SEVENTEEN YEARS OF AGE, BUT SHE IS A MASTER OF *IKEBANA* IN THE CLASSICAL ITOSHIKI STYLE, AND HAS 3,000 STUDENTS UNDER HER TUTELAGE.
*IKEBANA?* SHE TEACHES FLOWER ARRANGEMENT?

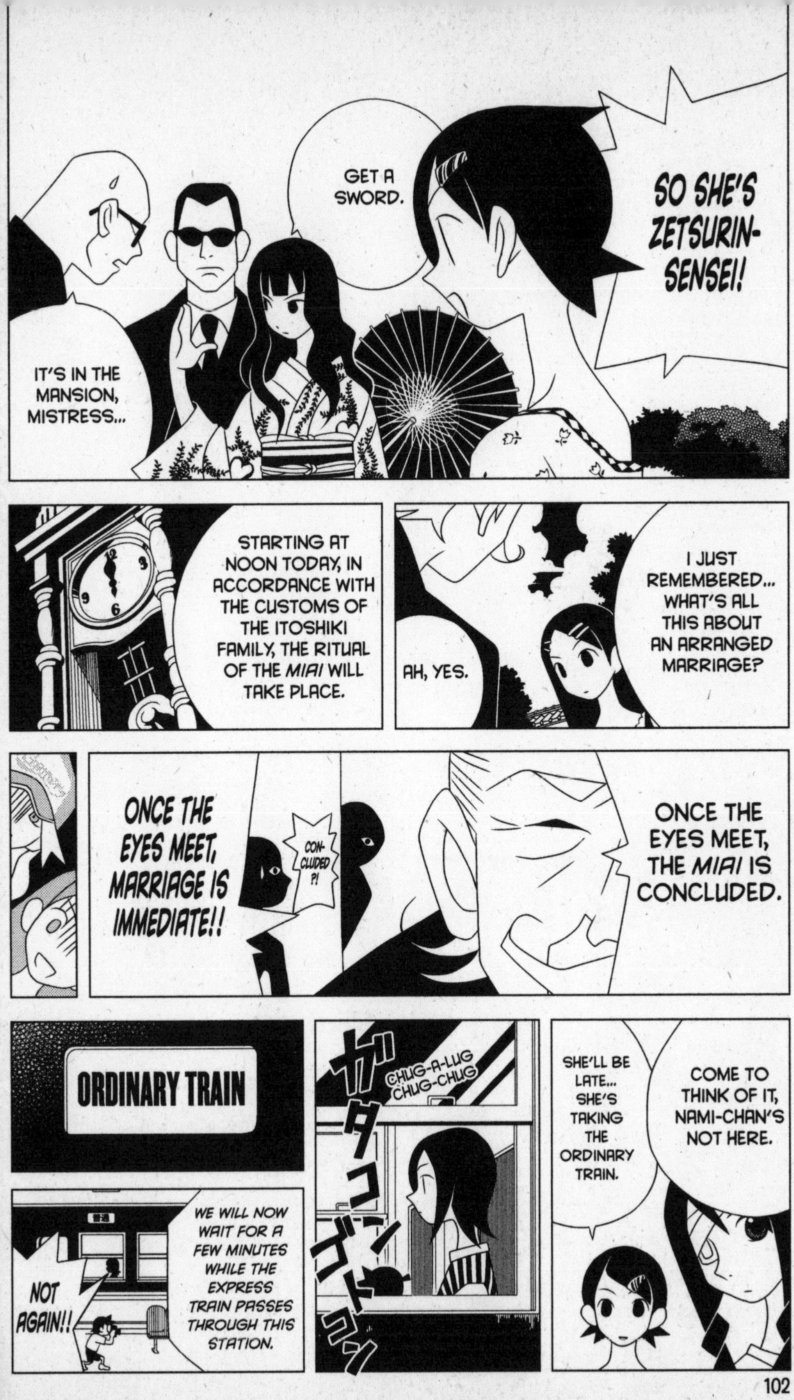
SO SHE'S ZETSURIN-SENSEI!
GET A SWORD.
IT'S IN THE MANSION, MISTRESS...
I JUST REMEMBERED... WHAT'S ALL THIS ABOUT AN ARRANGED MARRIAGE?
AH, YES.
STARTING AT NOON TODAY, IN ACCORDANCE WITH THE CUSTOMS OF THE ITOSHIKI FAMILY, THE RITUAL OF THE *MIAI* WILL TAKE PLACE.
ONCE THE EYES MEET, THE *MIAI* IS CONCLUDED.
CON-CLUDED ?!
ONCE THE EYES MEET, MARRIAGE IS IMMEDIATE!!
COME TO THINK OF IT, NAMI-CHAN'S NOT HERE.
SHE'LL BE LATE... SHE'S TAKING THE ORDINARY TRAIN.
CHUG-A-LUG CHUG-CHUG
ORDINARY TRAIN
普通
WE WILL NOW WAIT FOR A FEW MINUTES WHILE THE EXPRESS TRAIN PASSES THROUGH THIS STATION.
NOT AGAIN!!

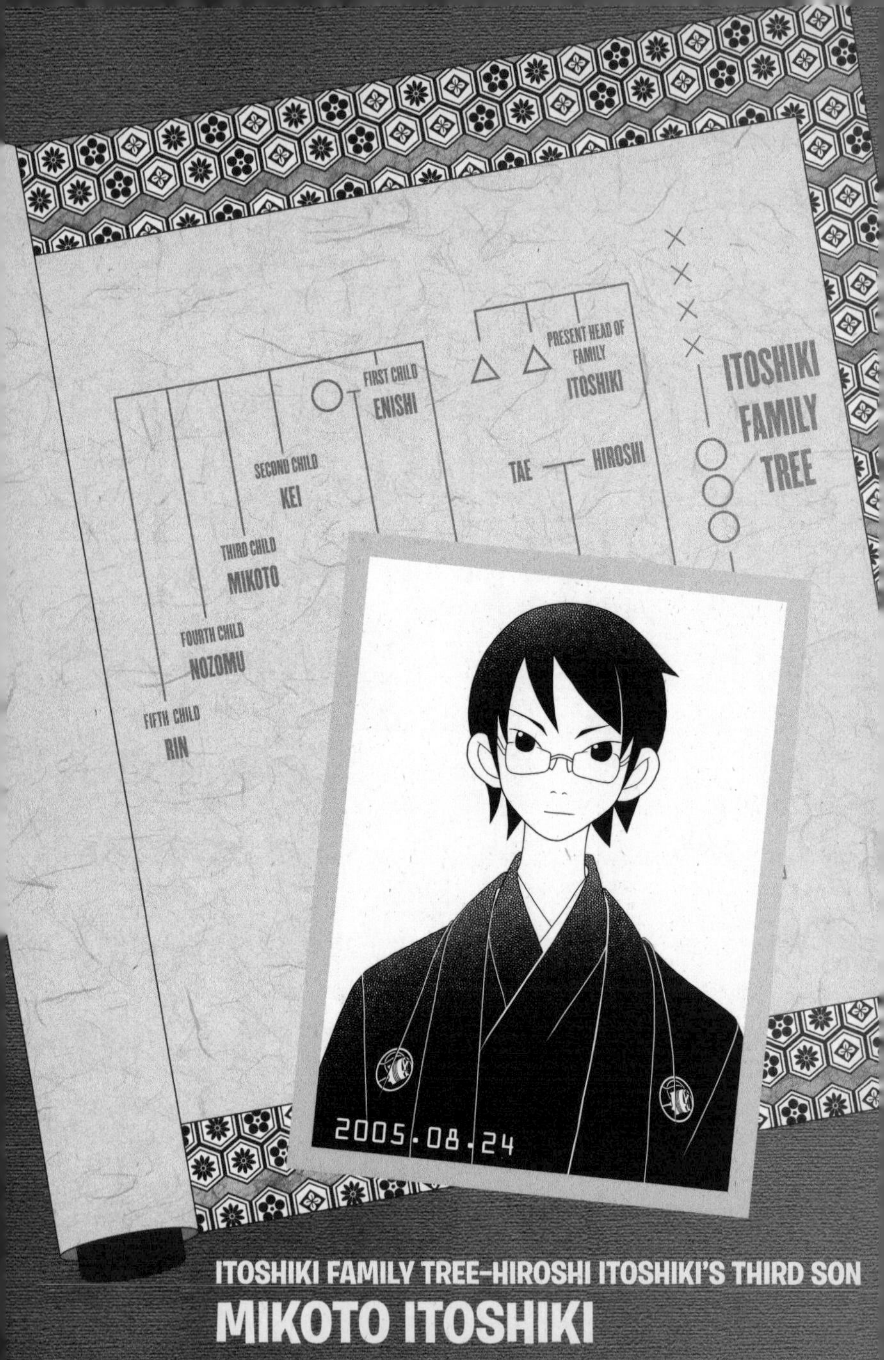
ITOSHIKI FAMILY TREE
PRESENT HEAD OF FAMILY
ITOSHIKI
HIROSHI
TAE
FIRST CHILD
ENISHI
SECOND CHILD
KEI
THIRD CHILD
MIKOTO
FOURTH CHILD
NOZOMU
FIFTH CHILD
RIN
2005.08.24

ITOSHIKI FAMILY TREE–HIROSHI ITOSHIKI'S THIRD SON

**MIKOTO ITOSHIKI**

DOCTOR AT THE ITOSHIKI CLINIC

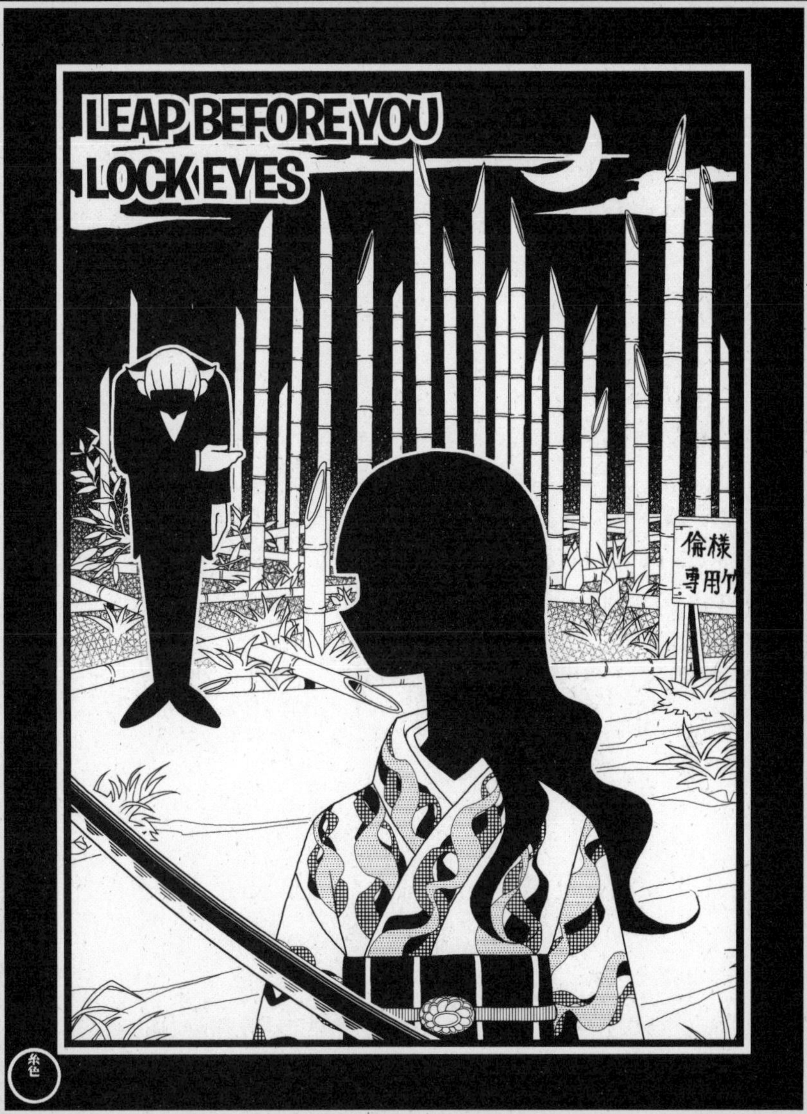
LEAP BEFORE YOU LOCK EYES
倫様
専用
糸色

# CHAPTER 18

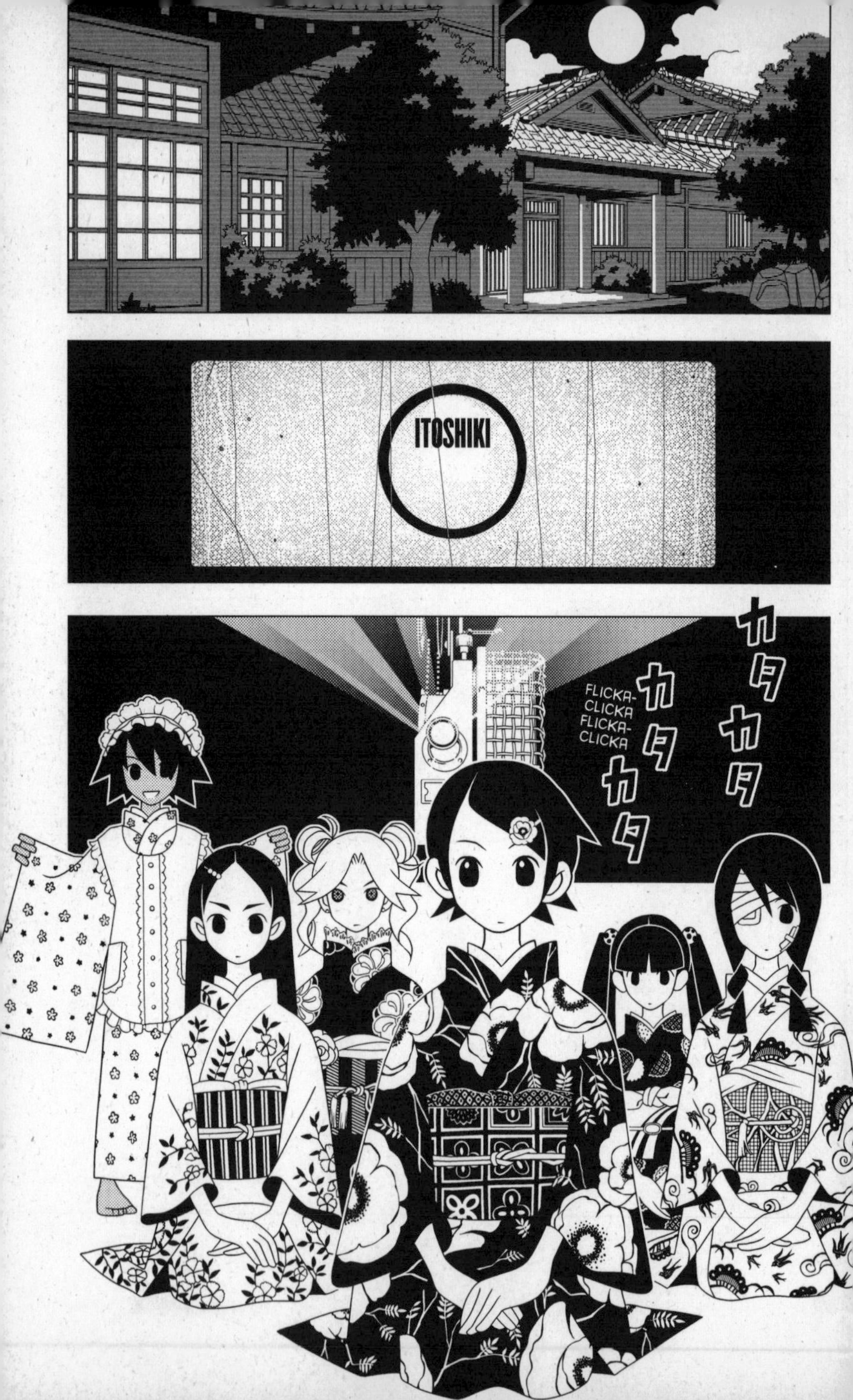
ITOSHIKI
カタカタ
カタカタ
FLICKA-
CLICKA
FLICKA-
CLICKA

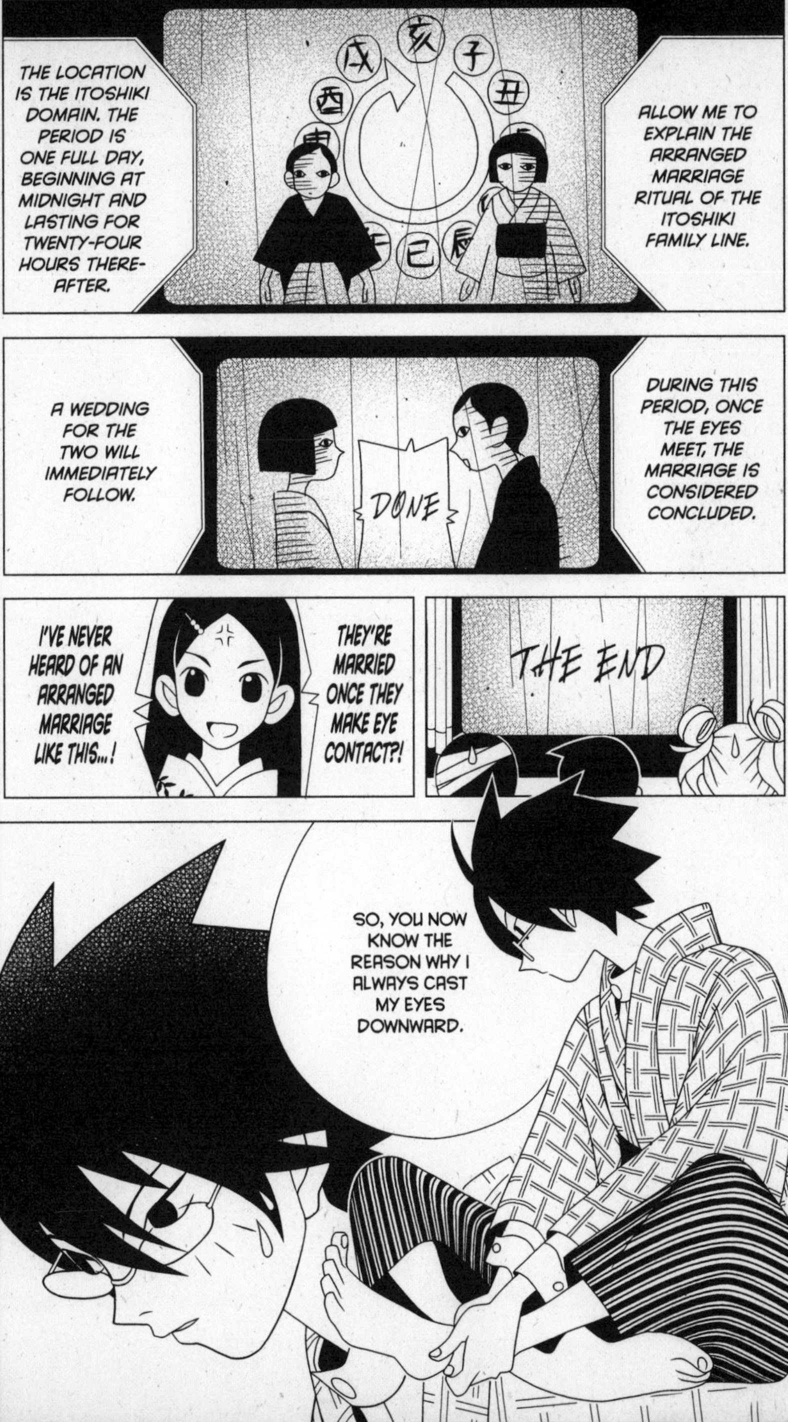
ALLOW ME TO EXPLAIN THE ARRANGED MARRIAGE RITUAL OF THE ITOSHIKI FAMILY LINE.
THE LOCATION IS THE ITOSHIKI DOMAIN. THE PERIOD IS ONE FULL DAY, BEGINNING AT MIDNIGHT AND LASTING FOR TWENTY-FOUR HOURS THERE-AFTER.
DURING THIS PERIOD, ONCE THE EYES MEET, THE MARRIAGE IS CONSIDERED CONCLUDED.
DONE
A WEDDING FOR THE TWO WILL IMMEDIATELY FOLLOW.
THE END
THEY'RE MARRIED ONCE THEY MAKE EYE CONTACT?!
I'VE NEVER HEARD OF AN ARRANGED MARRIAGE LIKE THIS...!
SO, YOU NOW KNOW THE REASON WHY I ALWAYS CAST MY EYES DOWNWARD.

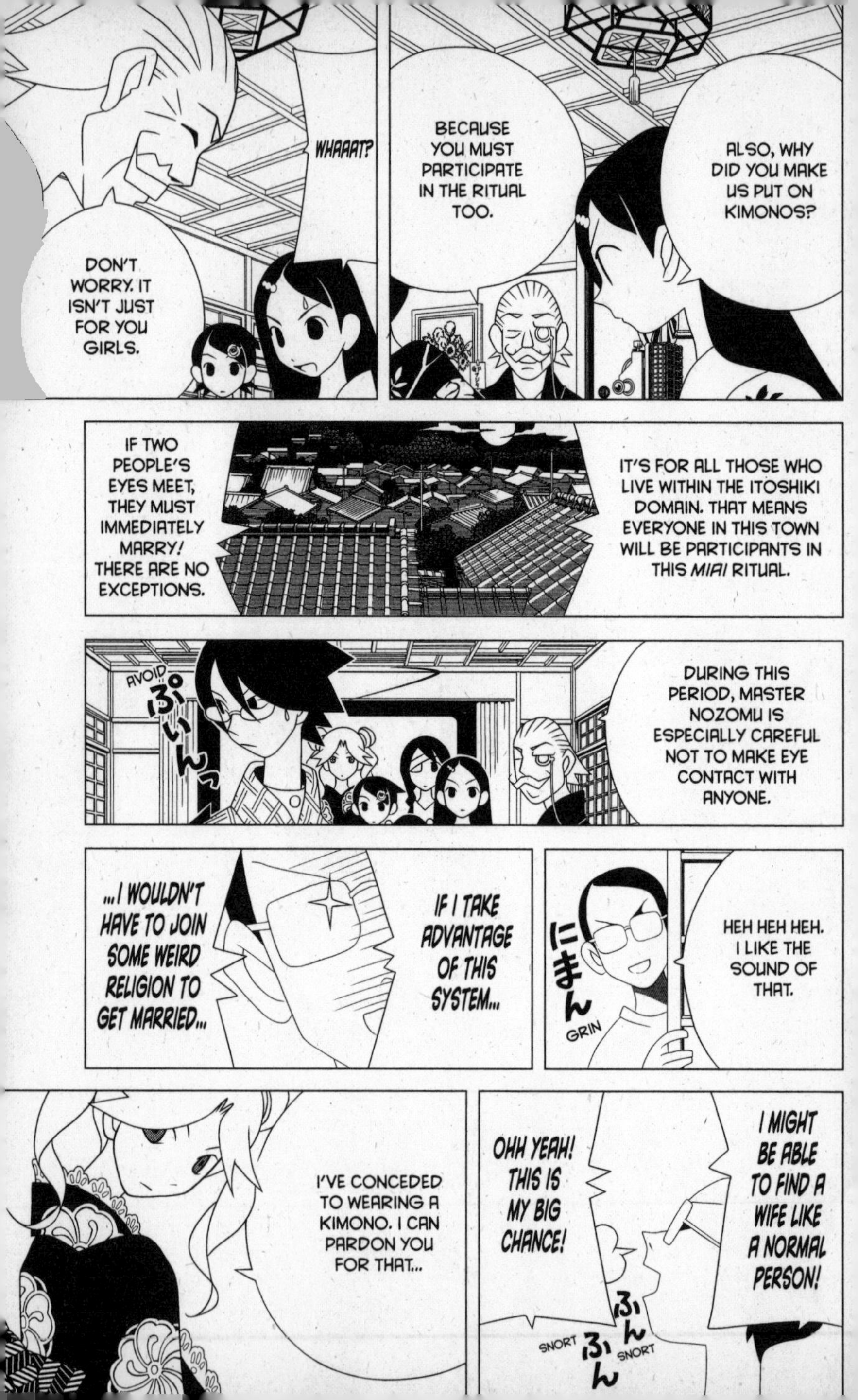
ALSO, WHY DID YOU MAKE US PUT ON KIMONOS?
BECAUSE YOU MUST PARTICIPATE IN THE RITUAL TOO.
WHAAAT?
DON'T WORRY. IT ISN'T JUST FOR YOU GIRLS.
IT'S FOR ALL THOSE WHO LIVE WITHIN THE ITOSHIKI DOMAIN. THAT MEANS EVERYONE IN THIS TOWN WILL BE PARTICIPANTS IN THIS *MIAI* RITUAL.
IF TWO PEOPLE'S EYES MEET, THEY MUST IMMEDIATELY MARRY! THERE ARE NO EXCEPTIONS.
DURING THIS PERIOD, MASTER NOZOMU IS ESPECIALLY CAREFUL NOT TO MAKE EYE CONTACT WITH ANYONE.
ぷいんっ
AVOID
HEH HEH HEH. I LIKE THE SOUND OF THAT.
にまん
GRIN
IF I TAKE ADVANTAGE OF THIS SYSTEM...
...I WOULDN'T HAVE TO JOIN SOME WEIRD RELIGION TO GET MARRIED...
I MIGHT BE ABLE TO FIND A WIFE LIKE A NORMAL PERSON!
OHH YEAH! THIS IS MY BIG CHANCE!
ふん
SNORT
ふん
SNORT
I'VE CONCEDED TO WEARING A KIMONO. I CAN PARDON YOU FOR THAT...

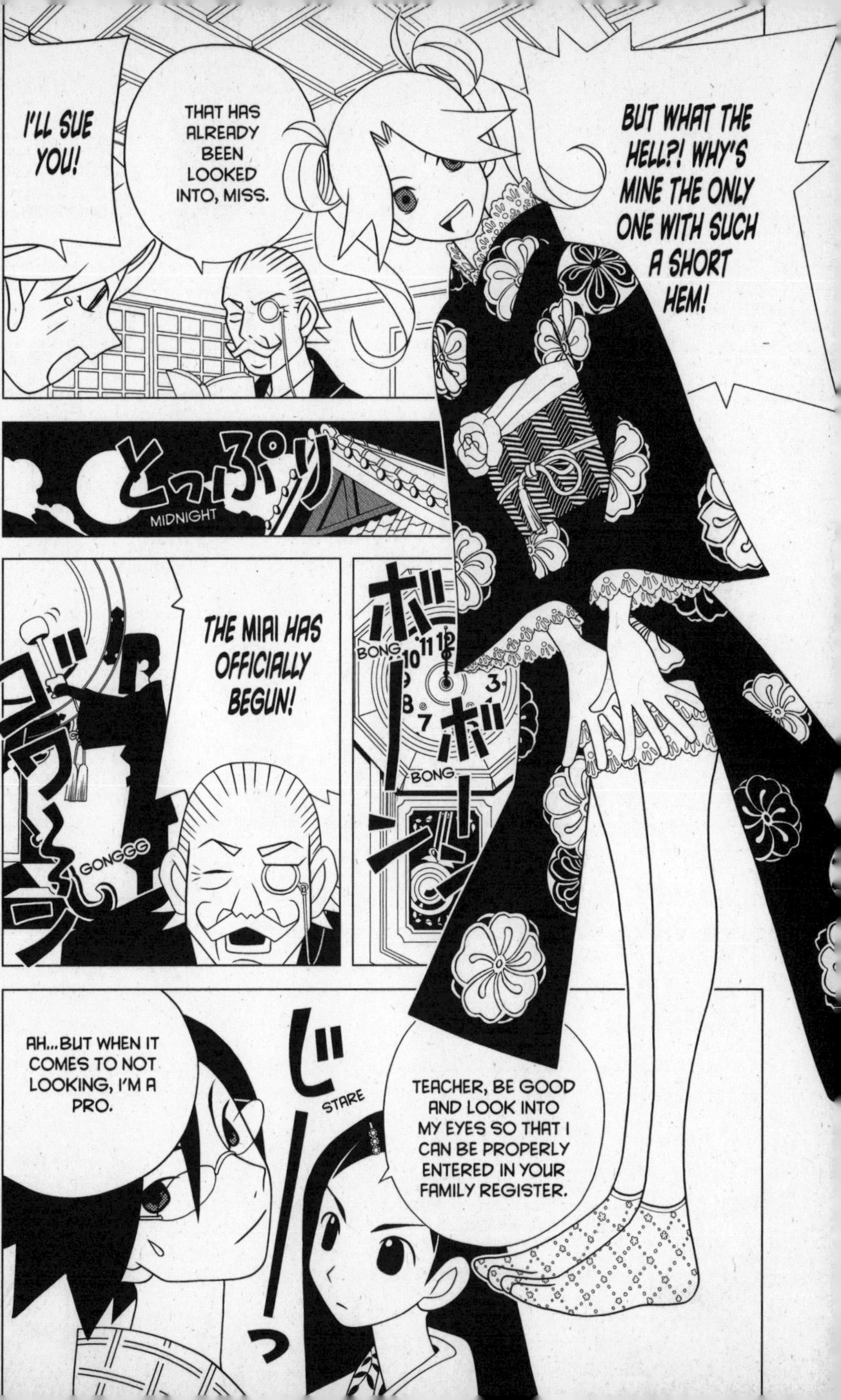
BUT WHAT THE HELL?! WHY'S MINE THE ONLY ONE WITH SUCH A SHORT HEM!
THAT HAS ALREADY BEEN LOOKED INTO, MISS.
I'LL SUE YOU!
とっぷり
MIDNIGHT
BONG
BONG
THE MIAI HAS OFFICIALLY BEGUN!
GONGGG
じーっ
STARE
TEACHER, BE GOOD AND LOOK INTO MY EYES SO THAT I CAN BE PROPERLY ENTERED IN YOUR FAMILY REGISTER.
AH...BUT WHEN IT COMES TO NOT LOOKING, I'M A PRO.

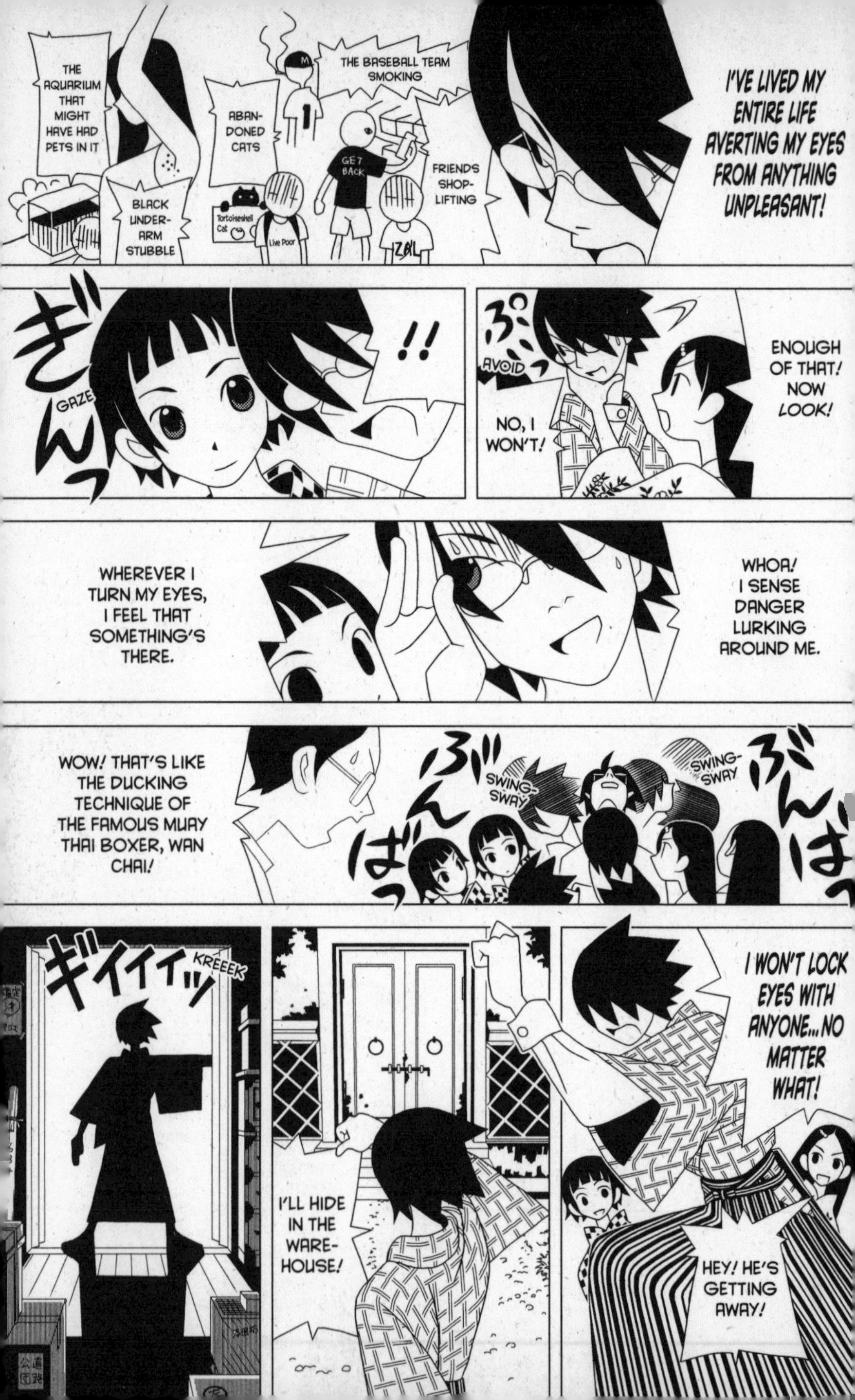
I'VE LIVED MY ENTIRE LIFE AVERTING MY EYES FROM ANYTHING UNPLEASANT!
FRIENDS SHOPLIFTING
GET BACK
THE BASEBALL TEAM SMOKING
ABANDONED CATS
Live Poor
Tortoiseshell Cat
BLACK UNDERARM STUBBLE
THE AQUARIUM THAT MIGHT HAVE HAD PETS IN IT
ENOUGH OF THAT! NOW LOOK!
ぷいっ
AVOID
NO, I WON'T!
!!
ぎんっ
GAZE
WHOA! I SENSE DANGER LURKING AROUND ME.
WHEREVER I TURN MY EYES, I FEEL THAT SOMETHING'S THERE.
ぶんはっ
SWING-SWAY
ぶんばっ
SWING-SWAY
WOW! THAT'S LIKE THE DUCKING TECHNIQUE OF THE FAMOUS MUAY THAI BOXER, WAN CHAI!
I WON'T LOCK EYES WITH ANYONE...NO MATTER WHAT!
HEY! HE'S GETTING AWAY!
I'LL HIDE IN THE WAREHOUSE!
ギイイイッ
KREEEK

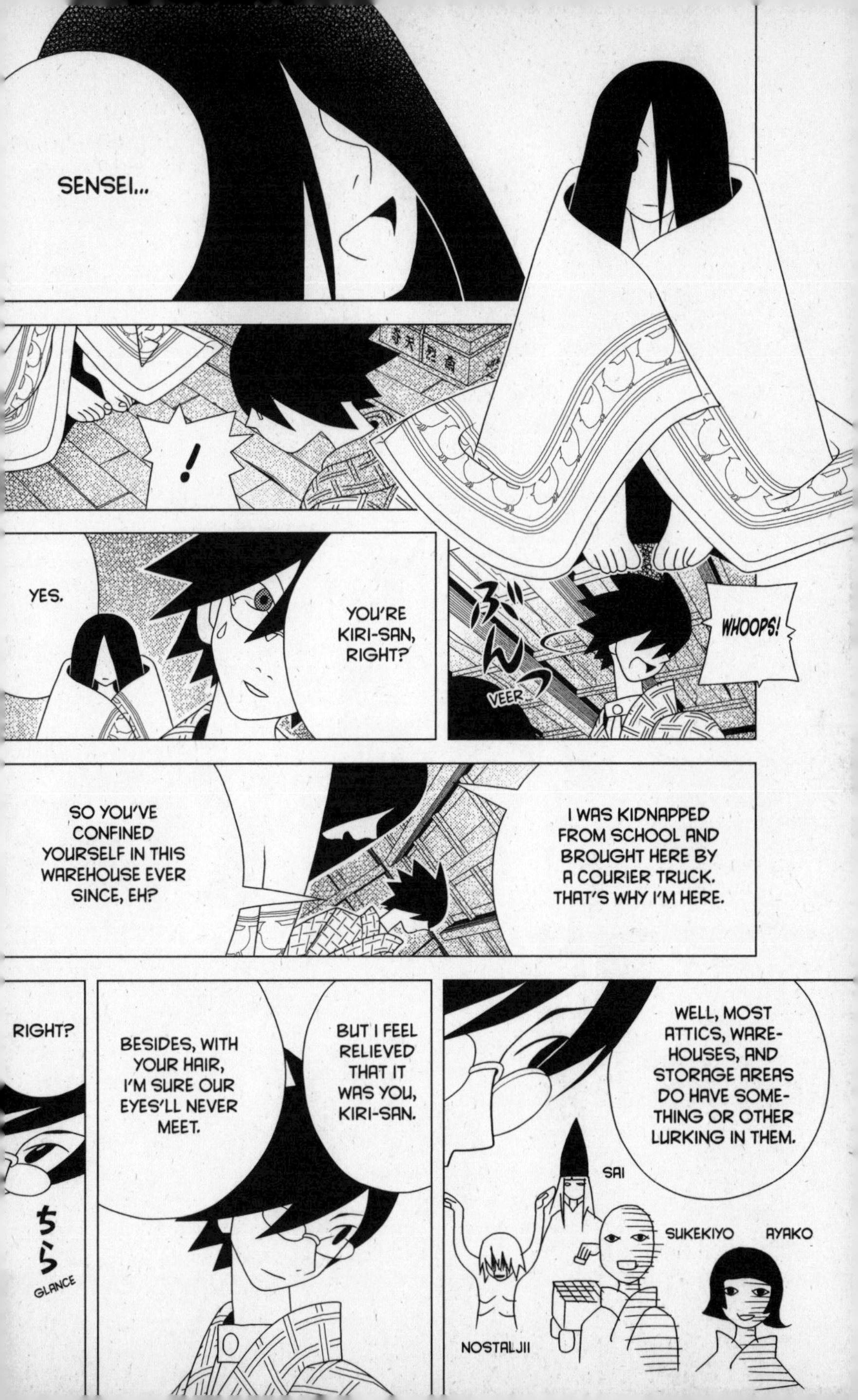
SENSEI...
!
WHOOPS!
ぶんっ
VEER
YOU'RE KIRI-SAN, RIGHT?
YES.
I WAS KIDNAPPED FROM SCHOOL AND BROUGHT HERE BY A COURIER TRUCK. THAT'S WHY I'M HERE.
SO YOU'VE CONFINED YOURSELF IN THIS WAREHOUSE EVER SINCE, EH?
WELL, MOST ATTICS, WARE-HOUSES, AND STORAGE AREAS DO HAVE SOME-THING OR OTHER LURKING IN THEM.
SAI
AYAKO
SUKEKIYO
NOSTALJII
BUT I FEEL RELIEVED THAT IT WAS YOU, KIRI-SAN.
BESIDES, WITH YOUR HAIR, I'M SURE OUR EYES'LL NEVER MEET.
RIGHT?
ちら
GLANCE

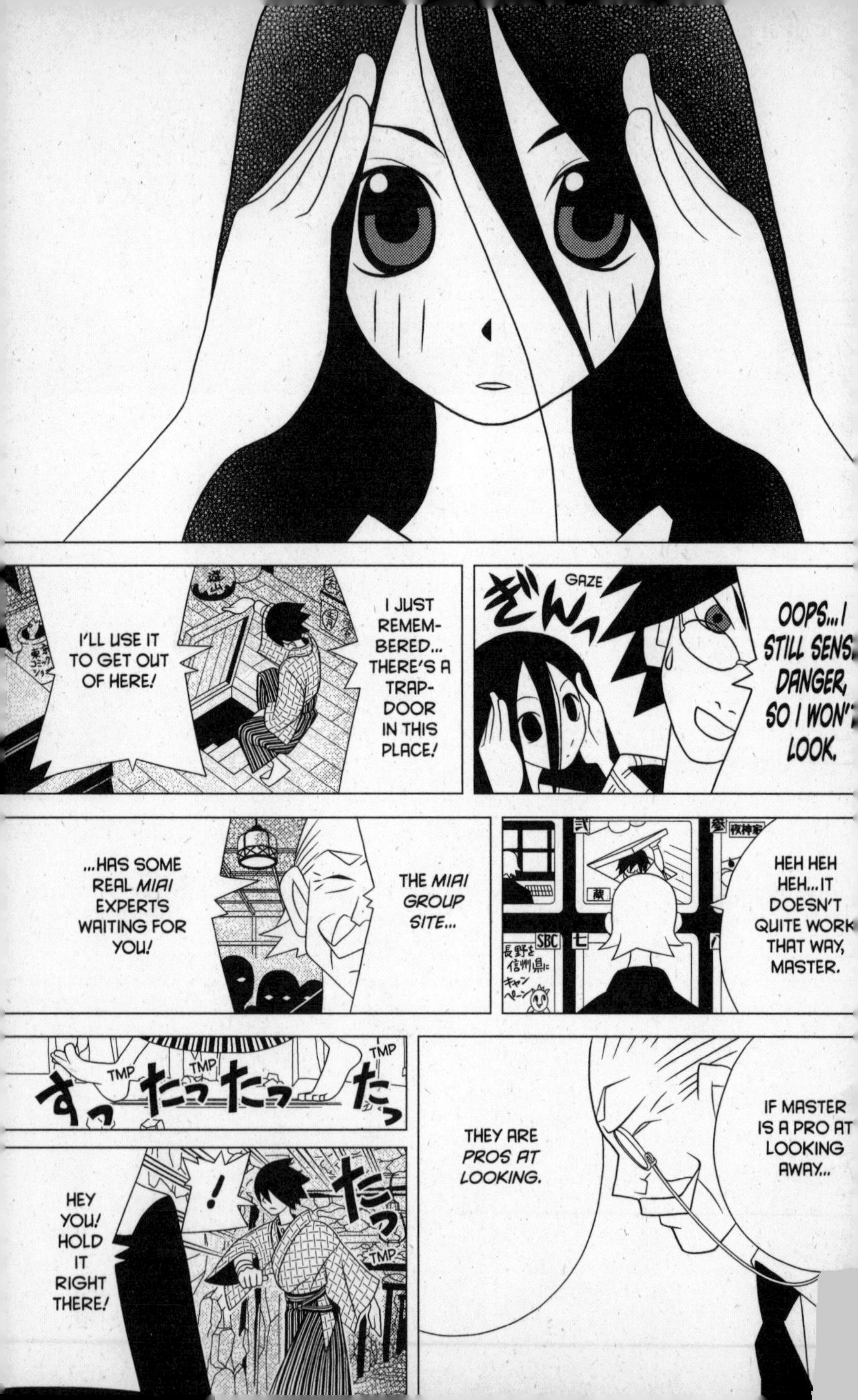
ぎん
GAZE
OOPS...I STILL SENS DANGER, SO I WON' LOOK.
I JUST REMEMBERED... THERE'S A TRAPDOOR IN THIS PLACE!
I'LL USE IT TO GET OUT OF HERE!
HEH HEH HEH...IT DOESN'T QUITE WORK THAT WAY, MASTER.
THE *MIAI* GROUP SITE...
...HAS SOME REAL *MIAI* EXPERTS WAITING FOR YOU!
IF MASTER IS A PRO AT LOOKING AWAY...
THEY ARE *PROS AT LOOKING.*
すっ
TMP
たっ
TMP
たっ
TMP
たっ
!
たっ
TMP
HEY YOU! HOLD IT RIGHT THERE!

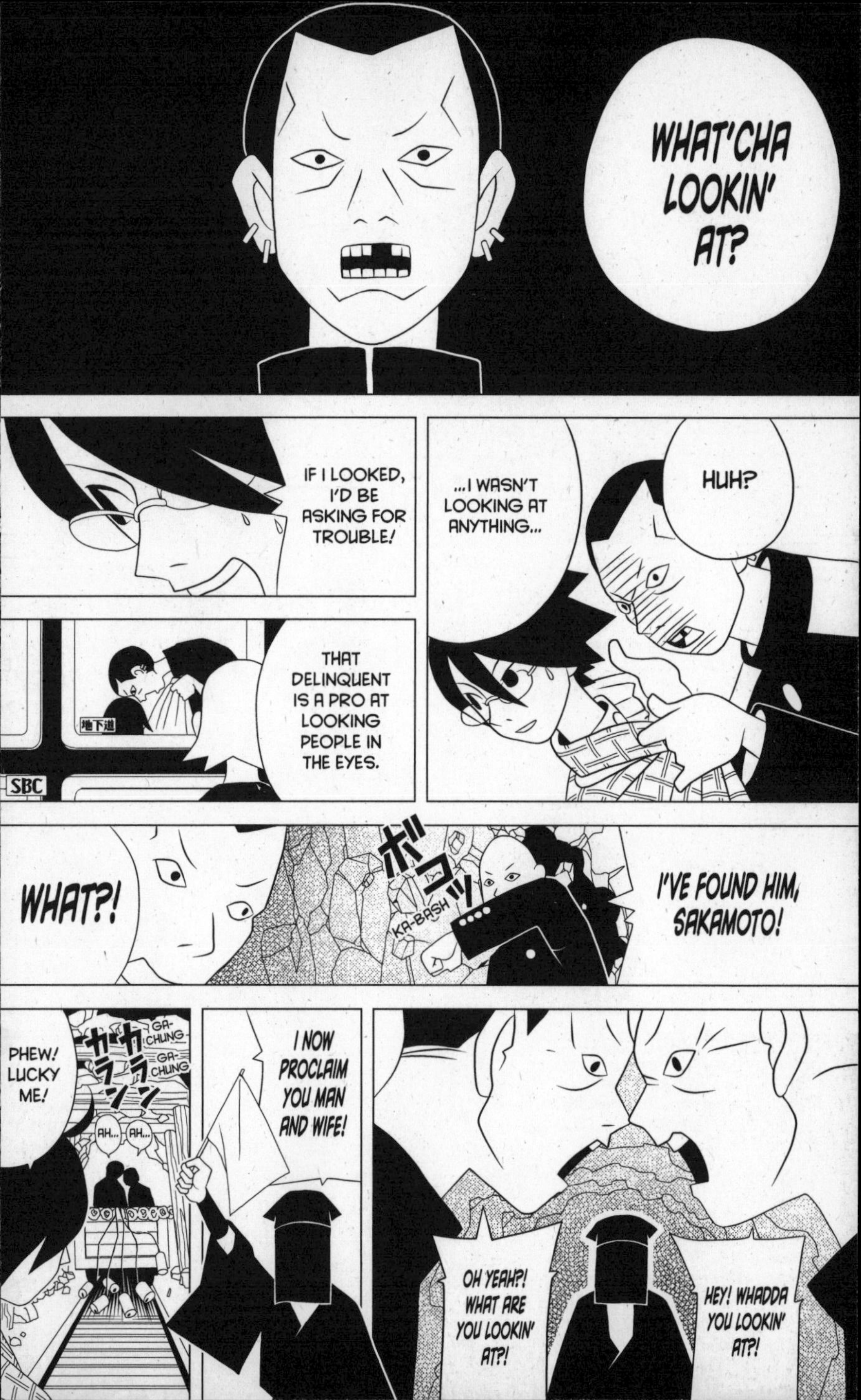
WHAT'CHA LOOKIN' AT?
HUH?
...I WASN'T LOOKING AT ANYTHING...
IF I LOOKED, I'D BE ASKING FOR TROUBLE!
THAT DELINQUENT IS A PRO AT LOOKING PEOPLE IN THE EYES.
地下道
SBC
I'VE FOUND HIM, SAKAMOTO!
ボコッ
KA-BASH
WHAT?!
HEY! WHADDA YOU LOOKIN' AT?!
OH YEAH?! WHAT ARE YOU LOOKIN' AT?!
I NOW PROCLAIM YOU MAN AND WIFE!
カラン
GA-CHUNG
カラン
GA-CHUNG
AH...
AH...
PHEW! LUCKY ME!

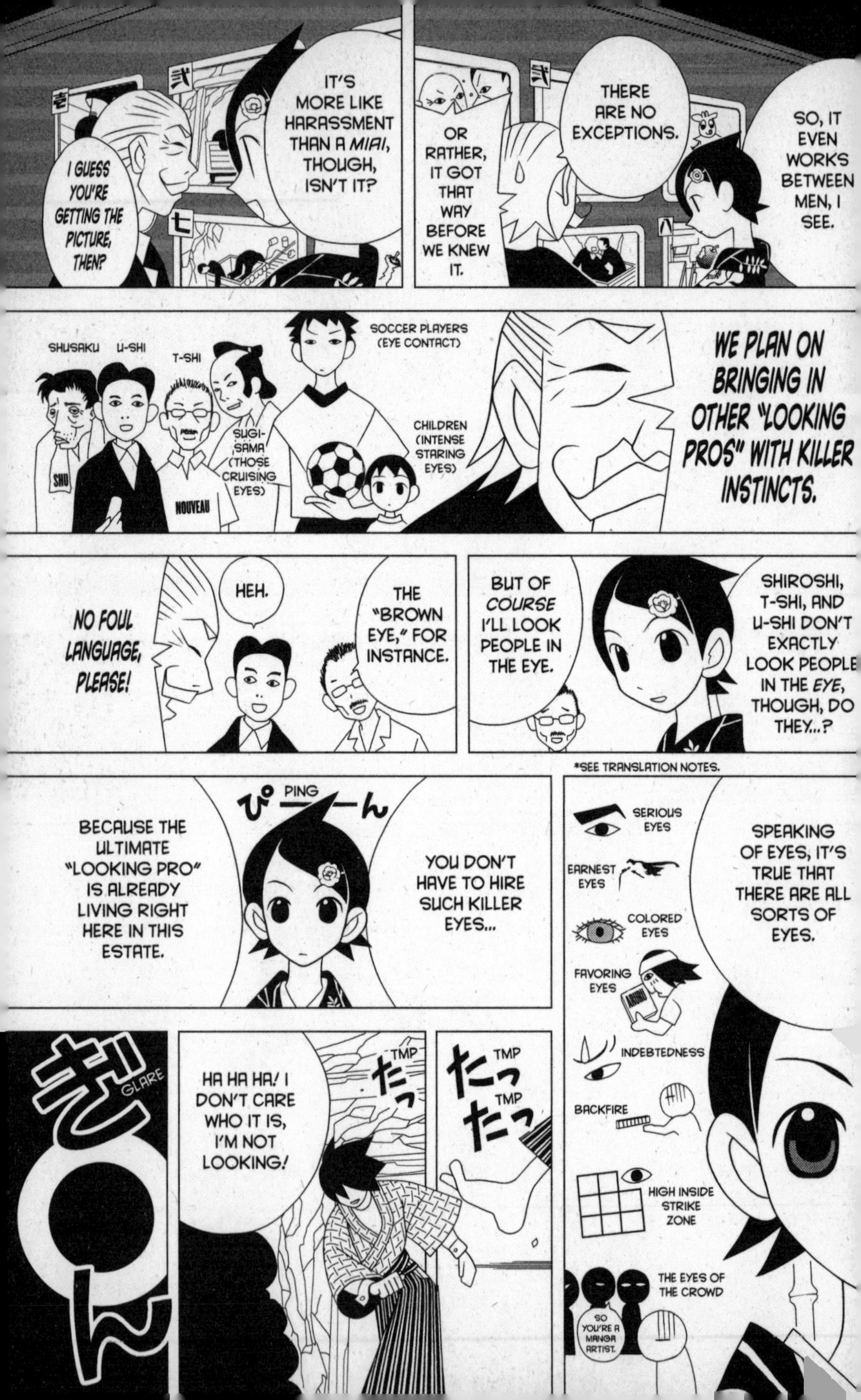

SO, IT EVEN WORKS BETWEEN MEN, I SEE.
THERE ARE NO EXCEPTIONS.
OR RATHER, IT GOT THAT WAY BEFORE WE KNEW IT.
IT'S MORE LIKE HARASSMENT THAN A *MIAI*, THOUGH, ISN'T IT?
I GUESS YOU'RE GETTING THE PICTURE, THEN?
WE PLAN ON BRINGING IN OTHER "LOOKING PROS" WITH KILLER INSTINCTS.
CHILDREN (INTENSE STARING EYES)
SOCCER PLAYERS (EYE CONTACT)
SUGI-SAMA (THOSE CRUISING EYES)
T-SHI
U-SHI
SHUSAKU
SHU
NOUVEAU
SHIROSHI, T-SHI, AND U-SHI DON'T EXACTLY LOOK PEOPLE IN THE *EYE*, THOUGH, DO THEY...?
BUT OF *COURSE* I'LL LOOK PEOPLE IN THE EYE.
THE "BROWN EYE," FOR INSTANCE.
HEH.
NO FOUL LANGUAGE, PLEASE!
*SEE TRANSLATION NOTES.
SPEAKING OF EYES, IT'S TRUE THAT THERE ARE ALL SORTS OF EYES.
SERIOUS EYES
EARNEST EYES
COLORED EYES
FAVORING EYES
INDEBTEDNESS
BACKFIRE
HIGH INSIDE STRIKE ZONE
THE EYES OF THE CROWD
SO YOU'RE A MANGA ARTIST.
YOU DON'T HAVE TO HIRE SUCH KILLER EYES...
ぴーーん PING
BECAUSE THE ULTIMATE "LOOKING PRO" IS ALREADY LIVING RIGHT HERE IN THIS ESTATE.
たっ TMP
たっ TMP
たっ TMP
HA HA HA! I DON'T CARE WHO IT IS, I'M NOT LOOKING!
ぎろん GLARE

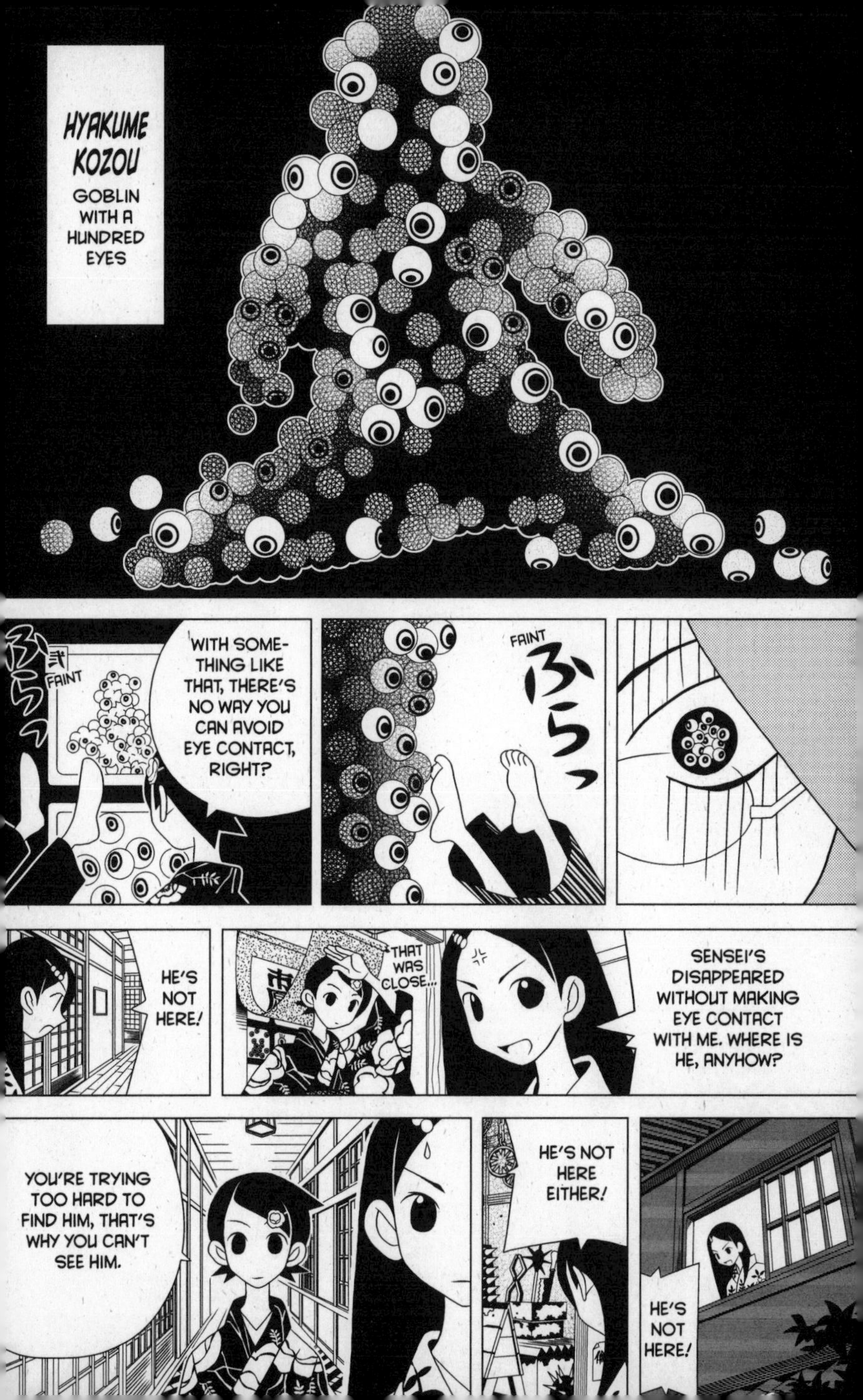
HYAKUME KOZOU
GOBLIN WITH A HUNDRED EYES
FAINT
ふらっ
WITH SOME-THING LIKE THAT, THERE'S NO WAY YOU CAN AVOID EYE CONTACT, RIGHT?
ふらっ
FAINT
SENSEI'S DISAPPEARED WITHOUT MAKING EYE CONTACT WITH ME. WHERE IS HE, ANYHOW?
THAT WAS CLOSE...
HE'S NOT HERE!
HE'S NOT HERE!
HE'S NOT HERE EITHER!
YOU'RE TRYING TOO HARD TO FIND HIM, THAT'S WHY YOU CAN'T SEE HIM.

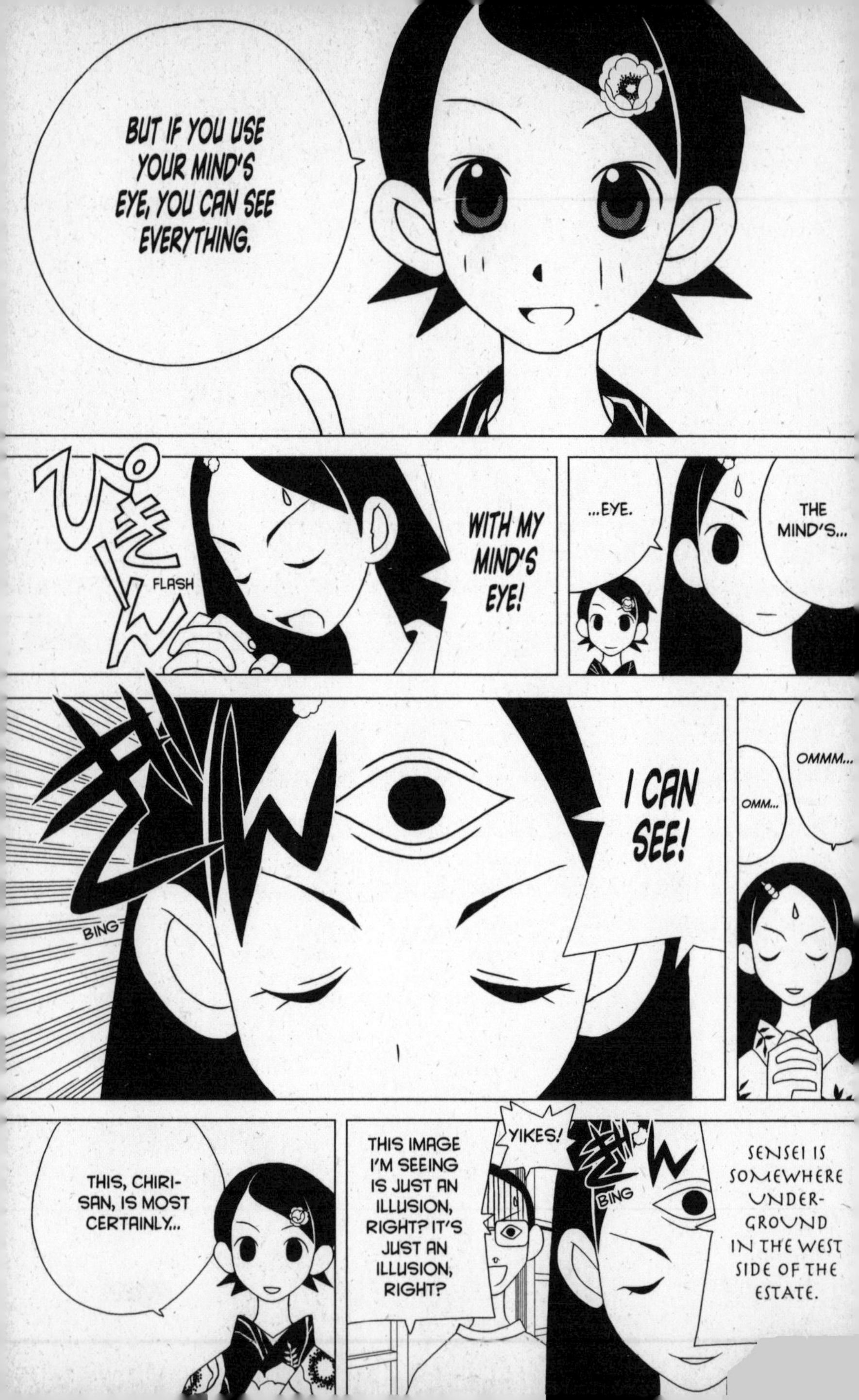

BUT IF YOU USE YOUR MIND'S EYE, YOU CAN SEE EVERYTHING.
THE MIND'S...
...EYE.
WITH MY MIND'S EYE!
FLASH
OMMM...
OMM...
I CAN SEE!
BING
SENSEI IS SOMEWHERE UNDER-GROUND IN THE WEST SIDE OF THE ESTATE.
BING
YIKES!
THIS IMAGE I'M SEEING IS JUST AN ILLUSION, RIGHT? IT'S JUST AN ILLUSION, RIGHT?
THIS, CHIRI-SAN, IS MOST CERTAINLY...

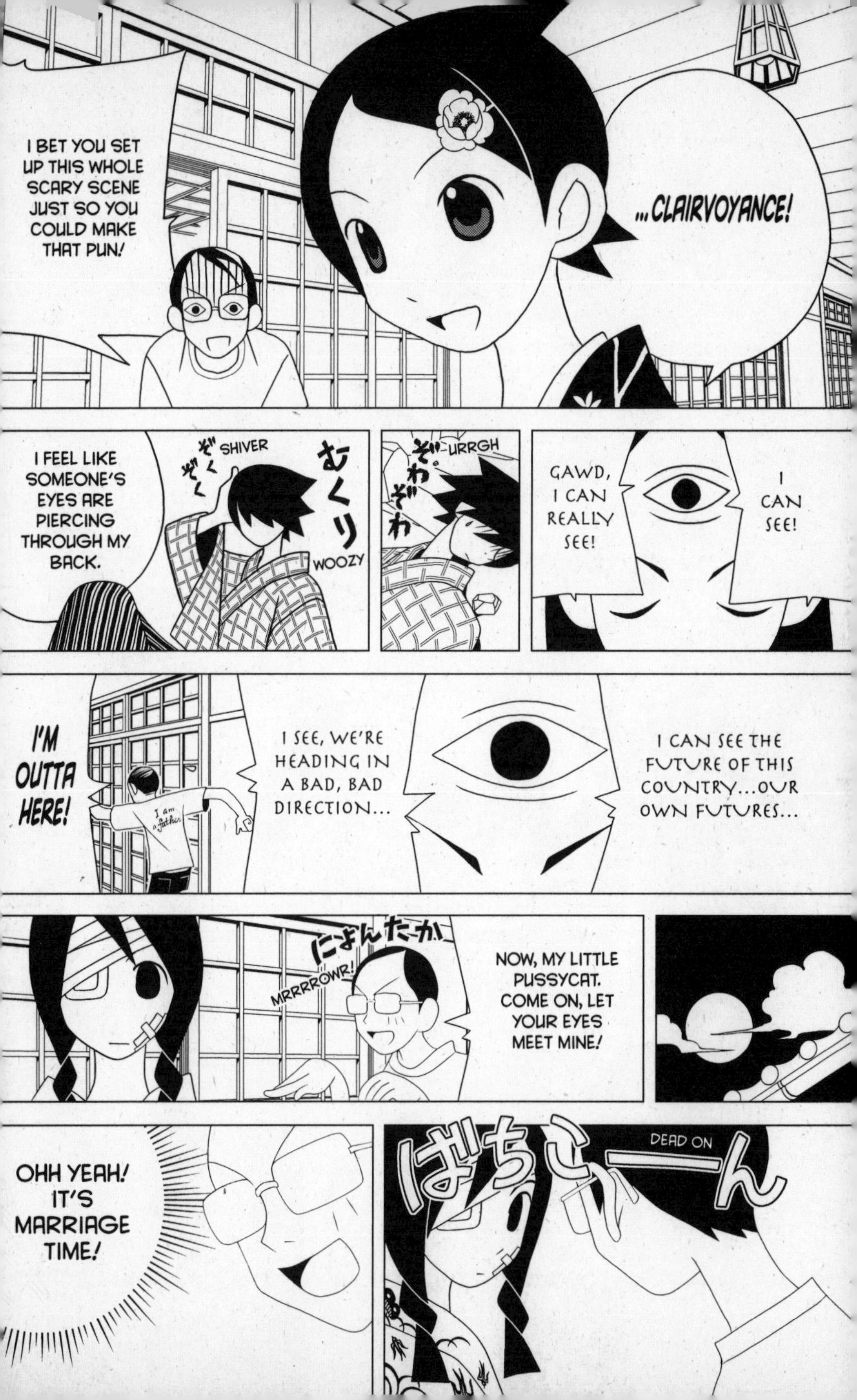
...CLAIRVOYANCE!
I BET YOU SET UP THIS WHOLE SCARY SCENE JUST SO YOU COULD MAKE THAT PUN!
I CAN SEE!
GAWD, I CAN REALLY SEE!
ざわざわ
URRGH
むくり
WOOZY
ぞくぞく
SHIVER
I FEEL LIKE SOMEONE'S EYES ARE PIERCING THROUGH MY BACK.
I CAN SEE THE FUTURE OF THIS COUNTRY...OUR OWN FUTURES...
I SEE, WE'RE HEADING IN A BAD, BAD DIRECTION...
I am a father
I'M OUTTA HERE!
NOW, MY LITTLE PUSSYCAT. COME ON, LET YOUR EYES MEET MINE!
にょんたか
MRRRROWR!
ぱちこーん
DEAD ON
OHH YEAH! IT'S MARRIAGE TIME!

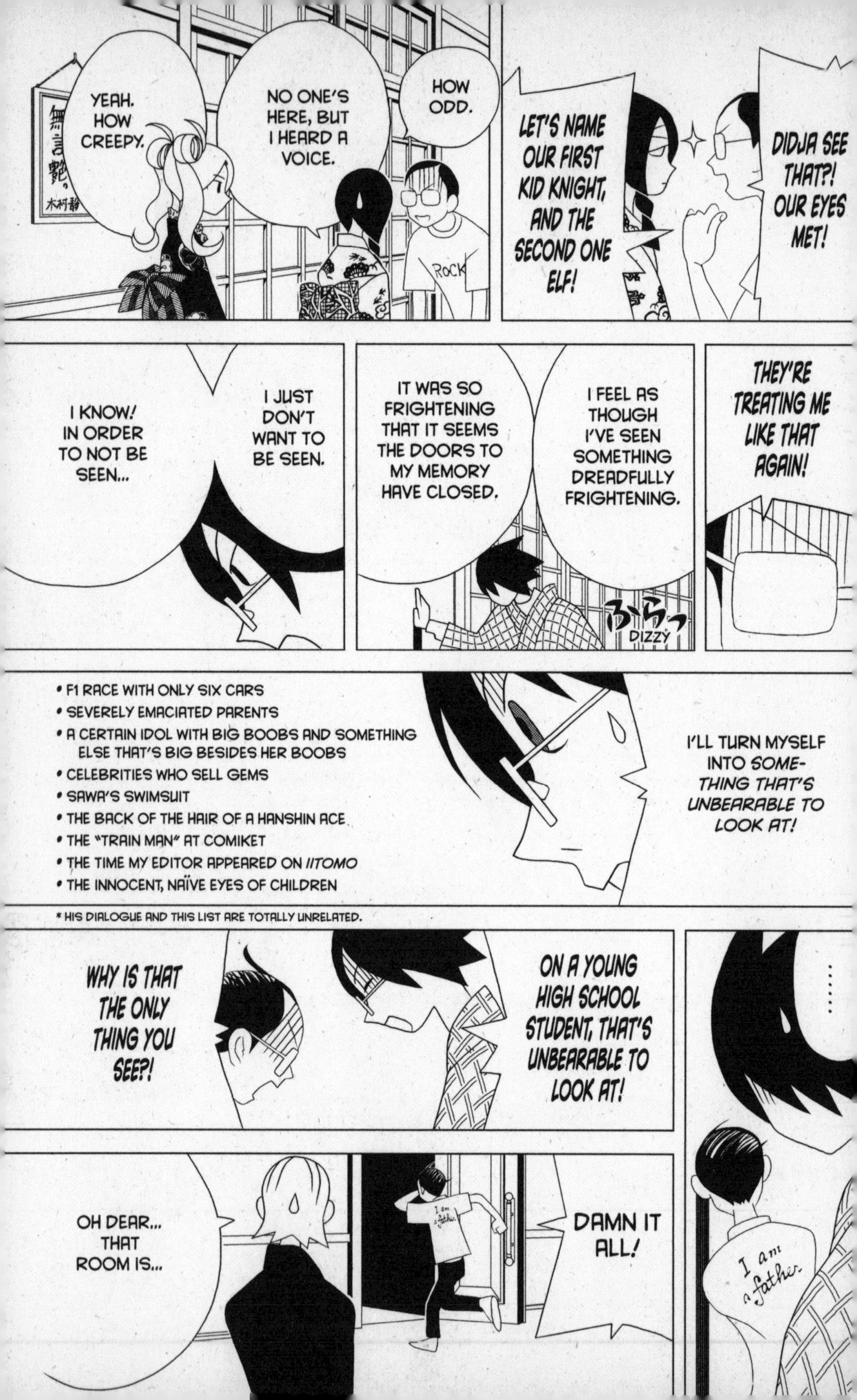
DIDJA SEE THAT?! OUR EYES MET!
LET'S NAME OUR FIRST KID KNIGHT, AND THE SECOND ONE ELF!
HOW ODD.
NO ONE'S HERE, BUT I HEARD A VOICE.
YEAH. HOW CREEPY.
ROCK
THEY'RE TREATING ME LIKE THAT AGAIN!
I FEEL AS THOUGH I'VE SEEN SOMETHING DREADFULLY FRIGHTENING.
IT WAS SO FRIGHTENING THAT IT SEEMS THE DOORS TO MY MEMORY HAVE CLOSED.
ふらっ DIZZY
I JUST DON'T WANT TO BE SEEN.
I KNOW! IN ORDER TO NOT BE SEEN...
I'LL TURN MYSELF INTO SOMETHING THAT'S UNBEARABLE TO LOOK AT!
• F1 RACE WITH ONLY SIX CARS
• SEVERELY EMACIATED PARENTS
• A CERTAIN IDOL WITH BIG BOOBS AND SOMETHING ELSE THAT'S BIG BESIDES HER BOOBS
• CELEBRITIES WHO SELL GEMS
• SAWA'S SWIMSUIT
• THE BACK OF THE HAIR OF A HANSHIN ACE
• THE "TRAIN MAN" AT COMIKET
• THE TIME MY EDITOR APPEARED ON IITOMO
• THE INNOCENT, NAÏVE EYES OF CHILDREN
* HIS DIALOGUE AND THIS LIST ARE TOTALLY UNRELATED.
......
I am a father.
ON A YOUNG HIGH SCHOOL STUDENT, THAT'S UNBEARABLE TO LOOK AT!
WHY IS THAT THE ONLY THING YOU SEE?!
DAMN IT ALL!
I am a father.
OH DEAR... THAT ROOM IS...

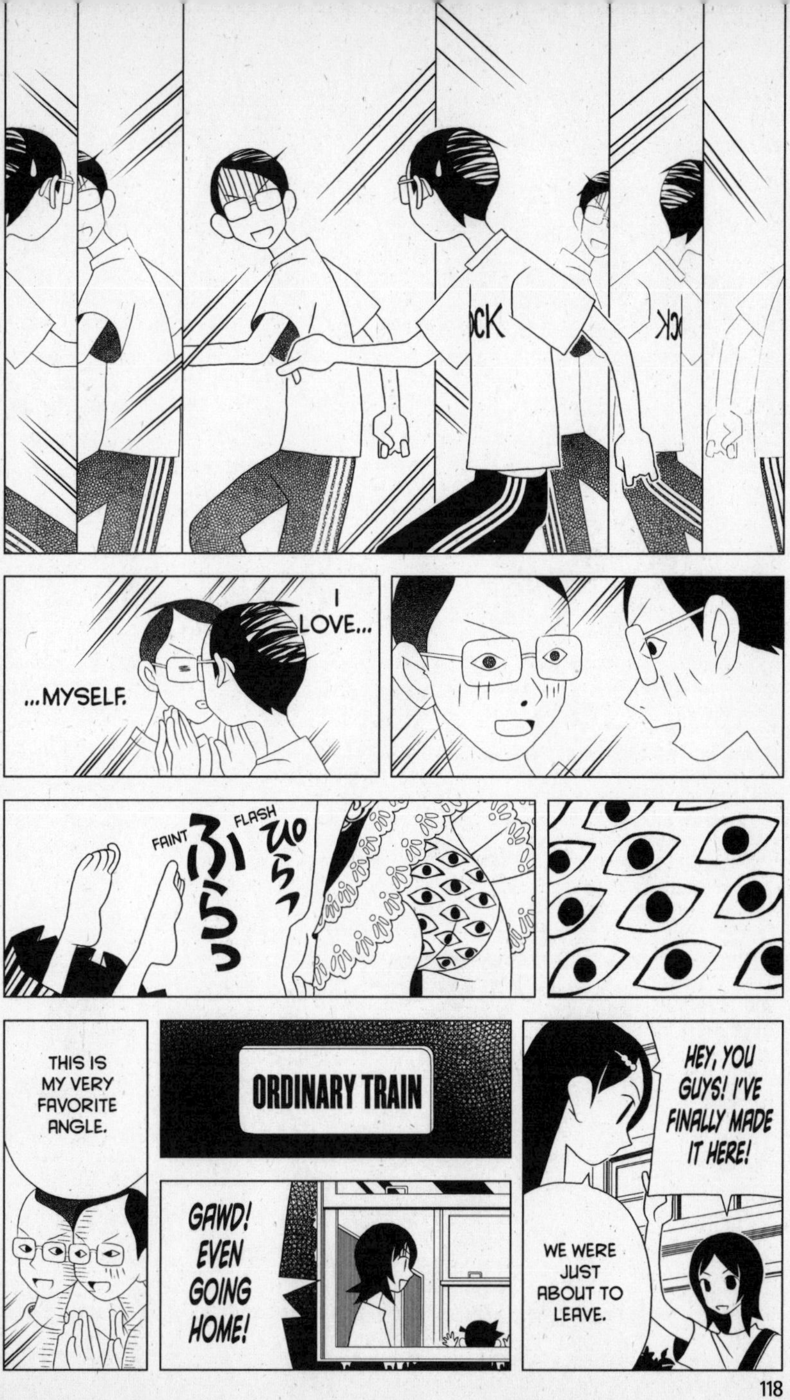

I LOVE...
...MYSELF.
FLASH ひらっ
FAINT ふらっ
HEY, YOU GUYS! I'VE FINALLY MADE IT HERE!
WE WERE JUST ABOUT TO LEAVE.
ORDINARY TRAIN
GAWD! EVEN GOING HOME!
THIS IS MY VERY FAVORITE ANGLE.

MEANWHILE, FUJIYOSHI-SAN...

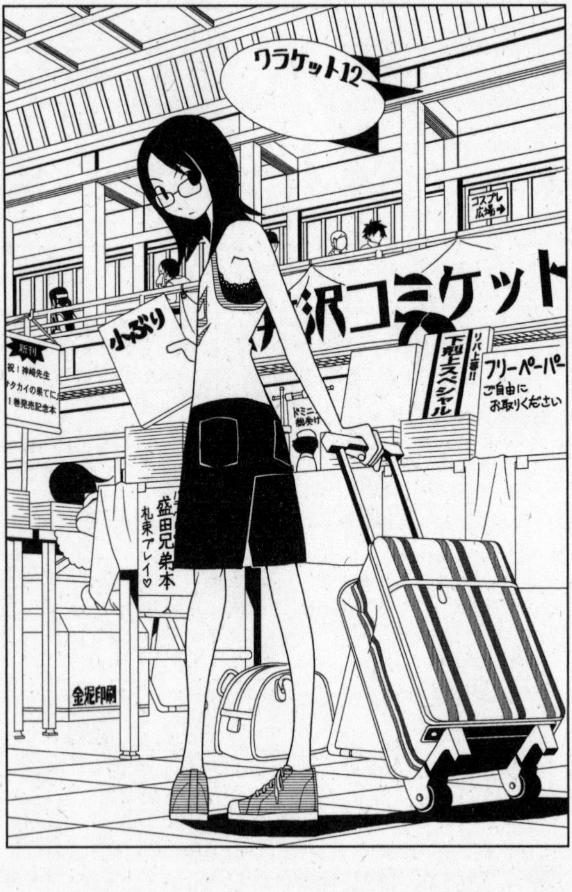
ワラケット12
コスプレ広場➜
沢コミケット
フリーペーパー
ご自由にお取りください
リバ上等!!
下剋上スペシャル
小ぶり
新刊
祝！神崎先生
盛田兄弟本
札束プレイ♡
金泥印刷

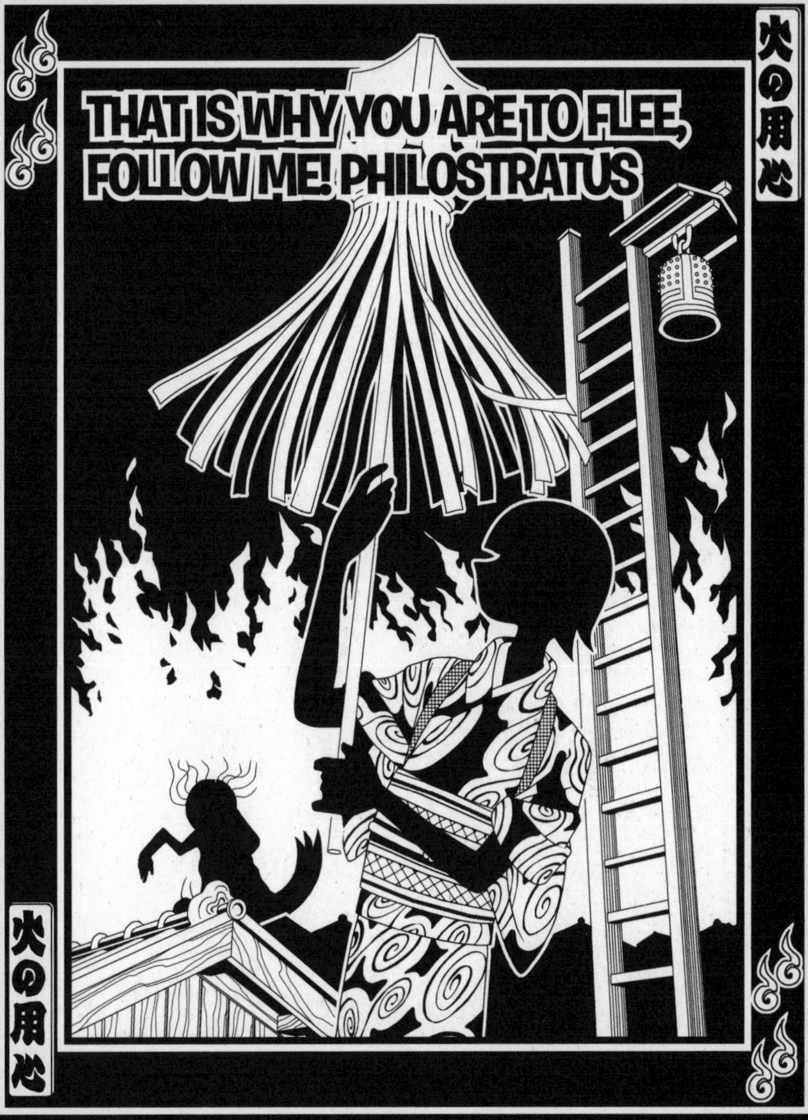
火の用心
THAT IS WHY YOU ARE TO FLEE, FOLLOW ME! PHILOSTRATUS
火の用心

# CHAPTER 19

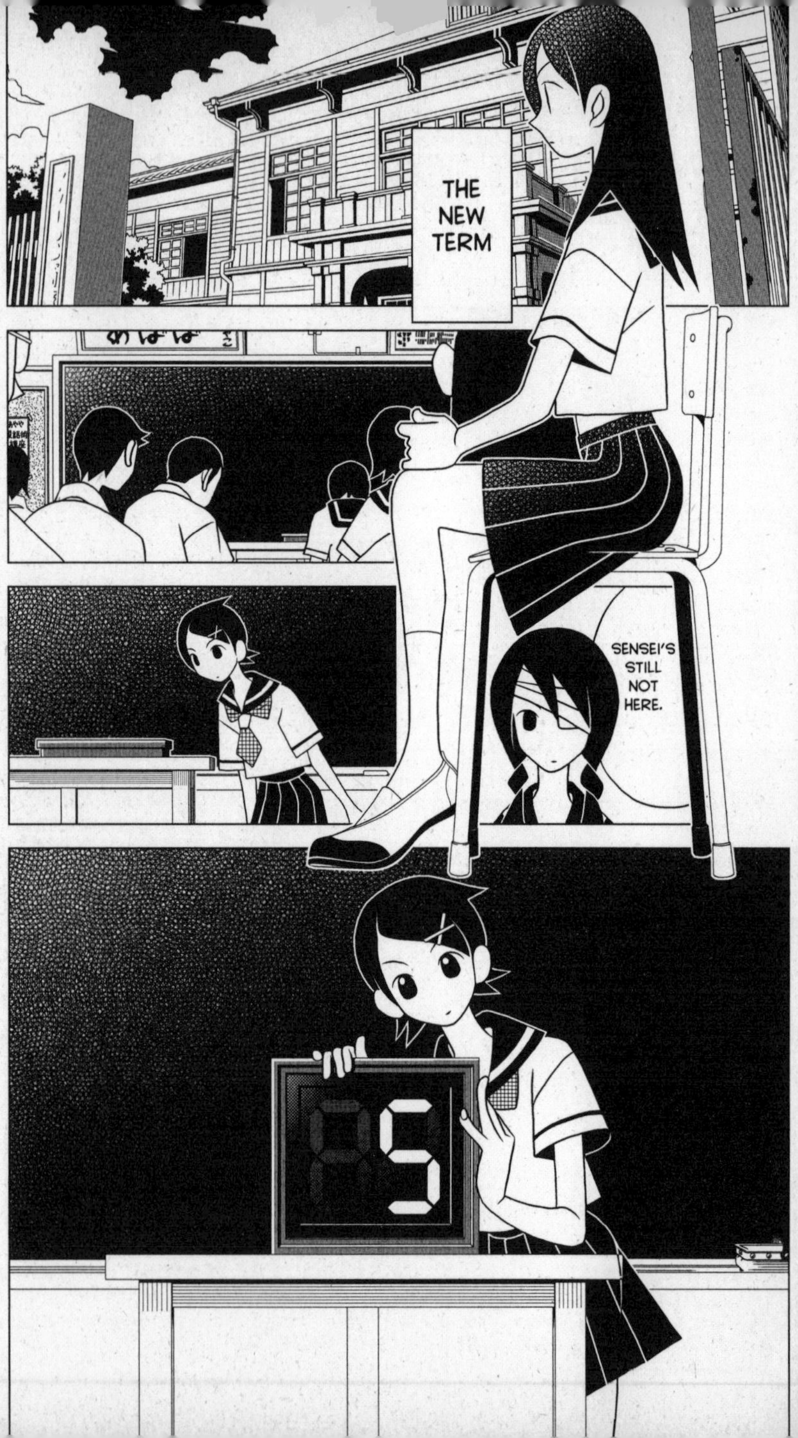
THE NEW TERM
SENSEI'S STILL NOT HERE.

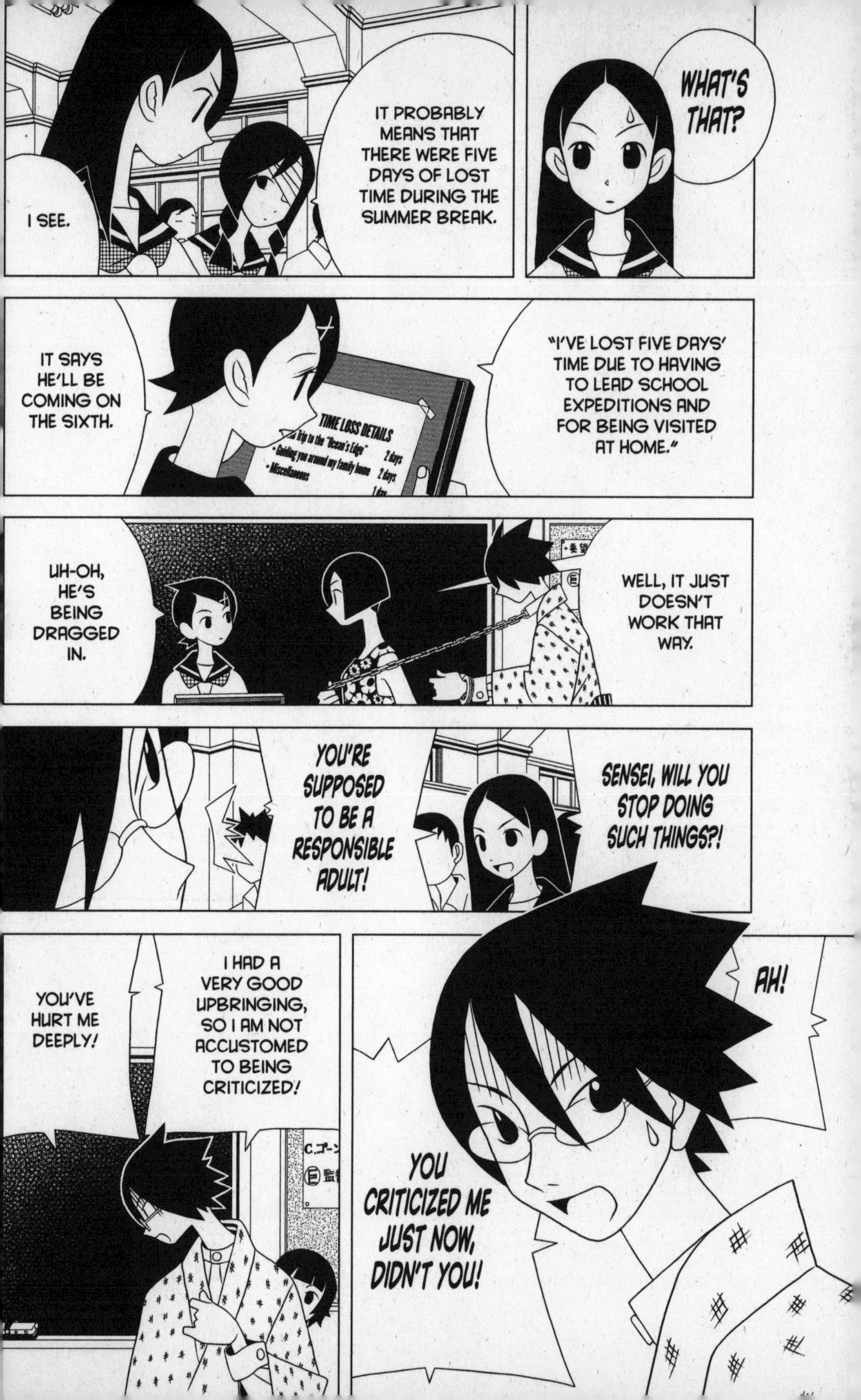
WHAT'S THAT?
IT PROBABLY MEANS THAT THERE WERE FIVE DAYS OF LOST TIME DURING THE SUMMER BREAK.
I SEE.
"I'VE LOST FIVE DAYS' TIME DUE TO HAVING TO LEAD SCHOOL EXPEDITIONS AND FOR BEING VISITED AT HOME."
TIME LOSS DETAILS
• Guiding you around my family home 2 days
• Miscellaneous
IT SAYS HE'LL BE COMING ON THE SIXTH.
WELL, IT JUST DOESN'T WORK THAT WAY.
UH-OH, HE'S BEING DRAGGED IN.
SENSEI, WILL YOU STOP DOING SUCH THINGS?!
YOU'RE SUPPOSED TO BE A RESPONSIBLE ADULT!
AH!
YOU CRITICIZED ME JUST NOW, DIDN'T YOU!
I HAD A VERY GOOD UPBRINGING, SO I AM NOT ACCUSTOMED TO BEING CRITICIZED!
YOU'VE HURT ME DEEPLY!

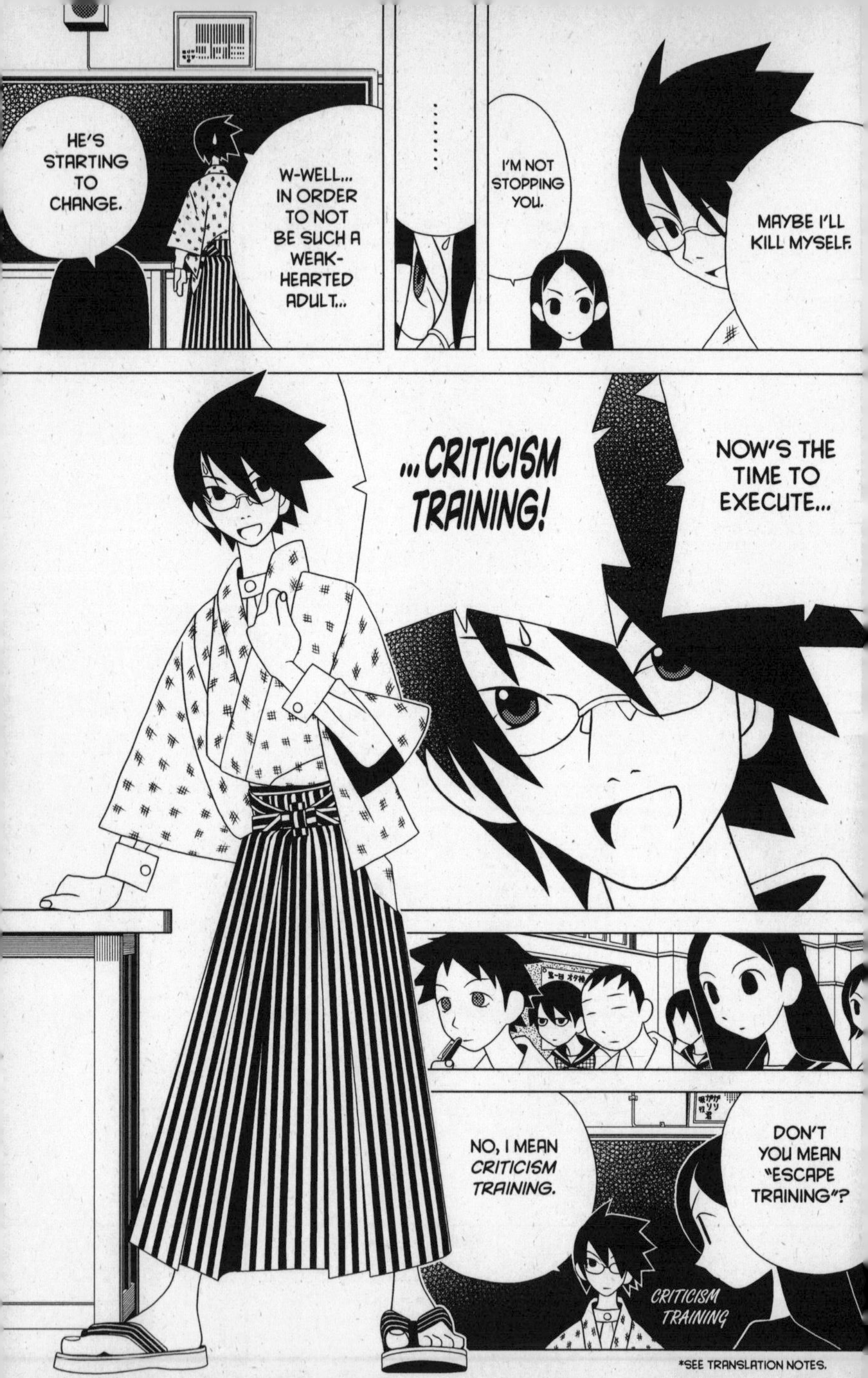
MAYBE I'LL KILL MYSELF.
I'M NOT STOPPING YOU.
......
W-WELL... IN ORDER TO NOT BE SUCH A WEAK-HEARTED ADULT...
HE'S STARTING TO CHANGE.
NOW'S THE TIME TO EXECUTE...
...CRITICISM TRAINING!
DON'T YOU MEAN "ESCAPE TRAINING"?
NO, I MEAN *CRITICISM TRAINING.*
*CRITICISM TRAINING*

*SEE TRANSLATION NOTES.

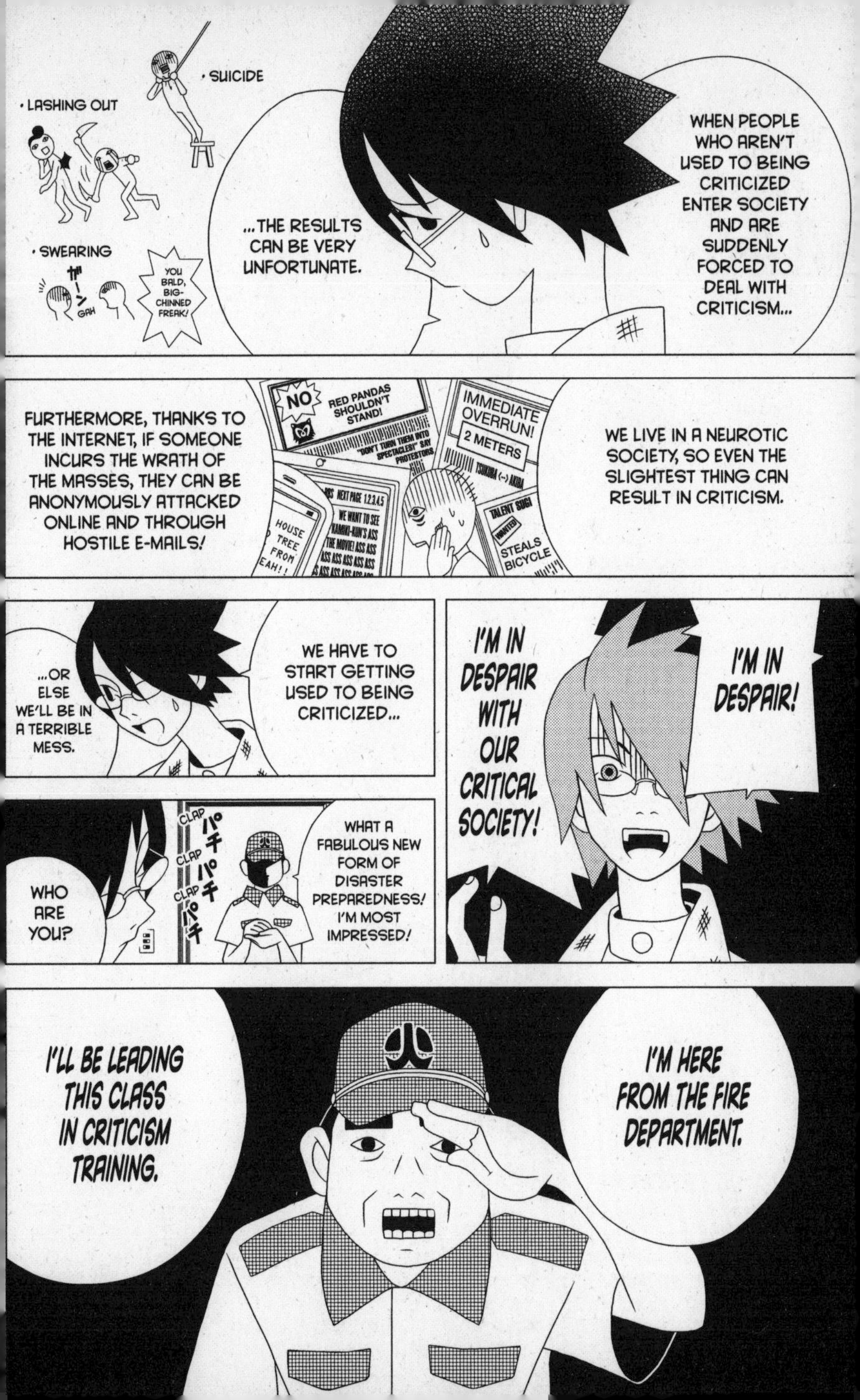
WHEN PEOPLE WHO AREN'T USED TO BEING CRITICIZED ENTER SOCIETY AND ARE SUDDENLY FORCED TO DEAL WITH CRITICISM...
...THE RESULTS CAN BE VERY UNFORTUNATE.
• SUICIDE
• LASHING OUT
• SWEARING
YOU BALD, BIG-CHINNED FREAK!
GAH
WE LIVE IN A NEUROTIC SOCIETY, SO EVEN THE SLIGHTEST THING CAN RESULT IN CRITICISM.
IMMEDIATE OVERRUN!
2 METERS
TSUKUBA (~) AKIBA
NO
RED PANDAS SHOULDN'T STAND!
"DON'T TURN THEM INTO SPECTACLES!" SAY PROTESTORS
TALENT SUGI
WANTED
STEALS BICYCLE
BBS NEXT PAGE 1.2.3.4.5
WE WANT TO SEE KAMIKI-KUN'S ASS THE MOVIE! ASS ASS ASS ASS ASS ASS
HOUSE TREE FROM
FURTHERMORE, THANKS TO THE INTERNET, IF SOMEONE INCURS THE WRATH OF THE MASSES, THEY CAN BE ANONYMOUSLY ATTACKED ONLINE AND THROUGH HOSTILE E-MAILS!
I'M IN DESPAIR!
I'M IN DESPAIR WITH OUR CRITICAL SOCIETY!
WE HAVE TO START GETTING USED TO BEING CRITICIZED...
...OR ELSE WE'LL BE IN A TERRIBLE MESS.
WHAT A FABULOUS NEW FORM OF DISASTER PREPAREDNESS! I'M MOST IMPRESSED!
CLAP パチ CLAP パチ CLAP パチ
WHO ARE YOU?
I'M HERE FROM THE FIRE DEPARTMENT.
I'LL BE LEADING THIS CLASS IN CRITICISM TRAINING.

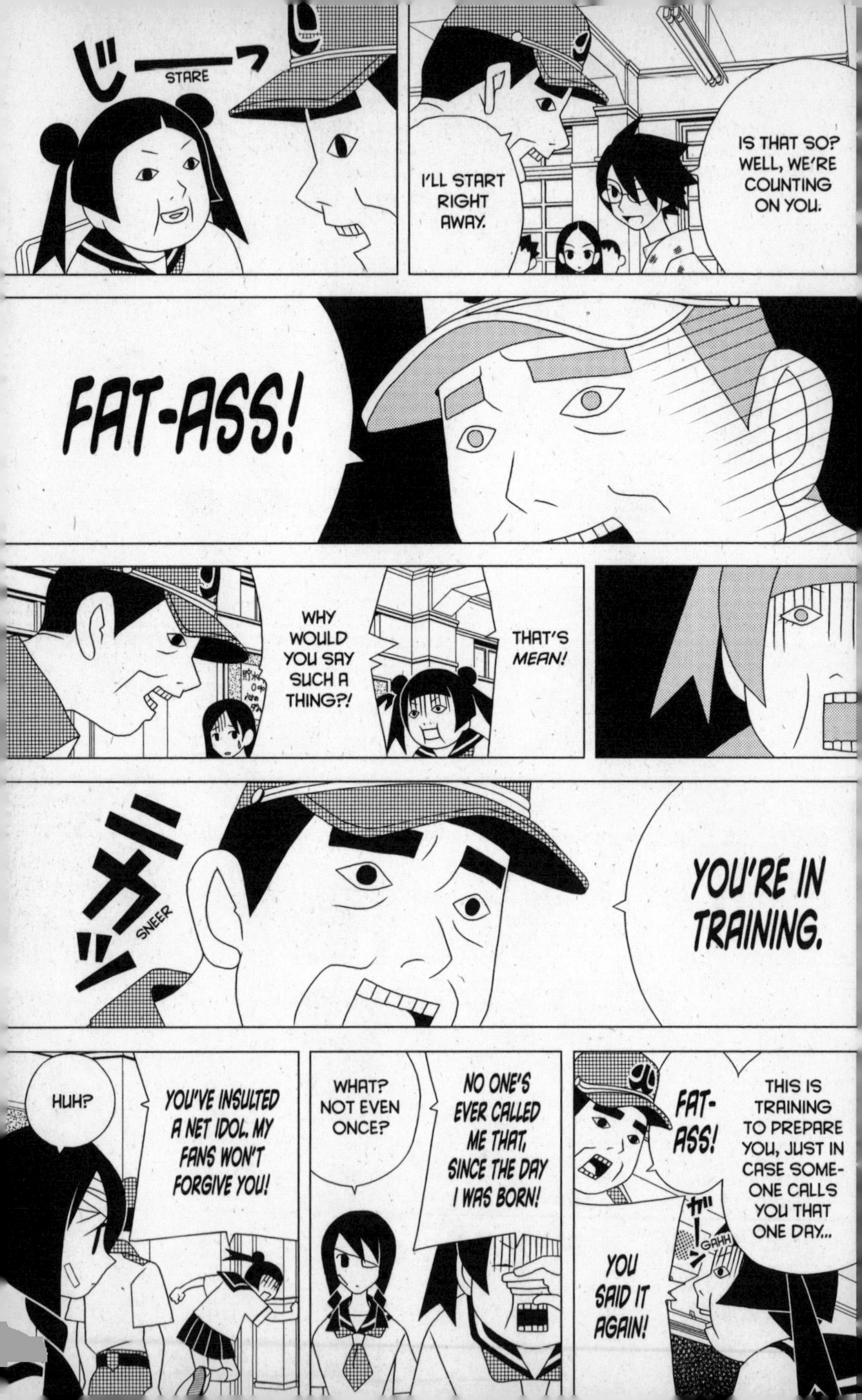
IS THAT SO? WELL, WE'RE COUNTING ON YOU.
I'LL START RIGHT AWAY.
STARE
FAT-ASS!
THAT'S MEAN!
WHY WOULD YOU SAY SUCH A THING?!
YOU'RE IN TRAINING.
SNEER
THIS IS TRAINING TO PREPARE YOU, JUST IN CASE SOME-ONE CALLS YOU THAT ONE DAY...
FAT-ASS!
GAHH
YOU SAID IT AGAIN!
NO ONE'S EVER CALLED ME THAT, SINCE THE DAY I WAS BORN!
WHAT? NOT EVEN ONCE?
YOU'VE INSULTED A NET IDOL. MY FANS WON'T FORGIVE YOU!
HUH?

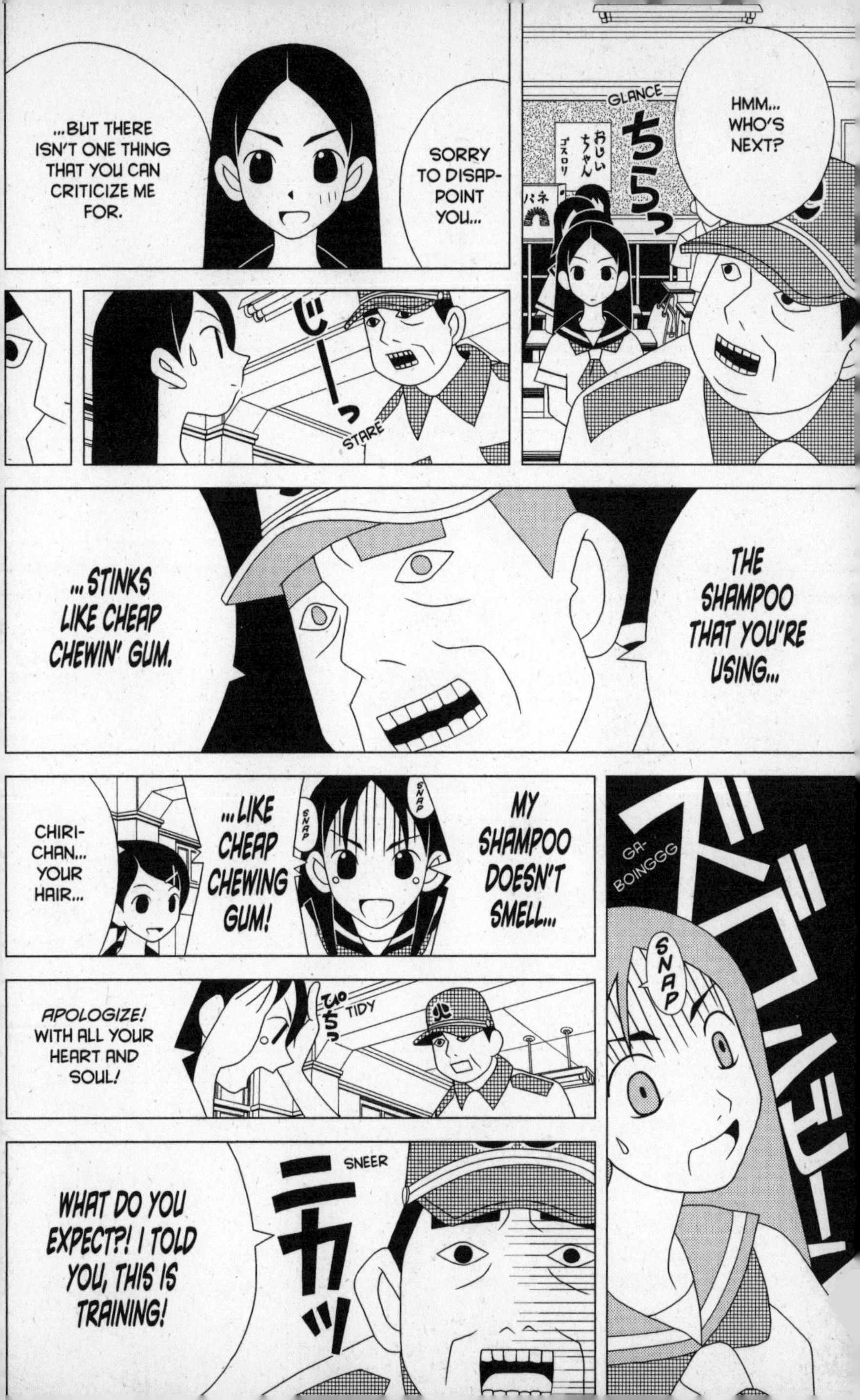
HMM... WHO'S NEXT?
GLANCE
ちらっ
おじいちゃん
ゴスロリ
バネ
SORRY TO DISAPPOINT YOU...
...BUT THERE ISN'T ONE THING THAT YOU CAN CRITICIZE ME FOR.
じーっ
STARE
THE SHAMPOO THAT YOU'RE USING...
...STINKS LIKE CHEAP CHEWIN' GUM.
GA-BOINGGG
SNAP
MY SHAMPOO DOESN'T SMELL...
SNAP
SNAP
...LIKE CHEAP CHEWING GUM!
CHIRI-CHAN... YOUR HAIR...
ぴっちっ
TIDY
APOLOGIZE! WITH ALL YOUR HEART AND SOUL!
テカッ
SNEER
WHAT DO YOU EXPECT?! I TOLD YOU, THIS IS TRAINING!

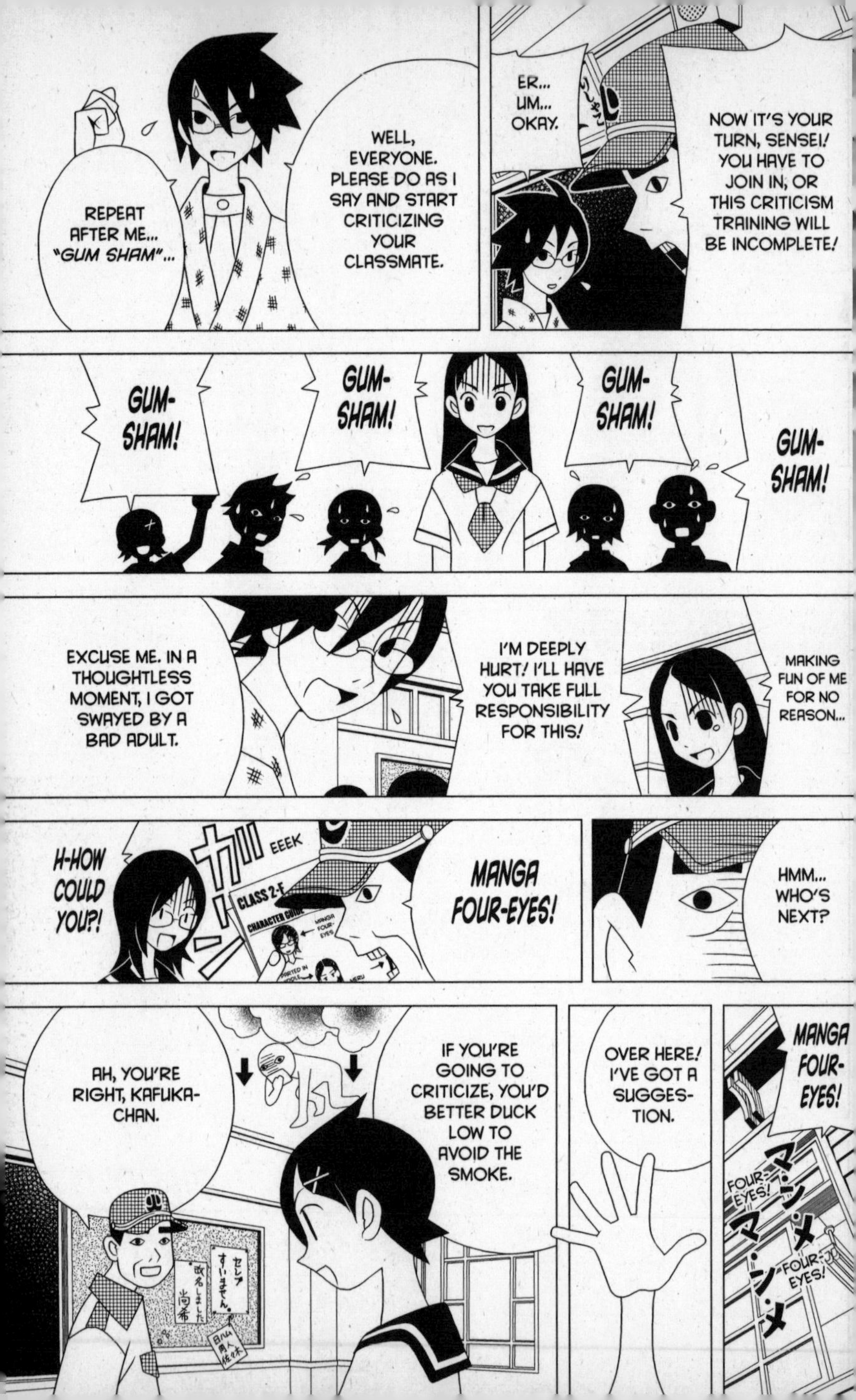
NOW IT'S YOUR TURN, SENSEI! YOU HAVE TO JOIN IN, OR THIS CRITICISM TRAINING WILL BE INCOMPLETE!
ER... UM... OKAY.
WELL, EVERYONE. PLEASE DO AS I SAY AND START CRITICIZING YOUR CLASSMATE.
REPEAT AFTER ME... "GUM SHAM"...
GUM-SHAM!
GUM-SHAM!
GUM-SHAM!
GUM-SHAM!
MAKING FUN OF ME FOR NO REASON...
I'M DEEPLY HURT! I'LL HAVE YOU TAKE FULL RESPONSIBILITY FOR THIS!
EXCUSE ME. IN A THOUGHTLESS MOMENT, I GOT SWAYED BY A BAD ADULT.
HMM... WHO'S NEXT?
MANGA FOUR-EYES!
CLASS 2-F
CHARACTER GUIDE
EEEK
H-HOW COULD YOU?!
MANGA FOUR-EYES!
FOUR-EYES!
FOUR-EYES!
OVER HERE! I'VE GOT A SUGGESTION.
IF YOU'RE GOING TO CRITICIZE, YOU'D BETTER DUCK LOW TO AVOID THE SMOKE.
AH, YOU'RE RIGHT, KAFUKA-CHAN.

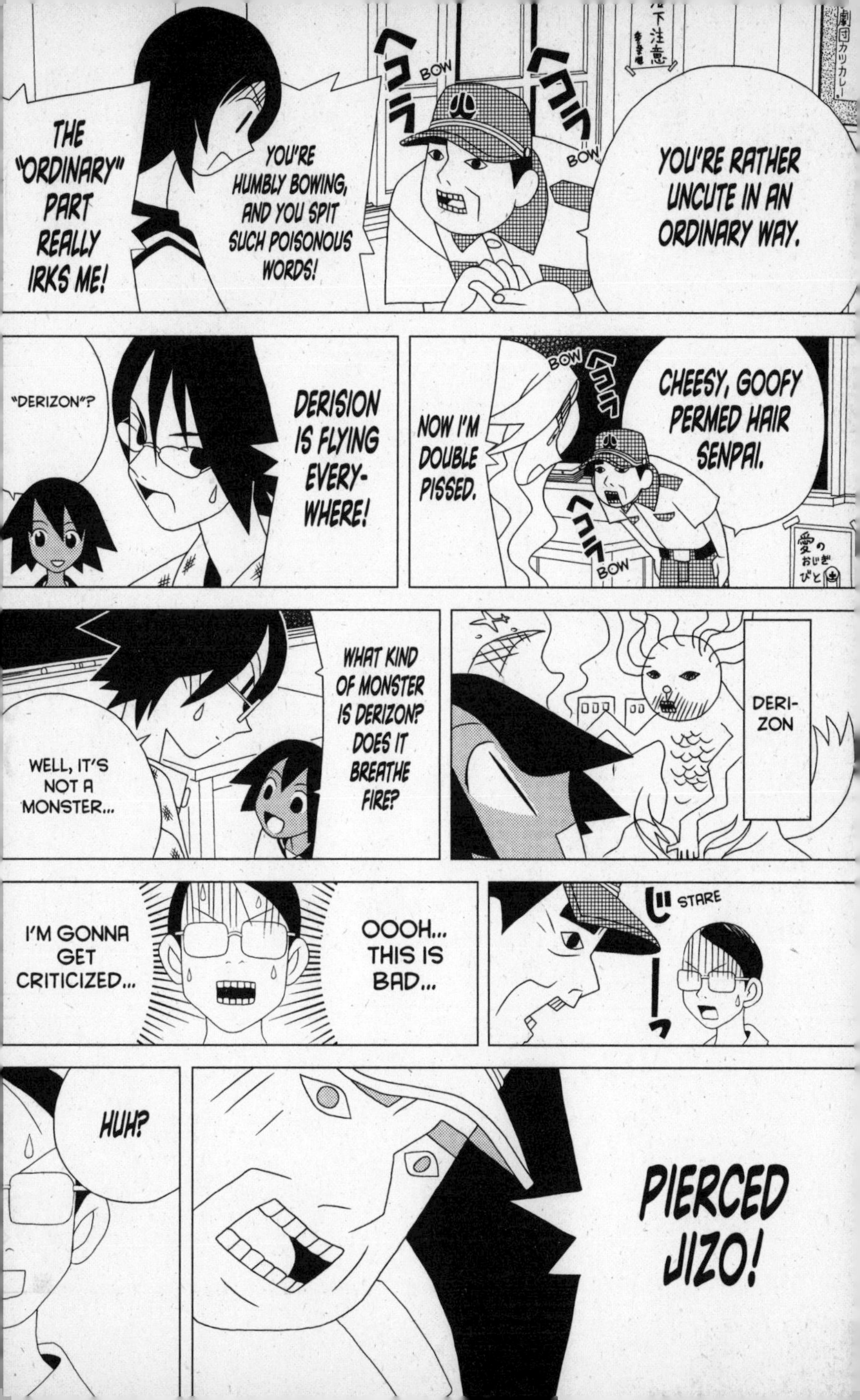
YOU'RE RATHER UNCUTE IN AN ORDINARY WAY.
BOW
BOW
YOU'RE HUMBLY BOWING, AND YOU SPIT SUCH POISONOUS WORDS!
THE "ORDINARY" PART REALLY IRKS ME!
CHEESY, GOOFY PERMED HAIR SENPAI.
BOW
BOW
NOW I'M DOUBLE PISSED.
DERISION IS FLYING EVERY-WHERE!
"DERIZON"?
DERI-ZON
WHAT KIND OF MONSTER IS DERIZON? DOES IT BREATHE FIRE?
WELL, IT'S NOT A MONSTER...
STARE
OOOH... THIS IS BAD...
I'M GONNA GET CRITICIZED...
PIERCED JIZO!
HUH?

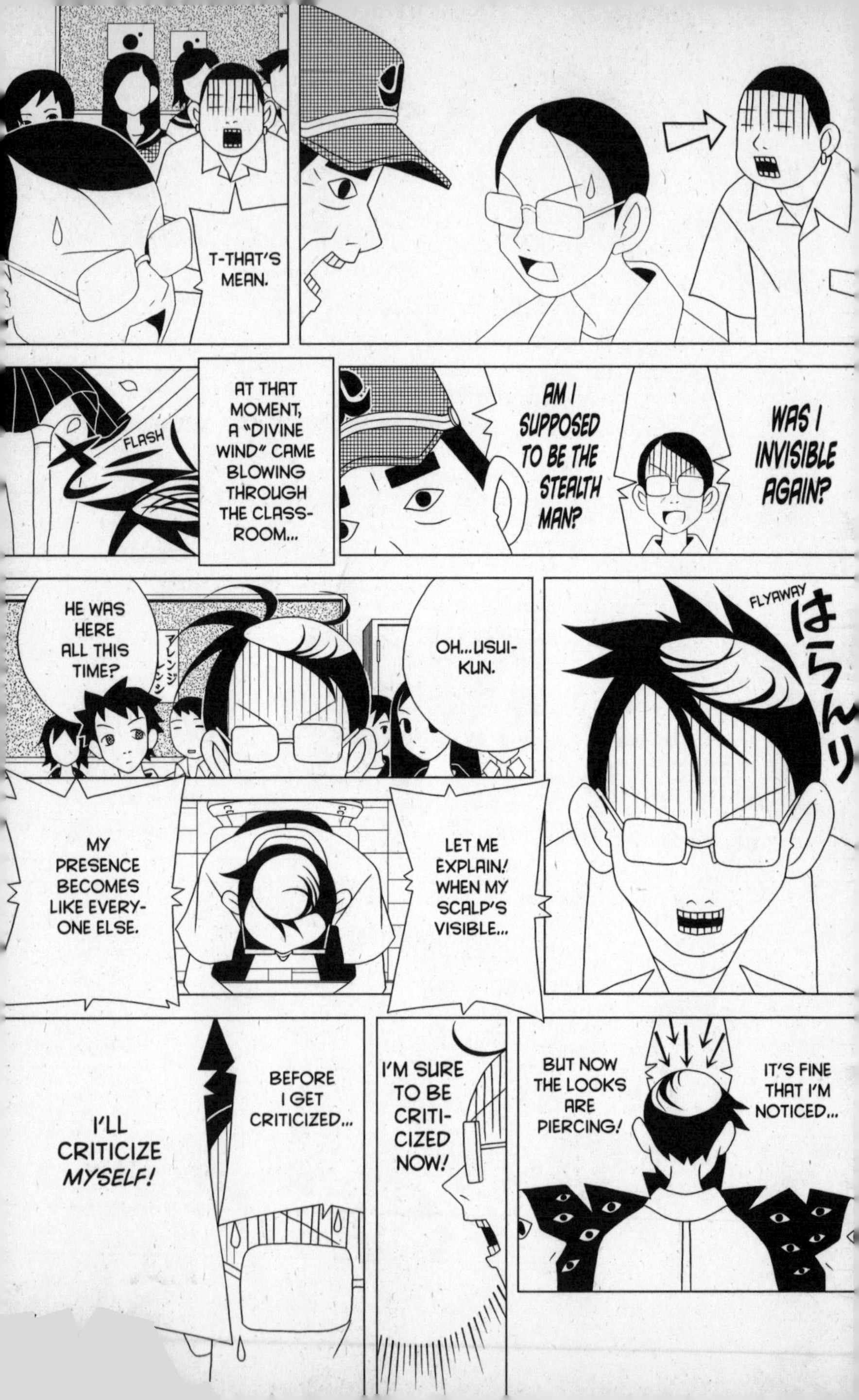
T-THAT'S MEAN.
WAS I INVISIBLE AGAIN?
AM I SUPPOSED TO BE THE STEALTH MAN?
AT THAT MOMENT, A "DIVINE WIND" CAME BLOWING THROUGH THE CLASSROOM...
FLASH
FLYAWAY はらんり
OH...USUI-KUN.
HE WAS HERE ALL THIS TIME?
LET ME EXPLAIN! WHEN MY SCALP'S VISIBLE...
MY PRESENCE BECOMES LIKE EVERYONE ELSE.
IT'S FINE THAT I'M NOTICED...
BUT NOW THE LOOKS ARE PIERCING!
I'M SURE TO BE CRITICIZED NOW!
BEFORE I GET CRITICIZED...
I'LL CRITICIZE *MYSELF!*

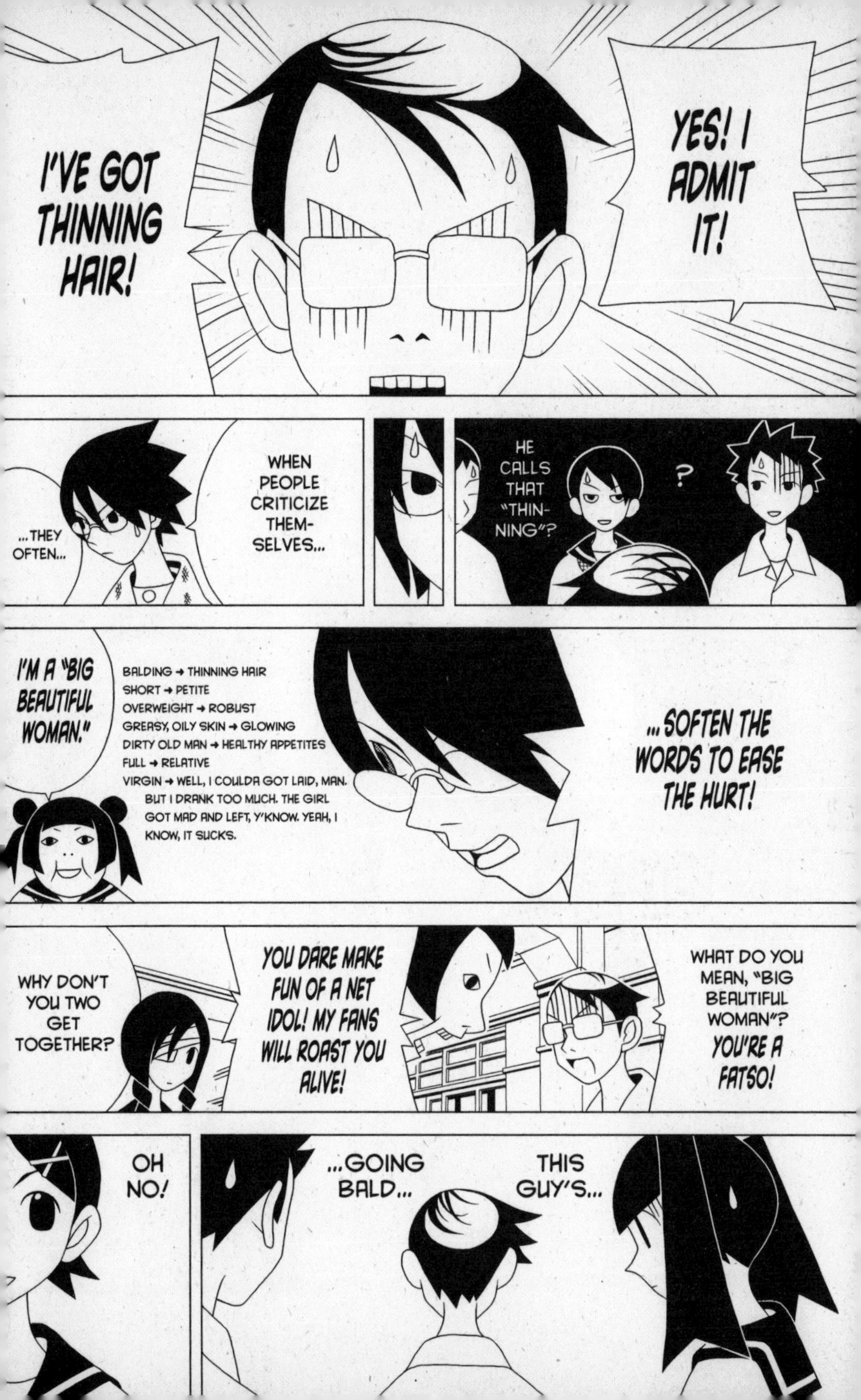
YES! I ADMIT IT!
I'VE GOT THINNING HAIR!
HE CALLS THAT "THINNING"?
?
WHEN PEOPLE CRITICIZE THEMSELVES...
...THEY OFTEN...
...SOFTEN THE WORDS TO EASE THE HURT!
I'M A "BIG BEAUTIFUL WOMAN."
BALDING → THINNING HAIR
SHORT → PETITE
OVERWEIGHT → ROBUST
GREASY, OILY SKIN → GLOWING
DIRTY OLD MAN → HEALTHY APPETITES
FULL → RELATIVE
VIRGIN → WELL, I COULDA GOT LAID, MAN. BUT I DRANK TOO MUCH. THE GIRL GOT MAD AND LEFT, Y'KNOW. YEAH, I KNOW, IT SUCKS.
WHAT DO YOU MEAN, "BIG BEAUTIFUL WOMAN"? YOU'RE A FATSO!
YOU DARE MAKE FUN OF A NET IDOL! MY FANS WILL ROAST YOU ALIVE!
WHY DON'T YOU TWO GET TOGETHER?
THIS GUY'S...
...GOING BALD...
OH NO!

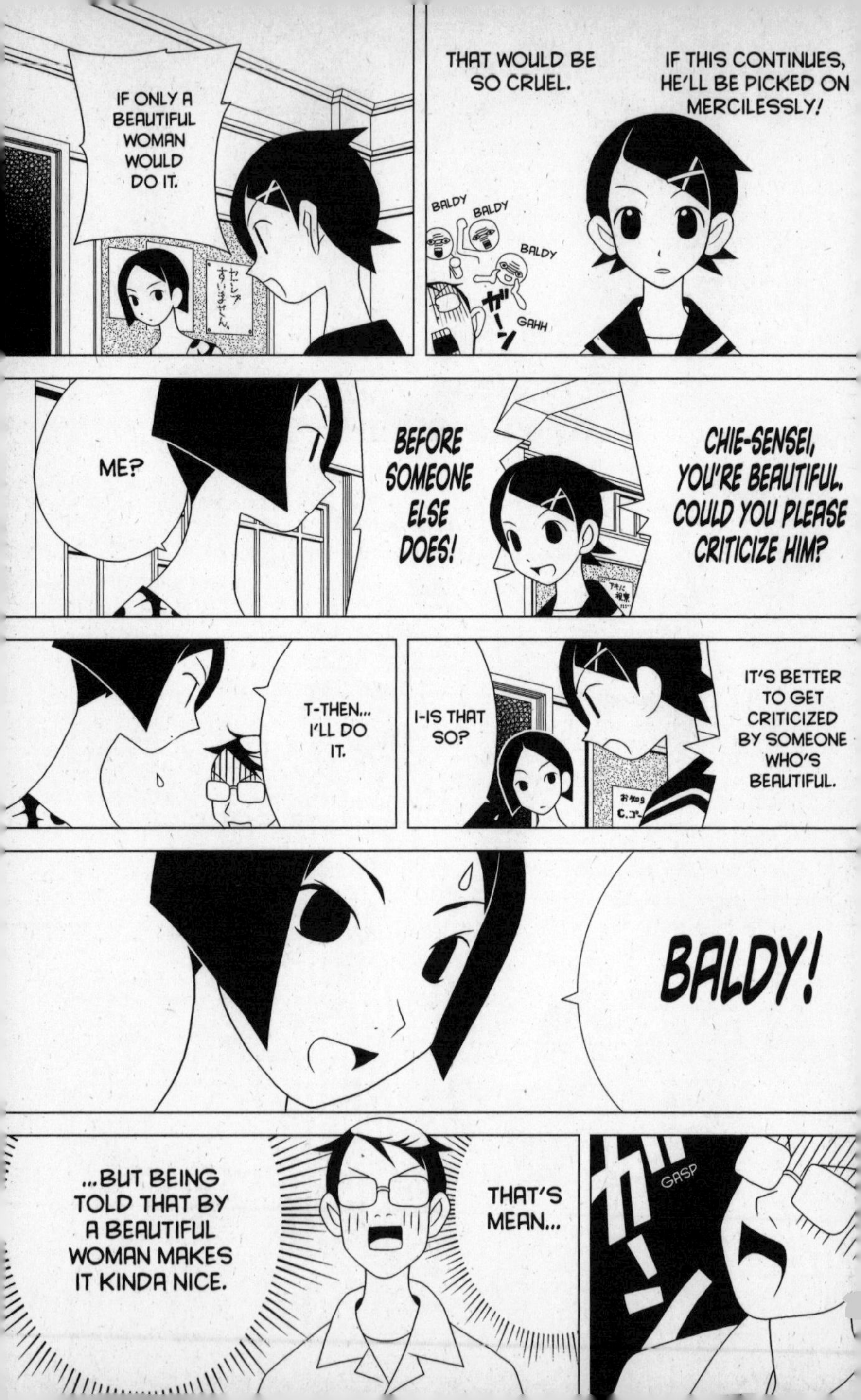
IF THIS CONTINUES, HE'LL BE PICKED ON MERCILESSLY!
THAT WOULD BE SO CRUEL.
BALDY
BALDY
BALDY
GAHH
IF ONLY A BEAUTIFUL WOMAN WOULD DO IT.
CHIE-SENSEI, YOU'RE BEAUTIFUL. COULD YOU PLEASE CRITICIZE HIM?
BEFORE SOMEONE ELSE DOES!
ME?
IT'S BETTER TO GET CRITICIZED BY SOMEONE WHO'S BEAUTIFUL.
I-IS THAT SO?
T-THEN... I'LL DO IT.
BALDY!
GASP
THAT'S MEAN...
...BUT BEING TOLD THAT BY A BEAUTIFUL WOMAN MAKES IT KINDA NICE.

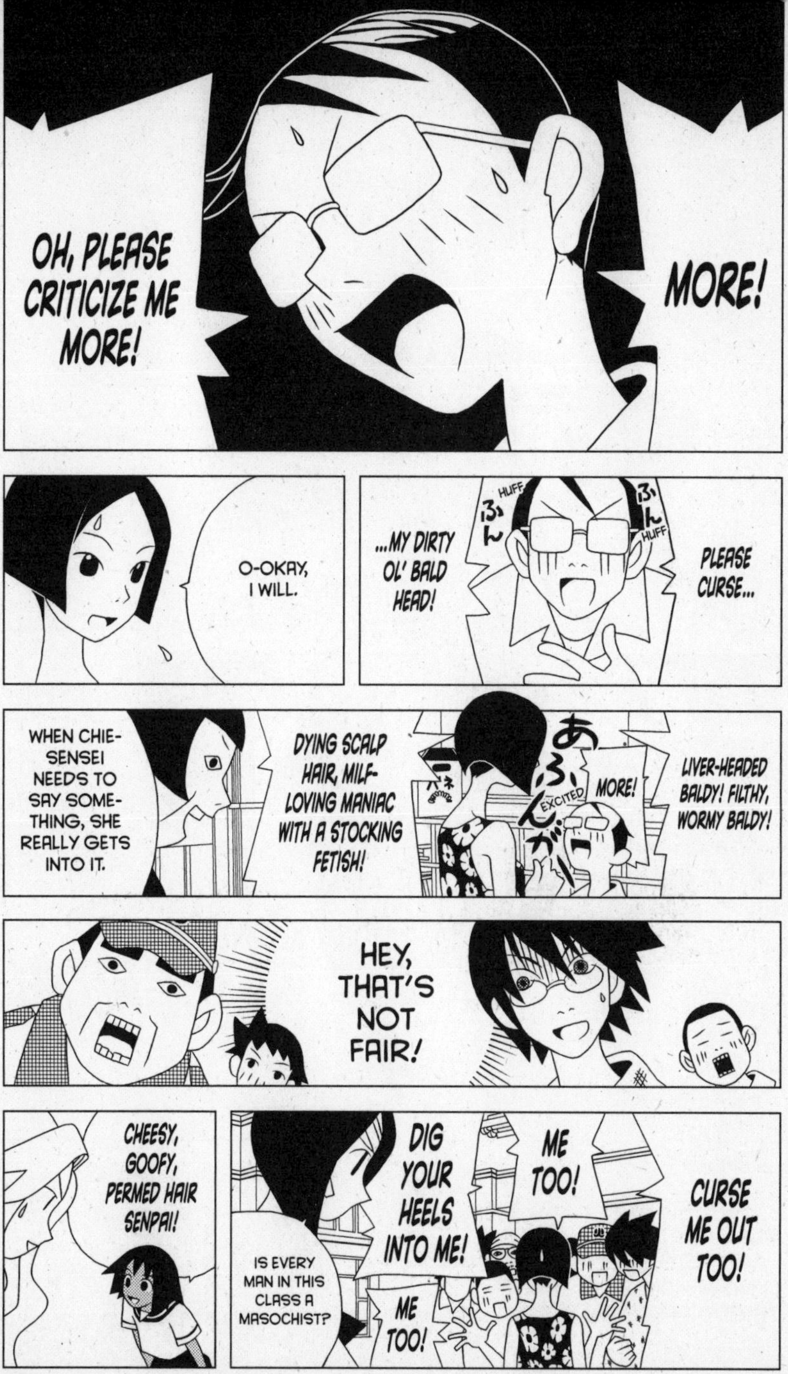
MORE!
OH, PLEASE CRITICIZE ME MORE!
ふん HUFF
ふん HUFF
PLEASE CURSE...
...MY DIRTY OL' BALD HEAD!
O-OKAY, I WILL.
LIVER-HEADED BALDY! FILTHY, WORMY BALDY!
MORE!
あふんが EXCITED
DYING SCALP HAIR, MILF-LOVING MANIAC WITH A STOCKING FETISH!
WHEN CHIE-SENSEI NEEDS TO SAY SOMETHING, SHE REALLY GETS INTO IT.
HEY, THAT'S NOT FAIR!
CURSE ME OUT TOO!
ME TOO!
DIG YOUR HEELS INTO ME!
ME TOO!
IS EVERY MAN IN THIS CLASS A MASOCHIST?
CHEESY, GOOFY, PERMED HAIR SENPAI!

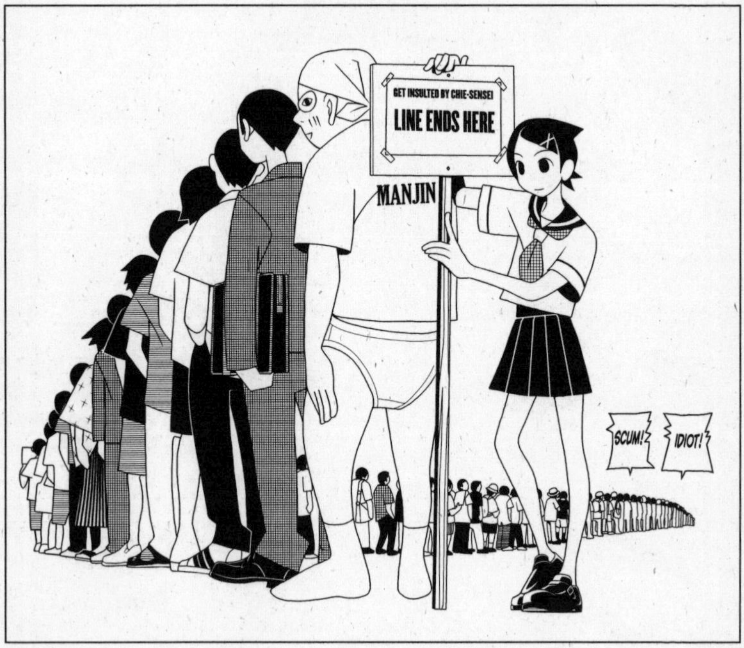
GET INSULTED BY CHIE-SENSEI
LINE ENDS HERE
MANJIN
SCUM!
IDIOT!

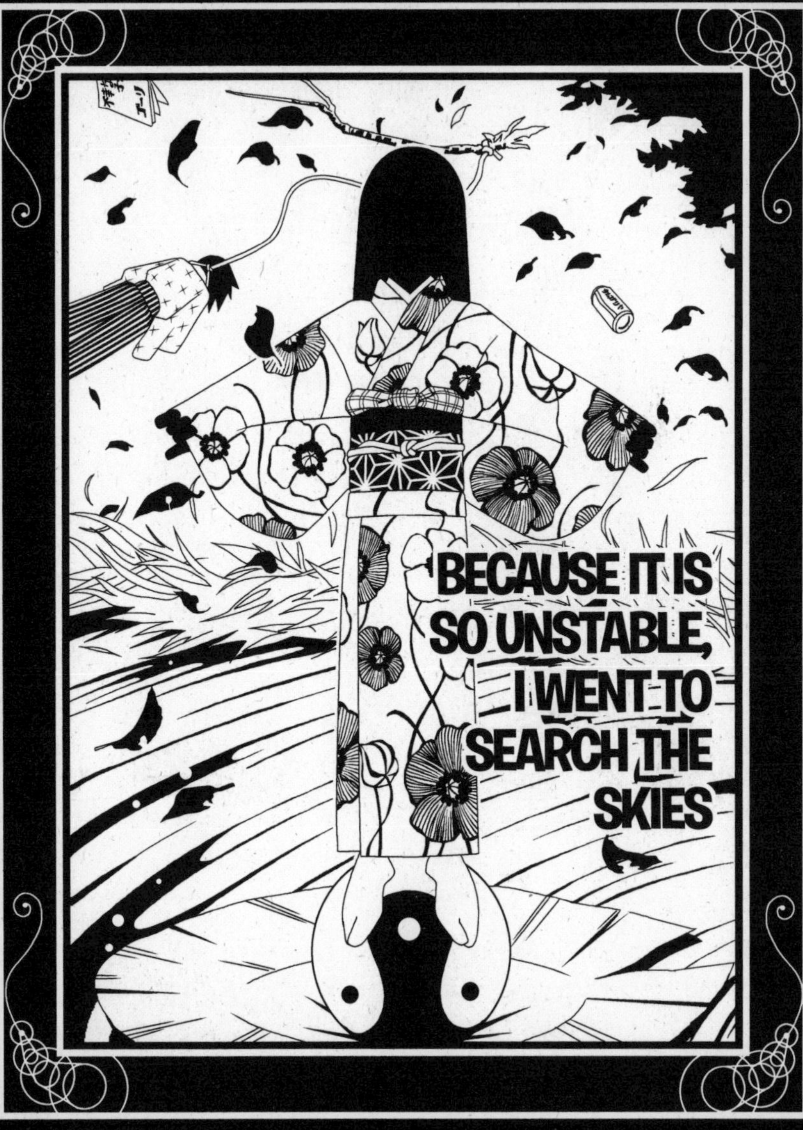
BECAUSE IT IS SO UNSTABLE, I WENT TO SEARCH THE SKIES

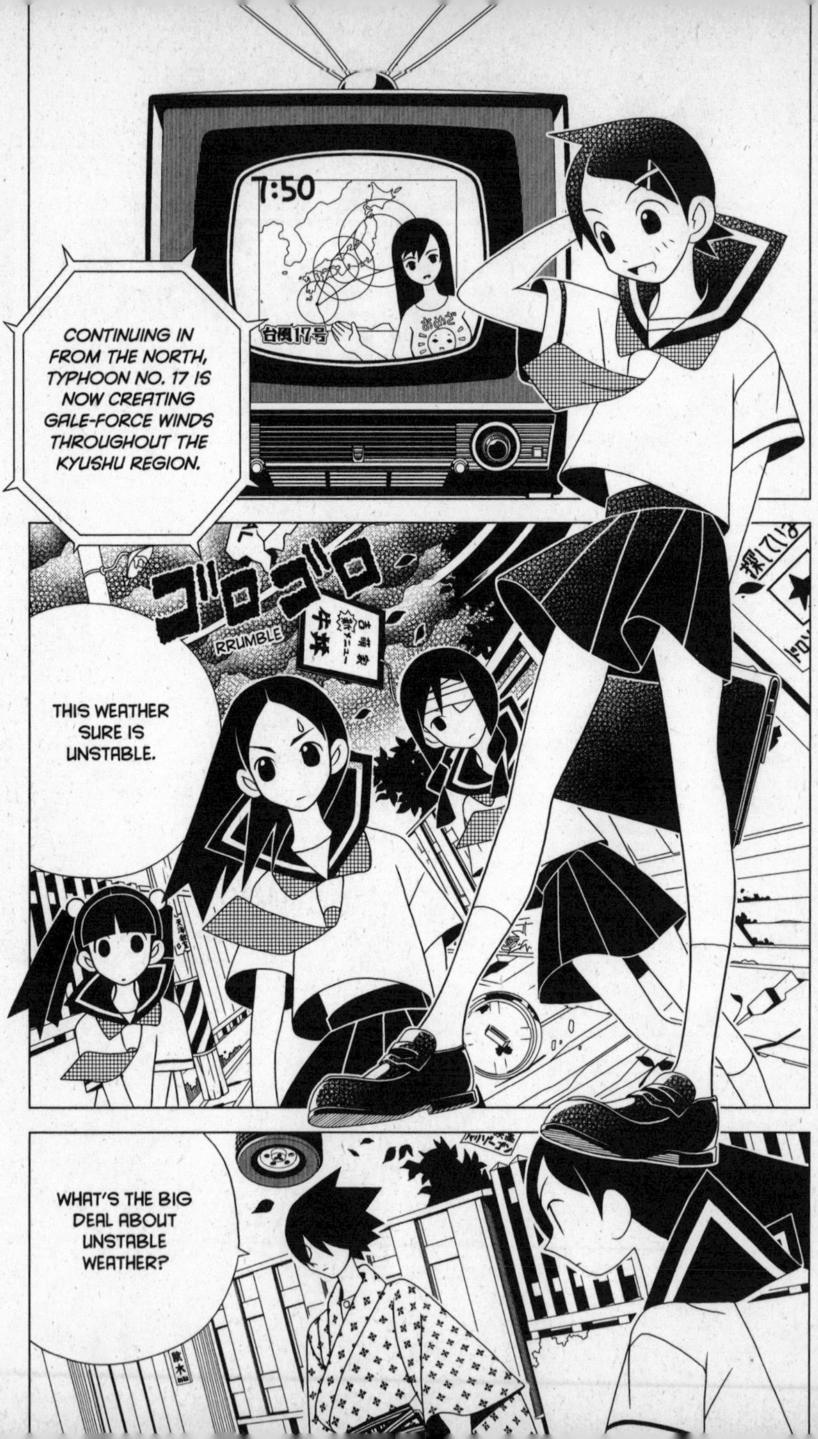
7:50
台風17号
おめざ
CONTINUING IN FROM THE NORTH, TYPHOON NO. 17 IS NOW CREATING GALE-FORCE WINDS THROUGHOUT THE KYUSHU REGION.
ゴロゴロ
RRUMBLE
THIS WEATHER SURE IS UNSTABLE.
WHAT'S THE BIG DEAL ABOUT UNSTABLE WEATHER?

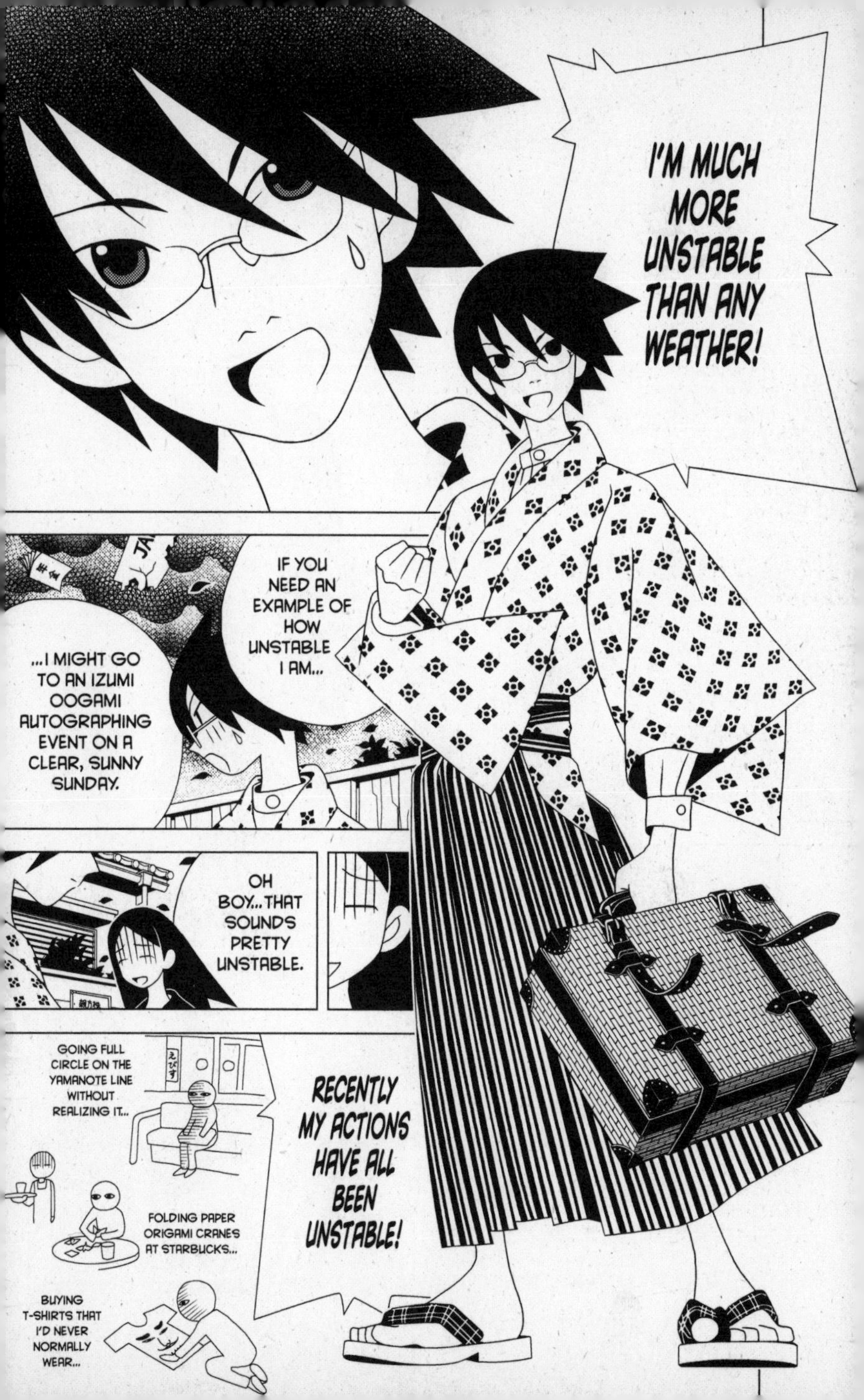
I'M MUCH MORE UNSTABLE THAN ANY WEATHER!
IF YOU NEED AN EXAMPLE OF HOW UNSTABLE I AM...
...I MIGHT GO TO AN IZUMI OOGAMI AUTOGRAPHING EVENT ON A CLEAR, SUNNY SUNDAY.
OH BOY...THAT SOUNDS PRETTY UNSTABLE.
RECENTLY MY ACTIONS HAVE ALL BEEN UNSTABLE!
GOING FULL CIRCLE ON THE YAMANOTE LINE WITHOUT REALIZING IT...
FOLDING PAPER ORIGAMI CRANES AT STARBUCKS...
BUYING T-SHIRTS THAT I'D NEVER NORMALLY WEAR...

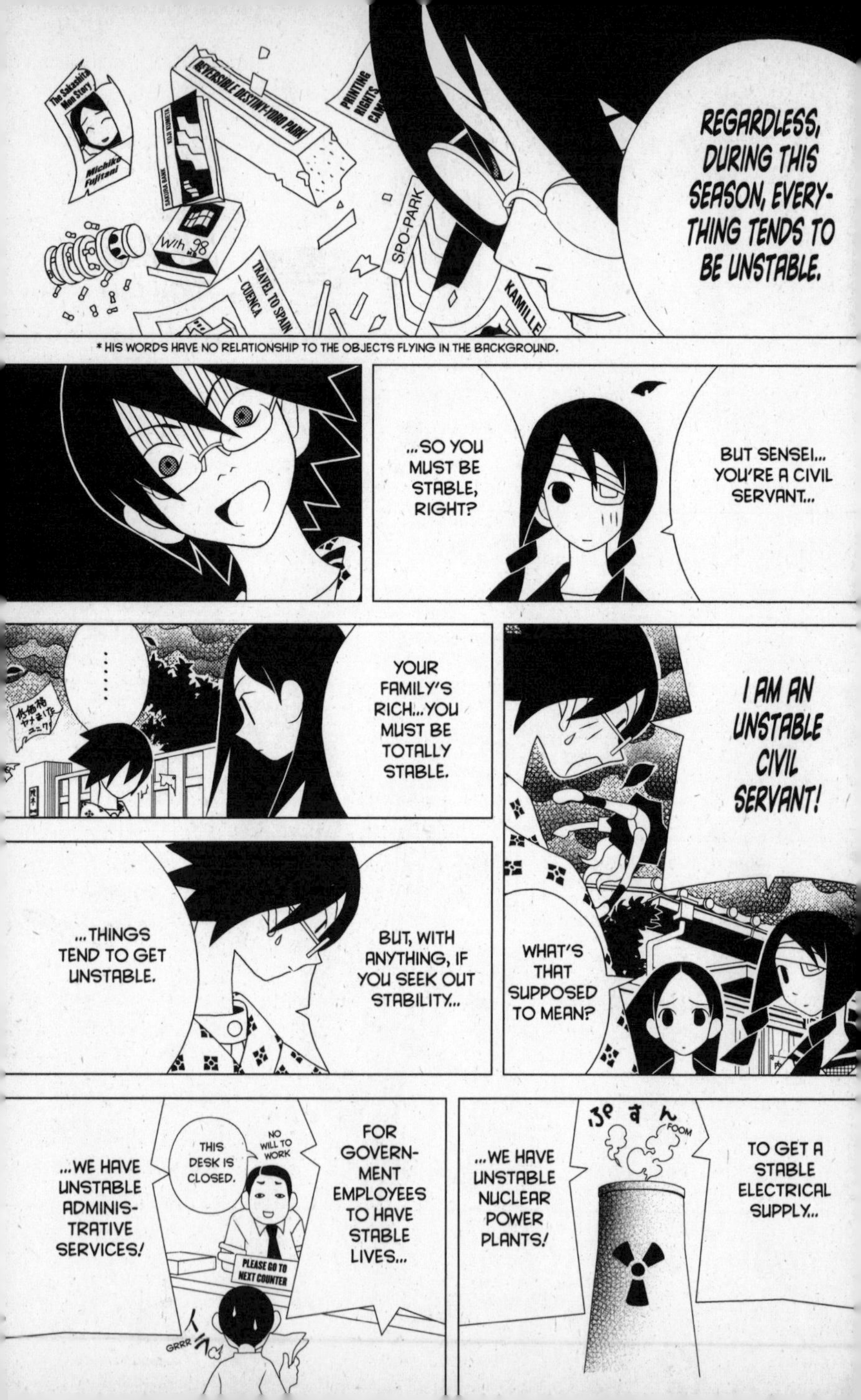
PRINTING RIGHTS
SPO-PARK
KAMILLE
REVERSIBLE DESTINY-YORO PARK
SAKURA BANK
Win 98
TRAVEL TO SPAIN —CUENCA
The Sakashita Mon Story
Michiko Fujitani
REGARDLESS, DURING THIS SEASON, EVERYTHING TENDS TO BE UNSTABLE.
* HIS WORDS HAVE NO RELATIONSHIP TO THE OBJECTS FLYING IN THE BACKGROUND.
BUT SENSEI... YOU'RE A CIVIL SERVANT...
...SO YOU MUST BE STABLE, RIGHT?
I AM AN UNSTABLE CIVIL SERVANT!
WHAT'S THAT SUPPOSED TO MEAN?
YOUR FAMILY'S RICH...YOU MUST BE TOTALLY STABLE.
......
BUT, WITH ANYTHING, IF YOU SEEK OUT STABILITY...
...THINGS TEND TO GET UNSTABLE.
TO GET A STABLE ELECTRICAL SUPPLY...
ぷすん
FOOM
...WE HAVE UNSTABLE NUCLEAR POWER PLANTS!
FOR GOVERNMENT EMPLOYEES TO HAVE STABLE LIVES...
NO WILL TO WORK
THIS DESK IS CLOSED.
PLEASE GO TO NEXT COUNTER
GRRR
...WE HAVE UNSTABLE ADMINISTRATIVE SERVICES!

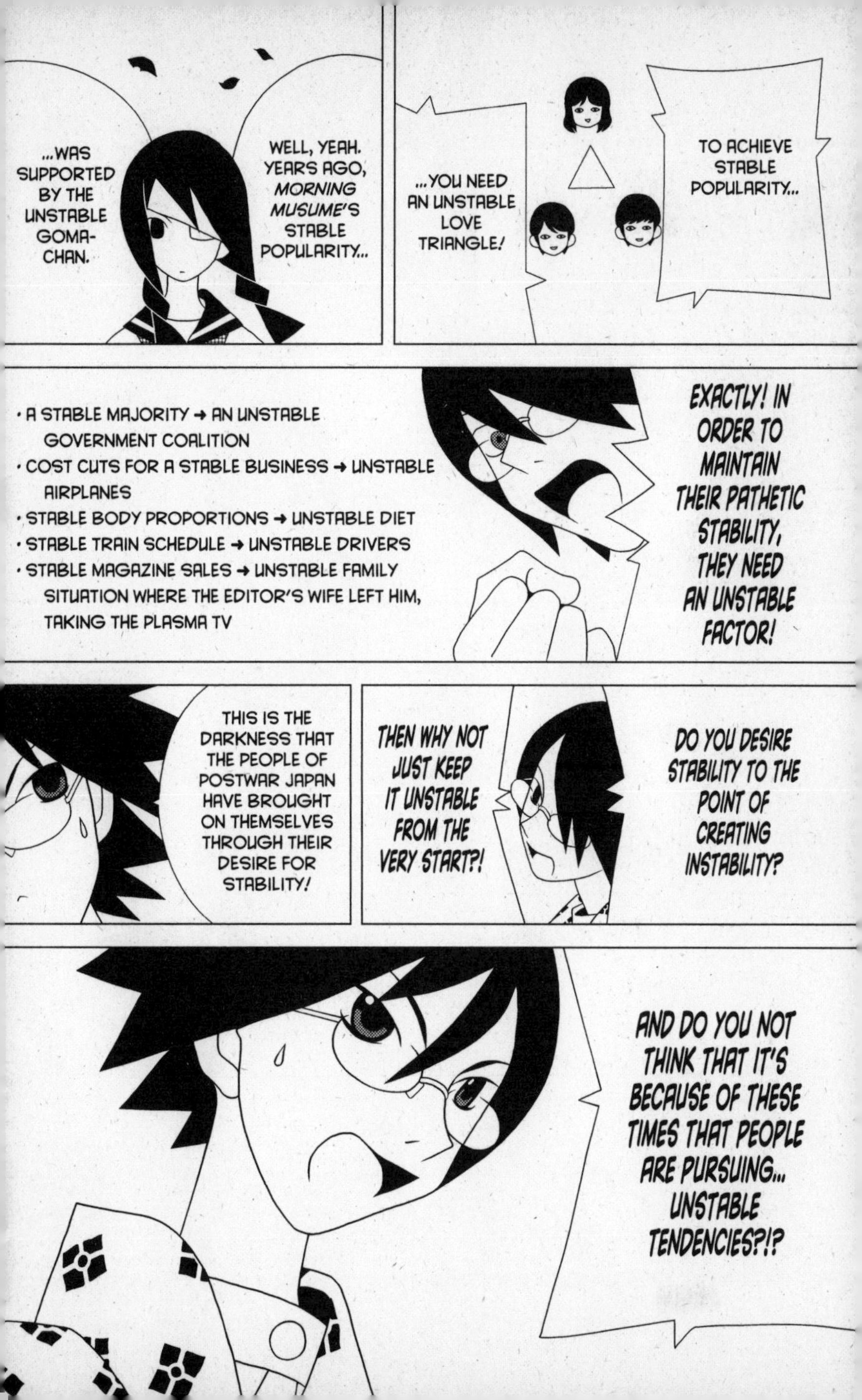
TO ACHIEVE STABLE POPULARITY...
...YOU NEED AN UNSTABLE LOVE TRIANGLE!
WELL, YEAH. YEARS AGO, *MORNING MUSUME*'S STABLE POPULARITY...
...WAS SUPPORTED BY THE UNSTABLE GOMA-CHAN.
EXACTLY! IN ORDER TO MAINTAIN THEIR PATHETIC STABILITY, THEY NEED AN UNSTABLE FACTOR!
• A STABLE MAJORITY → AN UNSTABLE GOVERNMENT COALITION
• COST CUTS FOR A STABLE BUSINESS → UNSTABLE AIRPLANES
• STABLE BODY PROPORTIONS → UNSTABLE DIET
• STABLE TRAIN SCHEDULE → UNSTABLE DRIVERS
• STABLE MAGAZINE SALES → UNSTABLE FAMILY SITUATION WHERE THE EDITOR'S WIFE LEFT HIM, TAKING THE PLASMA TV
DO YOU DESIRE STABILITY TO THE POINT OF CREATING INSTABILITY?
THEN WHY NOT JUST KEEP IT UNSTABLE FROM THE VERY START?!
THIS IS THE DARKNESS THAT THE PEOPLE OF POSTWAR JAPAN HAVE BROUGHT ON THEMSELVES THROUGH THEIR DESIRE FOR STABILITY!
AND DO YOU NOT THINK THAT IT'S BECAUSE OF THESE TIMES THAT PEOPLE ARE PURSUING... UNSTABLE TENDENCIES?!?

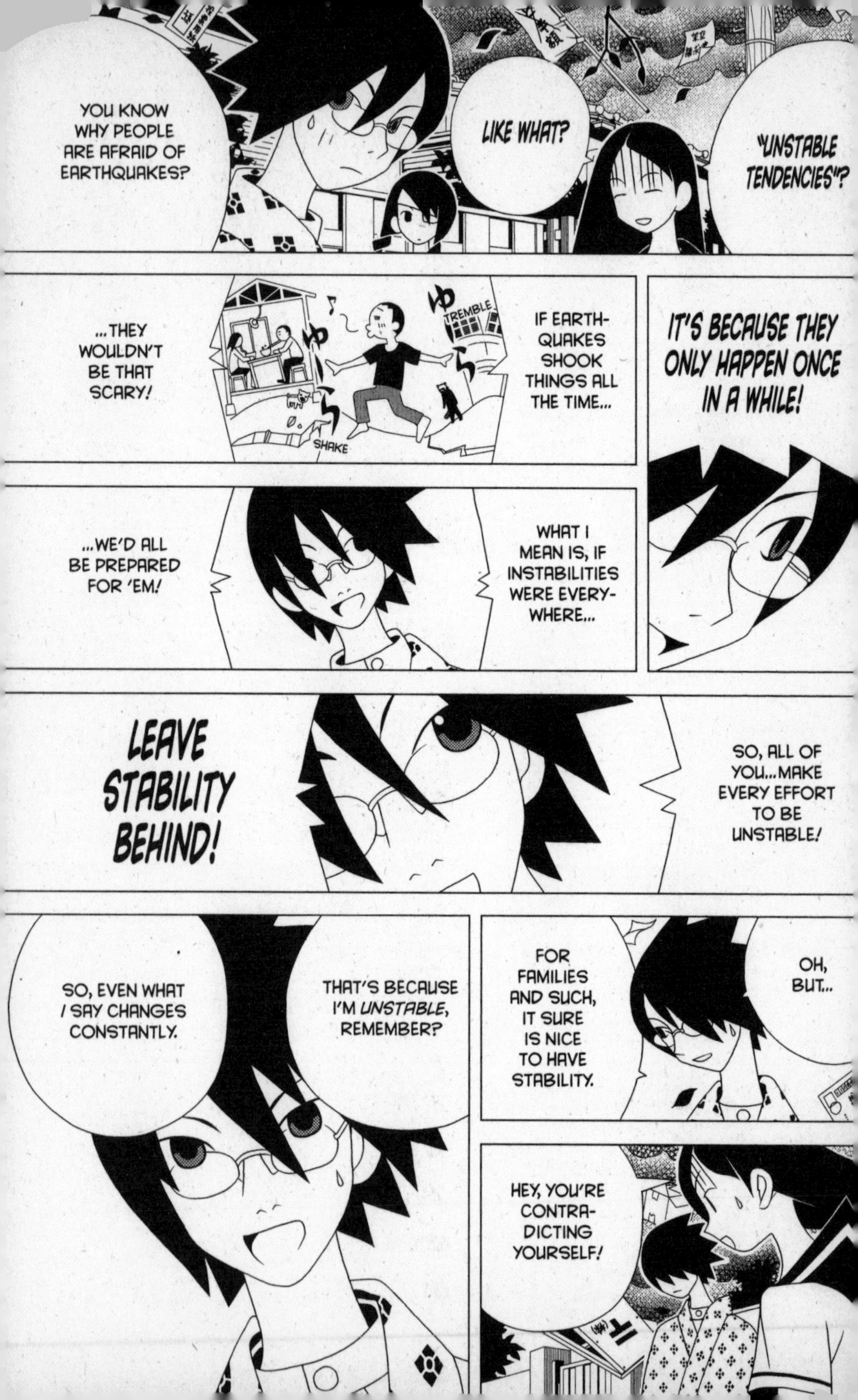
"UNSTABLE TENDENCIES"?
LIKE WHAT?
YOU KNOW WHY PEOPLE ARE AFRAID OF EARTHQUAKES?
IT'S BECAUSE THEY ONLY HAPPEN ONCE IN A WHILE!
IF EARTHQUAKES SHOOK THINGS ALL THE TIME...
TREMBLE
SHAKE
...THEY WOULDN'T BE THAT SCARY!
WHAT I MEAN IS, IF INSTABILITIES WERE EVERYWHERE...
...WE'D ALL BE PREPARED FOR 'EM!
SO, ALL OF YOU...MAKE EVERY EFFORT TO BE UNSTABLE!
LEAVE STABILITY BEHIND!
OH, BUT...
FOR FAMILIES AND SUCH, IT SURE IS NICE TO HAVE STABILITY.
HEY, YOU'RE CONTRADICTING YOURSELF!
THAT'S BECAUSE I'M *UNSTABLE*, REMEMBER?
SO, EVEN WHAT I SAY CHANGES CONSTANTLY.

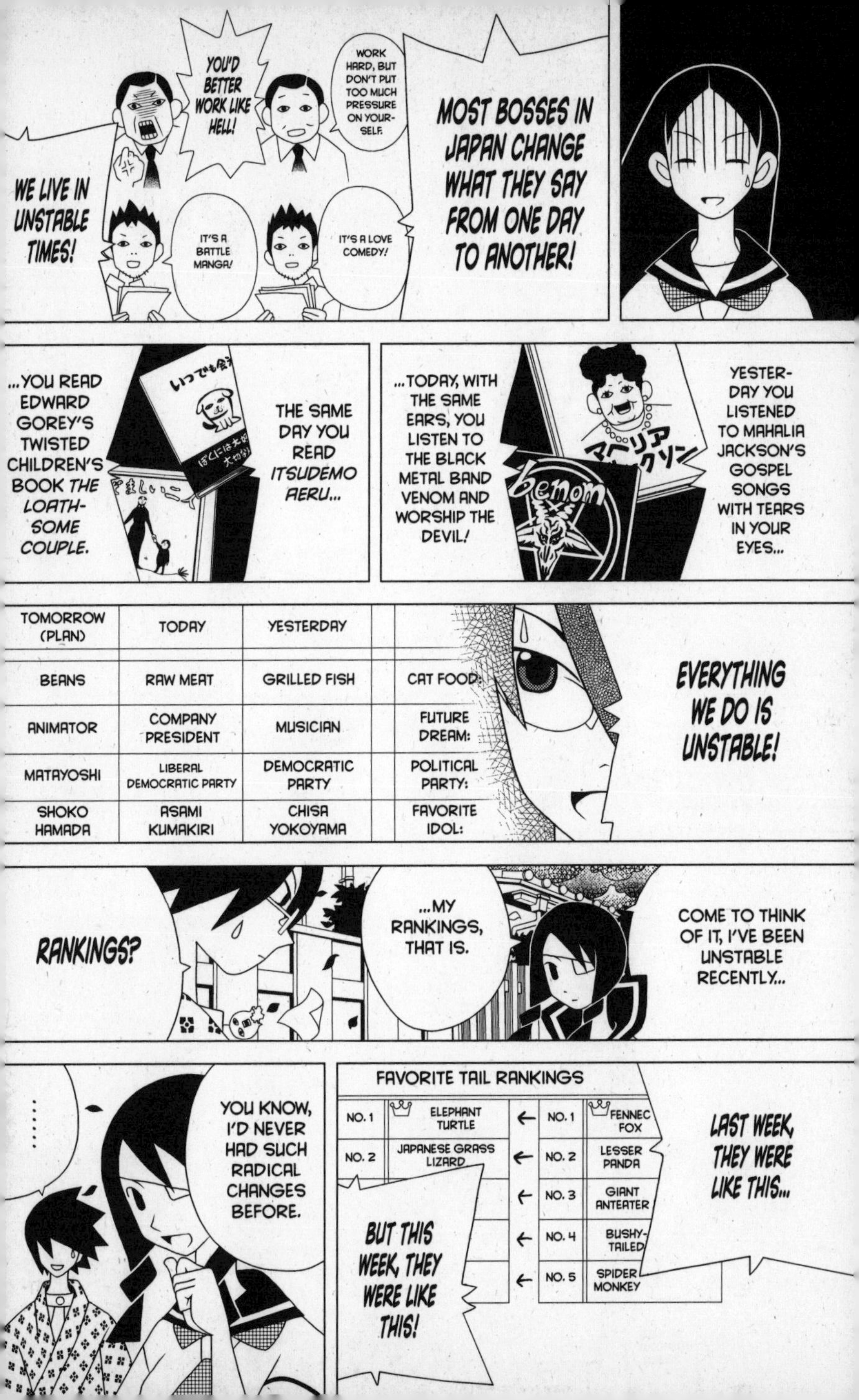

MOST BOSSES IN JAPAN CHANGE WHAT THEY SAY FROM ONE DAY TO ANOTHER!
WORK HARD, BUT DON'T PUT TOO MUCH PRESSURE ON YOURSELF.
YOU'D BETTER WORK LIKE HELL!
IT'S A LOVE COMEDY!
IT'S A BATTLE MANGA!
WE LIVE IN UNSTABLE TIMES!
YESTERDAY YOU LISTENED TO MAHALIA JACKSON'S GOSPEL SONGS WITH TEARS IN YOUR EYES...
...TODAY, WITH THE SAME EARS, YOU LISTEN TO THE BLACK METAL BAND VENOM AND WORSHIP THE DEVIL!
benom
THE SAME DAY YOU READ *ITSUDEMO AERU*...
...YOU READ EDWARD GOREY'S TWISTED CHILDREN'S BOOK *THE LOATHSOME COUPLE*.
EVERYTHING WE DO IS UNSTABLE!

| TOMORROW (PLAN) | TODAY | YESTERDAY | |
|---|---|---|---|
| BEANS | RAW MEAT | GRILLED FISH | CAT FOOD: |
| ANIMATOR | COMPANY PRESIDENT | MUSICIAN | FUTURE DREAM: |
| MATAYOSHI | LIBERAL DEMOCRATIC PARTY | DEMOCRATIC PARTY | POLITICAL PARTY: |
| SHOKO HAMADA | ASAMI KUMAKIRI | CHISA YOKOYAMA | FAVORITE IDOL: |

COME TO THINK OF IT, I'VE BEEN UNSTABLE RECENTLY...
...MY RANKINGS, THAT IS.
RANKINGS?
LAST WEEK, THEY WERE LIKE THIS...
FAVORITE TAIL RANKINGS
NO. 1 FENNEC FOX
NO. 2 LESSER PANDA
NO. 3 GIANT ANTEATER
NO. 4 BUSHY-TAILED
NO. 5 SPIDER MONKEY
NO. 1 ELEPHANT TURTLE
NO. 2 JAPANESE GRASS LIZARD
BUT THIS WEEK, THEY WERE LIKE THIS!
YOU KNOW, I'D NEVER HAD SUCH RADICAL CHANGES BEFORE.
......

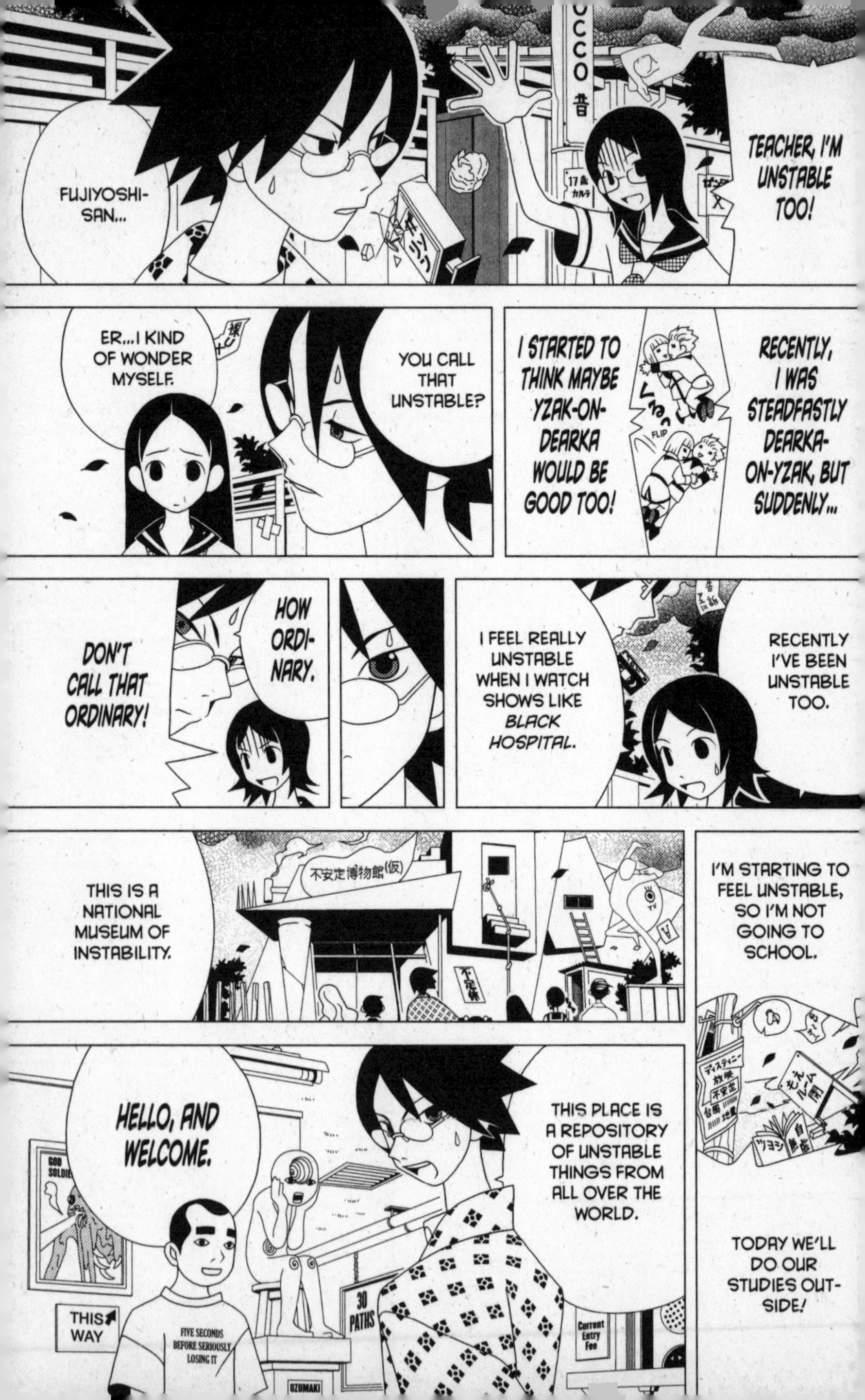
TEACHER, I'M UNSTABLE TOO!
FUJIYOSHI-SAN...
RECENTLY, I WAS STEADFASTLY DEARKA-ON-YZAK, BUT SUDDENLY...
I STARTED TO THINK MAYBE YZAK-ON-DEARKA WOULD BE GOOD TOO!
FLIP
YOU CALL THAT UNSTABLE?
ER...I KIND OF WONDER MYSELF.
RECENTLY I'VE BEEN UNSTABLE TOO.
I FEEL REALLY UNSTABLE WHEN I WATCH SHOWS LIKE *BLACK HOSPITAL*.
HOW ORDINARY.
DON'T CALL THAT ORDINARY!
I'M STARTING TO FEEL UNSTABLE, SO I'M NOT GOING TO SCHOOL.
TODAY WE'LL DO OUR STUDIES OUTSIDE!
不安定博物館(仮)
THIS IS A NATIONAL MUSEUM OF INSTABILITY.
THIS PLACE IS A REPOSITORY OF UNSTABLE THINGS FROM ALL OVER THE WORLD.
HELLO, AND WELCOME.
GOD SOLDIE
THIS WAY
FIVE SECONDS BEFORE SERIOUSLY LOSING IT
30 PATHS
Current Entry Fee
UZUMAKI

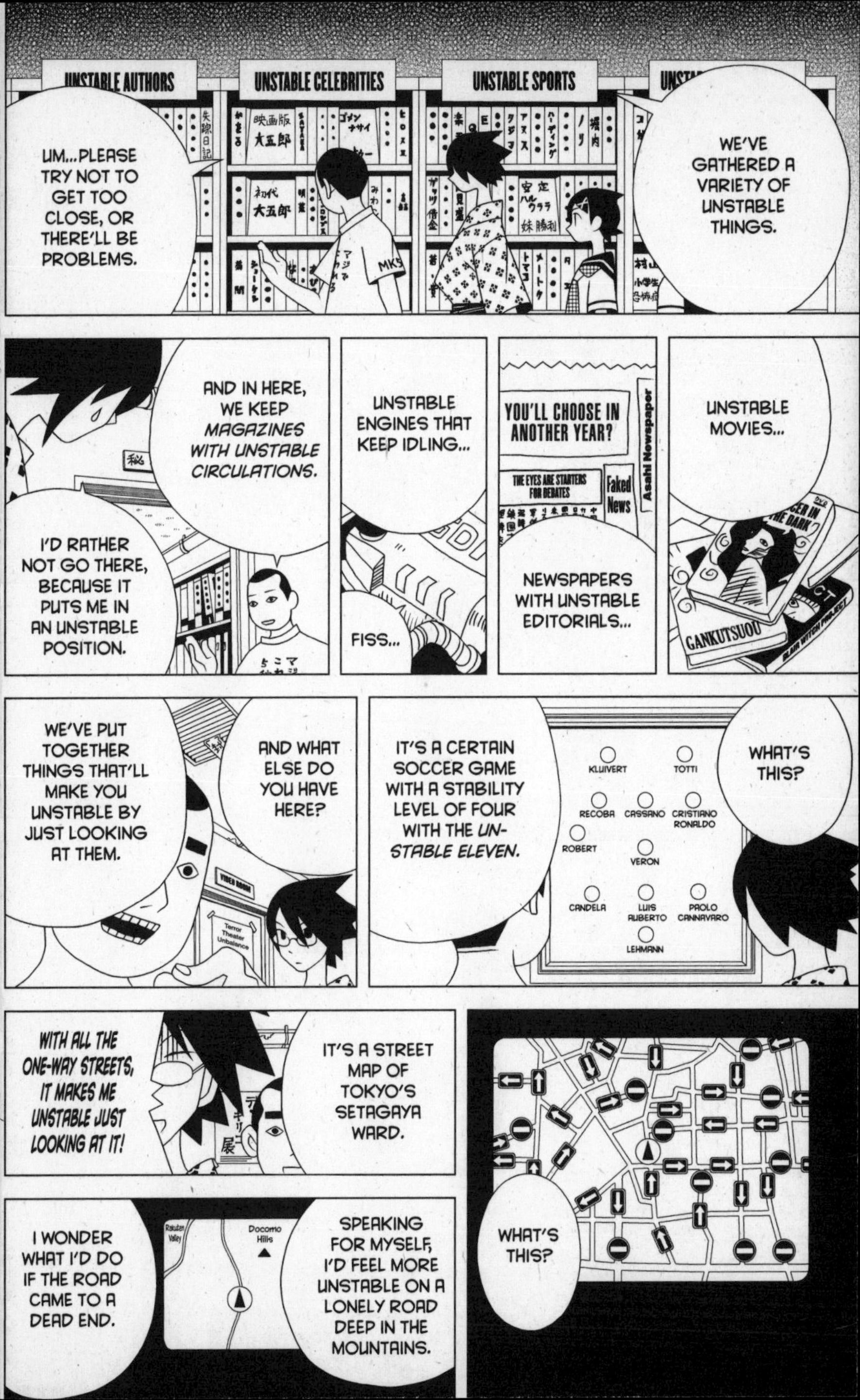
UNSTABLE AUTHORS
UNSTABLE CELEBRITIES
UNSTABLE SPORTS
WE'VE GATHERED A VARIETY OF UNSTABLE THINGS.
UM...PLEASE TRY NOT TO GET TOO CLOSE, OR THERE'LL BE PROBLEMS.
UNSTABLE MOVIES...
GANKUTSUOU
YOU'LL CHOOSE IN ANOTHER YEAR?
Asahi Newspaper
THE EYES ARE STARTERS FOR DEBATES
Faked News
NEWSPAPERS WITH UNSTABLE EDITORIALS...
UNSTABLE ENGINES THAT KEEP IDLING...
FISS...
AND IN HERE, WE KEEP *MAGAZINES WITH UNSTABLE CIRCULATIONS.*
I'D RATHER NOT GO THERE, BECAUSE IT PUTS ME IN AN UNSTABLE POSITION.
WHAT'S THIS?
IT'S A CERTAIN SOCCER GAME WITH A STABILITY LEVEL OF FOUR WITH THE *UNSTABLE ELEVEN.*
KLUIVERT
TOTTI
RECOBA
CASSANO
CRISTIANO RONALDO
ROBERT
VERON
CANDELA
LUIS ALBERTO
PAOLO CANNAVARO
LEHMANN
AND WHAT ELSE DO YOU HAVE HERE?
WE'VE PUT TOGETHER THINGS THAT'LL MAKE YOU UNSTABLE BY JUST LOOKING AT THEM.
VIDEO ROOM
Terror Theater Unbalance
WHAT'S THIS?
IT'S A STREET MAP OF TOKYO'S SETAGAYA WARD.
WITH ALL THE ONE-WAY STREETS, IT MAKES ME UNSTABLE JUST LOOKING AT IT!
SPEAKING FOR MYSELF, I'D FEEL MORE UNSTABLE ON A LONELY ROAD DEEP IN THE MOUNTAINS.
Docomo Hills
Rakuten Valley
I WONDER WHAT I'D DO IF THE ROAD CAME TO A DEAD END.

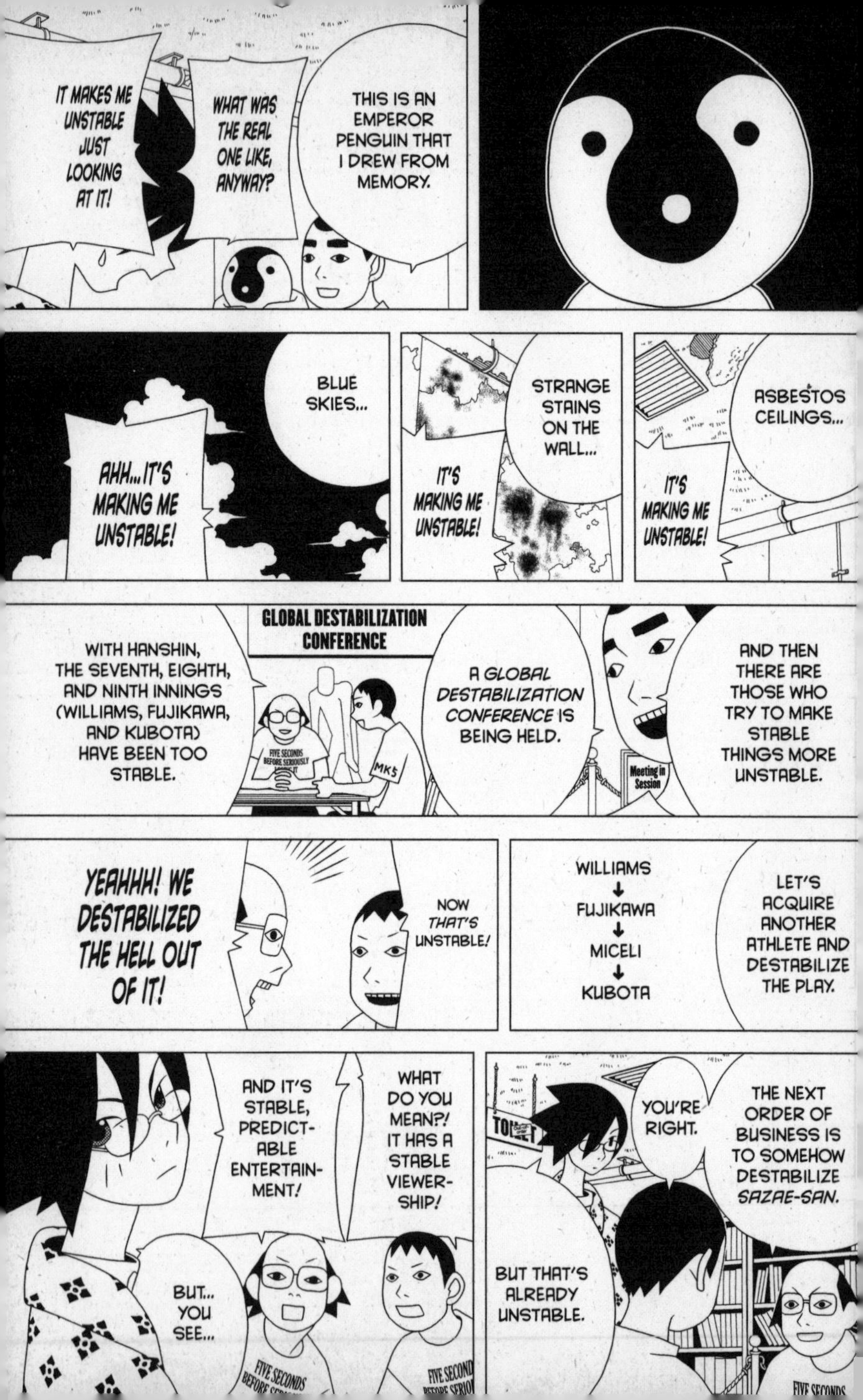
THIS IS AN EMPEROR PENGUIN THAT I DREW FROM MEMORY.
WHAT WAS THE REAL ONE LIKE, ANYWAY?
IT MAKES ME UNSTABLE JUST LOOKING AT IT!
ASBESTOS CEILINGS...
IT'S MAKING ME UNSTABLE!
STRANGE STAINS ON THE WALL...
IT'S MAKING ME UNSTABLE!
BLUE SKIES...
AHH...IT'S MAKING ME UNSTABLE!
AND THEN THERE ARE THOSE WHO TRY TO MAKE STABLE THINGS MORE UNSTABLE.
Meeting in Session
GLOBAL DESTABILIZATION CONFERENCE
A *GLOBAL DESTABILIZATION CONFERENCE* IS BEING HELD.
WITH HANSHIN, THE SEVENTH, EIGHTH, AND NINTH INNINGS (WILLIAMS, FUJIKAWA, AND KUBOTA) HAVE BEEN TOO STABLE.
MKS
LET'S ACQUIRE ANOTHER ATHLETE AND DESTABILIZE THE PLAY.
WILLIAMS ↓ FUJIKAWA ↓ MICELI ↓ KUBOTA
NOW *THAT'S* UNSTABLE!
YEAHHH! WE DESTABILIZED THE HELL OUT OF IT!
THE NEXT ORDER OF BUSINESS IS TO SOMEHOW DESTABILIZE *SAZAE-SAN*.
YOU'RE RIGHT.
BUT THAT'S ALREADY UNSTABLE.
WHAT DO YOU MEAN?! IT HAS A STABLE VIEWERSHIP!
AND IT'S STABLE, PREDICTABLE ENTERTAINMENT!
BUT... YOU SEE...

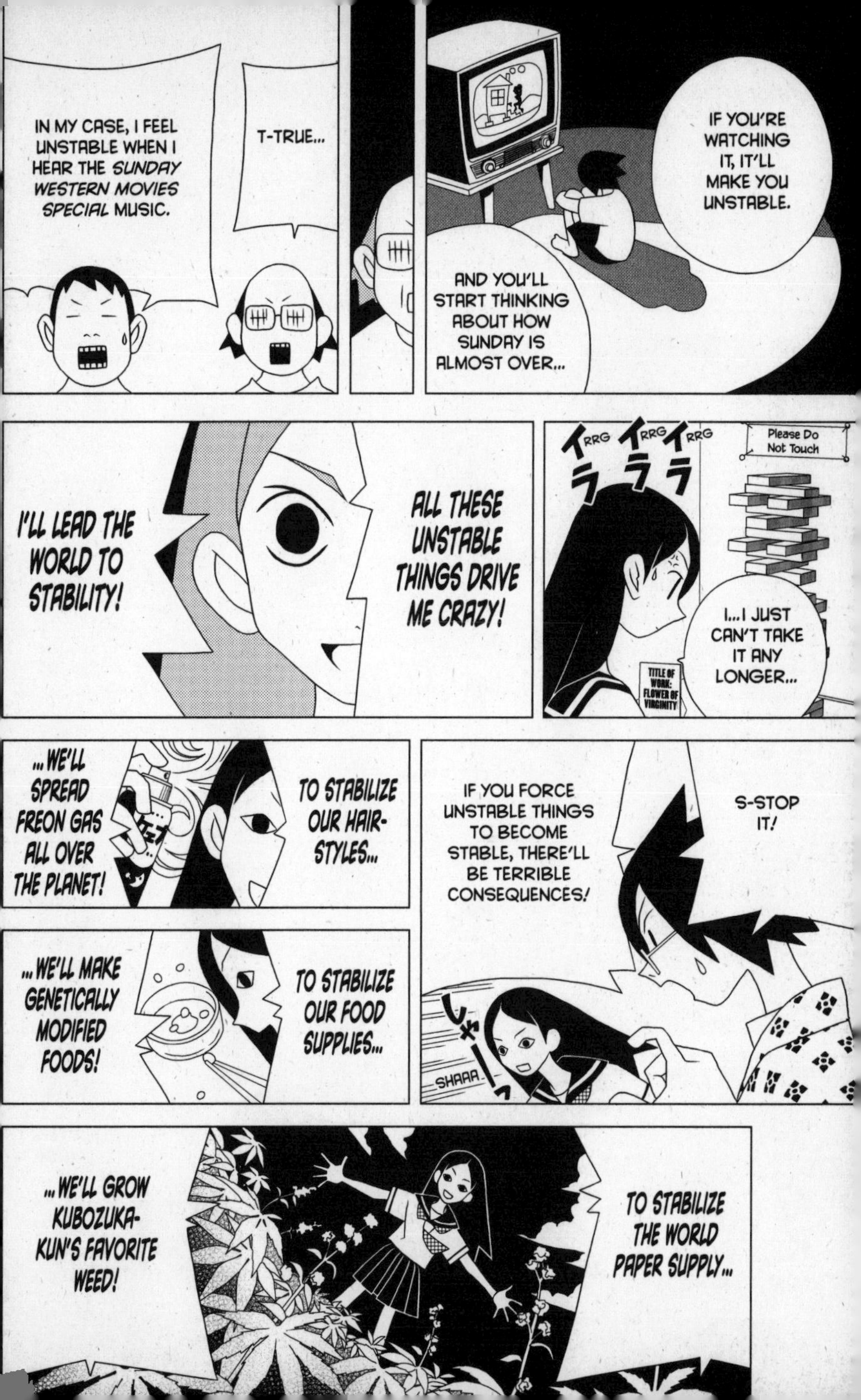

IF YOU'RE WATCHING IT, IT'LL MAKE YOU UNSTABLE.
AND YOU'LL START THINKING ABOUT HOW SUNDAY IS ALMOST OVER...
T-TRUE...
IN MY CASE, I FEEL UNSTABLE WHEN I HEAR THE *SUNDAY WESTERN MOVIES SPECIAL* MUSIC.
Please Do Not Touch
イラ RRG
イラ RRG
イラ RRG
I...I JUST CAN'T TAKE IT ANY LONGER...
TITLE OF WORK: FLOWER OF VIRGINITY
ALL THESE UNSTABLE THINGS DRIVE ME CRAZY!
I'LL LEAD THE WORLD TO STABILITY!
S-STOP IT!
IF YOU FORCE UNSTABLE THINGS TO BECOME STABLE, THERE'LL BE TERRIBLE CONSEQUENCES!
SHAAA
TO STABILIZE OUR HAIR-STYLES...
...WE'LL SPREAD FREON GAS ALL OVER THE PLANET!
TO STABILIZE OUR FOOD SUPPLIES...
...WE'LL MAKE GENETICALLY MODIFIED FOODS!
TO STABILIZE THE WORLD PAPER SUPPLY...
...WE'LL GROW KUBOZUKA-KUN'S FAVORITE WEED!

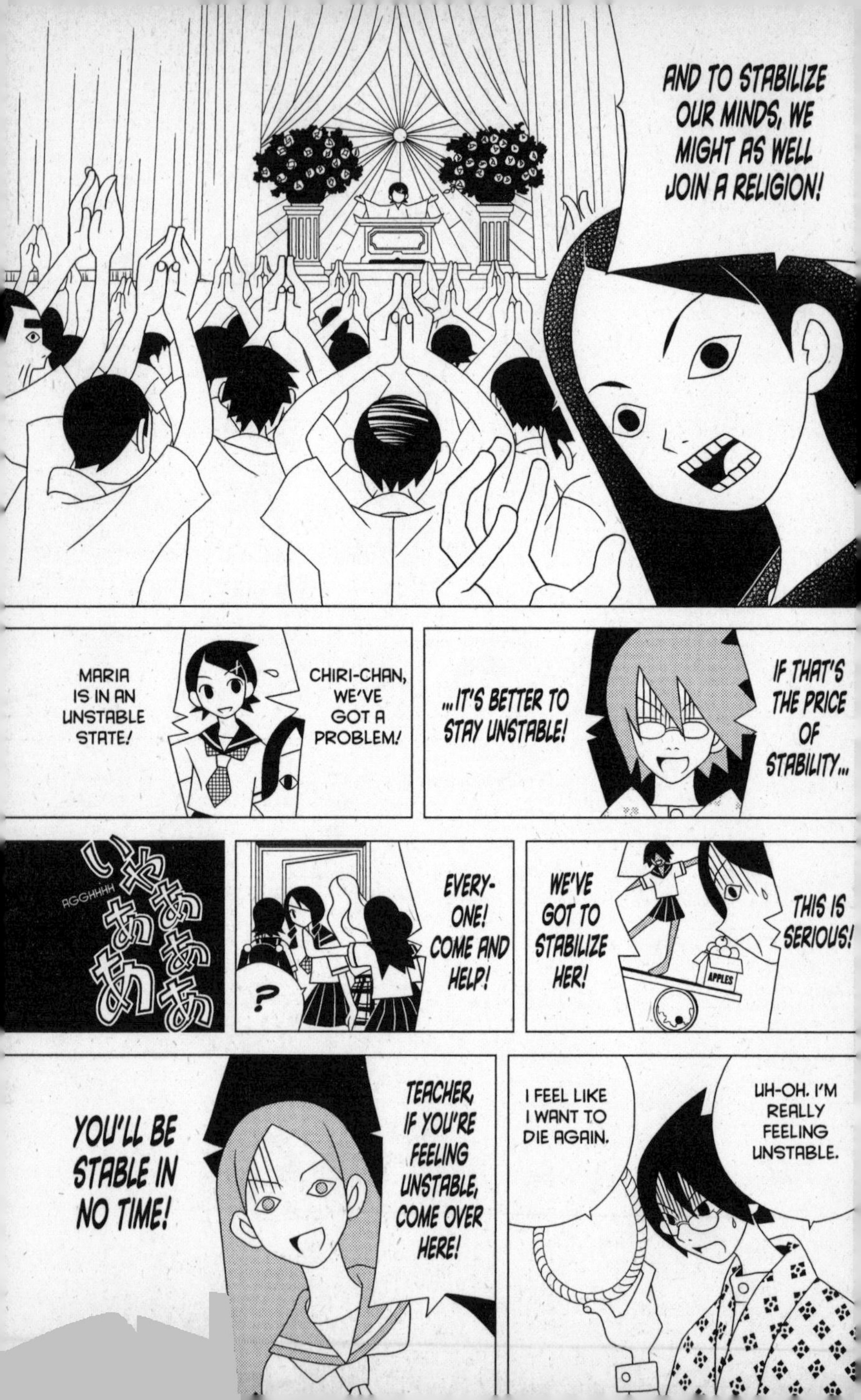
AND TO STABILIZE OUR MINDS, WE MIGHT AS WELL JOIN A RELIGION!
IF THAT'S THE PRICE OF STABILITY...
...IT'S BETTER TO STAY UNSTABLE!
CHIRI-CHAN, WE'VE GOT A PROBLEM!
MARIA IS IN AN UNSTABLE STATE!
THIS IS SERIOUS!
WE'VE GOT TO STABILIZE HER!
APPLES
EVERY-ONE! COME AND HELP!
?
いやあああああ
AGGHHHH
UH-OH. I'M REALLY FEELING UNSTABLE.
I FEEL LIKE I WANT TO DIE AGAIN.
TEACHER, IF YOU'RE FEELING UNSTABLE, COME OVER HERE!
YOU'LL BE STABLE IN NO TIME!

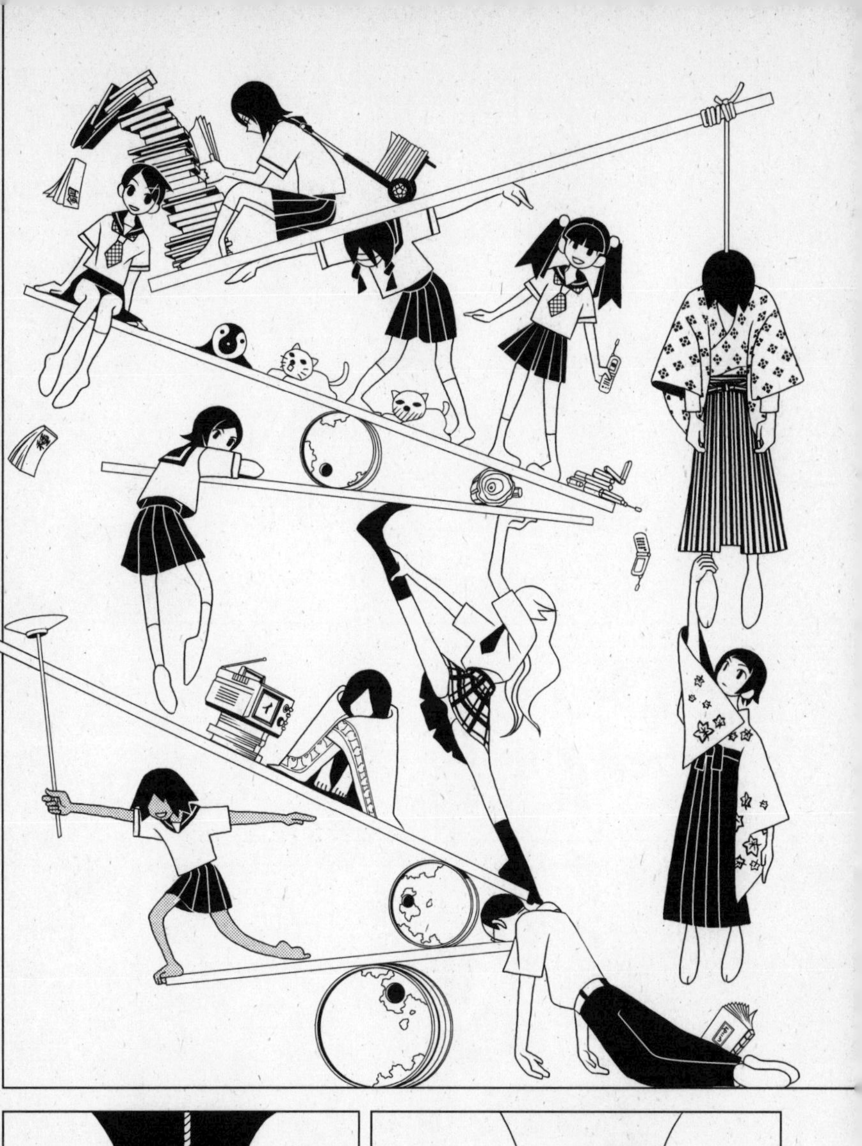

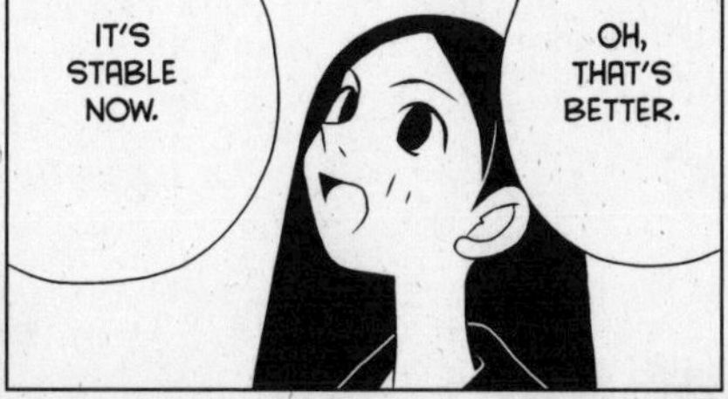
OH, THAT'S BETTER.
IT'S STABLE NOW.

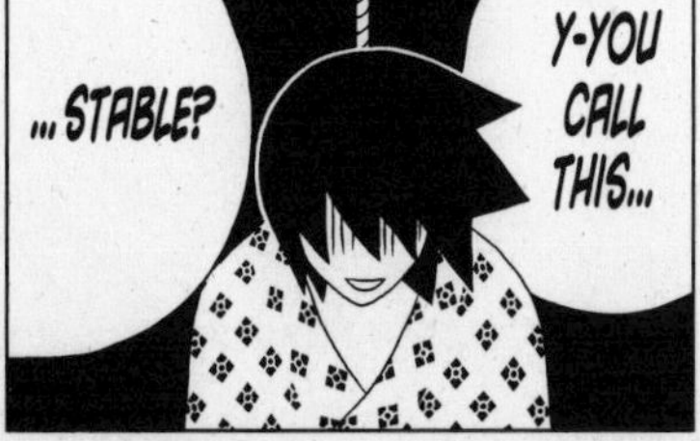
Y-YOU CALL THIS...
...STABLE?

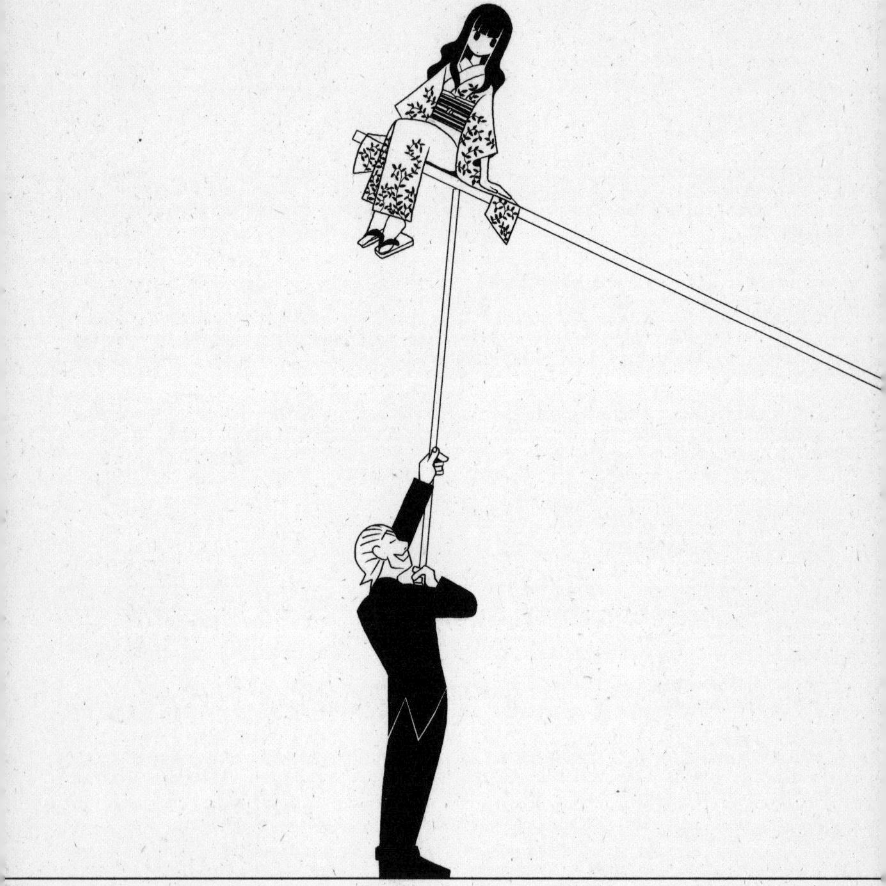

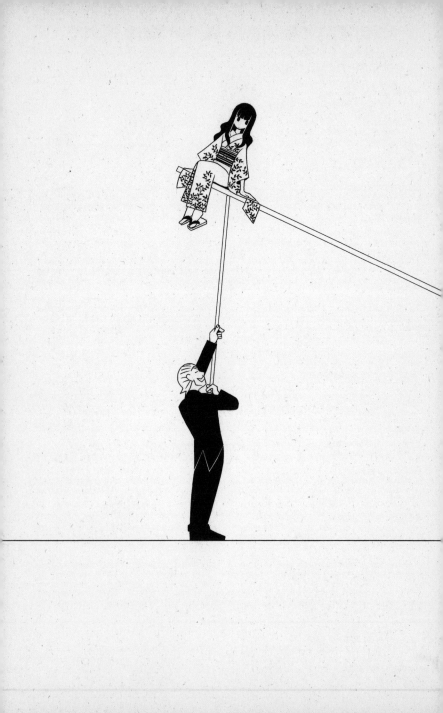

# CURRENT CHARGES FROM THIS ISSUE

LETTER OF ACCUSATION

PLAINTIFF:
OCCUPATION: STUDENT
NAME: KAERE KIMURA

DEFENDANT:
OCCUPATION: FORMER STORE OWNER
NAME: PERRY (ASSUMED NAME)

DATE: JULY 13
ATTN: CHIEF OF POLICE

- PURPOSE OF ACCUSATION
THE ACTS BY THE DEFENDANT, AS STATED BELOW, ARE DEEMED TO COME UNDER CRIMINAL LAW, ARTICLE 176 (FORCIBLE ACT OF LEWDNESS), AND THIS COMPLAINT IS MADE TO PURSUE SEVERE PUNISHMENT TO BE HANDED OUT TO THE DEFENDANT.

- FACTS OF THE ACCUSATION
AT ABOUT 1:00 P.M., WITHIN THE SCHOOL PREMISES, THE DEFENDANT SHOUTED, "HEY THERE, LITTLE GIRL, OPEN UP!" WHILE SIMULTANEOUSLY ASSAULTING ME.

AT THE TIME, I WAS CARRYING A BAG, AND WITH MY HANDS FULL, I WAS UNABLE TO FLEE FROM THE DEFENDANT. HE GRABBED ME BY MY ANKLES, HUNG ME UPSIDE DOWN, AND FORCIBLY PEEKED AT MY PANTIES, THEREBY COMMITTING A LEWD ACT.

THE ACT BY THE DEFENDANT IS CONSIDERED TO FALL UNDER CRIMINAL LAW, ARTICLE 176 (CRIME OF FORCIBLE ACT OF LEWDNESS), SO I HEREBY FILE A COMPLAINT SO THAT SEVERE PUNISHMENT MAY BE HANDED TO THE DEFENDANT.

EVIDENCE
1. WITNESS: NOZOMU ITOSHIKI
2. WITNESS: CLASSMATE A

---

LETTER OF ACCUSATION

PLAINTIFF:
OCCUPATION: STUDENT
NAME: KAERE KIMURA

DEFENDANT:
OCCUPATION: BUTLER
NAME: TOKITA

DATE: AUGUST 31
ATTN: CHIEF OF POLICE

- PURPOSE OF ACCUSATION
THE ACTS BY THE DEFENDANT AS STATED BELOW ARE CONSIDERED TO FALL UNDER CRIMINAL LAW, ARTICLE 230 (CRIME OF DEFAMATION OF CHARACTER), AND THIS COMPLAINT IS MADE TO PURSUE SEVERE PUNISHMENT TO BE HANDED OUT TO THE DEFENDANT.

- FACTS OF THE ACCUSATION
AT ABOUT 8:00 A.M., I WAS FORCED TO WEAR A KIMONO, ALONG WITH FIVE OTHER FEMALE STUDENTS, AT THE ITOSHIKI FAMILY RESIDENCE IN KARUIZAWA (NAGANO PREFECTURE). FURTHERMORE, WHILE THE KIMONOS WERE BEING ASSIGNED, I WAS SINGLED OUT AND FORCED TO WEAR A KIMONO WITH AN EXCEEDINGLY SHORT HEM.

WHEN I VOICED MY PROTESTS, THE REPLY WAS, "THAT HAS ALREADY BEEN LOOKED INTO." THIS WAS SAID OPENLY, IN FRONT OF EVERYONE, TO GIVE THE IMPRESSION THAT I ALWAYS ENJOY WEARING HIGHLY REVEALING CLOTHING.

THE AFOREMENTIONED ACTS ARE CONSIDERED TO FALL UNDER CRIMINAL LAW, ARTICLE 230 (CRIME OF DEFAMATION OF CHARACTER), AND IN ORDER FOR THE DEFENDANT TO BE GIVEN STRICT PUNISHMENT, I HEREBY MAKE MY CHARGES.

EVIDENCE
1. WITNESS: CLASSMATE A
2. IN-HOUSE VIDEO FROM THE BURGLARY SYSTEM DIVISION OF THE ITOSHIKI RESIDENCE

SUPPLEMENTARY DOCUMENTS
THE ABOVE-MENTIONED VIDEOTAPE – ONE TAPE

# PAPER BLOGS

**WISHES** | OPEN UP | NON-REPORTING | SHADOWY OUTCAST

WHEN A CONVERSATION STARTS WITH THE PHRASE "I HAVE A FAVOR TO ASK OF YOU," IT'S USUALLY SOMETHING THAT'S NOT COOL. THEY'RE LIKE: LEND ME MONEY, HURRY UP AND TURN IN YOUR MANUSCRIPT, I'VE GOT TO GO TO COMIKET, SO GIVE ME THE DAY OFF.

SO, JUST DON'T ASK. TRY IMAGINING WHAT IT FEELS LIKE TO BE THE STARS, WITH PEOPLE MAKING WISHES ON YOU ALL THE TIME, AND YOU'LL GET AN IDEA OF HOW TOUGH IT IS FOR THEM. WHEN IT'S "THE WISH OF A LIFETIME" THAT MAKES IT EVEN MORE OF A NUISANCE. YOU CAN'T MAKE ANY MORE WISHES, AND YOU DON'T WANT TO HEAR ABOUT THEM EITHER.

I DON'T LIKE PEOPLE WHO MAKE LOTS OF WISHES. IF ONE COMES TRUE, THEY'LL MAKE ANOTHER, AND IF THAT ONE COMES TRUE, THEY'LL MAKE ANOTHER. IT'S ALWAYS "GIMME, GIMME." THERE'S NO END TO IT. I DON'T WANT TO BE DISLIKED, SO I DON'T MAKE WISHES OR REQUESTS OF PEOPLE. EVEN IF MY WISHES WEREN'T GRANTED, I'D BE DISLIKED ANYWAY.

IN THAT CASE, IT MAKES ME WANT TO MAKE A WISH. WHEN SHOULD I MAKE THAT WISH OF A LIFETIME? CAN IT BE TRANSFERRED TO MY NEXT LIFE? I'LL USE IT ON ABOUT MY THIRD LIFE. SINCE IT'S A WISH FOR MY THIRD LIFE, COULD YOU PLEASE TURN ME INTO AN ANIMATED CHARACTER?

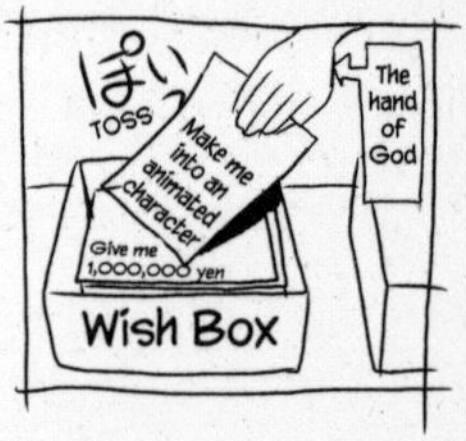
ぽいっ
TOSS
The hand of God
Make me into an animated character
Give me 1,000,000 yen
Wish Box

WISHES | **OPEN UP** | NON-REPORTING | SHADOWY OUTCAST

"I DON'T UNDERSTAND YOUR TRUE FEELINGS."

PEOPLE HAVE SAID THAT TO ME FOR AS LONG AS I CAN REMEMBER. EVEN MY PARENTS TOLD ME THAT. MY HOMEROOM TEACHER SAID THAT. YESTERDAY, I MET A PERSON FOR THE FIRST TIME, AND THEY TOLD ME THAT. (WE DIDN'T GET ALONG SO WELL.)

STRANGERS ASK ME TO OPEN UP MY HEART A LITTLE MORE. BUT THAT'S RIDICULOUS. IF I "OPENED MY HEART" AND SPOKE MY TRUE FEELINGS, PEOPLE WOULD CUT OFF RELATIONS WITH ME ON THE SPOT. AS LONG AS I KEEP THIS DISGRACEFUL HEART OF MINE CLOSED, I CAN SOMEHOW BE INVOLVED WITH OTHERS. YOU PUT A LID OVER SMELLY STUFF TO NOT CAUSE TROUBLE. IT'S JUST GOOD MANNERS TO GET ALONG WITH YOUR NEIGHBORS.

THOUGH PEOPLE TELL ME, "I DON'T UNDERSTAND YOUR TRUE FEELINGS," IN TRUTH, EVEN I DON'T KNOW MY TRUE FEELINGS. WHAT DO I REALLY WANT TO DO? WHAT AM I? WHO ARE YOU TO ME? SO, I'M NOTHING, YOU SAY? WELL, I'M SORRY.

MY HEART HAS TWO DOORS. EVEN I CAN'T OPEN THE ONE IN THE BACK.

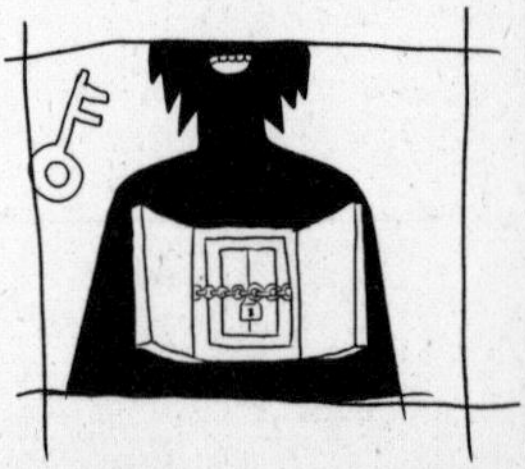

## WISHES | OPEN UP | **NON-REPORTING** | SHADOWY OUTCAST

GOD ISN'T HAPPY, BECAUSE HE KNOWS EVERYTHING...

GOD IS OMNISCIENT, BUT I'M SURE THAT THERE ARE ALL KINDS OF THINGS THAT HE'S BETTER OFF NOT KNOWING.

AS FOR MYSELF, I DON'T WANT TO KNOW, SO I'M NOT GOING TO KNOW. BUT THAT MIGHT MAKE LIFE A LITTLE DIFFICULT, SO I PRETEND THAT I KNOW. I OPEN MY MOUTH, LOOKING LIKE I KNOW. SO, ASK AWAY, KIDS.

Q: HOW MUCH DOES IT COST TO ERASE A NEIGHBOR'S WRINKLES?
A: ABOUT TEN MILLION YEN PER WRINKLE.

Q: WHY ARE THE MAIDS AT THE MAID TEA SHOP ETERNALLY SAID TO BE SEVENTEEN YEARS OLD?
A: EVEN IF SHE KILLS SOMEONE, MAID A WON'T HAVE HER REAL NAME MADE PUBLIC.

Q: WHY DOES PRIME MINISTER KOIZUMI LOOK LIKE DR. MASHIRITO?
A: BECAUSE THEY EVOLVED FROM THE SAME AMOEBA.

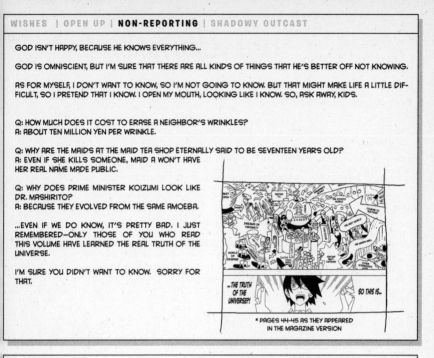

...EVEN IF WE DO KNOW, IT'S PRETTY BAD. I JUST REMEMBERED—ONLY THOSE OF YOU WHO READ THIS VOLUME HAVE LEARNED THE REAL TRUTH OF THE UNIVERSE.

I'M SURE YOU DIDN'T WANT TO KNOW. SORRY FOR THAT.

DREAMS OF VIRGINITY
WORLD OF DESPAIR
GROUP SELF-DEFENSE
SO THIS IS...
...THE TRUTH OF THE UNIVERSE?!

* PAGES 44-45 AS THEY APPEARED IN THE MAGAZINE VERSION

## WISHES | OPEN UP | NON-REPORTING | **SHADOWY OUTCAST**

I DON'T KNOW WHY YOU GOT ANGRY. CALLING YOU THE EMPEROR THAT'S PLACED AT THE SUNSET... IT'S ABOUT THE SHADOW EMPEROR.

I LIKE THE SHADE. EVERY TIME I MOVE, I CHOOSE A PLACE FACING NORTH. EVEN IN THE SHADE, I WEAR SUNBLOCK. OF COURSE, I HANG MY PANTS IN THE SHADE TO DRY.

I'M ATTRACTED TO SHADY WOMEN. I SUPPORT THE SHADOW LEADER YOSHIKO SAKURAI. IF THERE ARE RIGHTS TO SUNLIGHT, I THINK THERE OUGHT TO BE RIGHTS TO SHADE. TO THINK THAT SHADOW ART'S POPULAR NOW, WITH THE SPOTLIGHT BEING CAST ON SHADOWS—WE'RE IN STRANGE TIMES. THEY SAY THAT THE SHADOWS ARE GETTING MORE POPULAR, BUT PLEASE DON'T PUT THE SPOTLIGHT ON THEM. WHAT ARE YOU TRYING TO DO BY SHINING AN INQUISITIVE LIGHT?

I'M AN ADVOCATE FOR SHADE. I DON'T LIKE SUNLIGHT. I LOVE THE TOSHOGU SHRINE IN NIKKO, BECAUSE THERE ARE MONKEYS.

SEE NO EVIL, SPEAK NO EVIL, HEAR NO EVIL. SEE NO DREAMS. HEAR NO SURVEYS. AND SAY NOTHING WHEN PEOPLE ASK, "SO, WHAT TYPE OF WORK DO YOU DO?"

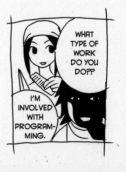

WHAT TYPE OF WORK DO YOU DO??
I'M INVOLVED WITH PROGRAM-MING.

**MANGA KOSHIEN** | EXTREME LIMITS | GOING HOME | MIAI

"OWW!" THERE WAS A STABBING PAIN IN MY RIGHT INSTEP. A CART RAN OVER MY FOOT, MAKING ME THINK THAT IT WAS ANOTHER FLARE-UP WITH MY CHRONIC GOUT. IT WAS A CART FULL OF DREAMS THAT WAS BEING PUSHED BY A YOUNG GIRL ON OTOME ROAD.

"I'M FINE. GO ON. DON'T WORRY 'BOUT ME."

"MAY ALL YOUR DREAMS TAKE TOP PRIORITY."

WITHOUT ASKING ABOUT ME, THE METALLIC-HAIRED MAIDEN KEPT GOING. THIS ROAD IS DANGEROUS. POLICEMEN, PLEASE CONTROL THIS AREA. THE MAIDENS' CARTS ARE OVERLOADED AND THEY'RE ALWAYS SPEEDING; IT'S A LAWLESS AREA.

THE NEXT THING YOU KNOW, WHILE DESPERATELY AVOIDING CARTS, I WAS NEARLY RUN OVER BY A REAL CAR. I SAW A BLACK CENTURY WITH A NOBLE EMBLEM AND THE SILHOUETTE OF THE BACK OF AN ELEGANT HAT. AS I EXPECTED, THEY WEREN'T STOPPED BY THE POLICE. I'M SURE THERE MUST HAVE BEEN SOME MISUNDERSTANDING.

♪ *LU LU LU* ♪ *LU LU LULU LU* ♪

OTOME ROAD, CHAPTER 13 BY TORA BURYU

EDA

MANGA KOSHIEN | **EXTREME LIMITS** | GOING HOME | MIAI

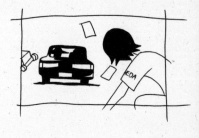

FOR EIGHT HOURS, I COULDN'T REMEMBER NAMES FROM VARIOUS PLACES, WHICH MADE ME IRRITATED. THE WORD "TAKUMACHINE" KEPT GETTING IN THE WAY, SO I COULDN'T REMEMBER A THING. I'M WORTH THREE GAVAS POINTS AND HAVE LESS THAN 1MB OF MEMORY. IT GETS MAXED OUT VERY QUICKLY.

MY HUMAN CAPACITY IS THE SAME WAY. I'M PETTY, SO I LOSE MY TEMPER WHEN THE SMALLEST THING HAPPENS. I'VE NEVER HELD ANYTHING HEAVIER THAN A PEN. I DON'T KNOW A WORLD BIGGER THAN MY MANUSCRIPT. I FRET OVER INSIGNIFICANT THINGS.

BUT YOU KNOW, BECAUSE MY CAPACITY'S SMALL, I CAN BE FULFILLED WITH LITTLE THINGS. EVEN GETTING A COURTEOUS SMILE THAT MIGHT MEAN NOTHING TO YOU MAKES ME SPEND THE ENTIRE DAY IN HAPPINESS.

THE CHARACTER FOR CAPACITY — 器 — LOOKS LIKE FOUR PEOPLE READY TO KILL EACH OTHER. IF THAT'S THE CASE, IT'S BETTER TO BE ARGUING OVER SOMETHING TRIVIAL.

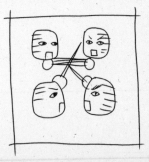

MANGA KOSHIEN | EXTREME LIMITS | **GOING HOME** | MIAI

I CAN'T FIND THE RIGHT TIME TO VISIT MY PARENTS' HOUSE. I'M BUSY DURING MANGA SERIALIZATION TIME, SO IT'S HARD TO FIND TIME TO GO HOME. AFTER A MANGA SERIES IS FINISHED, I CAN'T GO BACK HOME, BECAUSE MY PARENTS WILL WORRY THAT I'M UNEMPLOYED. DURING OBON AND THE NEW YEAR, THERE'S THE PROBABILITY OF LOTS OF DIFFERENT PEOPLE VISITING MY PARENTS' HOME, SO I CAN'T GO THEN. I DON'T HAVE ENOUGH "FACE" TO FACE ANYONE, SO TO SPEAK.

THERE WAS A TIME WHEN I MADE UP MY MIND TO GO, BUT WHEN I GOT THERE, NOBODY WAS HOME. I FELT RATHER RELIEVED. I HADN'T BEEN THERE IN QUITE A WHILE. I THOROUGHLY ENJOYED MYSELF, AND LEFT BEFORE ANYONE RETURNED.

IT SURE IS NICE TO VISIT MY PARENTS' HOME FROM TIME TO TIME.

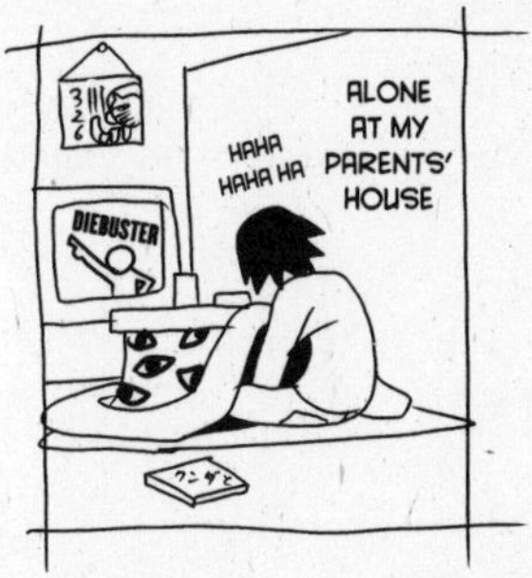
ALONE AT MY PARENTS' HOUSE
HAHA HAHA HA
DIEBUSTER

MANGA KOSHIEN | EXTREME LIMITS | GOING HOME | **MIAI**

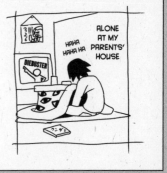

I LIKE THE BACK OF PEOPLE'S HEADS. NO MATTER HOW INTENTLY I STARE AT THEM, THERE'S NO WAY THAT OUR EYES WILL MEET.

I REALLY CAN'T LOOK SOMEONE IN THE EYE WHEN I TALK. I ALWAYS WALK BY WITH MY EYES CAST DOWNWARD, SO I NEVER HAVE TO LOOK ANYONE IN THE EYE. BUT ON RAINY DAYS, IF I'M NOT CAREFUL, I'LL LOOK IN MY OWN EYES BY ACCIDENT. I FEEL LIKE DYING WHEN I SEE MY REPULSIVE FACE REFLECTED IN A PUDDLE.

WHEN I WAS IN JUNIOR HIGH SCHOOL, I WAS SCOLDED BY MY HOMEROOM TEACHER, WHO TOLD ME TO LOOK INTO PEOPLE'S EYES WHEN I TALKED. BUT WHEN I DID LOOK INTO HIS EYES, HE TOLD ME, "WHAT DO YOU MEAN, LOOKING AT ME LIKE THAT?!" AND BEAT ME.

I DON'T LOOK INTO PEOPLE'S EYES WHEN SPEAKING ANYMORE. BUT IF SOMEONE TELLS ME TO LOOK INTO THEIR EYES, AND I HAVE NO OTHER CHOICE, I'LL LOOK INTO THE WHITES OF THEIR EYES. PEOPLE WITH LARGER PUPILS ARE A PROBLEM. PEOPLE WITH ALL-WHITE EYES ARE ALSO A PROBLEM.

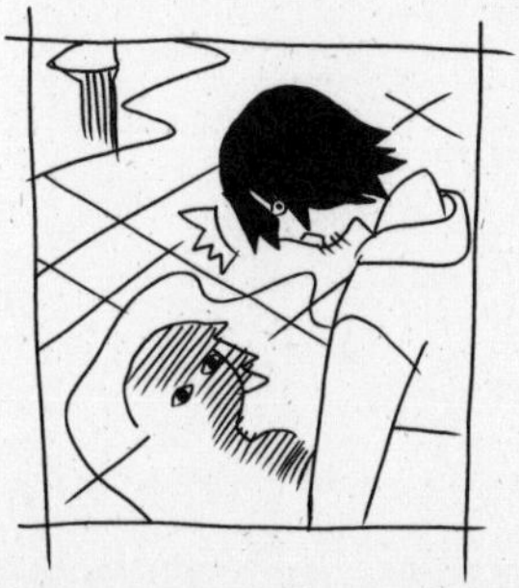

## CRITICISM TRAINING | INSTABILITY

I'M A GUY WHO'S USED TO CRITICISM, BUT SOMETIMES I FEEL AS IF I'M WORTH SOMETHING. LIKE THE TIME WHEN I HAPPENED TO SEE SOMEONE BUYING ONE OF MY MANGA, RIGHT IN FRONT OF MY EYES. TO HAVE SOMEONE READ MY WORK IS SO EMBARRASSING THAT IT MAKES ME WANT TO DIE, BUT AS AN ADULT, THE TRUTH IS THAT I'D BE IN TROUBLE IF THEY DIDN'T SELL.

ON A CERTAIN MONTH, ON A CERTAIN DAY, IN A CERTAIN BOOK STORE IN SHINJUKU, I OVERHEARD THIS CONVERSATION BETWEEN TWO ANGELS, WHO HAD TAKEN THE FIRST COLLECTIVE VOLUME OF *SAYONARA, ZETSUBOU-SENSEI* IN THEIR HANDS, AND WERE GETTING READY TO BUY...

"YOU KNOW, THIS THING HERE...YOU THINK I CAN USE IT AS A REFERENCE FOR DRAWING KIMONOS FOR *GINTAMA*?"

THANK YOU FOR YOUR PURCHASE. WE, THE STAFF, WILL CONTINUE TO WORK OUR HARDEST FOR YOU, OUR CUSTOMER, SO YOU CAN FIND REFERENCE MATERIAL FOR *GINTAMA DOJINSHI.*

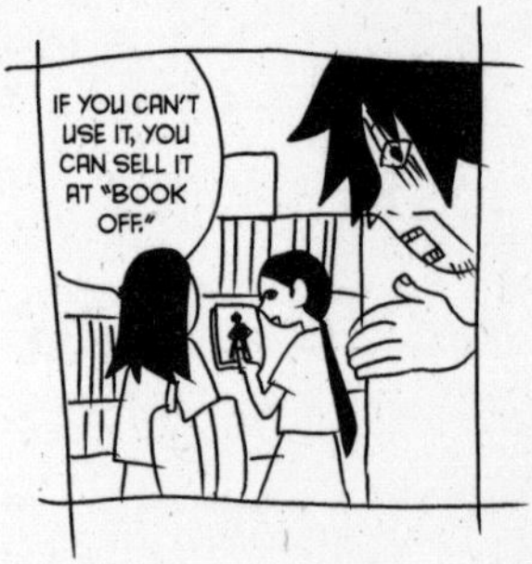
IF YOU CAN'T USE IT, YOU CAN SELL IT AT "BOOK OFF."

## CRITICISM TRAINING | INSTABILITY

WHEN I THOUGHT, "EARTHQUAKE?!" IT WAS ACTUALLY I WHO WAS SHAKING. EARTHQUAKES ARE SCARY, BUT WHEN I'M DOING THE SHAKING, IT'S EVEN SCARIER.

EVERY NOW AND THEN, THE WORLD LOOKS SHAPELESS AND DISTORTED TO ME. PEOPLE WALKING AROUND LOOK LIKE THE I-MODE LOGO.

I'M UNSTABLE. I CAN'T DRAW A STRAIGHT LINE. I ALWAYS HAVE ASHI-SAN CORRECT THEM FOR ME. WHEN I THINK I'M WALKING ON THE RIGHT SIDE OF THE ROAD, BEFORE I REALIZE IT, I'M ON THE LEFT. WHEN I USED TO DRAW A SPORTS MANGA, I ENDED UP WITH A MANGA WITH LOTS OF VULGAR STUFF. *SUNDAY* WAS THE MAGAZINE.

MY WORK WAS SUPPOSED TO BE A DREAM, SO THERE ARE PLENTY OF TIMES WHEN I GET DESPONDENT. I'D GO OUT AND BUY NEW CLOTHES, AND WEAR MY OLD ONES. ONE OF MY SOCKS ALWAYS DISAPPEARS. WHEN I GO OUT, CROWS ALWAYS FOLLOW ME.

I HAD THIS DREAM WHERE I HAD TO CHOOSE BETWEEN A LIFE WITHOUT A ROOF, AND A LIFE WITHOUT A FLOOR. I CHOSE THE LIFE WITHOUT A FLOOR. MY BODY WENT SINKING INTO THE DIRT. EVENTUALLY, MY WHOLE BODY WAS COVERED IN DIRT, SO THERE WAS NO LONGER ANY POINT FOR A ROOF.

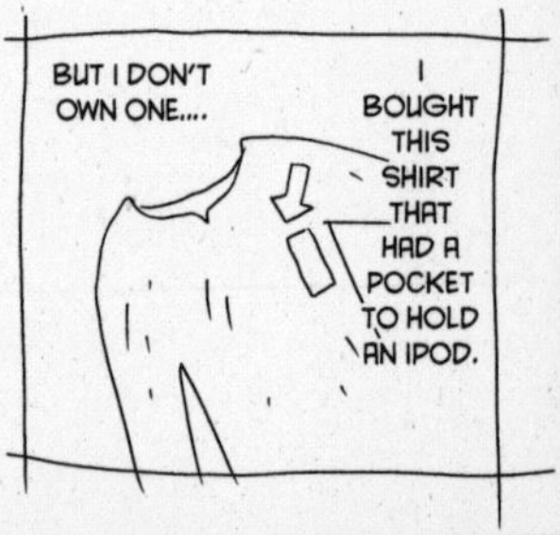
I BOUGHT THIS SHIRT THAT HAD A POCKET TO HOLD AN IPOD.
BUT I DON'T OWN ONE....

# THIS ISSUE'S SURVEY

THANK YOU SO VERY MUCH FOR PURCHASING VOLUME 2 OF *SAYONARA, ZETSUBOU-SENSEI.*

IF IT'S NOT TOO MUCH TROUBLE, WE WOULD GREATLY APPRECIATE YOUR ANSWERS TO THE FOLLOWING QUESTIONS, TO USE FOR OUR FOCUS MARKETING FOR FUTURE VOLUMES. WE APPRECIATE YOUR COOPERATION.

Q1: PLEASE LIST NINE STORIES THAT WERE BORING FOR YOU IN VOLUME 2 OF *SAYONARA, ZETSUBOU-SENSEI.*

Q2: PLEASE LIST TEN CHARACTERS APPEARING IN THIS VOLUME WHOM YOU DISLIKED.

Q3: OUT OF THE CHOICES BELOW, PICK FOUR GENRES THAT YOU WOULD *NOT* LIKE KOJI KUMETA TO DRAW:

    A. LOVE COMEDY
    B. SPORTS
    C. FIGHTING
    D. HUMOR
    E. SCI-FI/FANTASY

Q4: TELL US YOUR LEVEL OF SATISFACTION WITH VOLUME 2 OF *SAYONARA, ZETSUBOU-SENSEI.*

    A. RATHER SATISFIED
    B. DISSATISFIED
    C. EXTREMELY DISSATISFIED
    D. DISSATISFIED TO A LEVEL I'VE ALMOST NEVER EXPERIENCED BEFORE

Q5: TELL US YOUR REASON FOR BUYING *SAYONARA, ZETSUBOU-SENSEI.*

    A. AS RESEARCH MATERIAL FOR *GINTAMA DOJINSHI*
    B. I MISTOOK IT FOR A SUBCULTURE MANGA.
    C. I MISTOOK IT FOR A MANGA BY KENJIRO HATA
    D. I BOUGHT THE WHOLE LOT BECAUSE THERE WERE THINGS I DIDN'T WANT THE OFFICE TO TELL ME

SEND IN YOUR ANSWERS FOR QUESTIONS 1-5 ON AN OFFICIAL GOVERNMENT POSTCARD TO THIS ADDRESS:

    SAYONARA, ZETSUBOU-SENSEI
    ATTN: READER SURVEY DEPARTMENT
    12-21, 2-CHOME
    OTOWA, BUNKYO-KU, TOKYO 112-8001
    JAPAN

    THANK YOU VERY MUCH.

> PLEASE UNDERSTAND THAT THE POSTCARDS YOU MAIL IN, INCLUDING YOUR PERSONAL INFORMATION, MAY BE FORWARDED TO THE AUTHOR.

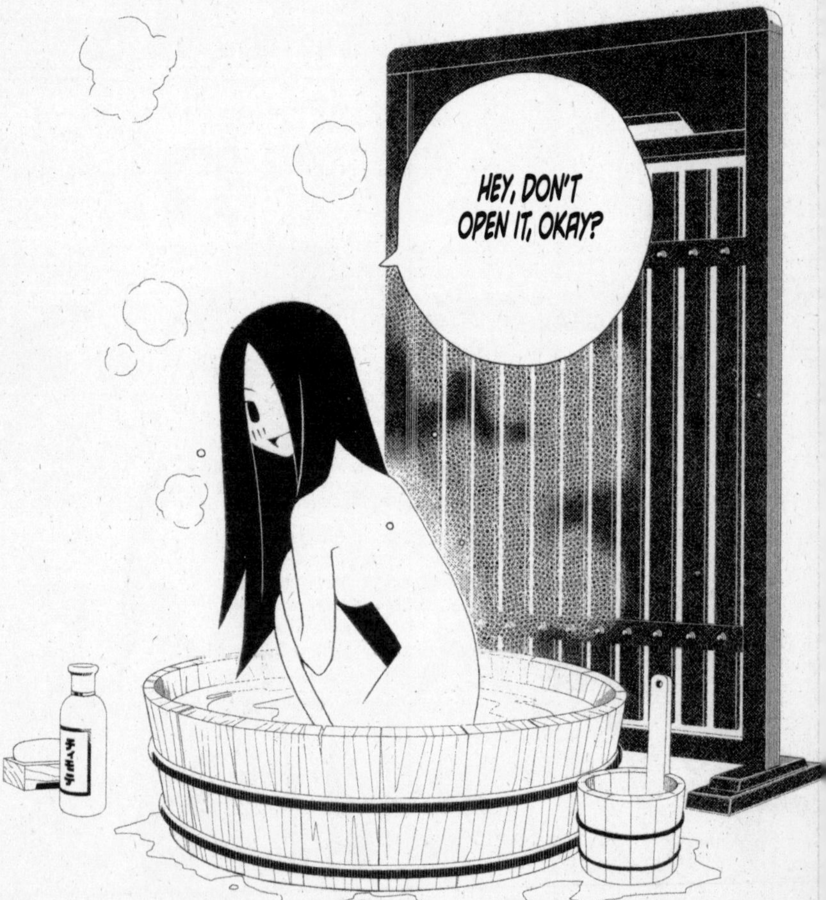
HEY, DON'T OPEN IT, OKAY?

# LITTLE MISS PRECISION

BY: KAFUKA

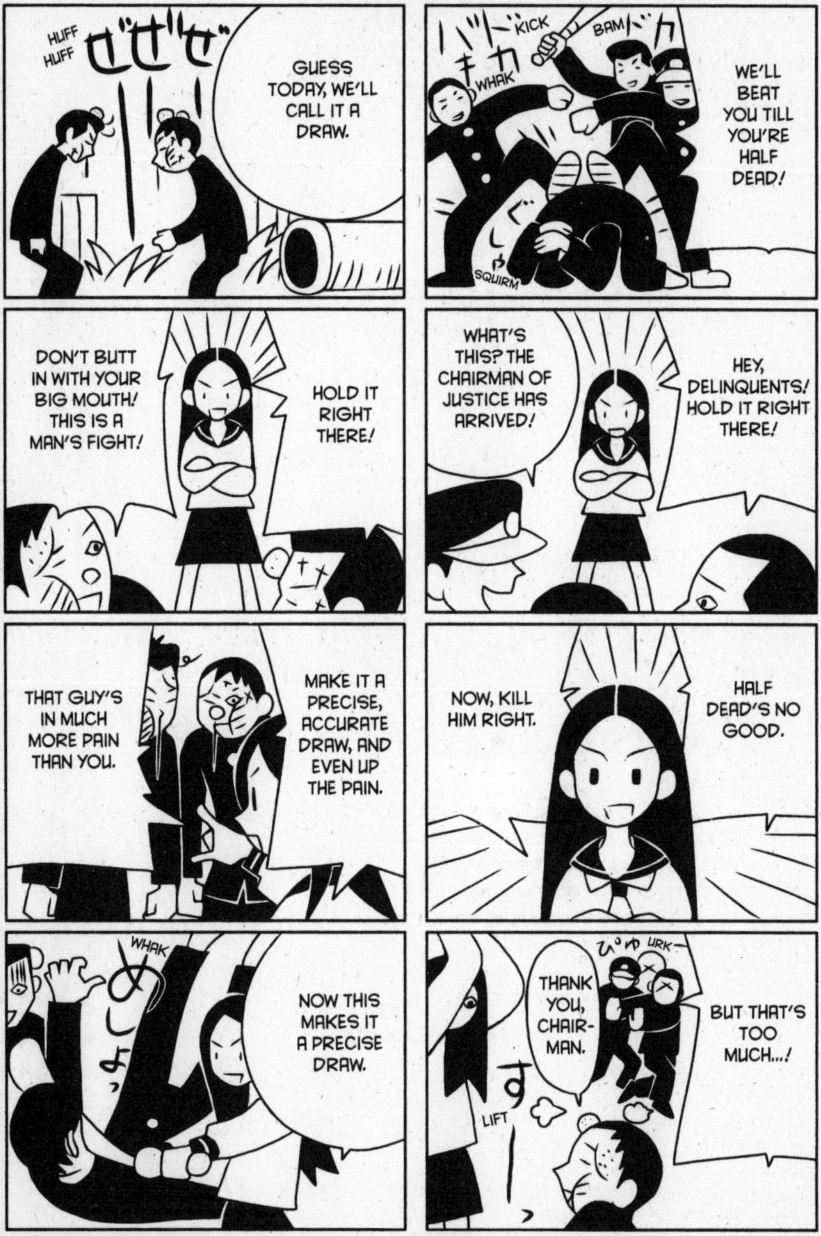
KICK
BAM
WHAK
SQUIRM
WE'LL BEAT YOU TILL YOU'RE HALF DEAD!
HEY, DELINQUENTS! HOLD IT RIGHT THERE!
WHAT'S THIS? THE CHAIRMAN OF JUSTICE HAS ARRIVED!
HALF DEAD'S NO GOOD.
NOW, KILL HIM RIGHT.
URK
BUT THAT'S TOO MUCH...!
THANK YOU, CHAIRMAN.
LIFT
HUFF HUFF
GUESS TODAY, WE'LL CALL IT A DRAW.
HOLD IT RIGHT THERE!
DON'T BUTT IN WITH YOUR BIG MOUTH! THIS IS A MAN'S FIGHT!
MAKE IT A PRECISE, ACCURATE DRAW, AND EVEN UP THE PAIN.
THAT GUY'S IN MUCH MORE PAIN THAN YOU.
WHAK
NOW THIS MAKES IT A PRECISE DRAW.

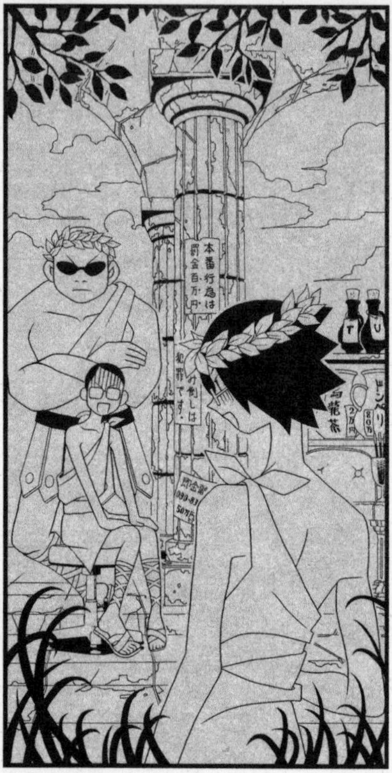
本番行為は罰金百万円
ドンペリ
80万
2万円

## ZETSUBOU LITERARY COMPILATION

## RUN, EROS!

MELOS WAS OUTRAGED.

"BUT THAT'S 70,000 YEN* FOR TWO BEERS! YOU SAID THERE'D BE NO CHARGE FOR ADDITIONAL BEERS!"

"NO, THIS IS OUR USUAL PRICE."

"I'LL GO AND GET THE MONEY, THEN."

"WE'LL KEEP YOUR FRIEND HERE AS COLLATERAL. IF YOU DON'T RETURN, WE'LL BURY HIM, SEE?"

MELOS RAN...

"SO SORRY...I MIGHT NOT BE ABLE TO RETURN."

*70,000 YEN=ABOUT $650 U.S.

# Translation Notes

Japanese is a tricky language for most Westerners, and translation is often more art than science. In the case of a text-dense manga like *Sayonara, Zetsubou-sensei*, it's a delicate art indeed. Although most of the jokes are universal, Koji Kumeta is famous for filling his manga with references to Japanese politics, entertainment, otaku culture, religion, and sports. Unless you're a true Japanophile, it's difficult to understand it all without some serious background knowledge of current events at the time the manga was running. Kumeta also uses references to foreign literature and politics, so even Japanese readers probably don't get all the humor. For your reading pleasure, here are notes on some of the more obscure references and difficult-to-translate jokes in *Sayonara, Zetsubou-sensei*.

## General Notes

### Sayonara, Zetsubou-sensei (title)

The title *Sayonara, Zetsubou-sensei* literally translates to "Good-bye, Mr. Despair." It's a possible reference to James Hilton's 1934 novel of a beloved teacher, *Good-bye, Mr. Chips* (known in Japan as *Chips-sensei, Sayonara*). The Del Rey edition preserves the original Japanese title, with *The Power of Negative Thinking* as a subtitle to express Itoshiki's philosophy. (The English subtitle is itself a reference to Norman Vincent Peale's 1952 self-help book *The Power of Positive Thinking*.)

### Signs

Koji Kumeta's highly detailed and realistic renderings of modern Japanese life present one special challenge to the letterer. Kumeta fills his panels with all the ephemera of everyday life—street signs, product labels, magazine covers, newspaper pages, and so on. It's difficult to replace this text with English lettering without interfering with the integrity of the original illustrations. Out of respect for Kumeta's unique artwork, many signs have retained their original Japanese lettering.

## Page Notes

### Takeshi Kaga, page iv
Takeshi Kaga (1950– ) is a Japanese actor best known as "Chairman Kaga" on the original Japanese *Iron Chef* TV series.

### Hikikomori, page 3
*Hikikomori* is a Japanese term for individuals who have chosen to withdraw from society and not leave their homes. The word comes from the verb *hikikomoru*, which means "stay indoors" or "be confined indoors." It is considered a serious social problem in Japan. Komori's name comes from the *hikikomori* phenomenon.

### May the Moon of This Month's Evening Cloud Over with My Tears, page 4
*Sayonara, Zetsubou-sensei*'s chapter titles are usually references to classic Japanese fiction. This title is a reference to Koyo Ozaki's 1897–1902 novel *Konjiki Yasha* ("The Golden Demon," also known as "The Usurer"), in which a wealthy suitor comes between a poor young couple.

### Hanging wishes, page 4
This chapter takes place during the beautifully lit-up, night-time festivities of the Tanabata Festival (or Star Festival), held annually in summer. During Tanabata, people write their wishes on strips of paper, known as *tanzaku*, and hang them on special bamboo branches in hopes that their wishes come true. The festival celebrates the meeting of the stars Orihime (Vega) and Hikoboshi (Altair) who, at other times of the year, are

separated by the Milky Way. According to mythology, these two lovers are allowed to meet only once a year, on the seventh day of the seventh lunar month.

## Assorted references, page 5

The Great King of Terror is a character from the prophecies of Nostradamus, who was supposed to begin his reign of terror in July 1999. "JR" stands for the Japan Railways Group, which operates most of Japan's railway network. The "Cool Biz" campaign was a 2005 Japanese environmental campaign to save electricity by dressing casually at work and using less air-conditioning. ("Warm Biz" was an unofficial counter-proposal to save electricity during winter by wearing heavy turtleneck shirts.) "May He Walk" refers to Futa-kun, a red panda at the Chiba Zoo who became a big attraction due to his ability to stand on his hind legs. Tamao Nishi is the name of a bearded seal who took up residence in a river in Yokohama's Nishi Ward, and was so beloved by the locals that he was registered as a citizen under the name Tamao Nishi. Dr. Nakamatsu (or as he calls himself, Dr. Nakamats) is a colorful inventor of strange devices who has repeatedly run for governor of Tokyo.

## President Kosaku Shima, page 9

This is a reference to *Shachô Shima Kosaku* ("President Kosaku Shima"), the manga by Kenshi Hirokane. Hirokane's businessman hero, Kosaku Shima, first appeared in 1983, and gradually rose through the corporate ranks, becoming company president in 2008 (a few years after this manga chapter first appeared, suggesting that Shima's wish came true).

## Assorted references, page 12

Ichiro Tanaka and Suzuki are characters who appeared in *Zetsubou-sensei*, volume 1, page 26, in which they previously expressed their dreams to join Japan's J. League soccer league, aka J2 (Tanaka) and study at Momogi Animation School, aka Mo-Ani (Suzuki). Evidently they're serious about their wishes. "The former Mr. Sekiutsu" is a character who appears in volume 1, page 121, having sold all that he possessed, including his internal organs. He sold his name to Maria Taro Sekiutsu.

## Assorted references, page 13

Ichiro Suzuki is a Japanese-born outfielder for the Seattle Mariners. Prince Peter Kropotkin (1842–1921) was a famous Russian anarchist, scientist, and author. "Horiemon" is short for Horie Takafumi, founder of the Japanese Internet portal livedoor. (He was known as an "alchemist" in the IT industry, hence the wish for "gold.") "Ayu" is short for Ayumi Hamasaki, the Empress of J-Pop, who easily sells a million CDs. The so-called Kano sisters are a pair of Japanese TV celebrities who are chiefly known for their flashy fashion sense and appearing nude together in photo books.

## "You, who sleeps, have you forgotten?" page 13

"You, who sleeps" (*Utatane no kimi*) is a verse from the poem *Hasu no Hanabune* ("Lotus Flower Boat"), from the book *Midaregami* ("Tangled Hair") by Akiko Yosano (1878–1942). The poems deal with love's awakening and carnal desire.

## Assorted references, page 15

Morning Musume is a famous all-girl J-Pop group, founded in 1997. They have a revolving lineup with new girls auditioning for spots as others "retire." Haru Urara is a Japanese racehorse, born in 1996, who became a sort of celebrity due to her unbroken string of 113 losses. Akira Kaji is a Japanese soccer player who lost a goal due to a controversial offside decision in a 2005 FIFA Confederations Cup against Brazil. "May I get together with Komuro" refers to the failed love affair between idol singer Tomomi Kahara and music producer/DJ Tetsuya Komuro. "May I be the chief mourner" refers to the public dispute between two popular sumo wrestlers, brothers Takanohana and Wakanohana, as to who was going to take over the honorable role of "chief mourner" at the funeral of their sumo wrestler father in 2005. (This incident is also referred to on page 35, and again on page 53.) Amuro and Lalah are characters from the 1979 anime series *Mobile Suit Gundam*. *Touch* is a famous 1981 baseball manga by Mitsuru Adachi, an artist Koji Kumeta admires.

## Assorted references, page 16

"May I practice birth control" refers to Shido Nakamura and Yoko Takeuchi, actors who met on the set of the movie *Be With You* in 2004. They had an affair, Yoko became pregnant, and they were briefly married and then divorced. Kazuyoshi Miura is a Japanese soccer player who was not selected as a main registered member in the '98 game and ended up unable to participate in the World Cup. Yama Hiraku is short for Taku Yamasaki, a Japanese Diet Member who was frequently embroiled in sex scandals and became famous for saying, "If I hadn't been a Diet Member, I definitely would have been an adult video actor." ("AV" is a Japanese abbreviation for "adult videos.") Goku and Vegeta are characters in Akira Toriyama's manga *Dragon Ball*, aka *Dragon Ball Z*. "Nacchi" is short for Natsumi Abe, a former member of Morning Musume, whose image was tarnished in 2004 by a plagiarism scandal. Kazuhide Uekusa was a former professor at Waseda University who was arrested in 2004 for peeping under girls' skirts at a train station using a mirror.

## I want to be a shellfish in my next life, page 17

This is a reference to the 1958 Japanese TV drama *Watashi wa Kai ni Naritai* ("I Want to Be a Shellfish"), which has been repeatedly remade, the most recent remake being in 2008.

## Your Front Hair Swept Back for the First Time..., page 18

This title is taken from the opening line to the poem *Hatsukoi* ("First Love"), part of the poetry collection *Wakanashu* ("A Collection of Young Herbs"), by Toson Shimazaki (1872–1943).

## "Opened Japan" vs. "Opened" the school, page 20

"Opened Japan" and "opened the school" are both pronounced *kaiko* (though the written characters are not the same) so, in the Japanese version, this is a pun. Commodore Perry (1794–1858) was the Commodore of the U.S. Navy who, in 1854, sailed a fleet of "black ships" to Japan and famously pressured Japan to open diplomatic relations to the United States, ending three hundred years of Japanese isolationism.

## *Shini Rurubu*, page 23

*Shini Rurubu*, "Rurubu for Dying," is a parody of the actual *Rurubu* series of Japanese travel guidebooks. Zetsubou-sensei uses it to find potential suicide spots.

## Ueno Clinic, page 28

The Ueno Clinic is a clinic that performs circumcisions, a fairly common form of cosmetic surgery among Japanese adult men. They frequently advertise in men's magazines.

## Surströmming, page 29

Baltic herring which has been soaked in brine and left to ferment for months, surströmming is considered a delicacy in Sweden. The cans' contents usually splatter when opened due to pressure from the fermentation inside.

## Signs on Perry Shop, page 31

Perrycan Courier Service is a takeoff on Japan's well-known Pelican Courier Service. *Kanten* is a Japanese dessert made with agar agar. Perrysienne is a takeoff of Parisienne, which is a type of gnocchi, among other things.

## Thou Shalt Not Know, page 32

This title is a reference to the poem *Kimi Shinitamo koto Nakare* ("Thou Shalt Not Die"), by Akiko Yosano (1878–1942). In Japanese, "Thou Shalt Not Know" is *Kimi Shiritamo koto Nakare*, just one letter's difference.

## One missed call, page 32

In addition to a common cellphone message, *Chakushin Ari* ("One Missed Call") is the name of a 2004 Japanese horror movie. An American remake was released in 2008.

## Dangerous Regions of Tokyo Death Map, page 36

The *Tokyo Kiken Chitai Shi no Map* ("Tokyo Dangerous Regions Map of Death") originated on a program broadcast on July 2, 2005, on Asahi TV, which claimed to show what buildings and parts of Tokyo would be most dangerous in case of a major earthquake. The program also warned viewers of the high probability of an earthquake.

## Takeo Omori, page 36

Takeo Omori is a character in Masashi Ueda's long-running family four-panel manga *Yorinuki Kobo-chan*, aka *Kobo the Li'l Rascal*. His marriage in the strip was a minor media event.

## Assorted references, page 37

"Train man" refers to the megahit 2004 love story *Train Man*, aka *Densha Otoko*, which was supposedly based on a real incident. *Ippai no Kakesoba* ("One Serving of Kakesoba Noodles") was a popular human-interest story written by Ryohei Kuri in 1989, and later adapted into a movie; however, its popularity was marred when the author was later convicted of crimes. "I thought I'd bought an 86 but I got an 85" refers to the AE85 and AE86 Toyota Corolla GTS. (The AE85 has a similar exterior but a less-powerful engine.) "That manga" may refer to *Hayate the Combat Butler*, the manga by Kumeta's former assistant Kenjiro Hata, currently running in *Weekly Shonen Sunday* (a rival of *Weekly Shonen Magazine*, where *Sayonara Zetsubou-sensei* appears).

## The Truth of the Universe Map, pages 44–45

Unfortunately, analyzing this map in detail would take as much space as the entire volume. However, readers will recognize references to many recurring jokes, such as the Ueno Clinic, Yoshiko Sakurai, etc.

## Murindô Bookstore, page 47

*Murindô* literally means "friendless."

## I'm Predestined to Be in the Shadows, page 48

This title is a reference to *Horoki* ("Vagabond's Song") by Fumiko Hayashi (1903–1951). The novel includes a famous line, *Watashi wa shukumeiteki na horosha de aru* ("I'm predestined to be a vagabond").

## Shinsengumi, page 52

The *Shinsengumi* ("New Select Squad") was a special police force of about three hundred ronin created at the end of Japan's Tokugawa era (about 1863–1869). Their mission was to keep the peace in Kyoto and defend the Tokugawa shogunate against the revolutionary elements, which would eventually lead to the Meiji Restoration. The members of the *Shinsengumi* have a special place in Japanese folklore and pop culture as some of the last samurai and loyal defenders of a doomed regime. Soji Okita, Toshizo Hijikata, and Isami Kondo were high-ranking members of the group, while Yoshimura is more obscure, as Kumeta points out.

## Assorted references, page 53

Sadaharu Oh and Katsuya Nomura are Japan's #1 and #2 ranked professional baseball players. The Saiyans are an alien race and Kuririn is a human character in Akira Toriyama's manga *Dragon Ball*, aka *Dragon Ball Z*. *Wuthering Heights* was produced as a play in Suzue Miuchi's classic manga about a young actress, *Glass no Kamen* ("Mask of Glass"). The manga's heroine, Maya Kitajima, played the young Cathy and outshined her counterpart who was playing Cathy as an adult. Yujiro Ishihara (1934–1987) was an actor and singer, while Tony Tani (1917–1987) was a vaudevillian, comedian, and singer who was most popular in the 1950s and 1960s. Takuya Kimura (aka Kimutaku) is the name of an actor and member of the Japanese idol group SMAP, while the other Takuya Kimura (pronounced the same but written using different Chinese characters) is a professional baseball player. "Sibling rivalry" and "father's death" refers to the feud between the sumo wrestlers Takanohana and Wakanohana (see notes for page 15). Hidetoshi Nakata is a famous soccer player, while a different Hide was a popular participant on the Japanese reality TV program *Ainori* ("Car Pool" or "Love Ride"), in which seven young single men and women ride around the world in a pink bus. "Madame Dewi" refers to Dewi Sukarno (1940– ), formerly Naoko Nemoto, a Japanese woman who married Sukarno (1901–1970), the first president of Indonesia. After Sukarno was overthrown in a 1967 coup and died three years later, Dewi became a wealthy international socialite.

## Hercules Beetle and Acteon Beetle, page 57

Hercules Beetle and Acteon Beetle are cards in *Mushiking: The King of Beetles*, an arcade collectible card game released by Sega in 2003. Each time a player deposits money to play, the machine dispenses a random card with a barcode, which can then be scanned into the machine and used to play.

## Assorted references, page 57

The *donjarahoi* is the name of the dance in the children's song *Mori no Kobito* ("Little People of the Forest"). It's a word which, to Japanese audiences, conjures up cute images of little elves dancing cheerfully. *Meitantei Kageman* ("Famous Detective Shadowman") is a classic children's manga and anime created by Aooni Yamane. Lum-chan is the romantic interest in Rumiko Takahashi's 1978–1987 manga *Urusei Yatsura*.

## Sunlight Monkey Troupe, page 59

The *Nikko Saru Gundan* ("Nikko Monkey Troupe") is a real tourist attraction in Nikko, Japan, in which costumed monkeys perform tricks. *Nikko* also means "sunlight," so Kumeta is making a pun.

## Assorted references, page 60

This page has some of the trickiest references in this volume. "Kage Utada" is a reference to the real-life singer Hikaru Utada (*kage* means "shadow" and *hikaru* means "light"). Keiko Fuji is Hikaru Utada's mother. "The night unfolds" is a reference to Keiko Fuji's hit song *Yume wa Yoru Hiraku* ("Dreams unfold at night"). "Stomp the shadow," aka *kagefumi,* is a Japanese game similar to tag, in which the person who is "it" stomps on the other players' shadows to tag them.

## Confessions of a Pen Name, page 65

This title is a reference to the novel *Kamen no Kokuhaku* ("Confessions of a Mask") by the famous author Yukio Mishima (1925–1970). It's a semi-autobiographical story of a young man coming to terms with his homosexuality.

## *Dôjinshi,* page 62

This entire chapter deals with *dôjinshi* (literally "same-person publications"), the Japanese term for small-press and self-published works. Although *dôjinshi* can be anything from literary journals to self-published computer software, the majority is manga fan-fiction, including a great deal of *yaoi,* a genre depicting imaginary romantic (and sexual) liasons between male characters from various manga, anime, and live-action shows. Female *yaoi* fans are known as *fujoshi,* an alternate reading for the name of the character introduced in this chapter, Harumi Fujiyoshi.

## Stuff in Fujiyoshi's room, page 63

Fujiyoshi's room is littered with evidence of her *dôjinshi* hobby, specifically *yaoi dôjinshi*. There's a poster for "Anaruto," which may be a reference to the manga *Naruto,* although it's also worth mentioning that "l" and "r" are the same letter in Japanese. There's also several mentions of "Dea x Yza," a reference to Yzak Joule and Dearka Elsman, characters from the 2002 anime series *Mobile Suit Gundam SEED*. The "x" refers to a *yaoi* couple, similar to the "slash" in American fan-fiction (e.g., "Kirk/Spock"). Other signs include references to the anime series *Fafner of the Azure* and various printing companies that do dôjinshi work. Judging from her calendar, Fujiyoshi is trying to prepare a *dôjinshi* for a summer convention, and the note taped to her mug reads "Taiyo Printing—noon—meet up with Kami Nasakino-san—Ikebukuro, 7:30—return the 'Dea x Yza' book."

## "Is it the Araragi School? Or is it the Shirakaba Movement?" page 65

*Araragi* was a Japanese literary/poetry magazine that ran from 1908 to 1997, and whose famous contributors were known as the "Araragi School." The *Shirakaba* ("White Birches") movement is a group of Japanese writers who were active in the second half of the twentith century. With Zetsubou-sensei's old-fashioned sensibilities, this is the type of *dôjinshi* he immediately thinks of.

## Athr x Caga, page 66

This is a reference to Athrun Zala and Cagalli Yula Athha from *Mobile Suit Gundam SEED*. It's a straight male-female pairing.

## *Dôjinshi* convention signs, page 67

This convention is a thinly fictionalized version of Comiket ("Comic Market"), the hugely popular *dôjinshi* convention held twice a year (summer and winter) in Japan. Most of the signs on pages 67–70 are normal signs that one might find at a *dôjinshi* convention: prices, catalogs, advertisements for printing companies, etc. One of the book covers reads *Okusama wa Maho Jukujo* ("My Wife Is a Magical Mature Woman"), a parody of the anime *Okusama wa Maho Shojo* ("My Wife Is a Magical Girl.")

## Cosplaying *Rurouni Kenshin*, page 67

Cosplay is short for "costume play": dressing up in costumes of manga, anime, or videogame characters. Cosplayers in Japan pay great attention to detail, and often go to events such as Comiket to show off their perfectly crafted alter egos. Nobuhiro Watsuki's *Rurouni Kenshin* (*Ruroken* for short) is a manga set in the Meiji Era (1868–1912). The convention attendees have mistaken Zetsubou-sensei's naturally retro clothing style for the elaborate kimonos of *Rurouni Kenshin*. (Actually, in the original Japanese, Koji Kumeta calls it *Uroken*, but Japanese readers would get the reference.)

## Zakuro Taisen, page 68

This is a reference to the video game, anime, and manga franchise *Sakura Taisen* ("Sakura Wars"), set in an alternate 1920s Japan. Due to Matoi Tsunetsuki's old-fashioned kimono, the convention attendees have mistaken her for a *Sakura Taisen* cosplayer, when actually she's just trying to dress like her beloved Zetsubou-sensei.

## *Ki sho ten ketsu*, page 70

*Ki sho ten ketsu* refers to the four-part structure of certain Chinese poetry. The four parts are *ki* (introduction), *sho* (development), *ten* (twist), and *ketsu* (conclusion).

## "No climax, no conclusion, no meaning," page 70

In the original Japanese, Chiri says, "*Yama nashi, ochi nashi, imi nashi*" ("No climax, no conclusion, no meaning"). She means it as an insult, but it's actually the famous phrase that was abbreviated in fandom to form the self-deprecating word *yaoi* (yama...ochi...imi.) *Yaoi* manga, indeed, are not known for their deep meaning or intricate plot structure.

## Manga Koshien, page 72

This is a big annual manga competition, patterned after the popular Koshien baseball tournament, which has high schools across Japan battling it out for the top award.

## "Are you going to see the fireworks, too?" page 72

The summer Comiket ("Comic Market") often coincides with the Tokyo Bay Fireworks Festival, making the area around the Tokyo Big Sight convention center incredibly congested.

## *Ki sho ten ketsu*, page 73

*Ki sho ten ketsu* in Maria's mind is entirely different. Due to her poor grasp of Japanese, she uses kanji which have the same sounds but different meanings: *ki* (devil), *sho* (injury), *ten* (heaven), and *ketsu* (blood).

## Assorted references, page 74

*An*, also written as *yami*, is Japanese for "darkness." The fireworks strip is a reference to the 1993 Japanese movie *Uchiage hanabi, shita kara Miruka? Yoko kara Miruka?* ("Fireworks, Should We See Them from the Side or from Below?"). The "protective custody" strip refers to an incident after a Japanese volleyball match, which ended with one of the players being taken into police custody for questioning. Pinko Izumi is a Japanese entertainer who went on a diet to lose weight, but gained some of it back. The Association for Those Falsely Accused of Engaging in Lewd Acts was an actual organization founded by a person in Japan, who was arrested for taking surreptitious photos of women on the Oedo Railway Line. "In reality, she's pregnant" is a reference to the lead actors of the movie *Be with You* (see notes for page 16). "Ramen Wars" refers to a 2005 incident in Japan when a jealous ramen shop owner kidnapped and beat a former business partner. The two men had

been business partners many years before, and the less successful businessman blamed the other one for using his recipes without crediting him.

## Coupling, page 75

"Coupling" is a Japanese term for coming up with imaginary pairings between fictional characters. The equivalent English slang term is "shipping."

## The People Are at the Breaking Point, page 76

This title is a reference to Sachio Ito's 1906 story *Noginiku no Hata* ("The Grave of the Wild Chrysanthemum," also known as "The Wild Daisy"). The original line reads *Tamisan ha nogiku no yo na hito da* ("The people are like a wild chrysanthemum"), and the *Zetsubou-sensei* chapter title reads *Tamisan ha ippai-ippai no hito da* ("The people are at the breaking point"). It could also be translated as "The people are at the extreme edge," hence the image of Zetsubou-sensei on the cliff.

## "On Edge" School, page 80

This chapter features the Ocean's Edge School and Ocean's Edge Boarding House. In Japanese, *rinkai* means "beachside" or "ocean's edge." However, using different kanji character with the same pronunciation can mean "in a critical state." The English adaptation uses "on edge" as an equivalent pun.

## Morihige's Narrow Escape, page 82

Sold in America under the name Pop-Up Pirate, these toys are known in Japan as Kurohige Kiki Ippatsu ("Blackbeard In the Nick of Time"). The game is played by inserting plastic swords into the barrel until a random slot ejects the pirate (Blackbeard) and ends the game. Kumeta replaces the pirate with "Morihige," a pun on the famous actor Hisaya Morishige (1913–). Like Blackbeard, Morishige has a beard (*hige*, in Japanese).

## "To The Max," page 82

The original Japanese adaptation uses another obsolete slang term, "MK5," meaning "five seconds before seriously losing it." (The M is short for *maji*, meaning "seriously.") It was a popular phrase in Japan in the 1990s. See also the guy's shirt on page 141.

## Passnet, page 85

Magnetic prepaid train fare cards. They're currently being phased out.

## Ippai Pub, page 86

The "ippai" in Ippai Pub has a double meaning. It can mean "one drink" or it can mean, "the very extreme edge," as in the Japanese title of this chapter (see the notes for page 76). Lastly, since the "b" and "v" sounds are the same in Japanese, it could also be a pun meaning "Extreme Perv." This would explain why Zetsubou-sensei thinks it's sleazy.

## Assorted references, page 87

Tsuneo Horiuchi (1948–) is a former Japanese baseball pitcher who was resigned as the manager of the Yomiuri Giants following a dispute. Ippei Hayashiya is a *rakugoka*, a practitioner of the traditional Japanese form of *rakugo* solo comedy performance. In Ippei's case, his entire family (sister, brother, mother, etc.) are *rakugo* performers dating back three generations, but Ippei is considered the least successful of the bunch. Cocco is a Japanese singer/songwriter who, in artist Kumeta's opinion, has already gone past "the breaking point" (evidently he liked her the way she used to be). The Platon Hotel is the setting of the occupational/business manga *Hotel* by famous manga artist Shotaro Ishinomori (1938–1998). The manager of the Platon often had to apologize to customers for story-related problems and goings-on.

## Butsumetsu, page 88

Butsumetsu is the day that Buddha died. (Due to Japan's old lunisolar calendar, it's not always on the same day every year.) It's considered a most unlucky day, and weddings are avoided on this day. The phrase "On the third offense, even the Buddha will get angry" is translated from a Japanese saying, *Hotoke no Kao mo Sandomade* ("Even the Buddha's face, on the third time...")

## Sister-in-law, I'm an Aristocrat, page 90

This is a reference to a line in *Shayo* ("The Setting Sun"), a famous novel by the pessimistic author Osamu Dazai (1909–1948).

## Zetsumei, page 93

The verb *zetsumei suru* means "to die." *Mikoto*, sometimes read as *inochi*, means "life."

## Satogaeri, page 95

*Satogaeri* literally means "paying the first visit to one's parents' home after getting married." But it can be used more loosely as a visit to one's parents' home for certain holidays, etc.

## Miai, page 95

*Miai*, or more formally, *omiai*, is a formal meeting with a view for marriage. It's the first step for an arranged marriage. The verb *miau* ("to look at each other," or "to exchange glances") is made of the same two kanji characters, but with a different inflection. In short, it's a pun.

## Sebastian, page 99

In Japanese pop culture, Sebastian is a stereotypical name for a Western-style butler.

## Genroku Era, page 99

Considered to be the Golden Age of the Edo Period, the Genroku Era (1688–1704) was a period of economic stability when the arts flourished. Evidently the noble Itoshiki family line dates back to these illustrious times.

## Zetsurin, page 102

*Zetsurin* means "matchless, unequalled, unsurpassed." It also has a meaning of sexual prowess, hence the pun, and Rin's irritation.

## Ordinary Train, page 102

In Japan, the *futsu* train, or "ordinary" train, is a slower, cheaper form of train service. Since Nami is so ordinary, obviously it's her means of transportation. (See *Zetsubou-sensei* volume 1, page 139.)

## Leap Before You Lock Eyes, page 104

This title is a reference to *Miru mae ni tobe* ("Leap Before You Look"), an anthology of stories by the famous author Kenzaburo Oe (born in 1935). The *Zetsubou-sensei* chapter title is *Miau mae ni tobe* (literally, "Leap Before You Exchange Glances," or "Leap Before the Eyes Meet").

## Assorted references, page 110

Ayako is the heroine of the 1972 mystery-drama manga *Ayako* by Osamu Tezuka. Sukekiyo is a character from Seishi Yokomizo's famous 1950 mystery novel *Inugamike no Ichizoku* ("The Inugami Clan"), who wore a white rubber mask to hide his war-scarred face. Sai is the Go-playing ghost from Yumi Hotta and Takeshi Obata's megahit manga *Hikaru no Go*. *Nostaljii* (a portmanteau of "nostalgia" and *jii*, Japanese for "old man") is a 1974 manga by Fujiko F. Fujio, about a soldier still hiding in the jungle thirty years after World War II, who tries to go back to his hometown.

### "Looking pros," page 113

Sugi-sama is the *jidaigeki* (period drama) actor Ryutaro Sugi, known for his sidelong glances. "T-shi" is short for Masashi Tashiro, a former Japanese TV performer and musician whose career imploded following his 2000 arrest for filming up women's skirts with a camcorder. (In the original Japanese, he says he looks into the *wareme*, a play on words which uses the word "eye" but can mean "cleavage" or "buttcrack.") The "Nouveau" T-shirt refers to a product he did TV commercials for, before his disgrace. "U-shi" is short for another famous voyeur, Kazuhide Uekusa (see notes for page 16). Shusaku is the revolting title character of an X-rated Japanese computer game released by ELF Corporation in 1998; the first character of his name is *shu,* also pronounced *kusai,* which means "stinky."

### All sorts of eyes, page 113

In Japanese, these are all words or phrases involving *me*, the kanji for "eye." *Majime* is Japanese for "serious" or " reliable" (actually, if you wanted to say "serious eyes," you'd have to say *majime na me*). *Honkime* means "earnest eyes" or "sober eyes." *Irome* literally means "colored eyes" but can also mean giving a person a seductive, come-hither look. *Hiikime* means "favoring, supporting eyes." (Aruru is a cute-girl character from the adult video game/fantasy anime *Utawarerumono*.) When you say you have an *oime,* it means you're in debt to someone. *Urame* literally means "backside eyes"; it's used in the same way as the English phrase "backfire," implying an action with undesired consequences. *In course takame* is Japanese for "high inside strike zone," a baseball term. "The eyes of the crowd" is *seken no me* ("the eyes of society"). All these work as "eye" gags in Japanese, but not necessarily in English.

### Clairvoyance = Chiri's eyes, page 116

When Kafuka uses the word "clairvoyance" after Chiri starts magically seeing things beyond her realm, Usui snidely remarks, "I bet you set up this whole scary scene just so you could make that pun!" In Japanese, *senrigan* ("clairvoyance") is written with three characters that can also be read as *Chirigan* ("Chiri's eyes"). It's all because the kanji for "thousand" can be read as either *sen* or *chi*. A similar *sen/chi* pun appears in the name of the heroine of Hayao Miyazaki's anime *Spirited Away*.

### Assorted references, page 117

"Sawa's swimsuit" refers to the Japanese idol Sawa Yamaguchi. "The back of the hair of a Hanshin Ace" refers to Kei Igawa, a starting pitcher for the New York Yankees, formerly an ace pitcher for the Hanshin Tigers. He declared that he wouldn't cut his hair while he was on a winning streak, and when his team had twelve successive wins over three months, his hair got really long. *Waratte Iitomo!* ("It's Okay to Laugh!") is a Japanese variety TV show.

### Meanwhile, Fujiyoshi-san... page 119

Meanwhile, Fujiyoshi is at Comiket, a *dōjinshi* convention (see the notes for page 67).

### That Is Why You Are to Flee, Follow Me! Philostratus, page 120

This is a reference to Osamu Dazai's 1940 short story *Hashire Melos* ("Run, Melos!"), based on the ancient Greek legend of Damon and Pythias. In the story, Melos is sentenced to death by the king, but asks for a reprieve to attend his sister's wedding. The king grants his wish, but takes Melos's friend Selinuntius hostage, promising to kill him in three days if Melos does not return. On the way back, Melos encounters many obstacles, but he valiantly struggles to return so that his friend may live.

### Criticism training vs. escape training, page 123

Nozomu talks about initiating into "criticism training." Then Chiri sarcastically butts in with, "Don't you mean escape training?" since Nozomu's always figuring out ways to get out of teaching class. It's a pun since both of these words are pronounced the same (*Hitan Kunren*); they're just spelled using different kanji characters.

### Derizon, page 128

In the original Japanese, "derision" is *barizogon* ("abusive language"). When Nozumu says, "The *barizogons* are flying about," Maria imagines it's a scary-looking monster, since her grasp of Japanese isn't all that great.

## Pierced Jizo, page 128

Jizo is a bodhisattva worshiped in Japan as the guardian deity of children, particularly children who died before their parents. He's sometimes depicted with pierced ears.

## Full -> Relative, page 130

This is a reference to phimosis, a medical condition in which the foreskin of the penis won't retract properly. Phimosis in older children and adults can vary in severity, with some men able to retract their foreskin partially (relative phimosis), and some completely unable to retract their foreskin even in the flaccid state (full phimosis). Cosmetic surgeons like the Ueno Clinic (see note for page 28) make a big deal about the dangers of phimosis.

## Is every man in this class a masochist? page 132

In the original Japanese, the word "masochist" is written simply with the abbreviation M (as in S&M).

## Manjin, page 133

The word *manjin* on the back of the man's shirt is written with the character for *man* (as in "manga") and *jin* (person). As the kanji *man* can be used to mean "morally corrupt," the word could mean either "manga man" or something like "degenerate man."

## Because It Is So Unstable, I Went to Search the Skies, page 134

This title is a reference to *Saekosho*, a novel by Haruo Sato (1892–1964). The original line reads *Anmari otenki dakara, watashi sora wo sagashi ni ittekimashitanoyo* ("Because it was too beautiful a day, I went to search the skies").

## Izumi Oogami, page 136

Izumi Oogami (1969–) is a Japanese announcer and voice actress.

## Assorted references, page 137

Kamille is a reference to Kamille Bidan, the hero of the 1986 anime series *Mobile Suit Zeta Gundam*. The Spo-Park Matsumori sporting facility in Sendai, Japan, opened on July 1, 2005 but closed a mere forty-seven days later after an earthquake caused its roof to collapse. "Reversible Destiny-Yoro Park" is a theme park in Yoro, Japan, whose main feature is a building with a surreal, disorienting interior (furniture partially sticking out of the walls, etc.). Sakura Bank is one of the former names of the Mitsui-Sumitomo Bank, which has changed its name several times in recent years, as part of a series of mergers. Cuenca is a famous tourist spot in Spain, a medieval walled city where houses hang precariously on the edge of a river gorge.

## Stable train schedule -> Unstable drivers, page 138

This is a reference to the 2005 Amagasaki rail crash in which the driver was speeding in order to make up lost time for a delay. One hundred and six people died, making it one of the most serious rail disasters in Japanese history.

## Assorted References, page 140

"It's a love comedy!" "It's a battle manga!" refers to stereotypical *shônen* manga of the *Shônen Jump* variety, which sometimes start out as a comedy and then, at the editor's insistence, turn to a fighting series (*YuYu Hakusho* being the most blatant example). *Itsudemo Aeru* ("But When I Meet") is a sweet book by Mariko Kikuta. Mitsuo Matayoshi (1944–) is an eccentric Japanese political figure who has repeatedly run for prime minister of Japan. He claims to be the messiah and refers to himself as Jesus Matayoshi or "The Only God Mitsuo Matayoshi Jesus Christ."

## Dearka-on-Yzak, page 141

See note for page 63.

### *Black Hospital,* page 141

*Black Hospital* is short for a Japanese TV show, *Saishyu Keikoku! Takeshi no Honto wa Kowai Katei no Igaku* ("Final Warning! Takeshi's Seriously Frightening Family Medical Science"). Hosted by actor and TV personality Takeshi Kitano (aka "Beat" Takeshi), it's a medical-horror-simulation show, somewhere between a reality show and a bizarre documentary about strange diseases. At the end of each show, the guest panel is tested for their chances of contracting the odd illness of the day. The results are given live on the show.

### Repository of unstable things, page 141

Among the items on display are a God Soldier (from Hayao Miyazaki's anime/manga *Nausicaä of the Valley of the Wind*) and a figure with a spiral hole in its forehead (possibly a reference to Junji Ito's horror manga *Uzumaki*).

### *Sazae-san,* page 143

*Sazae-san* is Machiko Hasegawa's classic 1946–1974 newspaper-strip manga about a Japanese family. The anime based on *Sazae-san* is the longest-running animated TV series in history, having been broadcast every Sunday night at 6:30 P.M. since 1969.

### Kubozuka-kun's favorite weed, page 148

Yosuke Kubozuka (1979–) is a Japanese actor whose controversial behavior included speaking out in favor of marijuana, a drug which carries harsh penalties in Japan.

### Dr. Mashirito, page 150

Dr. Mashirito is a character from Akira Toriyama's manga *Dr. Slump*.

### Yoshiko Sakurai, page 150

Yoshiko Sakura (1945–) is a Japanese newscaster.

### Assorted references, page 151

Otome Road (Maiden Road) is a nickname for a street in the Tokyo neighborhood of Ikebukuro. With its many bookstores specializing in *yaoi dôjinshi* and other female-oriented anime and manga products, it has a reputation as a haven for female *otaku*. "Takumachine" is a Japanese porn DVD label. "Gavas points" were a sort of toy money printed in the Japanese video game magazine *Famitsu*, which could be mailed in and redeemed for various products (mugs, pens, keychains, etc.).

### Assorted references, page 153

Book Off is a popular Japanese used-book-store chain. *Gintama* is a 2003 sci-fi comedy manga by Hideaki Sorachi, set in a parallel-world version of Meiji Era Japan. *Weekly Shônen Sunday*, published by Shogakukan, was the magazine in which Koji Kumeta debuted as a manga artist, but he later split off from Shogakukan and moved to the rival *Weekly Shônen Magazine,* published by Kodansha. *Sunday* has since been the target of several of Kumeta's barbs, such as volume 1, page 125. (The magazine *YS* floating down the river on volume 1, page 84, could also be a reference to the companion magazine *Young Sunday,* which was canceled in 2008.)

### Kenjiro Hata, page 154

Kenjiro Hata is Koji Kumeta's former assistant and the creator of the 2004 manga *Hayate the Combat Butler*.

### Run, Eros! page 157

See note for page 120.

# TOMARE!

You're going the wrong way!

MANGA IS A COMPLETELY DIFFERENT TYPE OF READING EXPERIENCE.

TO START AT THE **BEGINNING**, GO TO THE **END**!

## That's right!

Authentic manga is read the traditional Japanese way—from right to left, exactly the *opposite* of how American books are read. It's easy to follow: Just go to the other end of the book and read each page—and each panel—from right side to left side, starting at the top right. Now you're experiencing manga as it was meant to be!